# Washington during Civil War and Reconstruction
## *Race and Radicalism*

In this provocative book, Robert Harrison provides new insight into grassroots Reconstruction after the Civil War and into the lives of those most deeply affected, the newly emancipated African Americans. Harrison argues that the District of Columbia, far from being marginal to the Reconstruction story, was central to Republican efforts to reshape civil and political relations, with the capital a testing ground for congressional policy makers. The book describes the ways in which federal agencies such as the Army and the Freedmen's Bureau attempted to assist Washington's freed population and shows how officials struggled to address the social problems resulting from large-scale African American migration. It also sheds new light on the political processes that led to the abandonment of Reconstruction and the onset of Black disenfranchisement. Finally, *Washington during Civil War and Reconstruction* is a valuable case study of municipal government in an era when Americans faced the challenges of a new urban-industrial society.

Dr. Robert Harrison (1944–2007) was a member of the Department of History and Welsh History at the University of Wales, Aberystwyth, for more than thirty years. His numerous publications on nineteenth- and early-twentieth-century American politics, particularly on Congress and the District of Columbia, have been a significant contribution to the field. They include *State and Society in Twentieth-Century America* (1997) and *Congress, Progressive Reform, and the New American State* (Cambridge 2004). An active participant in the research community of American history, Dr. Harrison was a long-standing member of the British Association for American Studies and was closely involved with the British American Nineteenth Century Historians, organizing two major conferences on American history in 2000 and 2004.

# Washington during Civil War and Reconstruction

## Race and Radicalism

**ROBERT HARRISON**

*University of Wales, Aberystwyth*

CAMBRIDGE
UNIVERSITY PRESS

CAMBRIDGE UNIVERSITY PRESS
Cambridge, New York, Melbourne, Madrid, Cape Town,
Singapore, São Paulo, Delhi, Tokyo, Mexico City

Cambridge University Press
32 Avenue of the Americas, New York, NY 10013-2473, USA

www.cambridge.org
Information on this title: www.cambridge.org/9781107002326

First published 2011

Printed in the United States of America

*A catalog record for this publication is available from the British Library.*

*Library of Congress Cataloging in Publication data*
Harrison, Robert, 1944–
Washington during Civil War and reconstruction : race and radicalism / Robert Harrison,
Phillipp Schofield, Jean Harrison.
p.   cm.
Includes bibliographical references and index.
ISBN 978-1-107-00232-6 (hardback)
1. Reconstruction (U.S. history, 1865–1877) – Washington (D.C.)   2. Washington
(D.C.) – Politics and government – 19th century.   3. Freedmen – Washington (D.C.) –
History – 19th century.   4. Washington (D.C.) – Race relations – History –
19th century.   I. Schofield, Phillipp R., 1964–   II. Harrison, Jean.   III. Title.
F198.H37   2011
305.8009753–dc22        2011001936

ISBN 978-1-107-00232-6 Hardback

# Contents

# Abbreviations

| | |
|---|---|
| AQMR | Annual, Quarterly and Monthly Reports |
| BRFAL-DC | Records of the Assistant Commissioner for the District of Columbia, Bureau of Refugees, Freedmen, and Abandoned Lands, 1865–1869, RG105, National Archives Microfilm Publications, No. M1055 |
| CCF | Consolidated Correspondence File |
| CG, 39.1 | *Congressional Globe*, 39th Congress, 1st Session |
| CR, 45.2 | *Congressional Record*, 45th Congress, 2nd Session |
| fn | frame number |
| Ho. Exec. Doc. | House of Representatives Executive Document |
| Ho. Misc. Doc. | House of Representatives Miscellaneous Document |
| LR | Letters Received |
| LS | Letters Sent |
| NARA | National Archives and Records Administration |
| OR | *The War of the Rebellion: A Compilation of the Official Records of the Union and Confederate Armies.* 69 vols. Washington, D.C.: Government Printing Office, 1880–1900 |
| REO | Reports from Employment Offices |
| RG | Record Group |
| Sen. Misc. Doc. | Senate Miscellaneous Document |
| SO | Special Orders |
| ULR | Unregistered Letters Received |

# Foreword

Robert Harrison died on May 6, 2007. Robert's last book, *Washington during Civil War and Reconstruction: Race and Radicalism* is published here, with some minor emendations, just as it was left at the time of his death. Once it was evident that a completed volume existed, it was immediately decided that Robert's publication plans should be pursued. In realizing those plans, a number of people have been extremely helpful and accommodating. In particular, Professor Martin Crawford, of the American Studies Department at Keele, offered both expert advice and conscientious regard for the volume's production; staff at Cambridge University Press, especially Eric Crahan at the publisher's New York office and Barbara Walthall, project manager at Aptara, Inc., also provided great encouragement and their full support for the publication.

Robert lived near Aberystwyth, in Llandre, with his wife, Jean, and his sons, Matthew and Stephen, for more than thirty years. He had been a member of the Department of History and Welsh History at Aberystwyth University. From his native Sunderland, where his mother, Beatrice, lived until 2010, Robert Harrison earned his first degree at St. John's College, Cambridge, in 1966, and completed his Ph.D. in 1971; in the next year he took up his post at Aberystwyth. His numerous publications on nineteenth- and early-twentieth-century American politics, particularly on Congress and on the District of Columbia, have been a significant contribution to his field. They include two volumes on American politics in the nineteenth and twentieth centuries, *State and Society in Twentieth-Century America* (1997) and *Congress, Progressive Reform, and the New American State* (2004), as well as a number of associated articles.

Robert's peers remember him as an excellent colleague, entirely dependable and calmly efficient, with a gloriously dry sense of humor. He is greatly missed by all who knew him: family, friends, colleagues, and students alike. It is a great pleasure to know that this, his last piece of research, is to be published just as he left it.

Phillipp R. Schofield
Aberystwyth
November 1, 2010

# Introduction

## A "Western Palmyra"

The historian Henry Adams first visited Washington in 1850. As he ventured out from his aunt's house, "he found himself on an earth-road or village street, with wheel tracks meandering from the colonnade of the Treasury hard by, to the white marble columns and fronts of the Post Office and Patent Office, which faced each other in the distance, like white Greek temples in the abandoned gravel pits of a deserted Syrian city." Returning to the city ten years later, he discovered "the same rude colony...camped in the same forest, with the same unfinished Greek temples for workrooms and sloughs for roads."[1] Although recollected at some distance and marked with the author's special brand of ironic detachment, Adams's reaction mirrored that of many other visitors to the nation's capital before the Civil War. The "City of Magnificent Intentions," as Charles Dickens dubbed it, presented a startling juxtaposition of monumental splendor and miserable squalor. Public buildings in the classical style had arisen at key points in Pierre Charles L'Enfant's original plan for the capital, including the White House, the State Department and Treasury Department buildings, the Post Office, the Patent Office, and, of course, the Capitol. The Capitol had been massively extended over the previous decade, but in 1860, the dome remained to be completed, and only a few of the Corinthian columns designed to embellish the porticoes were in place. Piles of masonry, scaffolding, and workmen's huts gave

---

[1] Henry Adams, *The Education of Adams* (Modern Library Edition, New York: Modern Library, 1931 [1918]), 44, 99.

Capitol Hill the appearance of a builders' yard. The Mall, intended as an important celebratory and processional space, was little better than a "cow pasture," and the mighty obelisk designed to glorify the memory of the Father of His Country had stood unfinished for several years, an oddly abbreviated shaft of masonry that seemed to symbolize the uncompleted and unfulfilled character of the capital city.[2]

The most striking characteristic of antebellum Washington, in the eyes of both foreign and domestic visitors, was the acute discrepancy between the grandiose scale of the L'Enfant plan and the untidy reality that they saw around them. Although the public buildings were impressive, what lay between them fell far short of any expectation of what a capital city should look like. According to Dickens, who visited Washington in the early 1840s, "Spacious avenues that begin in nothing, and lead nowhere; streets, mile-long, that only want houses, roads, and inhabitants; public buildings that need but a public to be complete; and ornaments of great thoroughfares, which only lack great thoroughfares to ornament – are its leading features." Imposing government buildings stood alongside undistinguished hotels and commercial premises; elegant row houses were erected in proximity to frame dwellings, wooden shanties, and a great deal of open space. Settlement was concentrated inside an arc, the base of which rested on Pennsylvania Avenue between the White House and the Capitol, with extensions to the west of the White House and south of the Mall. Even the more densely inhabited sections contained "vacant lots rank with weeds or strewn with rubbish," and behind the main thoroughfares ran alleys "dotted with groggeries and ramshackle shanties." On the outskirts of the city, patches of field and forest separated the occasional scattered dwellings, and the street plan, broken up as it was by streams and gullies, was little more than hypothetical. Much of the area of the city, observed the novelist Anthony Trollope in 1862, was "wild, trackless, unbridged, uninhabited and desolate." There the

[2] John W. Reps, *Monumental Washington: The Planning and Development of the Capital Center* (Princeton, NJ: Princeton University Press, 1967), 50 and 27–53 passim; Constance M. Green, *Washington: From Village to Capital, 1800–1878* (Princeton, NJ: Princeton University Press, 1962), 239. For descriptions of antebellum Washington, see also Margaret Leech, *Reveille in Washington, 1861–1865* (New York: Harper, 1941), 5–16; Alan Lessoff, *The Nation and Its City: Politics, "Corruption," and Progress in Washington, D.C., 1861–1902* (Baltimore: Johns Hopkins University Press, 1994), 3–7, 20–26; Walter Erhart, "Written Capitals and Capital Topography: Berlin and Washington in Travel Literature," in Andreas W. Daum and Christof Mauch, eds., *Berlin – Washington, 1800–2000: Capital Cities, Cultural Representation, and National Identity* (Cambridge: Cambridge University Press, 2005), 51–78.

unwary traveler might lose himself as easily as "in the deserts of the Holy Land." From an uncultivated wilderness, "the unfinished dome of the Capitol will loom before you in the distance, and you will think that you approach the ruins of some western Palmyra."[3]

Washington appeared an exotic settlement, quite unlike other American cities. Foreign travelers looked to New York or Philadelphia, later to Chicago, for exemplars of the bustling spirit of enterprise, the unquenchable energy that drove the country forward; they did not look to the nation's capital.[4] Washington was an artificial growth that had not arisen naturally from the imperatives of commerce and industry but had been imposed on the landscape by an act of political will. It drew its identity from its status as capital. A capital city, especially a new one built from scratch like Washington, is intended to articulate the national identity and to establish a focus for an emerging national identity. It is designed as a focus for emotional allegiance, a site that, by its symbolic organization of space, its deployment of imposing architecture, its housing of national monuments and memorials, and its staging of major national events, will display the majesty of the state and reinforce the citizens' attachment to the nation. It is therefore inextricably associated with the process of nation-building. In Washington's case, the intention was to imitate the grandeur and aesthetic unity of baroque city planning, with its long vistas and its grand plazas, while emphasizing the republican ideals that animated the new nation through the adoption of an extensive plan that offered open access to its citizens and a classical architectural style that "evoked images of democratic Athens and republican Rome."[5]

---

[3] Charles Dickens, *American Notes* (New York: St. Martin's Press, 1985 [1842]), 106; Green, *Washington*, 239; Anthony Trollope, *North America* (Harmondsworth, UK: Penguin, 1968 [1862]), 161.

[4] See Erhart, "Written Capitals and Capital Topography," 58.

[5] Milton C. Cummings, Jr., and Matthew C. Price, "The Creation of Washington, D.C.: Political Symbolism and Practical Problem Solving in the Establishment of a Capital City for the United States of America, 1787–1850," in John Taylor, Jean G. Lengellé, and Caroline Andrew, eds., *Capital Cities – Les Capitales:Perspectives Internationales – International Perspectives* (Ottawa, 1993), 241–42. On Washington as capital, see also Daum and Mauch, eds., *Berlin – Washington, 1800–2000*, especially the essays by Daum, Kenneth R. Bowling and Ulrike Gerhard, and Carl Abbott; Alan Lessoff, "Gilded Age Washington: Promotional Capital of the Nation," in Lothar Hönnighausen and Andreas Falke, eds., *Washington, D.C.: Interdisciplinary Approaches* (Tübingen: Francke Verlag, 1993), 35–49. On Washington's architecture, see Kathleen S. Wood, "Capital Architecture: Grand Visions, Monumental Reality," in ibid., 117–39. For a more general consideration of the characteristics of capital cities, see also the essays in Taylor, Lengellé, and Andrew, eds., *Capital Cities.*

However, the scale of the L'Enfant plan represented a leap of faith, a confidence that one day the nation and its capital would expand to fill the open spaces in the grand design. In the medium term, it left a gap between vision and reality that seemed to point to the inadequacy of the federal project itself. Over the antebellum decades, an unwillingness to invest heavily in the construction of a national capital seemed to betoken a lack of commitment to a strong national government. The spirit of Jacksonian democracy was inimical to the concentration of political power. As the sectional crisis deepened in the years leading up to 1860, the unfinished quality of Washington became a metaphor for the fractured condition of the nation itself.

In fact, Washington's founders had never intended that its function should be solely political; they had envisaged for the city a radiant future as a commercial entrepôt that, by exploiting its access to the Ohio Valley and the Great Lakes through the "Potomac corridor," would build a huge trade with the nation's interior. The capital, says Carl Abbott, was to be "an eminently practical gateway to the new nation." That these dreams were unfounded was due to the greater financial resources enjoyed by merchants in other cities, with the often generous support of their state governments, and the failure of Congress to provide comparable invest-ment capital. Equally unfortunate was the reliance of Washington and the neighboring Potomac cities on a soon-to-be-outmoded technology, in the shape of the Chesapeake and Ohio Canal, which was rapidly displaced by the railroad serving the rival city of Baltimore. Further, Washing-ton did not develop more than an incidental interest in manufacturing. It remained primarily a center of government, the population of which consisted of transients elected or appointed to federal office for a period of years, together with a core of more permanent residents whose prin-cipal occupation was to cater to their needs. Although the number of federal employees located there had doubled since 1840, reaching 2,199 in 1861, their number was still insufficient to fuel a sizable expansion of the capital.[6]

---

[6] Carl Abbott, *Political Terrain: Washington, D.C. from Tidewater Town to Global Metropolis* (Chapel Hill: University of North Carolina Press, 1999), 28, 31, and 26–38 passim; Howard Gillette Jr., *Between Justice and Beauty: Race, Planning, and the Failure of Urban Policy in Washington, D.C.* (Baltimore: Johns Hopkins University Press, 1995), 18–23; Green, *Washington*, 112–18, 127–31, 156–57, 191–94; David R. Gold-field, "Antebellum Washington in Context: The Pursuit of Prosperity and Identity," in Howard Gillette Jr., ed., *Southern City, National Ambition: The Growth of Early Wash-ington, D.C.* (Washington, DC: George Washington University Press, 1995), 1–20; Walter

If Washington fared badly in the urban rivalries of nineteenth-century America, that was really no surprise. "The nation's capital occupied an anomalous position in this context," notes David R. Goldfield. "Washington belonged to everyone and to no one." Congressmen lacked the same loyalty to the city's residents that state legislators held toward their urban constituents, and they were much less likely to accede to their demands. Congress provided little support for local transportation projects, and it did not gladly make appropriations for municipal utilities or the improvement of streets. Despite repeated calls for a fairer and more generous treatment of the District, most notably in the oft-quoted Southard Report of 1835, congressmen repeatedly complained of lavish federal expenditure on local projects. "These demands on the public Treasury – the people's money – for purposes of expenditure in the cities of Washington and Georgetown, are shameful; and the manner in which our money is poured out to these people is shameless," complained Senator Richard Brodhead of Pennsylvania in 1856. Such attitudes would obstruct a resolution of the city's financial difficulties for many years to come.[7]

There has always been something problematic, if not anomalous, about the political status of the District of Columbia. Anxious to avoid leaving the officers of the federal government vulnerable to undue pressure from the citizenry of whatever part of the country the capital might be located, the authors of the Constitution allowed Congress to "exercise exclusive legislation in all cases whatsoever" in the hundred square miles that were to house the seat of government. In fact, for most of its first seventy years of existence, Washington was governed by an elected mayor and councils (the city of Georgetown and the rural sections of the District, known as Washington County, had their own separate governing

F. McArdle, "The Development of the Business Sector in Washington, D.C.," *Records of the Columbia Historical Society, 1973–74* (Washington, DC: 1976), 556–93. Statistics of federal employment are taken from U.S. Department of Commerce, Bureau of the Census, *Historical Statistics of the United States: Colonial Times to 1857* (Washington, DC: 1960), 710. The largely transient nature of Washington's population is emphasized by Goldfield, "Antebellum Washington in Context," 19; Abbott, *Political Terrain*, 2–5; Leech, *Reveille in Washington*, 12.

[7] Goldfield, "Antebellum Washington in Context"; Gillette, *Between Justice and Beauty*, 2, 16, 20–22; Green, *Washington*, 130–31, 204–7 (Brodhead quotation at 205). According to Steven J. Diner, "The government of the District by Congress has been inherently inefficient as well as unresponsive." "Statehood and the Governance of the District of Columbia: An Historical Analysis of Policy Issues," *Journal of Policy History* 4 (1992): 413.

arrangements). The conduct of municipal government in the antebellum period was not dissimilar to that in other cities of comparable size, with the important distinction that Washington, like the rest of the District, was subject to the supreme authority of Congress. That authority, however, was exercised fitfully by a national legislature whose preferred stance toward the District was one of benign neglect. Although owning roughly half the real property in the District, the U.S. government paid no taxes and contributed only intermittently to the costs of local government, with the result that the municipality was, even by antebellum standards, chronically short of money. With the best will in its world, Washington could not live up to the demanding requirements of the L'Enfant plan while providing adequate public services for its citizens. The result, as numerous foreign and domestic visitors observed, was unpaved streets, inadequate public services, and a mixture of dilapidation and monumental grandeur that ill suited the capital of a modern republic.[8]

## A Southern City

In the absence of a more diversified economy and a more vigorous national presence, Washington retained its predominantly southern character. Of the District's white residents in 1850, 52 percent had been born there, and 29 percent were natives of the neighboring states of Virginia and Maryland. Its leading families retained close connections with the inhabitants of the tidewater counties of Virginia and Maryland, with whom they shared a love of fast horses, lavish entertainment, dancing, and card playing. Northerners who visited Washington or who came to take up government employment there had no doubt that they had crossed the boundary separating North from South. Washington at the beginning of the Civil War was "a third rate Southern city," recalled Mary Clemmer Ames.[9] Henry Adams was equally struck by the city's southern complexion. "The want of barriers, of pavements, of forms; the looseness, the laziness; the indolent Southern drawl; the pigs in the streets; the negro

---

[8] For an historical review of the relationship between the federal government and the District of Columbia, see Diner, "Statehood and the Governance of the District of Columbia"; Donald C. Rowat, "Ways of Governing Capital Cities," in Taylor *et al.*, eds., *Capital Cities*, 149–71. On antebellum Washington, see Green, *Washington*, chaps. 5–8; Gillette, *Between Justice and Beauty*, 1–36; Gillette, ed., *Southern City, National Ambition*.

[9] Mary C. Ames, *Ten Years in Washington: Life and Scenes in the National Capital, as a Woman Sees Them* (Hartford, CT: A.D. Worthington, 1875), 67–69. See also Abbott, *Political Terrain*, 38–67; Goldfield, "Antebellum Washington in Context," 11.

babies and their mothers with bandanas; the freedom, openness, swagger, of nature and man" seemed as exotic as "the thick odor of the catalpa trees" that filled the air. Still more, "Slavery struck him in the face; it was a nightmare; a horror; a crime; the sum of all wickedness!"[10]

The pervasive presence of African Americans – driving carts and carriages, shoveling coal, serving at tables, selling fruits and vegetables, lounging and conversing on the streets – was the clearest evidence to northern visitors that they had entered the South. Eighteen percent of the city's population in 1860 was African American, but, as one visitor observed, the official enumeration appeared "inconsistent with the swarms of Negroes in the streets of Washington." Washington was a slaveholding community: 1,774 of its inhabitants were enslaved in 1860. Yet it contained fewer slaves than it had in 1820, and the proportion of slaves in the population had declined from 19.4 percent in 1800 to 2.9 percent in 1860.[11] Sixty percent of Washington's slaveholders possessed no more than one slave, and few held more than five, which suggests that most owners could find little use for their bondsmen and women other than as domestic servants. Although partly induced by the peculiarities of the capital's economy, this decline in the enslaved population was, in fact, shared with most Upper South cities in the generation leading up to the Civil War.[12] The partial ban on the slave trade in the District of Columbia introduced in 1850 had terminated Washington's status as a major slave mart, but local residents were still permitted to buy and sell slaves for their own use, local newspapers continued to carry advertisements for their human property, slave auctions were still held, and the occasional slave coffle could still be seen making its way through the streets of the capital. At the same time, the strengthened fugitive slave law gave added incentive to the local business of slave catching. The municipal

[10] Adams, *Education of Henry Adams*, 44.

[11] Constance, M. Green, *The Secret City: A History of Race Relations in the Nation's Capital* (Princeton, NJ: Princeton University Press, 1967), 63; Letitia W. Brown, "Residence Patterns of Negroes in the District of Columbia, 1800–1869," *Records of the Columbia Historical Society*, 47 (1971): 78.

[12] For alternative explanations for the decline of slavery in the cities, see Claudia D. Goldin, *Urban Slavery in the American South, 1820–1860: A Quantitative History* (Chicago: University of Chicago Press, 1976); Richard C. Wade, *Slavery in the Cities: The South, 1820–1860* (New York: Oxford University Press, 1964); Barbara Jeanne Fields, *Slavery and Freedom on the Middle Ground: Maryland during the Nineteenth Century* (New Haven, CT: Yale University Press, 1985), 40–62; Harold D. Woodman, "Comment," in Stanley Engerman and Eugene Genovese, eds., *Race and Slavery in the Western Hemisphere: Quantitative Studies* (Princeton, NJ: Princeton University Press, 1975), 451–54.

police spent much of its time acting as a slave patrol, and many of the cases heard by local magistrates concerned the legal status of persons claimed as human chattels. Although greatly reduced in scope, slavery remained in force in the federal District, and slaveholders retained their power within the community, buttressed by the support of influential congressmen and government officials from the slave states.[13]

Washington's free black population had grown rapidly since the city's foundation, as a result partly of the cumulative effect of local manumissions and partly of the city's attractiveness to freed slaves from the neighboring states. The city offered a wider range of employment opportunities than surrounding rural areas, along with the social attractions of a developed black community. In 1860, the city contained 9,209 free African Americans, 84 percent of the total black population.[14] As elsewhere in the South, free blacks were debarred from numerous economic activities, but there were important niches that they could exploit, occupations that local whites found menial or dishonorable because they entailed an element of personal service but offered a relatively secure livelihood, including barbering, catering, butchering, and the operation of laundries and livery stables. Free blacks also labored as stevedores, coal handlers, carters, draymen, hod carriers, bootblacks, waiters, bartenders, and cooks. Others made a living from market gardening and market trading. Although

[13] On slavery in the District, see Green, *Secret City*, 13–54; Stanley Harrold, *Subversives: Antislavery Community in Washington, D.C., 1828–1865* (Baton Rouge: Louisiana State University Press, 2003); Mary Beth Corrigan, "The Ties That Bind: The Pursuit of Community and Freedom among Slaves and Free Blacks in the District of Columbia, 1800–1860," in Gillette, ed., *Southern City*, 69–90; Walter C. Clephane, "The Local Aspect of Slavery in the District of Columbia," *Records of the Columbia Historical Society* 3 (1900): 224–56; William T. Laprade, "The Domestic Slave Trade in the District of Columbia, *Journal of Negro History* 11 (January 1926): 17–34.

[14] On free blacks in the District of Columbia, see especially Corrigan, "Ties That Bind"; Mary Beth Corrigan, "'It's a Family Affair': Buying Freedom in the District of Columbia, 1850–1860," in Larry Hudson Jr., ed., *Working toward Freedom: Slave Society and Domestic Economy in the American South* (Rochester, NY: University of Rochester Press, 1994), 163–91; Corrigan, "Ties That Bind"; Green, *Secret City*, 13–54; Letitia W. Brown, *Free Negroes in the District of Columbia, 1790–1846* (New York: Oxford University Press, 1972); Allan John Johnston, "Surviving Freedom: The Black Community in Washington, D.C., 1860–1880" (Ph.D. diss., Duke University, 1980), 114–45 (NB published by Garland in 1993 under the same title); Henry S. Robinson, "Some Aspects of the Free Negro Population of Washington, D.C., 1800–1862," *Maryland Historical Magazine* 64 (Spring 1969): 57–63. For a comparative perspective, see Ira Berlin, *Slaves without Masters: The Free Negro in the Antebellum South* (New York: Pantheon, 1974); James Oliver Horton, *Free People of Color: Inside the African American Community* (Washington, DC: Smithsonian Institution Press, 1993).

the great majority of African Americans were employed in some form of unskilled labor or domestic service, several had found more lucrative occupations. One hundred and fifty African American businessmen were listed in *Boyd's Directory* for 1860. In consequence, a sizeable black middle class had developed. The tax lists for 1860 record 1,175 of the District's 11,131 blacks as owning some property and 235 as owning property worth in excess of $1,000. Already by 1860, Washington had acquired something of a reputation as a favorable location for free blacks to live and work.[15]

A vigorous African American community established itself in the nation's capital over the course of the antebellum era. By 1862, it supported eleven black churches with 3,850 members, some boasting well-appointed buildings and excellent choirs. More than any other institutions, church organizations bound African Americans together and formed networks of solidarity and communication around which a black community could be built. The churches sponsored charitable work, arranged lectures, organized burial societies and fraternal associations, and ran Sunday schools. Some also provided accommodation, teachers, and financial support for day schools for African American children. In view of the poverty of most of the city's black residents and the refusal of the municipal government to make any provision for black schools, great sacrifices had to be made to provide any educational facilities at all. Nevertheless, one or two primary schools were maintained throughout the antebellum period and, for a while during the 1850s, a secondary school for girls operated by the white philanthropist Myrtilla Miner. As a result, literacy levels, although depressingly low in comparison with local whites, were higher than among the black communities of most other southern cities. In 1860, approximately 42 percent of the free black population was literate, and several hundred African American children attended school. The arduous struggle to establish and maintain churches

[15] On occupations and property holdings, see Dorothy Provine, "The Economic Position of Free Blacks in the District of Columbia, 1800–1860," *Journal of Negro History* 58 (1973): 61–72; Green, *Secret City*, 27–28; Melvin R. Williams, "A Blueprint for Change: The Black Community in Washington, D.C., 1860–1870," *Records of the Columbia Historical Society*, 48 (1972): 361–65; Melvin R. Williams, "A Statistical Study of Blacks in Washington, D.C. in 1860," *Records of the Columbia Historical Society*, 50 (1980): 174–75; Berlin, *Slaves without Masters*, 217–49. On residential patterns, see James Borchert, *Alley Life in Washington: Family, Community, Religion and Folklore in the City, 1850–1970* (Urbana: University of Illinois Press, 1980), 1–28; Brown, "Residence Patterns of Negroes in the District of Columbia," 75–77.

and schools served more than anything else to knit the black community together.[16]

Washington's free blacks were subject to a strict black code inherited from Maryland. Although they had not acquired some of the more punitive provisions later added to the black codes of neighboring states, the District's laws, supplemented by repressive city ordinances, were troublesome enough. Free blacks were supposed to carry free papers with them at all times. Any African American suspected of being a fugitive might be arrested and sold to pay for the costs of his incarceration, including the fees that went into the pockets of the policemen and magistrates involved in the case. Black testimony was excluded from the courts in any case involving white persons. African Americans were subjected to a 10 P.M. curfew, and they were not permitted to assemble in public in numbers exceeding five. Lashes could be inflicted for a host of minor offences, such as setting off firecrackers, bathing in the Washington City Canal (although the detrimental consequences of exposure to its waters should have been deterrent enough), or flying a kite within the city limits. Although many of these provisions were irregularly enforced, their presence on the statute books was both a source of continuous irritation and danger and a constant reminder of the second-class status of those to whom they applied.[17]

Washington, then, was a southern city, but very much a city of the Border South. The institution of slavery was in retreat, and in its place was emerging a system of free black labor that, although it reflected a continuing insistence on the imperatives of racial hierarchy, offered a more flexible set of economic and social possibilities. Slavery was numerically in decline, but its adherents clung fiercely to the institution, rejecting any attempts to eliminate it or to modify its terms, and they received strong support from southern representatives in the federal government, who were anxious that the defenses of slavery should not be breached in the nation's capital. However, the city's very status left it peculiarly open to outside influences. Although located in the South, it could never be wholly a southern city. The business of the government necessarily attracted northerners, many of whom did not approve of the South's

---

[16] Williams, "Blueprint for Change," 366–70; Corrigan, "Ties That Bind," 75–78, 80–82; Green, *Secret City*, 23–25, 50–52; John W. Cromwell, "The First Negro Churches in the District of Columbia," *Journal of Negro History* 7 (1922): 64–106.

[17] Green, *Secret City*, 18–19, 25, 37, 47–48; Leech, *Reveille in Washington*, 236; Berlin, *Slaves without Masters*, 316–40.

"peculiar institution" and at least some of whom refused to hide their disdain. In the nation's capital, their voices were not so easily suppressed.

A slaveholding city at the heart of a "slaveholders' republic," Washington laid itself open to inquiry and criticism from the enemies of the peculiar institution. It was accessible to antislavery whites in a way that other southern cities were not. Denied many of the controls that silenced expressions of antislavery opinion elsewhere in the South, slaveholders in the nation's capital could not prevent the development of a small but determined, and ultimately effective, clique of local whites and northern journalists and officeholders who worked together with elements of the free African American community to undermine the institution. Sometimes working through legal channels to secure the freedom of local blacks, sometimes acting illegally to help slaves escape from bondage, they added to the sense of vulnerability increasingly felt by slaveholders everywhere by challenging the viability of slavery in the District of Columbia. Their campaign linked local struggles with the broader debate over slavery and thereby added fuel to an already heated sectional crisis. The resulting conflict, which was so dramatically to transform the capital's social structure and political status, had its roots, in some small part, in the peculiar situation of antebellum Washington.[18]

The abolitionist movement hit on the special significance of the District at an early stage. The presence of slavery in the nation's capital and the prosecution of the slave trade in close proximity to the heart of U.S. government had long been an embarrassment to the institution's critics. "Slave coffles" in the nation's capital, says Don E. Fehrenbacher, were "shameful symbols of oppression that soiled the image of the United States before the rest of the world." A petition campaign, aimed at the eradication of slavery in the District of Columbia, served as an effective mobilizing device for the abolitionist movement, all the more so when, in May 1836, the House of Representatives resolved to reject abolitionist petitions without consideration. In so doing, the issue was widened beyond the emancipation of black slaves to embrace the political rights of freeborn white men and women. The ongoing controversy over the "gag rule" kept the issue before the country until its repeal in December 1844. Abolition of slavery in the District of Columbia formed part of

---

[18] Harrold, *Subversives*. A recent work that demonstrates effectively how the local freedom struggle could have a much wider impact on the articulation of sectional conflict is Josephine F. Pacheco, *The Pearl: A Failed Slave Escape on the Potomac* (Charlotte: University of North Carolina Press, 2005).

the platform of the Liberty Party and later antislavery parties. Although proposals for abolition received precious few congressional votes, a prohibition of the most public manifestations of the slave trade formed part of the body of legislation that would make up the Compromise of 1850. In other respects, slavery in the District remained intact until the outbreak of the Civil War.[19]

## A Model City

Washington was in many ways an anomalous presence in the United States of the 1850s. The dreams of imperial splendor attached to its foundation had by no means been fulfilled – and, indeed, had been inhibited by the democratic dynamic of mid-nineteenth-century America. Its geographic status was liminal, resting awkwardly between sections, and its constitutional status was anomalous, a seeming contradiction of the principles of U.S. government. Yet rather than being a deviant case by virtue of its exceptional status, the federal capital was central to the decision making that went into the making of emancipation and Reconstruction, and its experience can tell us something important about the purposes and possibilities of federal policy in the Civil War era. As Howard Gillette Jr. observes, "the very fact of federal control over its local affairs makes Washington's story exemplary."[20]

The District of Columbia, said a late-nineteenth-century historian, "has always been a kind of experimental station, from law-making to rain-making, for the country." Although, according to most nineteenth-century readings of the Constitution, the federal government possessed only limited authority over domestic policy making, there were no restrictions on its sovereignty within the boundaries of the federal District. There it held plenary power, serving as national, state, and municipal authority

---

[19] Don E. Fehrenbacher, *The Slaveholding Republic: An Account of the United States Government's Relation to Slavery* (Ward M. MacAfee, ed., New York: Oxford University Press, 2002), 67 and 49–88 passim; Harrold, *Subversives*, 30–32, 34–35, 107–10, 163–67; James B. Stewart, *Holy Warriors: The Abolitionists and American Slavery* (revised edn., New York: Hill & Wang, 1996), 81–88; Gilbert H. Barnes, *The Antislavery Impulse, 1830–1844* (New York: Harcourt, Brace and World, 1964 [1933]), 109–46; Robert P. Ludlum, "The Antislavery 'Gag Rule': History and Arguments," *Journal of Negro History*, 26 (April 1941): 203–43; William Lee Miller, *Arguing about Slavery: The Great Battle in the United States Congress* (New York: Knopf, 1966).

[20] Gillette, *Between Justice and Beauty*, xi. See also Alan Lessoff, *Nation and Its City: Politics, "Corruption," and Progress in Washington, D.C., 1861–1902* (Baltimore: Johns Hopkins University Press, 1994), 1–13.

all in one. There, unencumbered by the rival claims of other governmental authorities, it was free to formulate its own social and municipal policy. Although Congress did not always trouble itself greatly with the management of local affairs, the policy decisions that were made, or not made, for the federal District had a more than local significance. The social and political institutions that were established there might be said to carry the imprimatur of the United States. That meant that the affairs of the District were, at least potentially, the business of all Americans, and at certain junctures in the nation's history, that mattered a great deal.[21]

The changes brought by the Civil War and Reconstruction gave congressional policy for the District of Columbia an added significance. "The war . . . has made a new slate in many things relating to law as well as politics," observed Pennsylvania Representative M. Russell Thayer in January 1866.[22] Republican congressmen used the nation's capital as a proving ground for their policies of emancipation and Reconstruction. Washington's slaves, who were freed in April 1862, were the first to benefit from the emancipation program of the new Republican majority. Similarly, Congress decided to extend the right to suffrage to black citizens of the District months before it was imposed, through the Reconstruction Acts, on the occupied South. Racial distinctions were eliminated from the laws of the District, segregation was prohibited on the city's street railroads and in other public places, and the foundations were laid for a system of public schools for African American children. The Republican senator Charles Sumner described Washington as "the place where all the great reforms of the war have begun."[23] The federal district, therefore, played a pivotal role in the articulation of the congressional program of Reconstruction.

It might seem paradoxical to talk about Reconstruction in Washington, which was, after all, the nerve center of the Union. In fact, the District of Columbia went through a process of Reconstruction in many ways comparable to that which was experienced farther south. The architects of Reconstruction believed that their handiwork was as applicable to

---

[21] Edward Ingle, *The Negro in the District of Columbia* (Baltimore: Johns Hopkins University Press, 1893), 8. For an historical review of the relationship between the federal government and the District of Columbia, see Diner, "Statehood and the Governance of the District of Columbia." See also Robert Harrison, "The Ideal of a Model City: Congress and the District of Columbia, 1905–1909," *Journal of Urban History* 15 (1989): 435–63.

[22] CG, 39.1:282.

[23] *New National Era*, August 7, 1873.

the capital city in which they sat and legislated as to the states of the former Confederacy. In the first place, Washington looked and felt much like a southern city. In the eyes of the northern soldiers, politicians, journalists, bureaucrats, and businessmen who were drawn to the city during and after the Civil War, Washington badly needed an infusion of "Yankee vigor" to pull it out of its subtropical languor. Second, it retained much of the social atmosphere, as well as the legal paraphernalia, of a slaveholding community. It emerged from the war with a large freed population, expanded by the arrival of the "contrabands," whose rights and liberties needed protection against a local white population that was at best indifferent, at worst hostile to its claims to equal treatment. Third, although most of the city's white residents supported the Union and enlisted in proportionate numbers to defend its integrity, a sizable number did not. Many Washingtonians journeyed south to offer their services to the Confederacy; many who remained were known to harbor secessionist sympathies. Republicans tended to exaggerate the extent of disloyalty, but, however extensive it might have been, it gave them grounds for believing that Washington was, at least partially, rebel territory and sorely in need of reconstruction.[24]

The politics of Reconstruction in the nation's capital were given added meaning by the city's demographic transformation during the Civil War era. Washington's white population increased by 47 percent between 1860 and 1870, with most of the newcomers hailing from north of the Mason-Dixon Line. By 1870, more than 20 percent were born in the North and another 13 percent in Europe. This "carpetbagger generation," as Carl Abbott calls it, did much to change both the political complexion and the social orientation of the city. Still more important was the trebling of the District's black population, for during the troubled war years, thousands of freed men and women, mostly drawn from the neighboring slave states, took refuge in the relative security of federal territory. The enlarged black population provided the foundation for Republican control of the city government for several years after 1867, but it also gave rise to an array of social and economic problems that complicated the governance of the city for year to come. The scale of the movement, relative to Washington's antebellum population, was comparable to that of the "Great Migration" of African Americans from the

---

[24] See James H. Whyte, "Divided Loyalties in Washington during the Civil War," *Records of the Columbia Historical Society, 1960–62* (Washington, D.C., 1963), 103–22; Green, *Washington*, 248–51, 285–8; Leech, *Reveille in Washington*, 27–54.

rural South to the urban North after World War I and so were its effects. In Washington, as in other southern cities, many of the "necessary elements for ghetto formation" were present long before the dawn of the twentieth century.[25]

For a few short years after the Civil War, African Americans enjoyed a substantial measure of political power. Their enfranchisement opened up the space for an extraordinary efflorescence of political organizing, grassroots activism, and community development. Freedpeople attempted to convert the newly established Republican Party into an organization that would serve the social and economic needs of their communities, a forum in which they could give voice to their concerns about public education, civil rights and, above all, employment. However briefly and however imperfectly, the party acted as a force for social change. For a while, the interests of African American voters coincided with those of a group of influential white Republicans who were interested in the physical refurbishment of the capital. However, the improvements initiated by the Republican mayor Sayles J. Bowen between 1868 and 1870, largely to please his black constituents, and the still more grandiose projects of the territorial government between 1871 and 1874 strained the financial resources of local government far beyond what either taxpayers or Congress would tolerate. The reaction led to the eventual abrogation of home rule and the destruction of this particularly vital form of black politics.

If political Reconstruction came early to Washington, so did its demise. If Washington's blacks were the first to gain the suffrage, they were also the first to lose it. Many Republicans in Congress and many Republicans, especially black Republicans, in Washington commented on the irony: that at the heart of the republic, the right to self-government should be abrogated. "In this District," noted the Washington *National Republican*, "the experiment was first made of giving the black man the suffrage. Has it come to this, that the Republican party admits and acknowledges its failure?" Thus, having briefly stood as a model of interracial democracy,

---

[25] U.S. Office of Education, *Special Report of the Commissioner of Education on the Condition and Improvement of Public Schools in the District of Columbia*, Ho. Exec. Doc. 315, 41.2 (June 13, 1871), Series 1427, 28–38; Abbott, "Dimensions of Regional Change," 1375–79; Paul A. Groves, "The Development of a Black Residential Community in Southwest Washington, 1860–1897," *Records of the Columbia Historical Society*, 1973–74 (Washington, DC: 1976), 260–63; Groves and Edward K. Muller, "The Evolution of Black Residential Areas in Late Nineteenth-Century Cities," *Journal of Historical Geography* 1 (April 1975): 169–91.

Washington emerged from Reconstruction as an exemplar of a very different form of government.[26]

## The Capital and the Union

*Washington during Civil War and Reconstruction: Race and Radicalism* is primarily concerned with the working of Reconstruction at the grassroots; with how federal policies designed to reconstruct southern society after the Civil War and to protect the civil and political rights of freedpeople worked in practice; with their actual impact on the lives and opportunities of African Americans in the communities in which they lived; and with the importance of African American agency in shaping the postbellum world. It explores the ways in which African Americans contributed to their own emancipation and fought to secure their own civil and political rights. It therefore forms part of a growing body of research on "grassroots Reconstruction," which links political decisions to social change in southern communities after 1865. This includes the work of Julie Saville, Rebecca J. Scott, John C. Rodrigue, Steven Hahn, and Eric Foner, as well as a substantial body of work on race relations in postbellum southern cities by, among others, Michael Fitzgerald, Elsa Barkley Brown, and Wilbert Jenkins.[27]

[26] Washington *National Republican*, December 18, 1874. See also *CR*, 43.2:120–22, 1103–4. For an account of the rise and fall of territorial government and the termination of home rule, see Robert Harrison, "From Biracial Democracy to Direct Rule: The End of Self-Government in the Nation's Capital, 1865–1878," *Journal of Policy History*, 18 (Spring 2006): 241–69; William M. Maury, *Alexander "Boss" Shepherd and the Board of Public Works* (Washington: George Washington University Press, 1975); Mark W. Summers, *The Era of Good Stealings* (New York: Oxford University Press, 1993), 137–47; James H. Whyte, *Uncivil War: Washington during Reconstruction, 1865 – 1878* (New York: Twayne, 1958), 90–177, 203–36; Green, *Washington*, 332–62, 386–95; Lessoff, *Nation and Its City*, 44–129; Gillette, *Between Justice and Beauty*, 56–68.

[27] Julie Saville, *The Work of Reconstruction: From Slave to Wage Laborer in South Carolina, 1860–1870* (Cambridge: Cambridge University Press, 1994); Julie Saville, "Rites and Power: Reflections on Slavery, Freedom and Political Ritual,' in Sylvia R. Frey and Betty Wood, eds., *From Slavery to Freedom in the Atlantic World* (London: Frank Cass, 1999), 81–102; Rebecca J. Scott, "Stubborn and Disposed to Stand Their Ground: Black Militia, Sugar Workers and the Dynamics of Collective Action in the Louisiana Sugar Bowl, 1863–67," in ibid., 103–26; John C. Rodrigue, "Labor Militancy and Black Grassroots Political Mobilization in the Louisiana Sugar Region, 1865–1868," *Journal of Southern History* 67 (February 2001): 115–42; Michael W. Fitzgerald, *The Union League Movement in the Deep South: Politics and Agricultural Change during Reconstruction* (Baton Rouge: Louisiana State University Press, 1989); Steven Hahn, *A Nation under Our Feet: Black Political Struggles in the Rural South from Slavery to the Great Migration* (Cambridge, MA: Harvard University Press, 2003); Eric Foner, "Black

Far from an isolated case, separated from the mainstream of American experience by its unusual political status, Washington was absolutely central to the political dynamics of Reconstruction. An examination of its experience during the troubled years of Civil War and Reconstruction can tell us a great deal about the underlying political processes. In the first place, we can see Republican policy makers execute their policies of emancipation and Reconstruction under special laboratory conditions, without the interposition of state power. We can see how they behaved, what policies they enacted, when free of countervailing authority. Therefore, the first objective of this study is to examine congressional attitudes toward the District of Columbia, particularly in its role as a testing ground for the principles of Reconstruction. Second, we can investigate how federal policies of emancipation and Reconstruction worked themselves out under urban conditions. More specifically, we can analyze the efforts of government agencies, especially the Army and the Freedmen's Bureau, to assist the freed population of the District and the ways in which Republican congressmen and city officials after the war addressed the social problems resulting from the large-scale black migration. We shall examine the development of race relations in the District, and, more particularly, the way in which they were affected by the actions of government. In doing so, we can explore the ways in which social and economic developments interacted with political issues in determining the success or failure of Reconstruction. Some historians have argued that the ultimate failure of Reconstruction lay in Republicans' failure to provide an economic foundation for the civil and political freedoms that were promised to the formerly enslaved.[28]

The politics of Washington, D.C., provides evidence of the complex ways in which what Eric Foner calls the "Reconstruction of the North" intersected with the Reconstruction of the South. An examination of the

---

Reconstruction Leaders at the Grass Roots," in Leon Litwack and August Meier, eds., *Black Leaders of the Nineteenth Century* (Urbana: University of Illinois Press, 1988), 219–36; Eric Foner, *Nothing but Freedom: Emancipation and Its Legacy* (Baton Rouge: Louisiana State University Press, 1983). On grassroots Reconstruction in the cities, see Michael Fitzgerald, *Urban Emancipation: Popular Politics in Reconstruction Mobile, 1860–1890* (Baton Rouge: Louisiana State University Press, 2002); Elsa Barkley Brown, "Negotiating and Transforming the Public Sphere: African American Political Life in the Transition from Slavery to Freedom," *Public Culture* 7 (Fall 1994): 107–46; Wilbert Jenkins, *Seizing the New Day: African Americans in Post-Civil War Charleston* (Bloomington: University of Indiana Press, 1998).

[28] With reference to Washington, see, in particular, Johnston, "Surviving Freedom," 329–30.

factors influencing congressional policy toward the District of Columbia not only sheds light on the reasons for disfranchisement there but also illustrates the complexity of the process through which the national government withdrew its support for Reconstruction governments in the former Confederacy. The manner in which self-government in the national capital came to an end offers valuable insights into the political processes that led to the effective abandonment of Reconstruction. A primary objective, then, is to consider what an analysis of the experience of the District contributes toward an understanding of Reconstruction and its failure.[29]

At the same time, the project touches on the discussion of state formation and governance by historians such as Richard J. Bensel, Morton Keller, and William J. Novak.[30] An examination of governance in the nation's capital enables us to explore important aspects of the operation of the nineteenth-century American state as it responded to the challenges of a new urban-industrial society. It provides a valuable case study of the working of municipal government, with, of course, the municipal authority being, in the last analysis, the U.S. Congress. We shall analyze the social policies of municipal and federal governments, as well as their efforts to provide satisfactory public services and clean and passable streets. As Howard Gillette Jr. observes, "By intentionally setting out to make a city in the federal district, Congress had assumed for itself a role in urban policy." However, "federal oversight of Washington in practice proved uneven at best and at times disastrous." As at other times in the city's history, the federal government failed to provide the attention or the resources to create a model city on the banks of the Potomac and, in most cases, followed, rather than took the lead, in the adoption of new ideas and technologies. This study addresses the question of the power and reach of the nineteenth-century American state. It does so

[29] On the interrelatedness of the Reconstruction of the South and "the Reconstruction of the North," see Eric Foner, *Reconstruction: America's Unfinished Revolution, 1863–1877* (New York: Harper, 1988), 461–88; Heather Cox Richardson, *The Death of Reconstruction: Race, Labor, and Politics in the Post-Civil War North, 1865–1901* (Cambridge, MA: Harvard University Press, 2001); David Scobey, *Empire City: The Making and Meaning of the New York City Landscape* (Philadelphia: Temple University Press, 2002), 251–61; David Quigley, *Second Founding: New York City, Reconstruction, and the Making of American Democracy* (New York: Hill & Wang, 2004).

[30] Richard F. Bensel, *Yankee Leviathan: The Origins of Central State Authority, 1859–1877* (Cambridge: Cambridge University Press, 1990); Morton Keller, *Affairs of State: Public Life in Late Nineteenth-Century America* (Cambridge, MA: Harvard University Press, 1977); William J. Novak, *The People's Welfare: Law and Regulation in Nineteenth-Century America* (Chapel Hill: University of North Carolina Press, 1996).

in the special setting of the nation's capital. Thus, the history of federal policy toward the District of Columbia is used to explore some of the characteristics of American political development in the third quarter of the nineteenth century.[31]

Of course, policy making for the District was never just about the District. Every man in the United States had an interest in the city, said a Republican congressman during debate on legislation creating a new territorial government.[32] Yet their interests were diverse and, in some cases, incompatible. The kind of capital that Americans wished to see on the banks of the Potomac would ultimately depend on their convictions about what the United States stood for and how it should develop. Such convictions were diverse and sometimes conflicting. It was because it touched on so many different political projects and found a place in so many alternative narratives of the nation's future that determining the destiny of the District of Columbia proved so problematic and, ultimately, so paradoxical in its outcome.

---

[31] Gillette, *Between Justice and Beauty*, ix–x. On congressional governance in a later period, see Harrison, "Ideal of a Model City"; Lessoff, *Nation and Its City*, 130–63. For a more positive view of Washington's progress in relation to other cities, see ibid., esp. 26–30.

[32] CG, 41.3:642.

# Wartime Washington

## Introduction

The Civil War marked a clear rupture between the sleepy federal city of the antebellum era and the national capital that took its place after 1865. In the first place, the conflict greatly enlarged the federal presence in the city, not only in the shape of the men and materials that were hastily assembled to prosecute the war and then dispersed equally hastily on its conclusion but also in the shape of a more permanent expansion of federal power. Second, the wartime mobilization brought new people to the city. Soldiers, administrators, and businessmen from all across the North gravitated to the capital of the Union to play their part in the struggle – or to profit from it – and their coming brought a demographic transformation that had far-reaching implications for the future development of the city. Third, the election of 1860 and the subsequent secession of eleven southern states left most agencies of the federal government in the hands of the Republican Party, a party that had enjoyed only an embryonic existence in the city before the Civil War. Congressional Republicans did not hesitate to initiate a wide-ranging revision of the District's laws and institutions, beginning with the abolition of slavery in April 1862. They then set in motion processes leading to the creation of a viable local Republican Party that would eventually be strong enough to control the city government.

That outcome was made possible by another of the changes brought about by the war – namely, the coming of the "contrabands." The large-scale federal military presence around Washington, along with the loosening of the integuments of slavery in neighboring states, encouraged

thousands of fugitives to take refuge in and around the capital, where
the able-bodied among them could take advantage of the government's
almost insatiable demand for labor during the wartime emergency and
dependents could find at least some measure of relief in the contraband
camps established by the Army. Their arrival, however, greatly complicated the problems of racial adjustment that followed the emancipation
of slaves in the District. The needs of the large number of dependent freedpeople stretched the resources, and still more the patience, of the military
authorities. Fortunately, the social problems caused by the migration
drew the attention of freedmen's aid societies, both in Washington and
in the North, the endeavors of which did much to ease the problems of
caring for the contrabands but also led to tensions between volunteer
philanthropists and the army officers responsible for freedmen's affairs.
These tensions spilled over into controversies over the management of the
Freedmen's Bureau after the war.

## The Question of Loyalty

Those who lived in Washington during the troubled winter of 1860–
61, as sectional conflict evolved into secession and secession into civil
war, recalled it as a time of extreme anxiety. The breakup of the Union
left the city in a position of extreme jeopardy, located as it was close
to the boundary between North and South. Indeed, although the future
allegiance of Virginia and Maryland lay in the balance, there could be no
certainty that its position as federal capital would remain tenable. When
the chips had fallen, the city found itself on the frontier between the new
Confederacy and the old Union, ensuring that its political role would be
reinforced by its function as a base for frontline military operations. The
anxiety produced by these strategic calculations was intensified by a deep
uncertainty about the loyalties of Washingtonians themselves. During the
winter and early spring, until local militia units were supplemented by
federal troops, loyal citizens and federal officials not only feared invasion
from without but insurrection from within. Whether at the hands of units
of the Confederate Army or of local Confederate sympathizers, it seemed,
for a while, as if the capital was ripe for the taking.[1]

---

[1] For an account of these months of uncertainty, see Constance M. Green, *Washington:
from Village to Capital, 1800–1878* (Princeton, NJ: Princeton University Press, 1962),
230–43; Margaret Leech, *Reveille in Washington, 1861–1865* (New York: Harper, 1941),
27–29, 53–65; Ernest B. Furgurson, *Freedom Rising: Washington in the Civil War*

It was impossible, remembered the journalist Noah Brooks, to convey "any adequate idea of the atmosphere that pervaded Washington" during those months. Loyalists "were constantly haunted by suspicions of secret plotting all about them." Several hundred Washingtonians, including a number of prominent citizens, such as former mayor Walter Lenox and U.S. District Attorney Robert Ould, journeyed south to offer their services to the Confederacy, and at least four hundred citizens of the District enlisted in the Confederate Army. An unknown number of southern sympathizers remained, either keeping their counsel for the duration of the war or, in some cases, actively working on behalf of the enemy. Until captured, flamboyant female spies such as Rose Greenhow and Belle Boyd conveyed military secrets to the authorities in Richmond, and other local ladies expressed their appreciation for Confederate agents and prisoners of war with gifts and friendly visits. Nearly three hundred local residents were incarcerated in the Old Capitol Prison on suspicion of disloyalty – so many, indeed, that the overflow had to be accommodated in two houses on Duff Green's Row. Several local clergymen were censured for delivering disloyal sermons or for refusing to read a prayer of thanksgiving for the success of Union armies, and three of their churches were closed by order of the military governor of the District. The municipal police and fire services were believed to be riddled with Confederate sympathizers at the beginning of the war, and the imposition of a loyalty oath for municipal elections in 1862 led to a sharp reduction in turnout. To make things worse, Mayor James Berret unwisely refused to take a loyalty oath at the beginning of the war on the grounds that, as "the chief magistrate of the city, elected by popular suffrage," he should not be required to do so, and in consequence he was stripped of his office and required to spend a few weeks in a federal prison. Although probably motivated by a sense of the dignity and importance of his office rather than Confederate sympathies, his action did much to stir up fears that the population of Washington was riddled with subversion.[2]

(New York: Knopf, 2004), 19–85. On the questionable loyalty of local militia units and their replacement with more dependable companies, see also Wilhelmus B. Bryan, *A History of the National Capital* (2 vols., New York: Macmillan, 1914–16), 2:463–72; James H. Whyte, "Divided Loyalties in Washington during the Civil War," *Records of the Columbia Historical Society, 1960–62* (1963): 105–7.

[2] Noah Brooks, *Washington, D.C., in Lincoln's Time* (Herbert Mitgang, ed., Athens: University of Georgia Press, 1989 [1895]), 22; Bryan, *History of the National Capital*, 2:486–87. On the evidence of disloyalty, see *Evening Star*, May 30, 1862; *National Republican*, September 29, 1862; Whyte, "Divided Loyalties"; Bryan, *History of the National Capital*, 2:460–62; Green, *Washington*, 245–51, 285–88; Leech, *Reveille in Washington*, 49–50,

Congressman George W. Julian declared in January 1866 that "a very large majority of the white people of this District have been rebels in heart before the war, and are rebels in heart still." Republicans like Julian wildly exaggerated the extent of disloyalty. As the city's defenders were quick to point out, although some 400 local men might have joined the armed forces of the Confederacy, 16,872 Union soldiers were enrolled in the District, although not all of them would have been resident there at the outset. In view of its southern antecedents and connections, concludes the historian James H. Whyte, the loyalty shown by the population of the District was quite remarkable. Nevertheless, the charges of disloyalty that rebounded around the city during the Civil War gave Republicans grounds for believing that Washington was, at least partially, rebel territory and that its inhabitants could not be wholly relied on.[3]

## The Capital of the Union

The most obvious manifestation of Washington's newfound status as nerve center of the Union was the arrival of large numbers of soldiers. "The country town had been turned into a great, confused garrison town," observed Margaret Leech. Hundreds and thousands of soldiers awaited transportation to the front line in various barracks and encampments around the District or manned the elaborate network of fortifications that encircled it. Parades through the streets by newly arrived regiments, for a while a source of diversion to Washington residents, soon came to be regarded as routine events. In due course, many of those men returned as casualties to be treated in the makeshift hospitals that sprang up all over the city. Several buildings were converted into hospitals, including, for a time, the Capitol, the Patent Office, the insane asylum, and several church buildings, where thousands of desperate and wounded men received treatment for their injuries. At times, in the wake of major engagements, as many as fifty thousand men were treated in the local hospitals, a number roughly equivalent to the whole population

134–40; Furgurson, *Freedom Rising*, 113–16, 125–30. On divisions within the churches, see ibid., 181–84; Whyte, "Divided Loyalties," 119; Kathleen Trainor, "'But the Choir Did Not Sing': How the Civil War Split First Unitarian Church," *Washington History* 7 (1998): 54–71.

[3] *CG*, 39.1:259; Whyte, "Divided Loyalties," 121. For rebuttals, see the remarks of Councilman Samuel A. Peugh in *Journal of the 63rd Council* (Washington, DC, 1866), 412–17, and William W. Moore in *Journal of the 64th Council* (Washington, DC, 1867), 711–24.

of the city in 1850. "All Washington is a great hospital," noted Brooks during Grant's Virginia campaign of 1864. "Boatloads of unfortunate and maimed men are continually arriving."[4]

Besides housing two hundred thousand or more troops, Washington served as a distributing center for supplies bound for the armies in Virginia. Countless mules and wagons made their way through the city streets, destroying the small amount of paving that had already been installed and converting already difficult roads into a morass, while vast piles of fuel, timber, and other stores stood awaiting embarkation at the docks and railroad terminals. Government warehouses, cattle pens, slaughterhouses, corrals, and clothing depots sprang up around the city. "Washington is just the busiest place now, that I ever saw," remarked Benjamin B. French, the commissioner of public buildings and grounds, in December 1861, "and I rather guess the war will prove a blessing to us here."[5]

After an initial plunge in commercial fortunes, local businessmen soon began to derive substantial benefits from this new activity. Although most of the uniforms, tents, firearms, ammunition, and other military supplies were sourced outside the District, there was nevertheless an increased demand for a wide range of services, ranging from barbershops to livery stables. Tailors, blacksmiths, saddlers, hoteliers, and caterers all benefited from the temporary increase in the city's population. Several new banks were also formed during the war years. The new enterprises included numerous saloons and brothels that, for all the efforts of the provost marshals, catered to the needs and desires of an army of young men. Real estate values in the city soared, but so did rents and the cost of living for civilian workers, whose wages failed to keep up with the wartime inflation. Housing became both scarce and expensive, with the result that local newspapers reported that some federal employees found it

---

[4] Leech, *Reveille in Washington*, 75; P. J. Staudenraus, ed., *Mr. Lincoln's Washington: Selections from the Writings of Noah Brooks, Civil War Correspondent* (South Brunswick, NJ: Yoseloff, 1967), 320. For a general account of conditions in wartime Washington, see Furgurson, *Freedom Rising*; Leech, *Reveille in Washington*; Green, *Washington*, chaps. 10 and 11; Elden E. Billings, "Social and Economic Conditions in Washington during the Civil War," *Records of the Columbia Historical Society, 1963–65* (Washington, DC, 1966): 191–209; David C. Mearns, "A View of Washington in 1863," ibid., 210–20. On the neighboring cities of Georgetown and Alexandria, see Mary Mitchell, *Divided Town* (Barre, MA: Barre Publishers, 1968); James G. Barber, *Alexandria in the Civil War* (Lynchburg, VA: H. E. Howard, 1988).

[5] Benjamin B. French to Henry Flagg French, December 1, 1861, French MSS, Library of Congress.

more economical to commute by rail from Baltimore, where food and accommodation were cheaper.[6]

The concentration of so large a temporary population resulted in a dramatic increase in crime. Pickpockets and muggers patrolled the streets, especially outside the more densely populated areas and especially at night, and drunken brawls occurred all too frequently. William Owner, a local diarist prone to a highly jaundiced view of current events, complained of the large number of "counterfeiters and pickpockets" who had gravitated to the city and of the violent robbers who stalked the streets: "scarcely a night passes that some person is not garroted in the public highway."[7] Shortly after the beginning of the war, doubtful of the loyalty of the existing city police force, which was in any case too small to cope even with prewar levels of crime, Congress created the new Metropolitan Police Department, managed by a federally appointed board of commissioners and financed by a mixture of federal and municipal contributions. However, with 150 officers, the new force lacked the manpower to cope with the current emergency, and it tended to leave the supervision of off-duty military personnel to the provost marshals. Besides reorganizing the police force, Congress created a new professional fire service. The eight volunteer fire companies that had combatively, but not always efficiently, attended to fires in the antebellum period were no longer adequate to handle the increased risk of conflagration during wartime. The volunteer companies were persuaded to pool their forces, and a salaried fire department was set up in 1864.[8]

The war years also saw the completion of the Washington Aqueduct, work on which had commenced in 1853, at an eventual cost of $3.3 million. Supplies of fresh water drawn from above the Great Falls of the Potomac began to flow into the city in December 1863.[9] During the war years, Washington acquired its first street railroad. In 1862, a group of Philadelphia investors were awarded a charter to operate a railroad along Pennsylvania Avenue from Georgetown to the Navy Yard. The so-called

[6] Green, *Washington*, 244–45, 262–66; Furgurson, *Freedom Rising*, 206–8.

[7] William Owner Diary, May 5, 1862, March 14, 1863, Library of Congress. On the increase in crime levels, see also *Chronicle*, November 4, 1862; Kenneth G. Alfers, *Law and Order in the Capital City: A History of the Washington Police, 1800–1886* (Washington: George Washington University Press, 1976), 26–27; Green, *Washington*, 250–52.

[8] Alfers, *Law and Order in the Capital* City, 24–31; Bryan, *History of the National Capital*, 2:459–60, 481, 483–84; Green, *Washington*, 248–51, 256.

[9] Alan Lessoff, *The Nation and Its City: Politics, "Corruption," and Progress in Washington, D.C., 1861–1902* (Baltimore: Johns Hopkins University Press, 1994), 25.

Washington and Georgetown Railway was supplemented two years later by the Metropolitan Railroad, which ran from the intersection of New Jersey Avenue and A Street to 14th and I.[10] The grading and graveling of streets, although not carried out to a particularly high standard, proceeded throughout the war years. The city government, after relying on rented school buildings throughout its history, responded to congressional legislation requiring it to provide places for all school-age children by voting in 1862 to build a series of purpose-built schools for white children. The first of these, the Wallach School, was opened on July 4, 1864.[11] As a final demonstration that the improvement of the capital would not be interrupted by the sectional conflict, work proceeded on the dome of the Capitol, which was unveiled in all its splendor in December 1863. As a grace note, the massive nineteen-foot statue, "Freedom," which had been awaiting its apotheosis for some years, was finally elevated to its place of splendor on top of the dome, demonstrating to the world both the durability of the federal Union and the growing importance within that Union of its capital city.[12]

The population seemed to grow exponentially during the war years. The Metropolitan Police estimated in 1864 that approximately 140,000 persons resided in Washington, more than double the 1860 population. The local postmaster estimated that, including soldiers in the neighboring camps, he was distributing mail to a population of more than one million people. In 1870, when the dust had settled, the armies had been demobilized, and most of the temporary residents had gone home, the population remained at 109,199, still 77 percent higher than the 1860 total (the figures for the District as a whole were 131,700 and 75 percent, respectively). The most noteworthy component, as we shall see in the next section, was the explosive growth of the black population, with the coming of the "contrabands." However, Washington's white population increased by 47 percent between 1860 and 1870, with most of the newcomers hailing from north of the Mason-Dixon Line. In 1870, more than

---

[10] William Tindall, "Beginnings of Street Railways in the National Capital," *Records of the Columbia Historical Society* 21 (1918): 27–28, 35–36; Leroy O. King Jr., *One Hundred Years of Capitol Traction* (n.p., 1972), 3–9; Lessoff, *Nation and Its Capital*, 29–30; Bryan, *History of the National Capital*, 2:491–94.

[11] *Evening Star*, June 9, 1862; *Chronicle*, November 18, 1862; Green, *Washington*, 257–58; Bryan, *History of the National Capital*, 2:506–8.

[12] *New York Times*, December, 1863; Staudenraus, ed., *Mr. Lincoln's Washington*, 264–65. The elevation of "Freedom" is a recurrent theme in Ernest B. Furguson's account of wartime Washington. *Freedom Rising*, 3–5, 51–54, 179–80, 274–77.

20 percent of the District population had been born in the North and another 13 percent in Europe. This "carpetbagger generation," as Carl Abbott calls it, did much to change both the political complexion and the social orientation of the city.[13] Republicans like the editor of the *Washington Daily Morning Chronicle* pointed to the infusion of energy and enterprise that had come with the arrival of large numbers of northern army officers, civil servants, and businessmen. "New life has been infused into business by the inspiration of Northern ideas and industry," he proclaimed in February 1864. He pointed to the new buildings that had sprung up over the previous few years, the arrival of Potomac water, and the laying of street railroads. Another measure of progress was the huge increase in real estate values, from $41,084,985 in 1860 to $126,873,618 in 1870, an increase of 76 percent per capita. It seemed that, with the Civil War, Washington had crossed over an important divide. Not only was the integrity of the Union triumphantly affirmed, but Washington itself had commenced a social and political transformation that would replace the sleepy village of the antebellum era with a modern metropolis.[14]

### "An Asylum for Free Negroes"

Shortly after the outbreak of the Civil War, Colonel Alfred H. Terry, commanding the 2nd Connecticut Infantry on the outskirts of Washington, reported that "six men of color, representing themselves to be fugitive slaves from Howard County in the State of Maryland" and their masters to be "secessionists in sentiment and opinion" had entered his camp. Like Union commanders experiencing similar encounters all over the theatre of war, he asked for clarification of the fugitives' legal status and advice on what he should do with them.[15] The six runaways were among the first ripples of a tide of fugitive slaves, soon to be known as "contrabands," that flowed toward the District of Columbia during the course of the war. Some marched over the Long Bridge or seeped unobserved

---

[13] Green, *Washington*, 21, 264; U.S. Office of Education, *Special Report of the Commissioner of Education on the Condition and Improvement of Public Schools in the District of Columbia*, Ho. Exec. Doc. 315, 41.2 (June 13, 1871), Series 1427, 28–38; Carl Abbott, "Dimensions of Regional Change in Washington, D.C.," *American Historical Review* 95 (December 1990): 1375–79.

[14] *Chronicle*, February 22, 1864; Staudenraus, ed., *Mr. Lincoln's Washington*, 238–41; Lessoff, *Nation and Its City*, 19–20.

[15] Alfred H. Terry to Theodore Talbot, June 12, 1861, in Ira Berlin et al., eds., *Freedom: A Documentary History of Emancipation, 1861–1867. Series I, Vol. I. The Destruction of Slavery* (Cambridge: Cambridge University Press, 1985), 167.

into Washington and Georgetown; others traveled on foot, on mules and donkeys, and, in one case, in a gigantic ox cart bearing twenty people. Still others crossed the Potomac by boat, forming a lengthy human tail to returning Union armies or arriving in small family groups. Men and women, young and old, they brought with them no more than a few ragged clothes and the sketchiest personal belongings held together in ragged bundles, effectively placing their future in the hands of the federal authorities.

They came first from the adjacent counties of Maryland and Virginia. The *Washington Evening Star* reported in April 1862 that the slaves of Prince George's County, Maryland, were "running away in numbers." An estimated two hundred to three hundred a week crossed the bridge over the East Branch of the Potomac and got "in among their friends in the city." Prince George's County was stripped of 28.5 percent of its black population between 1860 and 1870, whereas Prince William County, Virginia, lost 36.9 percent and Stafford County 59.1 percent over the same period. As Union armies penetrated deeper into Virginia, they brought back hundreds of fugitives from a wide belt of counties between Alexandria and Richmond and between Hampton Roads and the Blue Ridge. For example, in two days after the Union defeat at Second Bull Run, four hundred contrabands arrived in the District, and in June 1864, during Grant's overland campaign, as many as 1466 arrivals were recorded. Each incursion opened up new avenues of escape.[16] By April 1863, an estimated 10,000 fugitive slaves had made their way into the District. By the time of Lee's surrender, Washington's black population had increased between two and three times. A census taken by the Army in May 1865, "not including house servants," found 16,092 refugees in the District, but that seriously undercounted the large number living independently in the city. A more detailed enumeration of the District population in 1867 found the black residents numbering 38,663, two-thirds of whom had arrived since 1860. The 1870 census recorded that,

---

[16] Washington *Evening Star*, April 7, August 29, August 30, 1862, and April 11, 1863; Allan John Johnston, "Surviving Freedom: The Black Community in Washington, D.C., 1860–1880" (Ph.D. diss., Duke University, 1980), 158, 189–93, 198–204. See also Oliver Otis Howard, *Autobiography of Oliver Otis Howard* (2 vols., New York: Baker & Taylor, 1907), 2:166–67; Lois E. Horton, "The Day of Jubilee: Black Migration during the Civil War and Reconstruction," in Francine C. Cary, ed., *Urban Odyssey: A Multicultural History of Washington, D.C.* (Washington, DC: Smithsonian Institution Press, 1996), 65–78; Barbara Jean Fields, *Slavery and Freedom on the Middle Ground: Maryland during the Nineteenth Century* (New Haven, CT: Yale University Press, 1985), 100–21; Green, *Washington*, 272–78; *Freedom*, I, 2:159–67.

of the 43,324 African Americans resident in the District, 16,785 were natives of Virginia and West Virginia and 11,720 of Maryland. However, the likelihood is that, counting those who moved on elsewhere, the total number of wartime arrivals may have been as high as 40,000.[17]

The fugitives "made their way to this city," observed the *Evening Star*, "having got the idea that they will be free here." Especially after the emancipation of the District's own slaves in April 1862, Washington acquired something of a reputation as "an asylum for free negroes."[18] However, the fugitives' legal situation was far from clear-cut, and their presence in the capital was not without danger. Certainly the slaves of Virginia masters could hope to exploit the legal fiction through which human property employed in support of rebel military operations was categorized as "contraband of war" and confiscated for employment by Union forces, a formula first devised by General Ben Butler at Fortress Monroe in May 1861, confirmed by the Secretary of War Simon Cameron, and widely applied by Union commanders as they encountered fugitive slaves on enemy soil. The First Confiscation Act, passed by Congress in July 1861, formalized the presumption that slaves employed in the Confederate war effort could rightly be seized from their owners.[19]

General Joseph K. F. Mansfield, commanding the Department of Washington, was quick to adopt that expedient, informing a local judge in July 1861 that the secretary of war had decided slaves should not be returned to rebel owners but should be considered as "contrabands" and put to work "for the improvement of public premises." An officer at the headquarters of the Army of the Potomac told General Joseph Hooker, in response to an inquiry about what to do with "runaway negroes," that if employed by the rebels for military labor, they should be detained

---

[17] *Evening* Star, April 11, 1863; Johnston, "Surviving Freedom," 162–69; Montgomery C. Meigs to Edwin M. Stanton, May 8, 1865, in Ira Berlin et al., eds., *Freedom: A Documentary History of Emancipation, 1861–1867. Series I, Vol. II. The Wartime Genesis of Free Labor: The Upper South* (Cambridge: Cambridge University Press, 1993), 360–62; Carl Abbott, "Dimensions of Regional Change," 1375–79; Green, *Washington*, 277. There were also approximately eight thousand fugitive slaves in and around Alexandria, on the Virginia side of the Potomac. *Freedom*, I, 2:348.

[18] *Evening Star*, April 7, 1862; Joint Resolution of Washington City Councils, April 1862, Senate Committee on the District of Columbia, Petitions and Memorials, 37A-J4, RG46, NARA.

[19] For Butler's formulation and the response of Secretary of War Simon Cameron, see *OR*, II, 1:752, 754–55. See also Louis S. Gerteis, *From Contraband to Freedman: Federal Policy toward Southern Blacks, 1861–1865* (Westport, CT: Greenwood, 1973), 11–17; *Freedom*, I, 1:15–16.

"for such labor as the public service may offer." However, "Those simply fugitive from the ordinary condition of labor for their class are to be dismissed from your camp." In practice, all slaves of rebel masters were liable to be treated as "contraband." "It is obvious," Cameron told Butler in August 1861, that in insurrectionary states where the laws of the United States could not be enforced, "rights dependent upon the execution of those laws must temporarily fail." Slaveholders whose property was wrongfully seized would have to appeal to Congress for compensation. The president ordered that Virginia slaves "employed in hostile service against the Government of the United States" who escaped to the District of Columbia should not be arrested by the city police "upon presumption arising from color that they are fugitives from service or labor." Under the terms of the Confiscation Act, such "hostile employment" rendered an owner's claim to their services null and void, and they should be received into the military protection of the United States.[20] The military authorities acted under the presumption that Virginia masters were disloyal. Of course, most of them were in no position to challenge that presumption. However, the president's order made it clear that the police were still in the habit of arresting contrabands "upon presumption arising from color," whatever their state of origin, and treating them as fugitive slaves.

In theory, Maryland slaves should have been arrested and returned to their owners; in practice, many of them were. After all, the Fugitive Slave Act, which required law enforcement authorities to return fugitives to the state from whence they came, was still on the statute books. Further, the government did not wish to antagonize slaveholders in Maryland, given that its support for the Union had so recently been in doubt. Federal officials assured the governor, as well as congressmen from that state, that the fugitive slave law had not been abrogated, that local officers would continue to apprehend runaways, and that "the relation of Master and Slave" would not be "interfered with." In July 1861, the Maryland Congressman Charles Calvert complained to General Mansfield that the concealment of slaves in the camps around Washington, and, even worse, their departure with the regiments to Virginia or other states, constituted a "monstrous abuse of our rights, and is rightfully causing a great deal

[20] Gen. J. F. K. Mansfield to Mr. Justice Dunne, July 4, 1861; Lt. Col. James A. Hardie to Gen. Joseph Hooker, December 1, 1861, in ibid., 167–68, 174–75; William Henry Seward to George B. McClellan, December 4, 1861, *OR*, II, 1:783. See also W. R. Montgomery to Simon Cameron, August 8, 1861; Cameron to Montgomery, October 2, 1861, *Freedom*, I, 1:162–63.

of censure upon the Government for permitting it." In response, Mansfield ordered that fugitive slaves should not be harbored in the camps or allowed to accompany troops on the march. When Maryland slaveholders protested that some of their slaves had taken refuge in part of Daniel Sickles's command, General George B. McClellan, the commander-in-chief of the Army of the Potomac, directed Sickles to "cause them to be returned to . . . the agent of their owners."[21]

Despite the grudging, and in McClellan's case wholehearted, cooperation of Union commanders in the field, even loyal slaveholders sometimes found it difficult to recover their slaves. Whether moved by abolitionist sentiment, sympathy for their plight, or a selfish desire to exploit their labor, rank-and-file Union soldiers often refused to deliver up fugitives. For example, Richard Green, although given permission to enter the encampment of a Massachusetts regiment and take possession of a person he claimed to be his slave, was twice driven away by the soldiers. Another slaveholder found no difficulty in obtaining authorization to search for his "boys," but "as soon as my purpose was known they were spirited away and concealed." Calvert protested that Mansfield's order that no slaves should be permitted to enter the camps had never effectively been enforced. As a result, the camps "with very few exceptions have been opened up as receptacles for our slaves."[22]

Republican congressmen, outraged that the Army was required to play the role of slave catcher, acted quickly to undermine enforcement of the fugitive slave law. As early as July 1861, the House of Representatives passed a resolution declaring that it was not the duty of U.S. soldiers to capture or return fugitive slaves. The following March, both houses approved an article of war forbidding Union forces to return fugitive slaves. Orders went out to all regiments serving in the defenses of Washington north of the Potomac that African Americans coming into the lines were "to be treated as persons and not as chattels." Commanders

---

[21] Charles B. Calvert to J. K. F. Mansfield, July 17, 1861; affidavit of Thomas Martin, October 25, 1861, in *Freedom*, I, 1:169–74; General Orders No. 33, Department of Washington, July 17, 1861, *OR*, II, 1:760; E. D. Townsend to Mansfield, July 11, 1861, LR, Department of Washington, RG393, NARA. See also *OR*, II, 1:755–59, 762, 765, 775–95; Johnston, "Surviving Freedom," 170–80; *Freedom*, I, 1:160–65.

[22] Affidavit of Richard Green, March 3, 1862; Charles Calvert to Edwin Stanton, March 31, 1862; F. B. F. Burgess to Calvert, March 27, 1862, *Freedom*, I, 1:177, 363–65. See also John H. Bayne to Edwin M. Stanton, July 25, 1862, *Freedom*, I, 1:367–69; Robert C. Schenck to James B. Fry, July 6, 1861 (with endorsements and enclosures), *OR*, II, 1:756–59; Edward Bates to A. W. Bradford, May, 10 1862, *OR*, II, 1:817; Field, *Slavery and Freedom on the Middle Ground*, 101–5.

should not surrender "persons claimed as fugitive slaves" without determining their character, and no civil process was to be served without the
permission of the commanding officer.[23]

The Second Confiscation Act, passed in July 1862, took the congressional attack on slavery a step further by declaring that all slaves of rebel
masters would be "forever free." Even more important in practice, it
incorporated provisions debarring slaveholders from securing the recap-
ture and return of fugitive slaves without satisfactory proof of their loyalty and forbidding military officers to decide on the loyalty of claimants
and the legal status of slaves. General John H. Martindale, commanding
the Military District of Washington, informed a Maryland slaveholder
in January 1863 that he was prohibited from surrendering fugitives but
was required to extend military protection to all fugitives as "Captures
of War." It was, he admitted, likely that, "in the confusion and disorder
incident in a state of war . . . loyal citizens may be deprived of their property," in which case they should present their claims for compensation
to Congress.[24] This, then, was the logic of federal policy regarding contrabands. Military authorities would act on the presumption that their
owners were disloyal and that the fugitives had a claim to freedom. It
was up to their owners to prove their loyalty, in most cases after the fact,
by appealing to the federal courts or to Congress.

Civil authorities in the District proved more amenable to requests for
the return of fugitive slaves and more willing to enforce the fugitive slave
law. Local newspapers continued to carry the familiar woodcuts that
accompanied advertisements for runaway slaves. They reported numerous instances of fugitives being apprehended and returned to their owners
or of men and women being kidnapped by slave catchers and spirited
away from the city. According to the *Daily Morning Chronicle*, one of
Washington's two Republican newspapers, "The Capital of free America
is full of men who anxiously catch at every opportunity to reenslave persons who are loyal to the government of the United States."[25] The police
arrested men and women on suspicion of being runaways and locked

[23] CG, 37.1:32; CG, 37.2:130–31, 376, 387–85, 955–59, 1142–43; Article of War 102,
March 13, 1862, OR, II, 1:810; U.S. Statutes at Large, 37.2, chap. 12 (March 13, 1862),
354; E. P. Halstead to J. D. Shaul, April 6, 1862, Freedom, I, 1:178–79.

[24] U.S. Statutes at Large, 12:589–92; John H. Martindale to William B. Hill, January 14,
1863, Freedom, I, 1:182–83. See also John H. Bayne to Edwin M. Stanton, July 25,
1862, Freedom, I, 1:367–69.

[25] Chronicle, July 31, 1863; Evening Star, May 17, 1862, May 17, 1863. For an example,
see affidavit of Grandison Briscoe, February 6, 1864, Freedom, I, 1:365.

them in the county jail, where sixty or more suspected fugitives were held in the expectation of an owner coming along to claim them and pay the fees for their delivery, which formed a substantial part of the warden's income, or, failing that, were sold to cover the costs of their incarceration. A Senate investigation of the jail uncovered evidence of abuse and false imprisonment. In February 1862, James W. Grimes, the chairman of the Senate Committee on the District of Columbia, reported a bill designed to secure the release of persons not indicted and to prevent the government jail being used "as a place of confinement for every person who, with a dark skin, is suspected of not owning himself." Despite the protest of a Maryland senator that it would operate as "a sort of act of emancipation" for the District, the Senate, although not the House, passed the measure. In response to such pressures from Capitol Hill, the marshal of the District promptly ordered the release of all those held without charge. However, the jails and police cells of the District were still available for the confinement of suspected fugitives against whom a slaveholder had taken out a warrant.[26]

Even after Congress had remodeled the District judiciary to replace the existing judges with Republican appointees, the local courts continued to enforce the law regarding fugitive slaves. In April 1863, the courts issued writs for the return of slaves claimed by three Maryland slaveholders. In May, in an important test case involving a young man called Andrew Hall, whose ownership was claimed by a former member of the Maryland legislature, two members of the District Supreme Court decided that the Fugitive Slave Act still applied in the District and that, objectionable though it might be, as long as it remained on the statute books, it should be enforced. Two justices, however, did not agree. Hall was released only for a new warrant to be issued for his arrest. The military authorities effectively resolved the dispute by taking him into their custody; once in their hands, he was effectively beyond the reach of the civil courts.[27] Military provost marshals frequently intervened to protect fugitives from arrest by agents of their former owners or the civil authorities.

[26] *Report of the Committee of the District of Columbia Instructed by a Resolution of the Senate to Inquire into the Condition of the Jail*, 37.2, Sen. Report 60, Ser. 1125, 1–5; CG, 37.2:264, 310–21; OR, II, 1:782; *Evening Star*, February 13, 1862; Leech, *Reveille in Washington*, 239–41.

[27] *Chronicle*, April 15, May 13, 1863; *Evening Star*, June 13, 1862, May 17, 22, 23, 27, 1863; Staudenraus, ed., *Mr. Lincoln's Washington*, 179–80. On the reorganization of the District judiciary, see CG, 37.3:1049–52, 1128–30, 1135–38, 1490–9, 1537–39; *Evening Star*, May 28, 1862.

In May 1862, the provost general sent a guard to the jail to remove a woman claimed, it was said, by a disloyal master. When the jailer refused, the provost marshals took him, along with the assistant U.S. marshal and the owner's counsel, to the guardhouse and posted a military guard at the jail, the inmates of which were themselves arrested by order of the marshal of the District. After the president's intercession, all parties were eventually released, and the woman, who was reported to have been General Wadsworth's cook, remained at liberty. Such cases continued to be heard until the repeal of the federal fugitive slave law in 1864.[28]

## Contraband Labor

As the logistical hub of the Union war effort, the Washington area generated a great demand for manual labor. Able-bodied contrabands found it easy to obtain employment behind Union lines, constructing the elaborate fortifications that ringed the capital, working as teamsters, stevedores, and laborers of all kinds, or, in the case of women, as seamstresses, washerwomen, and nurses. In June 1862, the engineer in charge of the defenses of Washington asked General James S. Wadsworth, the military governor in charge of the district, for a detail of "Contrabands to work on fortifications on the Maryland side of the Potomac. As the Government subsists them," he argued, "it would be advisable to get some return for the expense." He could easily employ 250 men, enabling him to discharge hired employees and thereby reduce costs. In denying his request, Wadsworth replied that there were only 100 contrabands under his direction, and they were needed for hospital duties.[29] By the middle year of the war, nearly 5,000 free and freed black laborers were working in the Washington area as laborers and teamsters, and hundreds more in the surrounding army camps. More than 300 were employed in military hospitals. Others worked to repair the public roads, which had suffered greatly from the repeated passage of government wagons.[30] An official in the Quartermaster Department, the agency most engaged in employing civilian laborers, recommended the replacement of white laborers, whom he found negligent and "much inclined to dissipation," with black.

---

[28] *Evening Star*, May 23, 1862; Leech, *Reveille in Washington*, 246–47. See also *Chronicle*, July 31, 1863.

[29] William E. Merrill to James S. Wadsworth, June 7, 1862, *Freedom*, I, 2:266–68.

[30] E. E. Camp to D. H. Rucker, July 31,1863, *Freedom*, I, 2:303–5; Thomas Gamble to Senate Committee on the District of Columbia, November 28, 1863, SEN38A-H4, RG46, NARA; *Freedom*, I, 2:253.

"The negroes are much superior workers, more attentive to their duties, less inclined to dissipation and readily controlled." An officer of the Commissary Department "found them very industrious, faithful and obedient."[31]

Good workers, however, were sometimes lured away by the attractions of private employment. This made it impossible to employ black workers under the terms of the Militia Act of July 1862, which authorized them to be received into the service of the United States at $10 a month plus rations, with a $3 deduction for clothing. Any such suggestion was rapidly dropped when it was pointed out that private employers were offering up to three times as much. His department, said Quartermaster General Montgomery C. Meigs, was forced to compete with private employers, hiring laborers "upon such terms as will be sufficient to secure their services." The application of the provisions of the Militia Act "will produce much dissatisfaction and suffering, and will probably deprive the Government of the services of a large portion of them." Such was the demand that laborers could command wages of between $20 and $25 a month with rations, well in excess of the pay of common laborers in the North. Hence it was concluded that the Militia Act should not apply to laborers hired by the Quartermaster Department.[32] A similar fate befell a proposal to resolve an acute shortage of labor by "the impressment of contrabands." The chief quartermaster of the Washington Depot, D. H. Rucker, feared that such a measure "would have a tendency to defeat the ends desired to be attained and probably cause them to run away at a time when their services might be most required." Instead, Rucker asked permission to import contraband laborers from Fortress Monroe, New Bern, or other points south.[33]

The work of freed black laborers in wartime Washington was arduous and demanding: toiling on fortifications, "cleaning cesspools, scrubbing privies and policing [that is cleaning] the grounds of hospitals," or transferring heavy loads from ship to wagon or from wagon to railroad carriage. Hard and unremitting, often carried out in large gangs under

---

[31] Charles H. Tompkins to D. H. Rucker, May 1, 1863, *Freedom*, I, 2:296–97; testimony of Danforth B. Nichols before the American Freedmen's Inquiry Commission, April 1863, ibid., 288.

[32] James S. Wadsworth to Edwin M. Stanton, September 25, 1862; Montgomery C. Meigs to Stanton, October 4, 1862, *Freedom*, I, 2:269–73

[33] D. H. Rucker to Montgomery C. Meigs, June 22, 1863; Rucker to Meigs, June 8, 1863, "Contrabands"; Rucker to Meigs, July 29, 1864, and Meigs to Edwin M. Stanton, July 30, 1864, "Negroes Ordered to Be Sent to Washington," RG92, NARA.

the direction of an "overseer," many of the tasks and the manner in which they were conducted must have been reminiscent of the work done under slavery. Army quartermasters were sometimes negligent in ensuring prompt payment of wages (although black laborers were not alone in suffering from this), or, in certain cases, even their payment at all, whereas freedpeople were frequently cheated and abused by private contractors. "From the moment the contraband lands within our lines and gets any money he is the victim of fraud and robbery," said Danforth B. Nichols, the local superintendent of contrabands. Nevertheless, formerly enslaved men and women were, for the first time, working for wages and soon learned to exploit market forces to secure better terms.[34]

So large a pool of deracinated men was a standing temptation to recruiting agents, once the enlistment of black soldiers got under way in the spring and summer of 1863. Two black regiments were raised in the city, formed largely from native black Washingtonians. Many contrabands, especially those without families to support, were attracted to the standard of the Union, but others, it seems, were forcibly impressed into the ranks. Nichols complained to his superiors that a squad of black troops entered Freedmen's Village at Arlington, Virginia, and took five or six male inmates by force. It appeared that a neighboring black regiment sent out squads of soldiers into the surrounding countryside "with a promise of a bounty for each recruit." However induced, an estimated 3,500 black residents of the District eventually served in the U.S. Army.[35]

## The "Contraband System"

Able-bodied men and women could be profitably employed by the U.S. Army, but elderly and infirm persons, as well as women with small children, could not. The War Department directed "that such of the old

[34] *Freedom*, I, 2:248–50. On nonpayment of wages, see Henry E. Alvord to John Eaton, December 15, 1865,

[35] On the recruitment of black regiments and the role of the local community, especially black churches, in their formation, see Henry M. Turner to Edwin M. Stanton, August 1, 1863; Salmon P. Chase and Owen Lovejoy to Stanton, September 4, 1863, in Ira Berlin et al., eds., *Freedom: A Documentary History of Emancipation, 1861–1867. Series II. The Black Military Experience* (Cambridge: Cambridge University Press, 1982), 358–59; *Chronicle*, May 8, 1863; *Evening Star*, May 19, 1863; C. R. Gibbs, *Black, Copper, & Bright: The District of Columbia's Black Civil War Regiment* (Silver Spring, MD: Three Dimes Publishing, 2002), 1–58. For complaints regarding the forced impressment of contrabands, see Danforth B. Nichols to Elias M. Greene, April 2, 1864; Albert Gladwin to Rolland C. Gale, October 1, 1864, *Freedom*, I, 2:332–36, 347–48.

and infirm negroes...as may be unable to provide for themselves, be furnished with such articles as the officers commanding...may approve and order." Thus, rations and articles of clothing were issued to those who could not support themselves; camps were set up for their accommodation and hospitals for their treatment when sick, all of which put the military authorities to a considerable expense.[36] Therefore, given that several hundred African American men were employed by the Quartermaster Department at wages in excess of $20 a month, and the government was supporting between six hundred and eight hundred women and children "of the same class," Wadsworth proposed that $5 a month should be deducted from their wages and allocated to the cost of their upkeep and medical treatment. This suggestion was approved, and in October 1862, all quartermasters were directed to make the proposed deductions, which would be administered "for the benefit of the women and children, and as a hospital fund for the sick among the men from whom it is derived."[37] The officer in charge of the so-called Contraband Fund was Chief Quartermaster Colonel Elias M. Greene, a New York merchant in civilian life. Although Greene complained that some of the officers responsible for collecting the tax were dilatory in remitting it to him, the contributions mounted up to form a generous sum, amounting to $30,000 by September 1863. The fund continued to accumulate: $63,799.83 had been received by January 1, 1864, of which an estimated $40,000 was reported to be in the hands of Greene and the collecting officers. The unexpended part of the fund was sufficient to finance a substantial part of the operations of the local Freedmen's Bureau during the first year of its existence and later to provide the seed corn for Howard University.[38]

The contraband tax was levied on all black laborers employed by the Quartermaster Department, whether freed or free, even though the

[36] Lorenzo Thomas to J. P. Taylor, January 3, 1862; George H. Day to Edwin M. Stanton, December 8, 1864, "Arlington, Va.," RG92, NARA; Lorenzo Thomas to Montgomery C. Meigs, January 2, 1862, *OR*, II, 1:798; Elias M. Greene to Charles Thomas, December 17, 1863, *Freedom*, I, 2:315–22.

[37] James S. Wadsworth to Edwin M. Stanton, September 25, 1862; Montgomery C. Meigs to Stanton, October 4, 1862, *Freedom*, I, 2:269–73; Lorenzo Thomas to Meigs, September 27, 1862, "Contrabands," RG92, NARA. See also *Freedom*, I, 2:251–53.

[38] Elias M. Greene to J. H. Taylor, January 30, 1864, "Contrabands," RG92, NARA; to Charles Thomas, September 29, 1863; E. H. Ludington and C. E. Compton to James E. Hardie, July 30, 1864, *Freedom*, I, 2:321, 340–41. On the failure of quartermasters to hand over the money, see Greene to Montgomery C. Meigs, February 22 and June 9, 1864, "Contrabands," RG92, NARA. On the Refugees and Freedmen's Fund, see Howard, *Autobiography*, 2:264–68.

benefits were confined to the families of the contrabands. Free laborers naturally objected to this arrangement. The freedmen and their families, declared a group of free laborers in Alexandria in August 1863, received "houses to live in, provision for them selves and families, and even wood a[nd] coal to cook with," whereas they were expected to support their families out of their own wages. As free men, they should be under no more obligation to "pay a tax for the benefit of the contrabands" than "white labor[er]s of our class." Another group of free laborers claimed to be in "a condition of utter destitution . . . many of us with large families and paying exorbitant rents."[39]

The authorities asked Greene for an opinion. Not surprisingly, Greene adjudged the Contraband Fund to be "a wise and prudent measure" that had "accomplished great good." The majority of black laborers received generous remuneration of $25 to $30 a month, well in excess of the wages of common labor in the North. The $5 deduction was necessary to care for children, the old and the infirm. The fund paid for the construction of Freedmen's Village, where dependent freedpeople subsisted in health and comfort. Without the tax, they "would be scattered in sickly camps through the city, as has been the case heretofore; living a life of idleness at the public expense; subject to the most demoralizing influences; . . . spreading the small pox and other infectious diseases." With it, they could be gathered in one place, those able to work could be provided with suitable employment, and the children could receive an education: "all will be taught self reliance, and sent into the world with a sense of their duties and obligations which they do not now possess." Green failed to address the issue of lumping free and freed persons together as belonging to "the same class." However, his argument made clear what his real concerns were, not only his desire to curtail the expense of caring for dependent freedpeople but also his belief that the government had a responsibility for their education and moral instruction, which was best fulfilled by gathering them together in one place and subjecting them to careful supervision and control. The War Department accepted Greene's recommendation that the deduction should continue.

---

[39] Coloured Laborers of Alexandria to Edwin M. Stanton, August 31, 1863, "Alexandria Virginia," CCF, ser. 225, CR, RG92, NARA; Robert A. Stanley, James C. Waters, and John H. Slocum to Stanton, 27 November 1863; Edward Thomas *et al.*, to Stanton, November 28, 1864, *Freedom*, I, 2:313–14, 353–5. Quartermasters warned that many "most excellent workmen" had threatened to leave government employment on account of the tax. See, for example, Charles H. Tompkins to D. H. Rucker, May 1, 1863, *Freedom*, I, 2:296–97.

Its only concession was to waive the tax for those earning less than $20 a month.[40]

Many of the fugitives arriving in Washington during the early months of the war had been housed in the Old Capitol Prison, which also served as a jail for political prisoners. There the contrabands came under the supervision of William P. Wood, the superintendent of the jail, who set about finding employment for as many as possible. Wood told a Senate committee in February 1862 that between two hundred and three hundred contrabands had come under his care, that he had found situations for those who were employable, and that all were "doing well."[41] However, early in 1862, acting on the advice of the surgeon in charge of contrabands that, "as a sanitary measure, they should be removed to some place where they can be kept more apart from respectable white people," the black inmates were moved to tenements on Duff Green's Row, east of the Capitol, where four hundred were housed in May. There, according to the *Evening Star*, "they were as well provided for, and as comfortable as that class of people can be made to keep themselves." Their supervision was transferred from Wood to Danforth B. Nichols, a Methodist minister and prison reformer who was working with the local freedmen's aid society. Nichols was appointed superintendent of contrabands in June. Like Wood, he worked hard to find employment for the new arrivals, most of whom remained in the tenements only a few weeks before moving on. However, the flow of newcomers and the onset of smallpox made it impossible to prevent a deterioration in sanitary conditions and mortality.[42]

In June, alarmed that the smallpox outbreak might spread and sensitive to criticism of their location in a residential neighborhood, the authorities removed the inhabitants of Duff Green's Row to a disused barracks complex known as Camp Barker at 12th Street and Vermont Avenue on the fringes of the city. It consisted of fifty wooden cabins (measuring ten feet by twelve, each normally holding twelve persons but frequently many

[40] Elias M. Greene to Charles Thomas, December 17, 1863, *Freedom*, I, 2:315–22; Thomas to Edwin M. Stanton, December 28, 1863, "Contrabands," CCF, RG92, NARA.

[41] *Condition of the Jail*, 24–27; Curtis C. Davis, "The 'Old Capitol' and Its Keeper: How William P. Wood Ran a Civil War Prison," *Records of the Columbia Historical Society* 52 (1989): 206–12. On the political prisoners, see Leech, *Reveille in Washington*, 141–58.

[42] *Evening Star*, May 9, 28, and 30, 1862; *National Republican*, October 31, 1862; Benjamin B. French to E. M. Stanton, February 13, 1862, *Freedom*, I, 2:262–63; Elaine C. Everly, "The Freedmen's Bureau in the National Capital" (Ph.D. diss., George Washington University, 1972), 33–37.

more), as well as a hospital and a school. There new arrivals were registered and provided with food and shelter, in most cases for a short time
until they could find employment. "Many find excellent employment at
good wages as soon as they arrive," noted the Washington *National
Republican*. Between June and October, approximately 3,600 passed
through; "all but 675 have gone out, either to do for themselves, labor in
private families, or work for the Government," and "quite a number of
the remainder go out during the day to work for the sick soldiers at the
hospitals." In April 1863, of 4,939 who had entered the camp since June
1862, only 557 remained. These were mostly the old, the sick, and the
infirm or mothers with small children whose husbands were away working for the Army. According to Nichols's successor as superintendent, "it
was a mass of Old folks." Something like eleven thousand freed persons
passed through Camp Barker during its lifetime. The military authorities
provided shelter and rations, and relief societies furnished clothing, sent
down in bundles from the North. The American Tract Society contributed
two teachers, who conducted a school for seventy-five children during the
day and one hundred adults at night, while the National Freedmen's Relief
Association of the District of Columbia (NFRADC) paid for a physician.
The barracks were small and cramped, offering little privacy. Owing to
the composition of the camp's long-term inhabitants and the distressed
condition of many of the new arrivals, disease, especially smallpox, was
rife. The camp's sanitary condition was far from perfect, partly owing to
inadequate cleaning and ventilation and an insufficient number of privies,
partly to its location alongside a large cavity, "practically a swamp," left
by an abandoned brickyard, and partly to its dependence for fresh water
on a well that dried up during the summer months. By December 1862,
311 of the camp's inmates had died, and another 490 expired between
June and December 1863.[43]

Although some newspaper accounts speak warmly of the camp, several inmates complained of their treatment at Nichols's hands. They complained of not receiving their full rations, being given inadequate bedding,

[43] *Evening Star*, October 24, 1862; *Chronicle*, November 11, December 1, 1862; Wash-
ington *National Republican*, July 21, 1862; testimony of Danforth B. Nichols, April
1863; testimony of James I. Ferree, January 1864, *Freedom*, I, 2:287–94, 325–29; John
A. Kress to Nichols, July 2, 1862, Military Department of Washington, LS, 98:155,
RG393, NARA; *Freedom*, I, 2:247–48; Everly, "Freedmen's Bureau," 37–51; Thomas
C. Holt, Cassandra Smith-Parker, and Rosalyn Tuborg-Penn, *A Special Mission: The
Story of the Freedmen's Hospital, 1862–1962* (Washington, DC: Academic Affairs Divi-
sion, Howard University, 1975), 2–5.

not being paid in full for work carried out in the camp, and being treating in an unkind and abusive fashion. "I speak from my heart before the Lord," said one, "when I say that the conduct of Mr. Nichols was worse than the general treatment of slave owners." "They think him better suited to be the overseer of a Southern plantation," a witness told the American Freedmen's Inquiry Commission in January 1864.[44] Nichols and other officers denied such charges and defended their management of affairs. However, they, too, were unhappy with the sanitary and moral condition of the camp. Nichols admitted that the "promiscuous herding of people," in one case as many as twenty-six to a cabin, was "promotive of immorality," and that camp life was itself demoralizing: "the longer they stay there the worse they become; the more vicious in their habits, and the less inclin[ed] to work."[45]

Troubled by the large number of dependent freedpeople congregating at Camp Barker and elsewhere around the city, Greene suggested in May 1863 that between 500 and 750 of their number should be relocated to abandoned estates on the Virginia side of the river where they could provide their own subsistence, enjoy "the salutary effect of good country air," and escape from the overcrowded camps and tenements of Washington. "The force of contrabands now idle in this city and a dead weight upon the Government" could be advantageously employed in cultivating the soil, returning to their "former healthy avocations" as field hands and more easily providing for their families. "The arrangement I propose will not only in my opinion conduce to the sanitary and moral improvement of the contrabands, but will save the Govt. an immense amount of money." The commander of the Department of Washington acceded to Greene's proposal, allowing him to make use of the abandoned property and to draw on the Contraband Fund to finance his operations. During the summer, five "government farms" were established, employing 260 workers by March 1864. They raised vegetables for military hospitals and made, according to Meigs, a clear profit for the government.[46]

---

[44] Testimony of Lewis Johnson and Lucy Smith, January 1864, *Freedom*, I, 2:295–96, 331–32; "Intemperance of Nichols and His Treatment of the Inmates of Camp Barker in Washington," RG393, NARA; testimony of William Slade, American Freedmen's Inquiry Commission, Records of the Adjutant General's Office, RG94, NARA, NA Microfilm No. M619, Reel 200.

[45] Testimony of Danforth B. Nichols before the American Freedmen's Inquiry Commission, April 1863, *Freedom*, I, 2:287–94; Testimony of James I. Ferree, January 1864, *Freedom*, I, 2:325–29.

[46] Elias M. Green to Samuel P. Heintzelman, May 5, 1863, *Freedom*, I, 2:298–99; Greene to Heintzelman, May 18, 1863, "Arlington, Va.," CCF, ser. 225, RG92, NARA;

A purpose-built camp to house the old and sick and women with children was erected on part of the Lee family's Arlington estate. The so-called Freedmen's Village contained a hundred individual family dwellings and gardens, described as neat and commodious, as well as a hospital, a chapel, gardens, workshops where freedpeople could learn useful trades, and a school operated by the American Tract Society. The society also constructed a home for invalid freedpeople. The rations that the government provided for those who could not support themselves were supplemented by gifts of clothing donated by northern philanthropic societies. The Freedmen's Village provided more appropriate work opportunities for those who were physically incapable of full-time paid employment and for mothers with children than were available in the city, and it provided a much healthier environment and a much lower mortality rate for the more vulnerable members of the freed community. In the eyes of the principal of the school, the contrast between the condition of the residents and the freedpeople brought from Camp Barker after its closure in December 1863 showed the wisdom of the project: "In a few words, *here* they are comparatively neat, tidy and *very* comfortable while *there* they were dirty, discontented and uncomfortable."[47]

When in the autumn of 1863 a decision on the future of Camp Barker was precipitated by the urgent need to do something about the hopelessly inadequate water supply and the unsatisfactory drainage, Greene had no hesitation in recommending that instead of making the necessary improvements, the camp should be closed and its occupants transferred to Freedmen's Village, where they would enjoy healthier conditions and escape the moral and epidemiological dangers of the city. On Greene's advice, the adjutant general decided that all contrabands in the care of the government should be concentrated on the Arlington estate and "all brought under a general system." This would avoid "many abuses inseparable from the existence of such camps in cities."[48] The removal, carried

*Freedom*, I, 2:344–45; Everly, "Freedmen's Bureau in the National Capital," 43–48. On the government's title to the Arlington estate, see Edwin M. Stanton to Hamilton Ward, February 24, 1866, "Arlington, Va.," CCF, ser. 225, RG92, NARA.

[47] Elias M. Greene to Charles Thomas, December 17, 1863, "Contrabands," CCF, ser. 225, CR, RG92, NARA; H. E. Simmons to Elias M. Greene, January 23, 1864, "Contrabands Tax," CCF, RG92, NARA; *Evening Star*, December 4, 1863; Joseph P. Reidy, "'Coming from the Shadow of the Past': The Transition from Slavery to Freedom at Freedmen's Village, 1863–1900," *Virginia Magazine of History and Biography*, 95 (October 1987): 409–14; *Freedom*, I, 2:254–55; Everly, "Freedmen's Bureau," 43–51.

[48] Elias M. Greene to Charles Thomas, October 14, 1863; Thomas to Edwin M. Stanton, October 23, 1863, and endorsement by C. C. Augur, November 12, 1863, "Contraband

out during December 1863, involved considerable hardship for the former inmates of Camp Barker. Not only was the weather chill and damp, they were forced to survive in tents while new homes were constructed for them, and insufficient clothes and blankets were provided. This was especially hard because most of the 120 freedpeople who made the move were old and infirm. The majority of the camp's 685 inhabitants chose not to go to Arlington, citing as reasons their "instinctive dread" of returning to slave territory, their reluctance to come once more under the control of Nichols, who had been placed in charge of the Village, and their desire to stay in touch with friends and job opportunities in Washington. Greene noted that the residents of Camp Barker "have a great many friends in this city who easily manage to get into the camp at night, and in a great measure subsist off the Government rations." The close contact between those inside and outside the camp, which to Greene posed problems of discipline and misuse of government property, to the inmates represented an important advantage of living close to the city and an important disadvantage of moving to the Village.[49]

From the start, Freedmen's Village was founded on contradictory principles. On one hand, Greene envisaged a self-supporting community of freedpeople who would, under the guidance and protection of the government, and with the benevolent assistance of northern philanthropists, negotiate the transition from slavery to freedom by engaging in agricultural labor on the nearby government farms or sewing garments in the camp workshops in exchange for modest wages, set at a level that would not deter them from seeking private employment. There they would be employed "profitably to the Government and themselves." There they would learn the "arts of life," the habits of industry and the technical skills that would prepare them for "a career of usefulness when they are thrown upon their own resources." In practice, most of the thousand or so residents of the Village were women and children, many of them the families of Union soldiers, old people, or invalids who were "clothed,

Camp (1863)," CCF, ser. 225, RG92, NARA. For correspondence relating to the supply of water to Camp Barker, see Alexander P. Augusta to R. W. Abbott, June 17, 1863; Edward P. Vollum to J. M. Cayler, September 20, 1863; to D. H. Rucker, September 23, 1863; Charles Thomas to Stanton, October 23, 1863, "Contraband Camp (1863)," CCF, ser. 225, CR, RG92, NARA.

49 Testimony of J. B. Holt and Georgiana Willetts, January 1864, *Freedom*, I, 2:328–31; R. C. Terry to Elias M. Greene; H. E. Simmons to Greene; Danforth B. Nichols to Greene, January 23, 1864; Greene to J. H. Taylor, January 30, 1863, "Contrabands Tax," CCF, ser. 225, CR, RG92, NARA.

sheltered, and fed" out of the proceeds of the Contraband Fund. The Village became a repository for dependent freedpeople that the government found itself obliged to support. Only just over a hundred of the inhabitants were able-bodied men, mostly employed in nearby Army camps. Nevertheless, the residents had gone some way toward making the farms productive and had, by the end of 1863, made considerable progress in the creation of a viable community of freed slaves. Unfortunately, that achievement in itself confounded Greene's intentions because, rather than seeing their sojourn there as a transitional step toward full independence, many of the residents showed every intention of converting it into a permanent community. "So well satisfied are the colored people with their present condition at Arlington," observed Greene, "that they can hardly be induced to accept service with private families or individuals in this City and vicinity, and generally endeavor to return to the public quarters provided for them." Their reluctance to leave and take up employment elsewhere made it difficult to accommodate the newcomers that continued to find their way to Washington during the later stages of the war.[50]

The "contraband department" of the Army and its successor, the Freedmen's Bureau, never solved the problem of managing the Village. While seeking to inculcate appropriate habits of self-reliance and encourage freedpeople to become a self-supporting community, the Army ruled with an iron hand and maintained a tight discipline over its charges. While offering a channel through which relief could be distributed, it struggled to combat dependency. The rules of the Village were designed to inculcate appropriate habits. Those not gainfully employed were denied food and clothing unless they were incapable of labor. All but the most dependent were expected to pay rents to force them into the labor market. The collection of rents was the occasion for recurrent disputes. Set at between $1 and $3 a month when most workers in the camp received $10, the level of rents was burdensome, especially for the wives of laborers and soldiers, some of whom who were paid irregularly and sometimes not at all. Nichols was sometimes brutal, sometimes neglectful in his management. The wife of a laborer who was away working for the Army was, by her own account, tied up by the thumbs, on Nichols's orders, then asked to leave the camp because she had begged for rations and clothing.

[50] Elias M. Greene to Charles Thomas, October 14, 1863, "Contraband Camp (1863)," CCF, ser. 225, CR, RG92, NARA; Green to Thomas, December 17, 1863; to J. H. Taylor, January 30, 1863 [from the content clearly 1864], *Freedom*, I, 2:315–25, 256–58.

Green, while defending Nichols, regretted "having to trust to Citizen Employés, there is not that promptness and exactness in the administration that there ought to be." Soon after, Nichols was replaced by Captain James M. Brown of the Quartermaster's Department. The management of the Village remained in military hands throughout the rest of its existence.[51]

By the summer of 1864 the population of the Village had risen to 2,166, with another 600 individuals living on the nearby farms. At that point, an inspection by two members of the Inspector General's Department, although founded on highly prejudiced assumptions about the freedpeople's capacity for productive labor and a serious misapprehension of the financial basis of the operation, forced the officers in charge of freedmen's affairs to reexamine their assumptions. The inspectors reported that the site was "well located" and clean, the houses comfortable, the sick well cared for, and the children attending the school making good progress. Nevertheless, they regarded the project as an "expensive burden on the Government" and suggested that it contributed to the "erroneous" idea on the part of the freedpeople that emancipation "signified a claim upon Government for support in idleness."[52] Meigs and his colleagues denied both the factual basis of and the premises behind the inspectors' report. They pointed out that the costs were borne entirely out of the Contraband Fund, which was made up of the contributions of the freedpeople themselves. They reiterated the government's responsibility to support the families of men fighting and laboring for the government and the benefits of housing them in a healthy rural rather than a crowded urban environment. "The education of 900 children; the support in comparative health and comfort of some 5000; the saving of hundreds of lives," suggested Greene, justified the Village's existence, "for without the police, control and discipline and shelter of this establishment, very many would have died."[53] Nevertheless, they responded to the criticisms by striving all the harder to reduce the population of the Village and reduce the number of freedpeople dependent on the government. Able-bodied adults were

---

[51] Testimony of Luisa Jane Barker in case of Lucy Ellen Johnson, January 14, 1864, *Freedom*, I, 2:308–11; Reidy, "Coming from the Shadow of the Past," 413–14; Holt, *Special Mission*, 5.

[52] E. H. Ludington and C. E. Compton to James E. Hardie, July 30, 1864, *Freedom*, I, 2:337–46.

[53] Montgomery C. Meigs to Edwin M. Stanton, August 15, 1864, *Freedom*, I, 2:344–45; Elias M. Greene, "Notes on Prospects of Freedmen's Village," August 9, 1864, "Contraband Camp (1863)," CCF, ser. 225, CR, RG92, NARA.

pressurized to hire themselves out to local farmers or to go into service; children were bound out, sometimes in abusive apprenticeship agreements that were later the subject of complaint. Others left the Village, discouraged by Brown's harsher regime. As a result of such measures, by March 1865, the population of the Village had fallen to 1,400. At the end of the year, the population stood at about 1,200 and remained close to that figure over the next few years, during which the responsibility for management fell on the Freedmen's Bureau.[54]

In June 1864, the "contraband department" took possession of an unused camp on Mason's Island (now Theodore Roosevelt Island) in the Potomac, which was closer to employment opportunities in the city. Greene's intention was to use this as "a general depot for hiring out Contrabands," while dependent freedpeople would continue to reside in the Village. No effort was made to provide comfortable accommodation. In any case, the tide of fugitives from the war in Virginia soon swelled the population to nearly 1,200, most of whom were women and children. An inspection of Mason's Island in July 1864 found "dirt and disorder reigning supreme," overcrowded dwellings, with males and females housed indiscriminately in the same barracks, and an absence of hospital facilities. The disease environment was catastrophic. According to Louisa J. Roberts, an agent of the Association of Friends of Philadelphia, "the Island was a very charnel house where malignant fevers of every type rioted almost unchecked for a time." Of 800 freedpeople resident on the island in August, 118 died; of 507 living there in September, 60 did not survive. Improved sanitation and medical care eventually ameliorated health standards, and a school was opened by the Philadelphia Friends, but there remained a powerful reluctance to make the place comfortable for its residents. Nichols, who was placed in charge of the camp, did all he could to find prospective employers but, in doing so, was far from scrupulous in checking their credentials. Several children were bound out in unsatisfactory and sometimes abusive apprenticeship agreements with Maryland farmers. Captain Brown, who took over responsibility for the supervision of contrabands, seemed willing to let people go without firm evidence that they would be able to support themselves. An inspection in October reported that "The object of the present management appears to be to get rid of these people in any way; often by throwing them upon the community at large; the prevention of which was the object of the

---

[54] *Freedom*, I, 2:260–61; William F. Spurgin to Charles H. Howard, January 1, 1866, AQMR, Reel 13, BRFAL-DC. On the later history of the Village, see Chapter 3.

establishment of the Freedmen's Village." Over the course of the following winter, the population was run down. After the end of the war, in
June 1865, the camp at Mason's Island was closed, and its residents were
transferred to the Village.[55]

"The contraband system is peculiarly a military system," observed the
Washington *National Republican* in 1862, "and it belongs to the military authorities, who have the exclusive control of the matter."[56] The
contraband department was an appendage of the Quartermaster Department, the agency most involved in the employment of freed laborers and
therefore most responsible for the care of their families. The department
set up a series of camps for the reception of fugitives and the long-term
care of those adjudged incapable of supporting themselves. The system
was motivated by a desire to facilitate contraband labor while minimizing
the cost of caring for dependents. However, the officers responsible were
also concerned with preparing former slaves for their future lives as free
men and women; their policies reflected their preconceptions about what
the appropriate place of freedpeople should be. Greene and his associates
were desperately anxious that they should not be confirmed in habits of
idleness by handing out relief too readily and permitting able-bodied men
and women to live in idleness. They therefore put pressure on men to leave
their families in pursuit of work and on mothers to support themselves
and their children; they required the payment of rent by all but the most
dependent. Their goal was a self-supporting community of freedpeople
that would not pose an undue burden on the resources of the government
and would form a launching-pad for their involvement in free society.
However, as Joseph P. Reidy points out, "Although the point was to
encourage self-sufficiency and independent participation in free society,
federal officials could not help treating former slaves as children."[57]

[55] E. H. Ludington and C. E. Compton to James E. Hardie, July 30, 1864; Kilburn Knox
to James A. Hardie, October 13, 18, 1864, *Freedom*, I, 2:337–46, 349–52; Louisa J.
Roberts to Oliver Otis Howard, June 30, 1865, ULR 159, Reel 12; John Eaton to
George Carse, June 24, 1865, LS 1:6, Reel 1, BRFAL-DC; Everly, "Freedmen's Bureau,"
51–53. For examples of apprenticeships arranged by Nichols, see Selden N. Clark to John
V. W. Vandenburgh, December 22, 1865, LS 1:306, Reel 1; Carter Holmes to William
M. Beebe, April 22, 1867, LR 2:1716, Reel 8, BRFAL-DC. Nichols denied binding out
children, claiming that Greene and Brown had inaugurated the system and signed the
indentures. Danforth B. Nichols to John Eaton, August 26, 1865, ULR 619, Reel 12,
BRFAL-DC.
[56] *National Republican*, July 21, 1862.
[57] Reidy, "Coming from the Shadow of the Past," 407. Cf. Gerteis, *From Contraband to
Freedman*, 5, 7, 33.

## Freedmen's Aid

The "contraband system" never embraced more than a fraction of the District's freed population. According to Greene, the government had no more responsibility for freed men and women in private service than for other "servants or hired men, who were not formerly slaves." If not, he asked, "when, under what circumstances and after what lapse of time do the colored refugees become really independent?"[58]

The majority of contrabands found their own employment and made their own homes in various parts of the city. They rented rooms in alley tenements, "made of the cheapest lumber, covered with felt and tar," for which they paid between $4 and $8 a month, or erected shanties on disused land on the back alleys and alongside the Washington City Canal. "The huts and shanties, more like pig pens than human dwellings," said a writer in the *Freedmen's Record*, were "filled to overflowing by these miserable creatures." They cooked on open fires, drew their water from a common pump, and lacked proper facilities for disposal of sewage. The rents were high, as were prices of the necessities of life in wartime Washington. Although wages were generally good, much of the work available to unskilled manual laborers was highly seasonal and came to halt in the winter months – an endemic problem for manual workers in nineteenth-century urban America. "I have visited the freedmen in their cabins," wrote a correspondent of the *National Freedman* during the hard winter of 1865; "their sufferings are most heart rending. The weather is cold; they have little or no wood. Snow covers the ground; and they have a scanty supply of rags called clothes. The hospital is crowded with the sick. . . . Many will die," he warned. Indeed, the Quartermaster Department of the Army received regular requests from the local police to collect and bury the bodies of unknown contrabands, particularly during the winter months.[59]

---

[58] Elias M. Greene to Montgomery C. Meigs, August 9, 1864, "Contrabands (1864)," CCF, RG92, NARA. There were 3,728 freedpeople in camps and on government farms in July 1864, at which date the total number of contrabands in the District was probably around 15,000 and may well have been higher. E. H. Ludington and C. E. Compton to James E. Hardie, July 30, 1864, *Freedom*, I, 2:337–46,

[59] *Freedmen's Record* 1 (March 1865): 43; Charles C. Leigh, letter to the editor, *National Freedman* 1 (March 1, 1865): 60; *National Intelligencer*, July 25, 1865; John Rogers to James Moore, February 6 and 20, 1864, "Unknown Contrabands," CCF, ser. 225, RG92, NARA; Elizabeth Keckley, *Behind the Scenes, Or Thirty Years a Slave and Forty Years at the White* House (New York: G. W. Carleton & Co., 1868), 11–12; Green, *Washington*, 277–78; Thomas R. Johnson, "The City on the Hill: Race Relations in Washington, D.C., 1865–1885" (Ph.D. diss., University of Maryland, 1975), 36–38;

Especially vulnerable were the wives and families of the many freed-men who worked for the government at various military posts around Washington or who were enrolled in the U.S. Colored Troops. Army pay frequently arrived late and sometimes not at all. In December 1864, the abolitionist and women's rights activist Josephine S. Griffing, now work-ing for the NFRADC, found several families of women and children with husbands in government service who were unable to buy food because of the high rents that they were forced to pay. "It is this exorbitant Rent, that is starving these women and children to death," she told Secretary of War Edwin M. Stanton. There were, she said "hundreds of families without the possibility of obtaining Wood or Blankets – and in several instances women and children... are so badly frozen as to be unable to walk at all." Griffing repeatedly drew the attention of the military authorities to the urgency of their situation during the hard winter of 1864–65.[60]

Established white residents showed little sympathy for the contrabands and sometimes downright hostility. The frequent incidence of insults and assaults on the newcomers was evidence of the continuation of antebellum racial prejudices.[61] So was the refusal to tender material assistance to the sick and the needy. Regarding the contrabands as an imposition inflicted on them by Republican antislavery policies, the local authorities disowned responsibility for their welfare. As early as May 1862, the Washington Board of Common Council complained that the city had been overrun by contrabands and demanded that it be relieved of responsibility for their support. Although they offered to care for destitute freedpeople who had been residents of the city before the Civil War, municipal officers regarded the recent arrivals, in the words of Mayor Richard Wallach, as "a class that the General Government is in justice bound to provide for." They proved unwilling to acknowledge the freedpeople's claims to citizenship and to equal treatment in law. "I have found among the Officers and Magistrates a bitter prejudice against the colored population," reported

Donald E. Press, "South of the Avenue: From Murder Bay to the Federal Triangle," *Records of the Columbia Historical Society*, 51 (1984): 58–60.

[60] Josephine S. Griffing to Edwin M. Stanton, December 27, 1864, *Freedom*, I, 2:356–57; Griffing to Stanton, December 7, 1864, 9 January 1865; to Montgomery C. Meigs, March 7, 1865, "Josephine S. Griffing," CCF, ser. 225, CR, RG92, NARA; Griffing to William Lloyd Garrison, August 19, 1864, *Liberator* 34 (26 August 1864): 139.

[61] For evidence of prejudice, see William Owner Diary, May 5 and 29, 1862, December 26, 1865, LC; *Evening Star*, May 6, 1862; *National Freedman* 1 (March 1, 1865): 60; Green, *Washington*, 279–80. For reports of assaults, see, for example, *Chronicle*, December 5, 9, and 19, 1862; *National Republican*, July 3, 1862. For attacks on black soldiers, see Gibbs, *Black, Copper, & Bright*, 39–40, 52–3.

a solicitor working for the Freedmen's Bureau. They exhibited, with a few exceptions, "if not a spirit of malignity and bitter hatred a spirit of cruel oppression and unkindness."[62]

Considering its limited resources, Washington's free black community responded generously to the plight of the refugees, raising money through its churches and its fraternal societies. In October 1862, members of the Union Bethel Church, a congregation patronized by many of Washington's black elite, organized a Union Relief Association "to collect provisions and clothing to be distributed among the freedmen." The association raised substantial sums through appeals in the *Christian Recorder*, a journal that circulated widely among members of African Methodist Episcopal churches in the North. The Contraband Relief Association, organized at Fifteenth Street Presbyterian, another church favored by the more affluent members of Washington's black community, at the suggestion of Elizabeth Keckley, a seamstress employed at the White House, was similarly successful in attracting donations of clothing from northern relief societies. A Boston branch of the society sent eighty boxes of goods collected by local blacks, and Frederick Douglass contributed $200 and the proceeds of a series of lectures. Mr. and Mrs. Lincoln also made donations, as did a number of British antislavery societies. Altogether, the society received $839 in subscriptions and donations during 1862–63, its first year of operation, and $1,228 in its second year, as well as 5,150 items of clothing. At the annual meeting of the association in August 1863, a banner was presented to a recently formed black regiment, and in the latter years of the war, its members devoted their attentions increasingly to the support of black soldiers and their families.[63]

---

[62] *Evening Star*, May 6, 1862; John V. W. Vandenburgh to William F. Spurgin, November 22, 1865, LR 1:263, Reel 4; Spurgin to Clark, August 31, 1865, AQMR, Reel 13; A.K. Browne to Selden N. Clark, November 5, 1867, LR 3:803, Reel 9, BRFALDC.

[63] Katherine Masur, "Reconstructing the Nation's Capital: The Politics of Race and Citizenship in the District of Columbia, 1862–1878" (Ph.D. diss., University of Michigan, 2001), 43–45 [editorial note: Dr. Masur's Ph.D., cited here in its unpublished form, has now been published in revised form as K. Masur, *An Example of All the Land: Emancipation and the Struggle over Equality in Washington, D.C.* (Chapel Hill, University of North Carolina Press, 2010). I am grateful to Professor M. Crawford for this information]; *Evening Star*, May 19, 1862; *Chronicle*, August 14, 1863; Keckley, *Behind the Scenes*, 110–16; Carol Faulkner, *Women's Radical Reconstruction: The Freedmen's Aid Movement* (Philadelphia: University of Pennsylvania Press, 2004), 79–82; G. C. Eggleston, "The Work of the Relief Societies during the Civil War," *Journal of Negro History* 14 (1929): 285; Gibbs, *Black, Copper & Bright*, 115–16. On Washington's early black churches, see John W. Cromwell, "The First Negro Churches in the District of Columbia, "*Journal of Negro History* 7 (1922): 64–106.

A white relief organization, the NFRADC, was formed in March 1862, with Vice President Hannibal Hamlin in the chair, "its object being to relieve the immediate wants of the contrabands by furnishing them with clothing, temporary homes, and support, and as far as possible to teach them to read and write, and bring them under moral and religious instruction." It was composed, for the most part, of federal officials and their wives who were temporary residents of the District. The new society distributed clothing from its office at 4½ and C Street on the island, helped freedpeople find employment, paid for a physician at Camp Barker, sponsored an orphanage, and operated schools at E Street Chapel between 9th and 10th Streets, SW; at Asbury Court, 11th and K, NW; and at 3rd Baptist Church, 4th and L, NW, which were attended daily by an average three hundred pupils a day. According to its annual report for 1864, "A considerable sum has also been expended in defending the legal rights of freedpeople, and in rescuing them from the remorseless grip of slave-catchers." Having a limited local constituency, the NFRADC, like other District societies devoted to the welfare of the freedpeople, was dependent on wealthier northern societies for assistance, including the U.S. Christian Commission and the National Freedmen's Aid Society of New York. During its first year, it raised $1,830, mostly in the North, and in 1863–64, its receipts amounted to $2,890.[64]

Like other relief societies, the association in the early years devoted itself primarily to the promotion of freedmen's education. From 1864, under the guidance of Josephine Griffing, the association became more strongly committed to material assistance. Griffing, who became the society's general agent, was especially sensitive to the problems of women and children. Writing directly to the secretary of war, she repeatedly begged the Army for rations, blankets, and fuel, to be paid for out of the Contraband Fund. The Army issued three thousand blankets and three hundred cords of wood, to be distributed by Griffing on behalf of the NFRADC, but refused later requests. Griffing also opened two industrial schools

---

[64] *Evening Star*, March 22, April 10, 1862, April 11, 1863; *Chronicle*, April 13, 1863, February 8, 1864; *First Annual Report of the National Freedmen's Relief Association of the District of Columbia* (Washington, DC: 1863); *Second Annual Report of the National Freedmen's Relief Association of the District of Columbia* (Washington, DC: 1864); Eggleston, "Work of the Relief Societies," 274, 284–85; Everly, "Freedmen's Bureau," 57–58. On the society's membership, see also Stanley Harrold, *Subversives: Antislavery Community in Washington, D.C., 1828–1865* (Baton Rouge: Louisiana State University Press, 2003), 229–31.

where women with families to support could earn a little money to support them.[65]

In addition, the National Association for the Relief of Destitute Colored Women and Children, a group of sympathetic and influential white women that included the wives of Republican Senators Wade, Trumbull, and Pomeroy, opened the Colored Orphans' Home. Believing that the Army would care for "helpless adults," the association concentrated on the large number of children who had lost touch with their parents or whose parents were unable to care for them. The extent of the problem became manifest when, after the closing of Camp Barker in December 1863, some fifty or so children remained without families or guardians to care for them. The society sought to provide a suitable home for as many children as possible, to give instruction, and to "bring them under Christian influences." The managers of the home would "govern the inmates, preserve order, enforce discipline, impart instruction in useful knowledge and some regular course of labor." Where appropriate, they would bind out children to suitable employers. Securing a charter from Congress in 1863, the society opened an orphans' home in Georgetown on the abandoned property of Richard S. Cox, a former mayor of the city who had deserted to the Confederacy.[66] After his return in 1866, the association purchased a lot on the outskirts of Washington where the Freedmen's Bureau erected a new building. For the next few years, the Colored Orphans' Home was supported by the Bureau, which referred to it all orphans and dependent children who came under its supervision.

[65] Josephine S. Griffing to Edwin M. Stanton, December 27, 1864, *Freedom*, I, 2:356–57; Griffing to Stanton, January 24, 1865; George E. Day et al. to secretary of war, December 30, 1864, "Freedmen's Relief Association of D.C.," CCF, RG92, NARA; Griffing to Stanton, December 7, 1864, January 9, 1865; Griffing to Montgomery C. Meigs, March 7, 1865; Joseph M. Brown to Meigs, March 12, 1865; Charles Thomas to Brown, January 30, 1865, "Josephine S. Griffing," CCF, RG92, NARA. On Griffing's career, see Keith E. Melder, "Angel of Mercy in Washington: Josephine Griffing and the Freedmen, 1864–1872," *Records of the Columbia Historical Society, 1963–65* (1967), 243–72; Faulkner, *Women's Radical Reconstruction*, 31–32, 57–60, 83–99, 117–31; James M. McPherson, *The Struggle for Equality: Abolitionists and the Negro in the Civil War and Reconstruction* (Princeton, NJ: Princeton University Press, 1964), 389–92; Everly, "Freedmen's Bureau in the National Capitol," 22–23; Elizabeth Cady Stanton et al., eds., *History of Woman Suffrage* (2 vols., New York: Arno, 1969 [1881]), 2:28–39.

[66] Mrs. D. Hay et al. to House Committee on the District of Columbia, March 28, 1864, HR38A-G4.1, RG292, NARA; *CG*, 37.3:818–19, 888; *Evening Star*, April 29, 1865, January 9, 1866; Howard, *Autobiography*, 2:260–61; Eggleston, "Work of the Relief Societies," 289–90.

Thereafter, it relied on regular appropriations from Congress along with the help of benevolent societies in the North.[67]

The NFRADC, said the *Freedmen's Record*, was "a weak body, being, like all other Washington organizations, without a constituency." Its resources were dwarfed by those of the national organizations that proliferated during the Civil War. Many abolitionist and church groups took up the cause of freedmen's relief after 1861; the movement grew out of the tradition of grassroots antislavery activism established over the previous generation. Strongly localized in character, it depended on the willingness of thousands of supporters across the North, most of them women, to donate their time and energy, through sewing bees and other fund-raising activities, and of hundreds more to go south themselves as teachers and relief workers. Many of those societies turned their attention to the District of Columbia, which was not only the site of the nation's capital but the location where the need for assistance most visibly showed itself. At least twenty societies operated in the District at one time or another between 1861 and 1870. The American Tract Society provided teachers for the school that opened at Camp Barker in 1862 and later at the Freedmen's Village. Schools were also supported by the American Missionary Association, the National Freedmen's Relief Association of New York, the American Freedmen's Aid Commission, the Pennsylvania Freedmen's Relief Association, the Friends' Association of Philadelphia, the New England Freedmen's Aid Society, and the African Civilization Society, an African American organization, as well as several other societies. The Pennsylvania Freedmen's Relief Association supported seventeen teachers in the Washington area in 1865, the Friends Association seven, and the American Missionary Association nineteen. By May 1865, 29 day and 18 night schools had opened their doors. However, although nearly all the societies gave priority to freedmen's education over immediate relief, the urgent need that they saw around them forced them to distribute clothes, shoes, and medicines as well. Thus, the New England Friends distributed supplies from a store on 13th Street and the Philadelphia Friends from a soup house on New Jersey Avenue;

---

[67] *Evening Star*, 9 January 1866; Howard, *Autobiography*, 2:260–61; Memorandum of Officers and Managers of the National Association for the Relief of Destitute Colored Women and Children, February 2, 1867, SEN39A-H4, RG46, NARA; Charles H. Howard to O. O. Howard, November 3, 1866; to Eliza Heacock, November 7, 1866, LS 1:682, 690; Charles H. Howard to O. O. Howard, October 10, 1867, LS 3:758a, Reel 1; Heacock to W. W. Rogers, May 29, 1866, LR 1:[131], Reel 6, BRFAL-DC; Masur, "Reconstructing the Nation's Capital," 71–73.

many other societies funneled supplies through local agencies such as the NFRADC.[68]

The relief societies existed in an oddly symbiotic relationship with the contraband department of the Army. They supplemented its efforts by providing clothing and other articles and by opening schools and infirmaries at the contraband camps. They provided relief and opened schools for freedpeople living outside the purview of the military authorities, in the allies and shantytowns of Washington itself. Yet they also prodded the Army to devote more resources to the care of freedpeople and to give more attention to their needs, and they were sharply critical of the military authorities when they did not. This led to recurrent friction between the superintendents of contrabands and the often female relief workers with whom they uneasily cooperated. Thus, Julia A. Wilbur, an agent of the Ladies Antislavery Society of Rochester, New York, who acted as a "visitor, advisor, and instructor," as well as an almoner, to the freedpeople of Alexandria, developed a bitterly adversarial relationship with the local military authorities. She persistently accused them of indifference and cruelty to the women and children, "the most wretched of God's creatures," particularly by demanding the payment of rents for government tenements and evicting those who would not pay. The local provost marshal, for his part, maintained that they were generally well cared for. The main difference, he stated, was that the Army tried to make the freedpeople "self-sustaining," whereas Wilbur "seems to labor under the belief that the chief object is to make life easy, and obtain for them the largest possible grants from the Gov't." Although "respecting Miss Wilbur's goodness of heart and broad benevolence, I regard her as an interfering, and troublesome person." Officers were evidently irritated by

---

[68] *Chronicle*, 12 December 1864; *Freedmen's Record* 1 (March 1865): 41–43; Everly, "Freedmen's Bureau," 58–69; Lois Elaine Horton, "The Development of Federal Social Policy for Blacks in Washington, D.C. after Emancipation" (Ph.D. diss., Brandeis University, 1977), 70, 122. For a detailed survey of freedmen's schools at the close of the war see John Kimball to John Eaton, December 8, 1865, LR 1:348, Reel 5, BRFAL-DC. On the broader activities of freedmen's aid societies, see McPherson, *Struggle for Equality*, 160–77; Robert H. Bremner, *The Public Good: The Impact of the Civil War* (New York: Knopf, 1980), 102–10; Carol Faulkner, "A Proper Recognition of Our Manhood: The African Civilization Society and the Freedman's Aid Movement," *Afro-Americans in New York Life and History* 24 (2000): 41–62; Faulkner, *Women's Radical Reconstruction*; Eggleston, "Work of the Relief Societies"; Joe M. Richardson, *Christian Reconstruction: The American Missionary Association and Southern Blacks, 1861–1890* (Athens: University of Georgia Press, 1986). The crucial role of women's participation in the movement is demonstrated by Faulkner, *Women's Radical Reconstruction*, while its roots in earlier antislavery societies can be seen in Julie Roy Jeffrey, *The Great Silent Army of Abolitionism: Ordinary Women in the Antislavery Movement* (Chapel Hill: University of North Carolina Press, 1998), 210–32.

both Wilbur's encroachment on their management of freedmen's affairs and her apparent indulgence toward the freedpeople's claims to material assistance.[69] Griffing developed a similar adversarial relationship with the military authorities as she struggled to persuade them to provide more generous assistance, especially for freed women and children. As Carol Faulkner points out, although they did not always get their way, women like Wilbur and Griffing compelled the military authorities to confront the implications of caring for the freedpeople: "the presence of abolitionist women . . . kept the issue of the care and treatment of former slaves in the nation's view."[70]

The abolitionists who gave their time to the voluntary relief agencies and the Army officers who were most concerned with freedmen's affairs held many views in common. They tended to agree that the freedpeople had been severely damaged by slavery, that they would need some instruction and guidance to prepare them for full freedom, that they must be encouraged to be independent and self-sufficient to operate in a free labor society, and that excessive generosity in the distribution of material assistance would promote idleness and dependency. However, there were significant differences in emphasis. The Army officers were primarily governed by military priorities and the economical expenditure of resources. When they did consider the welfare of the former slaves, which was almost always a secondary consideration, they did so from a paternalistic viewpoint that perceived their charges as a childlike people prone to indolence and mendicancy who needed to be taught sharp lessons. They also tended, when pressed, to resort to military modes of discipline and methods for enforcing compliance. At their best, they acted like stern school masters; at their worst, they were arbitrary, unfeeling, and sometimes cruel.

The abolitionists, on the other hand, operated on the basis of a broad sympathy for the freedpeople and a belief that they should be regarded

[69] Julia A. Wilbur to Abraham Lincoln, November 7, 1862; John C. Wyman to John P. Slough, November 24, 1862; Wilbur to Stanton, March 24, 1863; H. H. Wells to Slough, April 12, 1863, *Freedom*, I, 2:275–78, 280–87; Faulkner, *Women's Radical Reconstruction*, 15–26. See also Samuel Shaw to J. R. Bigelow, June 14, 1863, *Freedom*, I, 2:299–303.

[70] Faulkner, *Women's Radical Reconstruction*, 26. On Griffing's relations with the Army, see the correspondence collected in "Josephine S. Griffing," CCF, RG92, NARA. On Wilbur, see Julia A. Wilbur to Abraham Lincoln, November 7, 1862; John C. Wyman to John P. Slough, November 24, 1862; Wilbur to Stanton, March 24, 1863; H. H. Wells to Slough, April 12, 1863, *Freedom*, I, 2:275–78, 280–87; Faulkner, *Women's Radical Reconstruction*, 15–26. See also Samuel Shaw to J. R. Bigelow, June 14, 1863, *Freedom*, I, 2:299–303.

essentially as victims who would need help for some considerable time. Griffing considered it unreasonable to expect them to "organize civilization out of the chaos and curse of slavery" in a short time and without considerable assistance. Hence, fairly generous assistance from public and private agencies was warranted. "The relief of the freedmen," said the members of one local society, was called for by "consideration of justice to a race which for so many years has been the victim of oppression, and by the dictates of common humanity towards brethren in need." Being mostly women, the agents of freedmen's aid societies tended to view the sufferings of the freedpeople with greater sympathy than most Army officers, and they were readier to set aside theoretical objections to charity in favor of immediate and much-needed relief. They could not help but be moved by the pitiful condition, the "nakedness and homelessness," of so many of the freedpeople; they could not help but provide what little clothing and shelter they could.[71]

Yet even the most conscientious whites could only go some way toward appreciating the experience and culture of the former slaves whom they sought to assist, advise, and uplift. A note of condescension sometimes crept into their dealings with the freedpeople. This was evident in a newspaper account of a religious service at Camp Barker in December 1862. The residents sang a number of spirituals including "Go Down, Moses," which the reporter described as "very long and extemporized for the occasion," and "Jesus Is Coming," the words of which he could not distinguish. "While singing this piece they became very excited, their movement nearly resembling dancing, so much so that one of the teachers present thought in necessary to check them." The enthusiastic elements of African American religion were evidently not considered appropriate to a sober Christmas celebration. They were clearly regarded as part of the primitive inheritance that the freedpeople had brought with them from slavery and that should be shed along with their passage to freedom.[72]

## Conclusion

After the surrender of the principal Confederate forces and before the demobilization of the Union armies, a Grand Review of the Armies was

---

[71] Melder, "Angel of Mercy," 251; Faulkner, *Women's Radical Reconstruction*, 13–15, 31–33, 52–55.

[72] *Chronicle*, December 1, 1862. See also Faulkner, *Women's Radical Reconstruction*, 132–47.

held in Washington. For six hours on May 23, 1865, the Army of the Potomac paraded along Pennsylvania Avenue, marching proudly from the Capitol to the White House to the cheers of the crowds that packed the sidewalks and leaned out of buildings. The following day, Sherman's western armies followed the same route. The Grand Review provided an opportunity for the people of Washington, along with the thousands of visitors who came especially for the occasion, to see the armies that had won the war and celebrate their achievements, and for the soldiers themselves, many of them for the first time, to see the capital that they had fought so doggedly to defend. Washington put on its best face for the occasion. The weather was clear and sunny, without being too hot or sultry, and recent rain showers had quieted the dust that normally plagued the streets in summer. Crowds of onlookers, numbered at approximately two hundred thousand, filled the streets, while the floral displays, the patriotic bunting that was draped over public buildings, and the many flags that flew proudly in the breeze added to the spectacle.[73]

The Grand Review was more than just a pageant; it expressed, according to *Harper's Weekly*, "a deep, glorious, solemn sentiment" and a pride in the "youthful strength of a republic tried and found stead-fast." As William McClay puts it, "The river of blue was a visual confirmation of a sea change, the emblem of a powerful new political order whose authority would emanate increasingly from Washington." The victory of the Union armies had affirmed the unity of the nation, but it also brought a renewed sense of national power and a dramatic change in the relationship between the states and the federal government. However, the full nature of the new political order remained to be determined, and so did the position within it of the federal capital itself.[74]

When the troops had packed up their knapsacks and filed into the railroad carriages that would take them home, and when the crowds who had poured into Washington to witness the Grand Review had dispersed, the city began gradually to return to something like normality. However, the *status quo ante bellum* could not be fully restored. Too

---

[73] For an account, see *New York Times*, May, 1865; Ulysses S. Grant, *Memoirs of U.S. Grant* (2 vols., New York, 1887), 2:534–36; Staudenraus, ed., *Mr. Lincoln's Washington*, 471–81; Allan Nevins *War for the Union: The Organized War, 1864–1865* (New York: Charles Scribner's Sons, 1971), 364–67; Stuart McConnell, *Glorious Contentment: The Grand Army of the Republic, 1865–1900* (Chapel Hill: University of North Carolina Press, 1992), 1–17; Melinda Lawson, *Patriotic Fires: Forging a New American Nation in the Civil War North* (Lawrence: University Press of Kansas, 2002), 179–80.

[74] *Harper's Weekly*, June 10, 1865; McClay quoted in Lawson, *Patriotic Fires*, 180.

much had changed, and the conditions under which the capital operated had been modified too substantially for that to be possible. For one thing, loyal Washingtonians had to consider their reaction to those of their relatives, friends, and neighbors who had cast their lot with the Confederacy. A number of meetings were held, and in May 1865, the Board of Common Council debated resolutions stating that the return of former rebels at this juncture would be repugnant to the feelings of citizens. Over time, rebel sympathizers like W. W. Corcoran would filter back into the economic and social fabric of the city, although few of them played any further part in public life.[75] Second, wartime traffic had accentuated and exacerbated the woeful condition of Washington's streets. Even Pennsylvania Avenue, one of the few thoroughfares to have been paved before the war, was so damaged by the repeated passage of government wagons that it urgently needed to be resurfaced. The temporary expansion of the city's population had put increased pressure on municipal utilities and shown their inadequacy. In a more general sense, the war brought exposure to Washington, enabling more people from across the Union to visit the city and to see for themselves how far short of the planners' expectations it fell. Of course, the war itself gave added importance to the capital. What might have passed muster as a seat of government for the disjointed antebellum republic was far from suitable as the capital of a renewed and reinvigorated nation. This was "the filthiest and altogether the worst governed city of the Union," said the *Chronicle* in September 1865. After the war, a significant movement arose to move the capital to a Midwestern city, supposedly closer to the demographic and economic heart of the nation and untarnished by the imputations of disloyalty and atavistic southernism that had become attached, in some eyes, to the name of Washington. The threat of removal would hang over deliberations about the future development of the capital for some years to come.[76]

Third, the war had brought about the end of slavery, and that applied as much to the federal capital itself as to any of the former slave states. From that emancipatory moment flowed a series of questions about race relations and civil rights that were to form the primary issues of Reconstruction, in Washington as elsewhere in the South. Republican congressmen expressed the desire to remove all traces of slavery from the national

---

[75] *Evening Star*, May 9, 10, 31, 1865; Green, *Washington*, 294–95.
[76] *Chronicle*, September 16, 1865; Green, *Washington*, 328–29; Lessoff, *Nation and Its City*, 30.

capital, and they had already commenced the process during the war by repealing the local black code, acting against segregation in street-cars, and making some initial provision for the creation of black schools. Already Charles Sumner and other Radical Republicans were pressing for the enfranchisement of African American males and for other guarantees of civil rights. Of course, African Americans themselves were organizing to ensure that their voice was heard on behalf of equal rights. The District, therefore, was to become "a proving ground for federal race and reconstruction policies."[77]

The problems of racial adjustment were, of course, complicated by the coming of the contrabands. Their arrival resulted in a threefold increase in the city's African American population and introduced into the population a large number of people who were much less familiar with the ways of urban living than the established black community; it did so under conditions of mounting deprivation and overcrowding, as the running down of the wartime economy curtailed the opportunities available to unskilled laborers. The migration created a number of social and economic problems that neither the federal nor the city government was able to address successfully.

The capital, then, faced a number of challenges as it emerged from the war. How these challenges were to be addressed, of course, depended not only on the responses of Washingtonians, black and white, but also on the decisions of federal policy makers responsible for the management of the District. That, in turn, would depend on decisions about the kind of capital Americans wanted – the kind of capital they considered appropriate to the new nation that had been forged in the fires of sectional conflict. It would depend on decisions regarding the political relationship between the United States and the District of Columbia, a relationship that would change more than once over the next thirteen years. After sixty-one years of steady, if not soporific, progress, the nation's capital had experienced four years of startling and disruptive change. Disruption and uncertainty about the city's future were to continue for the next decade and a half.

---

[77] Steven J. Diner, "Statehood and the Governance of the District of Columbia: An Historical Analysis of the Policy Issues," *Journal of Policy History* 4 (1992): 395.

# 3

# The Freedmen's Bureau in the District of Columbia

## Introduction

On a summer's day in 1866, the citizens of New York were witnesses to an unfamiliar sight: a party of about sixty African Americans, whose garb and manner betrayed that they had not long been out of slavery, making their way across the city to the New Haven Railroad terminal.

Filing through the streets, the anxious wandering women dressed partly in neat garments given them, with others of their own selection in less good taste; while on the men an occasional damaged silk hat topped off a coat that would have made old Joseph's of old look plain; with iron-clad army shoes; or a half-worn wedding swallow-tail eked out by a plantation broad-brim, and boots too much worn for either comfort or beauty. This motley band, led by a gentle and spiritual-faced woman, will not soon be forgotten by those who saw it depart.[1]

The woman in question was Josephine S. Griffing, a veteran antislavery and women's rights activist who devoted the last years of her life to the relief of freedpeople in Washington, D.C. The party that she conducted across the city consisted of recently freed slaves, or "contrabands," who had settled in the District of Columbia, although originating in the neighboring counties of Maryland and Virginia. They were now bound for jobs and, it was hoped, new lives in the farming communities and small towns of New England. They were one among many such parties leaving the District for various parts of the Union in an ambitious attempt to

[1] This account is by Caroline A. F. Stebbins, in Elizabeth Cady Stanton et al., eds., *History of Woman Suffrage* (6 vols., New York: Arno, 1969), 2:31. There is a similar description, which may be the original source for Stebbins's, in an article by the feminist lecturer Frances Dana Gage in *National Anti-Slavery Standard*, September 1, 1866.

ease the problems of poverty and overcrowding that the coming of the contrabands had created. Although much of the initiative for the enterprise came from former abolitionists like Griffing, many of them women, it was organized and largely paid for by the District of Columbia office of the Bureau of Refugees, Freedmen, and Abandoned Lands, commonly known as the Freedmen's Bureau. The employment program was a central part of the Bureau's operations in the District, and it exemplifies well the imagination and energy that the agency showed in tackling the problems that confronted it in postwar Washington.

It might seem strange that an agency created to manage the transition from slavery to freedom in the states of the former Confederacy should establish a branch in the capital of the Union. Yet the head of the Freedmen's Bureau, Commissioner Oliver Otis Howard, was confronted with "such an accumulation of subjects relating to the District of Columbia" that he found it necessary to appoint an assistant commissioner to take charge of them.[2] Although the District had contained only 3,185 slaves in 1860, its freed population was greatly swollen by an influx of fugitives from neighboring counties in Maryland and Virginia. In consequence, the African American population of the District increased from 14,316 in 1860 to 38,663 in 1867. At least two-thirds were recent migrants unfamiliar with urban life and the workings of an urban economy.[3] Irregularly employed and dependent for much of the year on public or private charity, many of the newcomers lived in conditions of extreme destitution, inhabiting overcrowded tenements and dilapidated shanties on the fringes of the city or in neighborhoods like the so-called Murder Bay, on

[2] Oliver Otis Howard, *Autobiography of Oliver Otis Howard* (2 vols., New York: Baker & Taylor Co., 1907), 2:224–25. Under the terms of the Freedmen's Bureau Act of March 1865 the bureau was given "control of all subjects relating to refugees and freedmen" not only in "rebel states" but also in "any district of country within the territory embraced in the operations of the army," which applied to the District of Columbia. *U.S. Statutes at Large*, 38.2, ch. 90 (March 3, 1865), 507–8. The assistant commissioner for the District of Columbia was also responsible for neighboring counties of Maryland and Virginia, which presented the agency with problems similar to those confronted by bureau officers farther south: protecting civil rights, contesting abusive apprenticeship arrangements, and supervising labor contracts that were similar to those confronted by bureau officials farther south. On the Bureau's work in Maryland, see Richard Paul Fuke, *Imperfect Equality: African Americans and the Confines of White Racial Attitudes in Post-Emancipation Maryland* (New York: Fordham University Press, 1999), 23–45.

[3] For population figures, see U.S. Office of Education, *Special Report of the Commissioner of Education on the Condition and Improvement of Public Schools in the District of Columbia*, 41.2 (June 13, 1871), Ho. Exec. Doc. 315, Serial 1427, 28–38. See also Carl Abbott, "Dimensions of Regional Change in Washington, D.C.," *American Historical Review* 95 (December 1990): 1375–79.

the site of the present-day Federal Triangle.[4] It was the size of Washington's contraband population, as well as the unwelcoming attitude of the municipal authorities, that made the presence of the Freedmen's Bureau seem necessary.[5]

In response to the unemployment, poverty, and overcrowding that confronted African Americans in the nation's capital, the bureau initiated a series of ambitious projects that went far beyond the normal limits of state power in nineteenth-century America. Besides its characteristic emphasis on education and relief, they included an extensive program of sanitation, the provision of public housing, and, most strikingly, a massive project to relocate unemployed workers to other parts of the Union, including several northern states that were unaccustomed to receiving large-scale black migration. The relocation project clearly illustrates both the agency's capacity for vigorous social action and the conservative ends to which that action was sometimes put.

Since the late 1980s a welcome efflorescence of historical interest in the Freedmen's Bureau has been seen. A cluster of detailed local studies has explored the diverse social and political circumstances in which the bureau operated, the differing strategies and assumptions of its agents, and the complex interactions between bureau personnel, freedpeople, and white Southerners. Whereas a previous generation of so-called postrevisionist historians, writing during the late 1960s and 1970s, had focused on the bureau's limitations, pointing out the extent to which its personnel failed to subscribe to late-twentieth-century standards of racial

---

[4] Constance M. Green, *The Secret City: A History of Race Relations in the Nation's Capital* (Princeton, NJ: Princeton University Press, 1967), 58–65; Lois E. Horton, "The Day of Jubilee: Black Migration during the Civil War and Reconstruction," in Francine C. Cary, ed., *Urban Odyssey: A Multicultural History of Washington, D.C.* (Washington, DC: Smithsonian Institution Press, 1996), 65–78; Ira Berlin et al., eds., *Freedom: A Documentary History of Emancipation, 1861–1867. Series I, Vol. I: The Destruction of Slavery* (Cambridge: Cambridge University Press, 1985), 159–67; ibid., Vol. II: *The Wartime Genesis of Free Labor: The Upper South* (Cambridge: Cambridge University Press, 1993), 243–62; Margaret Leech, *Reveille in Washington, 1860–1865* (New York: Harper, 1941), 235–52; James Borchert, *Alley Life in Washington: Family, Community, Religion, and Folklore in the City, 1850–1970* (Urbana: University of Illinois Press 1980); Donald E. Press, "South of the Avenue: From Murder Bay to the Federal Triangle," *Records of the Columbia Historical Society*, 51 (1984), 51–70.

[5] On local attitudes, see John V. W. Vandenburgh to William F. Spurgin, November 22, 1865, LR, 1:263, Reel 4; A. K. Browne to Selden N. Clark, November 5, 1867, LR, 3:803, Reel 9; Spurgin to Clark, August 31, 1865, AQMR, fn 267, Reel 13, BRFAL-DC. Selden N. Clark was one of a number of assistant adjutant generals who handled the assistant commissioner's correspondence. Others are William W. Rogers, Stuart Eldridge, Franklin E. Town, and David G. Swain.

justice, the "New Freedmen's Bureau Historiography" offers a more balanced interpretation that acknowledges the elements of paternalism and prejudice that animated bureau officials and the many legal and practical constraints under which they worked. More recent work recognizes the positive assistance that the bureau gave to former slaves in negotiating the transition from bondage to freedom. "Considering the obstacles of racism, southerners' distrust of outsiders, the temporary status of the Bureau as an agency, the Bureau's limited resources, the lack of a significant military presence to support the Bureau, among a host of constraints, it is a wonder the Bureau succeeded at all," observe Paul A. Cimbala and Randall M. Miller in their introduction to a recent collection of essays. For all its weaknesses, "the Bureau altered the assumptions and calculus of local power and race relations" in communities all over the South and prevented the former ruling class from claiming "complete economic and social power" over blacks.[6]

Not surprisingly, this research has focused primarily on the rural South, where the great majority of freedpeople lived. There are few studies of the bureau in urban areas; otherwise excellent accounts of the

---

[6] Paul A. Cimbala and Randall M. Miller, eds., *The Freedmen's Bureau and Reconstruction: Reconsiderations* (New York: Fordham University Press, 1999), x. For other prominent examples of the New Freedmen's Bureau Historiography, see Paul A. Cimbala, *Under the Guardianship of the Nation: The Freedmen's Bureau and the Reconstruction of Georgia, 1865–1870* (Athens: University of Georgia Press, 1997); Barry A. Crouch, *The Freedmen's Bureau and Black Texans* (Austin: University of Texas Press, 1992); Randy Finley, *From Slavery to Uncertain Freedom: The Freedom's Bureau in Arkansas, 1865–1869* (Fayetteville: University of Arkansas Press, 1996); Donald G. Nieman, *To Set the Law in Motion: The Freedmen's Bureau and the Legal Rights of Blacks, 1865–1868* (Millwood, NY: KTO Press, 1979); Eric Foner, *Reconstruction: America's Unfinished Revolution, 1863–1877* (New York: Harper, 1988), 142–70. For a review of recent scholarship, see John David Smith, "'The Work It Did Not Do Because It Could Not': Georgia and the 'New' Freedmen's Bureau Historiography," *Georgia Historical Quarterly* 82 (Summer 1998): 331–49. Examples of "postrevisionist" work include William S. McFeely, *Yankee Stepfather: General O.O. Howard and the Freedmen* (New Haven, CT: Yale University Press, 1968), 1–9 and 149–65; Louis S. Gerteis, *From Contraband to Freedman: Federal Policy toward Southern Blacks, 1861–1865* (Westport, CT: Greenwood, 1973), 183–92; and Leon F. Litwack, *Been in the Storm So Long: The Aftermath of Slavery* (New York: Knopf, 1979), 364–86. Earlier historiography is examined in LaWanda Cox, "From Emancipation to Segregation: National Policy and Southern Blacks," in John B. Boles and Evelyn T. Nolen, eds., *Interpreting Southern History: Essays in Honor of Sanford W. Higginbotham* (Baton Rouge: Louisiana State University Press, 1987), 224–28. George R. Bentley, *A History of the Freedmen's Bureau* (Philadelphia: University of Pennsylvania Press, 1955) remains the only general history of the bureau. However, Paul A. Cimbala, *The Freedmen's Bureau: Reconstructing the American South after the Civil War* (Malabar, FL: Krieger, 2005), is an excellent brief synthesis written for a student audience.

African American experience in cities such as Mobile, Lynchburg, Richmond, and Charleston devote only a few pages to its activities.[7] Yet there is much to be gained from a detailed analysis of the bureau's operations in an urban setting. First, one of the principal themes of the New Freedmen's Bureau Historiography is the agency's attempt to apply northern free labor principles to the very different social and economic conditions of the rural South.[8] In Washington, as in other cities, the bureau confronted an economy already attuned to the operation of a free labor market in which it had to find a place for freed workers only recently transplanted from plantation slavery. Rather than seeking to reconstitute the labor market, it worked to prepare freed workers to participate in an already established one, which entailed inculcating values of industriousness, frugality, and regularity. However, in the nation's capital, bureau agents faced mass unemployment and severe overcrowding resulting from a mass migration of African Americans that in its relative scale anticipated

---

[7] There is some useful information on the work of the bureau in Howard N. Rabinowitz, *Race Relations in the Urban South, 1865–1890* (New York: Oxford University Press, 1978), 20–21, 32–34, 128–32, and 153–57. Michael W. Fitzgerald deals briefly with the agency in his study of popular politics in Mobile but says little about the ways in which it addressed specifically urban problems. *Urban Emancipation: Popular Politics in Reconstruction Mobile, 1860–1890* (Baton Rouge: Louisiana State University Press, 2002), 43–48. Much the same is true of recent accounts of the black experience in other southern cities. See, for example, Steven E. Tripp, *Yankee Town, Southern City: Race and Class Relations in Civil War Lynchburg* (New York: New York University Press, 1997); Michael B. Chesson, *Richmond after the War, 1865–1900* (Richmond: Virginia State Library, 1981); Wilbert L. Jenkins, *Seizing the New Day: African Americans in Post-Civil War Charleston* (Bloomington: University of Indiana Press, 1998); George C. Wright, *Life behind a Veil: Blacks in Louisville, Kentucky, 1865–1930* (Baton Rouge: Louisiana State University Press, 1985); and John W. Blassingame, *Black New Orleans, 1860–1880* (Chicago: University of Chicago Press, 1973). There is some discussion of the bureau's operations in New Orleans in Howard A. White, *The Freedmen's Bureau in Louisiana* (Baton Rouge: Louisiana State University Press, 1970), 96–89, 166–200. Despite its title, Caryn Cossé Bell, "'*Une Chimère*': The Freedmen's Bureau in Creole New Orleans," in Cimbala and Miller, eds., *Freedmen's Bureau and Reconstruction*, 140–60, has little to say about the agency's activities in the city itself.

[8] On the free labor ideology, see Eric Foner, *Politics and Ideology in the Age of Civil War* (New York: Oxford University Press, 1980), 97–127; Foner, *Free Soil, Free Labor, Free Men: The Ideology of the Republican Party before the Civil War* (New York: Oxford University Press, 1970), 11–39; Berlin et al., eds., *Wartime Genesis of Free Labor*, 2–6, 15–16; Jonathan A. Glickstein, *Concepts of Free Labor in Antebellum America* (New Haven, CT: Yale University Press, 1991). For the influence of the free labor ideology on Freedmen's Bureau agents, see in particular Foner, *Reconstruction*, 143–70; James D. Schmidt, "'A Full-Fledged Government of Men': Freedmen's Bureau Labor Policy in South Carolina, 1865–1868," in Cimbala and Miller, eds., *Freedmen's Bureau and Reconstruction*, 219–60.

the larger  migrations of the twentieth century. These conditions forced them to consider new approaches to questions of sanitation, housing, and employment.

Second, Washington housed a large number of the agents of northern freedmen's aid societies who not only provided a great deal of support and assistance to the bureau but also worked to influence its policies. To a greater degree than anywhere else, these policies emerged from a complex series of negotiations between the agency and the civilian agents, many of them women, on whose efforts and enthusiasm it heavily depended. The role of female activists in particular has been sensitively explored in a recent book by Carol Faulkner.[9] Finally, as James D. Schmidt observes, the Freedmen's Bureau "represents the first broad effort in American history to build the apparatus of a modern administrative state."[10] Although clearly a legacy of the expanded wartime state and always regarded as temporary, the Freedmen's Bureau explored the possibilities as well as the limitations of government action in guiding social change. This was especially evident in a city like Washington. The challenge of the urban environment probed the limits of its capabilities and revealed unexpected elements of its character. Therefore, it is impossible fully to understand the role of the bureau in the postbellum American state without considering the urban dimension of its activities.

This chapter examines the work of the Freedmen's Bureau in the District of Columbia. The only full-length study of the bureau in the District, a dissertation submitted in 1971, reflected then current trends in Reconstruction historiography. "Hampered by its own personnel, who were neither conditioned to work with the poor nor greatly interested in the

---

[9] Carol Faulkner, *Women's Radical Reconstruction: The Freedmen's Aid Movement* (Philadelphia: University of Pennsylvania Press, 2004); Faulkner, "A Proper Recognition of Our Manhood: The African Civilization Society and the Freedmen's Aid Movement," *Afro-Americans in New York Life and History* 24 (January 2000): 41–62; James M. McPherson, *The Struggle for Equality: Abolitionists and the Negro in the Civil War and Reconstruction* (Princeton, NJ: Princeton University Press, 1964), 160–77, 393–405; Robert Bremner, *The Public Good: Philanthropy and Welfare in the Civil War Era* (New York: Knopf, 1980), 98–110, 129–33; Joe M. Richardson, *Christian Reconstruction: The American Missionary Association and Southern Blacks, 1861–1890* (Athens: University of Georgia Press, 1986); Jacqueline Jones, *Soldiers of Light and Love: Northern Teachers and Georgia Blacks, 1865–1873* (Chapel Hill: University of North Carolina Press, 1980), 14–30; Ronald E. Butchart, *Northern Schools, Southern Blacks and Reconstruction: Freedmen's Education, 1862–1875* (Westport, CT: Greenwood, 1980), chaps. 1, 5.

[10] James D. Schmidt, *Free to Work: Labor Law, Emancipation, and Reconstruction, 1815–1880* (Athens: University of Georgia Press, 1998), 6.

freedmen, by the urgent need to get blacks off relief, and aware that its own mission would expire in July, 1868," concludes Elaine C. Everly, the Freedmen's Bureau was "a moderately successful relief agency and nothing more." Allan Johnston, writing a decade later, described the bureau's efforts as piecemeal and incomplete. It failed, he said, to address issues of economic inequality and was reluctant to provide welfare services for freedpeople. Despite genuine concern for the welfare of their charges, its agents were unable "to step outside their own system of values to appraise the freedmen's real needs more realistically." We must acknowledge the force of these criticisms, but, like much postrevisionist writing, their work tends to judge bureau agents by anachronistic standards and fails to place their ideas and actions in the context of contemporary ideologies and political possibilities. Nor does their assessment do justice to the often imaginative and usually conscientious efforts of bureau officials to assist Washington's freedpeople. Above all, these earlier studies do not address the specific questions of ideology and state power that concern us here or consider the wider implications of the bureau's adjustment to urban conditions.[11]

## The Work of the Bureau

As elsewhere in the South, bureau officials in the District of Columbia worked to facilitate the reunification of families that had been parted by the disruptive impact of slavery and civil war and to encourage the formalization of marriage relations. They took responsibility for the welfare of freed children separated from their parents by bereavement or

---

[11] Elaine C. Everly, "The Freedmen's Bureau in the National Capital" (Ph.D. diss., George Washington University, 1971), 101, 126; Allan John Johnston, "Surviving Freedom: The Black Community in Washington, D.C., 1860–1880" (Ph.D. diss., Duke University, 1980), 298a and 291–300 passim. (Johnston's thesis was published by Garland in 1993 under the same title, with few changes to the text apart from a new introduction.) See also the discussion of the Freedmen's Bureau in Lois Elaine Horton, "The Development of Federal Social Policy for Blacks in Washington, D.C. after Emancipation" (Ph.D. diss., Brandeis University, 1977), 63–78, 87–90, 92–100, 123–27. Carol Faulkner's *Women's Radical Reconstruction* contains a good deal of material on the District of Columbia because of the presence there of several prominent woman activists. See especially chaps. 5 and 7. However, its primary focus is on the ideas and actions of the female activists themselves rather than the bureau. Sections of Katherine Masur's recent dissertation also deal with the Freedmen's Bureau, but in this case, the primary focus is on black political culture and citizenship. "Reconstructing the Nation's Capital: The Politics of Race and Citizenship in the District of Columbia, 1862–1878" (Ph.D. dissertation, University of Michigan, 2001), 53–71.

the accidents of war, even sometimes asserting their authority against the wishes of single parents and other relatives. Younger orphans were consigned to the Colored Orphans' Home established during the Civil War and for a while to the Farm School on the outskirts of the city, whereas older children were apprenticed to employers who were adjudged suitable. On the other hand, bureau agents helped freedpeople reclaim children who had been bound out in restrictive and sometimes abusive apprenticeship arrangements in Maryland and Virginia, including those made at Mason's Island during the last months of the war. The agency maintained two hospitals, one on the outskirts of Washington and another in the Freedmen's Village that occupied part of the confiscated estate of Robert E. Lee at Arlington, Virginia, and between five and eight surgeons attended to patients in their homes.[12]

The bureau made an indispensable contribution to the establishment of schools for African American children. Confronted by the continuing refusal of the city government to make the provision for black education demanded by congressional legislation, the bureau cooperated with the various freedmen's aid societies that operated schools in the District, as well as the local black community, to provide resources for black schools. The benevolent societies continued for a few years to provide teachers and textbooks, and the bureau furnished unused government buildings for educational purposes, furniture, and equipment for schoolrooms, as well as food and fuel at government rates for schoolteachers. In addition, the agency encouraged the societies, by agreeing on a common curriculum and a common approach to pedagogy, to harmonize their activities and lay the foundations for a coordinated black school system. By 1868, the Board of Trustees of Colored Schools, set up by Congress in 1862, had secured sufficient resources to take over responsibility for the education of black children, and the bureau was able, at a much earlier date than in the southern states, to wind up most of its educational activities. Besides its aid to primary education, the bureau supported seven industrial schools where freedwomen were trained in sewing.[13]

---

[12] For a summary of the bureau's operations in the District, see the annual reports of the assistant commissioner: *House Executive Documents*, 39.1, No. 70: *Reports of Assistant Commissioners* (Serial 1256, Washington, DC, 1865), 378–86; Charles H. Howard to Oliver Otis Howard, October 22, 1866, LS, 2:152; C. H. Howard to O. O. Howard, October 10, 1867, LS, 3:758a, Reel 1; C. H. Howard to O. O. Howard, October 10, 1868, LS, 4:1128, Reel 2, BRFAL-DC.

[13] John Eaton to O. O. Howard, September 22, December 11, 1865, LS, 1:153, 273; C. H. Howard to O. O. Howard, October 10, 1867, LS, 3:758a, Reel 1; to O. O. Howard,

The bureau did what it could to provide legal protection for freedpeople. Agents discovered that African Americans were arrested on the least provocation and, after their cases were "summarily disposed of," usually on the testimony of the arresting officer, committed to the workhouse or the jail. The local bureau superintendent William F. Spurgin noted that "Colored persons... are too often arrested for very *trivial* offenses by the police, when the same offenses are overlooked in white persons."[14] The agency retained the services of a solicitor, A. K. Browne, who was authorized to represent freedpeople without charge if they were unable to pay for legal assistance. Over the next two years, he claimed to have defended freed persons in hundreds of criminal cases and to have represented hundreds more in civil cases involving nonpayment of wages, threatened evictions, and the custody of children – acting in 883 cases in all during the year ending October 1868.[15]

Bureau agents in the District of Columbia did not have the responsibility of establishing a system of agricultural labor contracts, unlike their colleagues farther south. Instead, they confronted an established urban labor market in which they attempted to find a place for the freedpeople. They worked to protect black laborers from discriminatory treatment, in particular, nonpayment of wages, which occurred all too regularly during the early postbellum years. Many employers seemed ready to deny full payment of wages on the most trivial of pretexts, "always making some shallow excuse such as dishonesty, disability, &c., &c.," according to John V. W. Vandenburgh, who succeeded Spurgin as local superintendent. For example, workers at the canal wharf had several dollars deducted from their wages for no apparent reason; one freedman claimed that he had worked for seven months without pay, another that he and

October 10, 1868, LS, 4:1128, Reel 2; John Kimball to Eaton, December 8, 1865, LR, 1:348, Reel 5; to W. W. Rogers, September 13, 1866, LR, 1:2184; to Rogers, April 15, 1867, LR, 2:1656; to C. H. Howard, July 1 1867, LR, 2:2517, Reel 8; to S. N. Clark, November 1, 1867, LR, 4:857, Reel 9; to S. Eldridge, March 1, 1868, LR, 4:424, Reel 10, BRFAL-DC.

[14] W. F. Spurgin to S. N. Clark, November 6, 1865, ULR, fn 779, Reel 12; A. K. Browne to Clark, November 5, 1867, LR, 3:803, Reel 9, BRFAL-DC.

[15] A. K. Browne to C. H. Howard, October 10, 1868, AQMR, fn 786, Reel 13, BRFAL-DC. See also Browne & Smithers to Howard, October 31, 1866, AQMR, fn 412, Reel 13; Browne to Howard, July 15, 1868, LR, 4:214, Reel 10; C. H. Howard to O. O. Howard, October 10, 1867, LS, 3:758a, Reel 1; October 10, 1868, LS, 4:1128, Reel 2, BRFAL-DC; Howard C. Westwood, "Getting Justice for the Freedman," *Howard Law Journal* 16 (1971): 492–537. On Browne's appointment, see C. H. Howard to Justices of the Peace, September 1, 1866, LS, 2:128, Reel 1, BRFAL-DC.

his fellow laborers were paid for their services in whiskey. Several freedmen complained after the municipal elections of 1867 that they had been discharged for exercising their right to vote. In each case, bureau agents were ordered to investigate and, where possible, take remedial action. When a woman employed in a hotel asked for assistance in recovering her wages, the proprietor refused to accept either a note from Vandenburgh, then serving as a bureau agent, or an official letter from Spurgin as local superintendent. "For the contempt shown and the manner in which he has treated this woman," wrote Spurgin, "I respectfully request that he be arrested and made answerable to the charges this woman brings against him. The *moral* influence of such a course will be greater than if we were to take the case into the courts." Many such cases were taken to the courts, if they could not be settled informally, and suits for the recovery of unpaid wages formed a large part of the caseload of the bureau solicitor.[16]

According to Spurgin, many such disputes arose from "the loose way in which contracts are made by the Freedmen," whom, he recommended, should be strongly advised to put their contracts in writing to avoid such difficulties in the future. An insistence on written agreements was, of course, one of the keystones of Freedmen's Bureau labor policy in the South. However, it was less easily applied in northern cities, where, as Amy Dru Stanley observes, urban laborers, especially unskilled laborers, rarely signed formal contracts. Thus, bureau officials were prescribing for the freedpeople a more rigid, perhaps a more restrictive, system of agreements than was customary in contemporary urban labor markets.[17] Apart from attempting to protect freed workers from maltreatment and fraud, the agency did little to reform Washington's highly segregated labor market or to expand job opportunities for African Americans.

---

[16] J. V. W. Vandenburgh to W. W. Rogers, July 20, 1867, AQMR, fn 525, Reel 13; Mary Contin to W. F. Spurgin, August 11, 1865, ULR, fn 422 (and endorsement by Spurgin), Reel 12, BRFAL-DC. For examples, see John Eaton to M. Summers, June 20, 1865, LS, 1:2; to Capt. Hallow, August 23, 1865, LS, 1:41; C. H. Howard to A. K. Browne, December 18, 1866, LS, 2:592; to William M. Beebe, January 25, March 2, 6, 1867, LS, 2:715, 950, 979, Reel 1; George E. H. Day to Montgomery Meigs, June 26, 1865, ULR, fn 156; Mary Contin to W. F. Spurgin, August 11, 1865 ULR, fn 422, Reel 12; and Browne & Smithers to C. H. Howard, October 31 1866, AQMR, fn 412, Reel 13, BRFAL-DC.

[17] W. F. Spurgin to S. N. Clark, August 4, 1865, AQMR, fn 259, Reel 13, BRFAL-DC; Amy Dru Stanley, *From Bondage to Contract: Wage Labor, Marriage, and the Market in the Age of Slave Emancipation* (Cambridge: Cambridge University Press, 1998), 36–37, 63–68; Foner, *Reconstruction*, 166–67. Spurgin's report sets out the terms for labor contracts recommended by the bureau.

Although it intervened on occasions to prevent employers, particularly government departments, from discriminating against black laborers, it could do little to open up alternative avenues of employment.[18] Instead, the Bureau directed its interventions in the labor market to the manipulation of its relief policies to encourage workforce participation and a massive program to induce unemployed freedpeople to seek their livelihood elsewhere.

### Sanitation and Housing

Owing to the concentration of impoverished freedpeople and the scarcity of suitable housing, many freed families lived in appalling conditions. They inhabited crowded tenements or hastily erected shanties, "contracted, filthy, and not protecting them from the inclemency of the weather," in the words of Oliver Otis Howard's brother Charles, who served as assistant commissioner for most of the life of the agency.[19] On a tour of inspection in the summer of 1867, Vandenburgh found freed families on the "Island" in South Washington "living in the most miserable of shanties" and "literally wallowing in filth." Murder Bay he discovered to be in its usual wretched condition. "Why must this abominable place be tolerated? Or, why do not the City authorities compel the landlord of that sink of iniquity to renovate their own tenements? For I assure you that there is not a more unpleasant duty can be conceived of than to visit that degraded place where lewd and insulting language assails you from all sides." It was, he suggested, "the 5 Points of Washington where sin and misery steeped in licentious amalgamation is allowed to exist." Bureau officials like Vandenburgh clearly considered such conditions to be detrimental to the moral welfare of the freedpeople as well as to their physical health and comfort.[20]

---

[18] See, for example, Stuart Eldridge to C. W. Perkins, April 13, 1868, LS, 4:519, Reel 2; Anthony Bowen to O. O. Howard, February 20, 1868, LR, 4:B43, Reel 10, BRFAL-DC. On racial discrimination in the labor market, see Johnston, "Surviving Freedom," 35–43, 253–55, 314–21; Thomas R. Johnson, "The City on the Hill: Race Relations in Washington, D.C., 1865–1885" (Ph.D. diss., University of Maryland, 1975), 152–66, 351–58; Borchert, *Alley Life in Washington*, 167–81.

[19] C. H. Howard to O. O. Howard, October 22, 1866, LS, 2:152, Reel 1, BRFAL-DC. See also W. F. Spurgin to S. N. Clark, November 20, 1865, AQMR, fn 312, Reel 13; to W. W. Rogers, April 3, 1866, LS, 2:82, Reel 1, BRFAL-DC; Johnston, "Surviving Freedom," 242–50.

[20] J. V. W. Vandenburgh to W. W. Rogers, June 20, 1867, LR, 2:2317, Reel 8 (on the "Island"); to W. W. Rogers, July 13, 1867, LR, 2:2348; to Stuart Eldridge, July 13,

They responded in a number of ways. One was to order the cleansing of properties occupied by freedpeople to reduce the danger of epidemic disease and as a measure of "social and moral reform." In March 1866, Charles Howard secured large quantities of lime to be used as a disinfectant and the services of ten noncommissioned officers, seconded from black regiments, to supervise the cleansing and whitewashing of all the habitations of freedpeople in Washington and Georgetown. The occupants were required to cleanse their dwellings thoroughly and to apply a coat of whitewash to external and internal walls. The city authorities agreed to remove accumulations of refuse and attend to drainage problems that were reported to them. Under Spurgin's supervision, the force moved systematically through the city. According to Spurgin, the inhabitants entered into the work with alacrity once they understood its purpose, although it is not clear that they were given much choice in the matter.[21]

The following year the procedure was repeated, this time by the city's sanitary police, with the bureau providing wagons and teams and whitewashing materials. The tenements were left, in Vandenburgh's words, "in as good a sanitary condition as was possible," although he doubted that anything could be done with some of the structures short of razing them to the ground.[22] A similar operation was conducted during the following summer, in the course of which some 3,225 houses were visited, with 12,549 inhabitants, and 350 barrels of lime expended. In the opinion of the bureau's chief medical officer, the sanitary operations were

1868, LR, 4:600, Reel 10 (on Murder Bay), BRFAL-DC. On Murder Bay, see also the letter written by Police Superintendent A. C. Richards to Senator Lot M. Morrill, March 6, 1861, printed in CG, 39.1:1507–08.

[21] C. H. Howard to Max Woodhull, March 3, 1866, LS, 1:451 (quotation); W. W. Rogers to W. F. Spurgin, March 17, 1866, LS, 1:515; C. H. Howard to O. O. Howard, October 22, 1866, LS, 2:152, Reel 1, BRFAL-DC. The cleansing may be traced in Spurgin's reports to Rogers, March 22, 27, 29, April 3, 1866, LR, 1: 1239, 1268, 1262, 1201; Reel 5, BRFAL-DC. For sanitary measures carried out by the bureau in other cities, see William L. Richter, *Overreached on All Sides: The Freedmen's Bureau Administration in Texas, 1865–1868* (College Station: Texas A & M University Press, 1991), 33–5; Reggie L. Pearson, "'There Are Many Sick, Feeble, and Suffering Freedmen': The Freedmen's Bureau's Health-Care Activities during Reconstruction in North Carolina, 1865–1868," *North Carolina Historical Review* 79 (April 2002): 153.

[22] J. V. W. Vandenburgh to W. W. Rogers, July 13, 1867, LR, 2:2348, Reel 8, BRFAL-DC. For an account of the whitewashing, see also Rogers to J. M. Brown, June 19, 1867, LS, 3:287; C. H. Howard to O. O. Howard, October 10, 1867, LS, 3:758a, Reel 1; Vandenburgh to Rogers, June 20, July 13, July 20, August 14, 1867, LR, 2:2317, 2436, 2471, 2587, Reel 8.

largely responsible for the absence of serious epidemic disease.[23] Even by the intrusive standards of nineteenth-century public health regulation, this was a dramatic exercise of state power, conducted with military efficiency and thoroughness, without regard for the wishes of the inhabitants, who were at no point consulted and who were more or less compelled to cooperate, as, indeed, were the owners of the property. It exhibited contemporary concerns about sanitation and moral order and the importance of good "policing" – that is, of removing unwelcome detritus and other "nuisances" from public space.

Because, as one of Howard's headquarters staff explained, "many of the habitations now occupied by freedmen are not fit for human beings to live in," the bureau decided in autumn of 1865 to divide up some of the unused buildings of Campbell Hospital in Washington into tenements to be rented to freedpeople at $3 a month, roughly a third of the "exorbitant rents" paid elsewhere in the city. Preference would be given to "poor, industrious men who have large families, – widows, and soldiers wives." Rents were to be paid in advance, but superintendents of tenement buildings were told that "No family will be evicted on account of inability to pay rent." Men and women cohabiting would be required to show formal proof of marriage. No pigs or poultry would be allowed, and the rooms would be regularly inspected to ensure a good standard of cleanliness. The following year further tenements were made available at East Capitol, Wisewell, and Kendall Green Barracks.[24]

By October 1867, the four tenement complexes housed 277 families, composed of 1,060 persons. According to Howard, "strict sanitary regulations" were enforced, and the tenements were supposed to be regularly inspected to ensure a good standard of cleanliness. In practice, the residents showed little desire to keep their rooms as clean and tidy as bureau officials thought appropriate and even less to clean out privies, yards, and other public spaces. Repeated inspections found some of the

---

[23] Stuart Eldridge to T. A. Lazenby, June 1, 1868, LS, 4:669; C. H. Howard to O. O. Howard, October 10, 1868, LS, 4:1128, Reel 2.; J. V. W. Vandenburgh to Eldridge, July 22, 1868, LR, 4:C269, Reel 10; to D.G. Swain, September 29, 1868, AQMR, fn 757, Reel 13, BRFAL-DC.

[24] W. W. Rogers to O. O. Howard, March 21, 1866, LS, 1:519; S. N. Clark to W. F. Spurgin, September 25, 1865, LS, 1:157; to John L. Roberts, February 20, 1866, LS, 1:417, Reel 1, BRFAL-DC. See also Clark to Spurgin, April 27, May 17, 1866, LS, 2:592, 45a; Charles H. Howard to Oliver Otis Howard, October 22, 1866, October 10, 1867, LS, 2:152, 3:758a, Reel 1; J. V. W. Vandenburgh to D. G. Swain, September 29, 1868, AQMR, fn 757, Reel 13, BRFAL-DC; Washington *Evening Star*, 3 April 1866; Johnston, "Surviving Freedom," 295.

tenements to be "in an extremely filthy condition" and the grounds "in a bad state of police." "There is a great want of cleanliness exhibited in the manner in which the houses are kept by the inmates," observed one inspector's report. The tenants were quick to turn the rooms to their own purposes, storing large amounts of paper, cardboard, rags, and even oysters, which had been collected for resale, posing both health and fire hazards. Repeated complaints from bureau inspectors suggest that such behavior was difficult to stamp out.[25] In the absence of compulsion to pay rent, many residents fell heavily into arrears, especially at Kendall Green, which, because of its smaller rooms and peripheral location, was regarded as the least desirable accommodation. It contained, explained Vandenburgh, many of the "poorer class" of tenants, "quite another class of people" from those to be found at Wisewell Barracks. Many who did not pay rent were removed in 1867 from Wisewell and East Capitol Barracks to Kendall Green to make room for more "deserving colored people" who would; others were discharged altogether.[26]

As the bureau wound up its affairs during 1868, the tenements were dismantled one by one, and many of their residents moved to newly erected apartments on Capitol Hill and Delaware Avenue. The new tenements were intended to provide better, more permanent accommodation. They were to be let out to "renters of good character"; none would be admitted who were known to be "dishonest or habitually slow in the payment of their rents," which would disqualify many of the bureau's former tenants. Because the new tenements were financed out of the Refugees and Freedmen's Fund established to finance a number of educational institutions, including Howard University, they were expected to make a profit, initially set at 6 percent, on the capital invested. Rents would be $4 to $6 a month, low for rental property of that quality in Washington but markedly higher than for the former tenements. Vandenburgh considered the change to be beneficial: "the people have learned . . . that they could not depend upon the Bureau for quarter for an indefinite period,

[25] Charles H. Howard to Oliver Otis Howard, October 10, 1867, LS, 3:758a; S. N. Clark to C. H. Howard, November 5, 1866, LS, 1:679, Reel 1; J. H. McBlair Jr. to O. O. Howard, May 12, July 17, 1866, LR, 1:1437, 1838, Reel 6, BRFAL-DC. For further reports, see to E. G. Townsend, November 10, 1866, LS, 1:707; to W. W. Rogers, October 6, 1866, LS, 2:137; McBlair to O. O. Howard, May 15, July 13, 1866, LR, 1:1453, 1836; Clark to Rogers, October 6, 1866, LR, 1:2330, Reel 6; Clark to Rogers, November 10, 1866, LR, 2:130, Reel 7; Willett A. Coulter to Clark, October 18, 1867, LR, 3:510, Reel 9, BRFAL-DC.

[26] S. N. Clark to J. V. W. Vandenburgh, October 11, 1867, LS, 2:663, Reel 1; Vandenburgh to D. G. Swain, September 29, 1868, AQMR, fn 757, Reel 13, BRFAL-DC.

but that they must depend upon themselves" and that this was a step toward "the ultimate withdrawal of Government assistance through this Bureau." The new tenements clearly served a different function to the old. Like "model tenements" elsewhere, while providing better accommodation at lower rents than could be obtained in the private housing market, they were rented on terms and at rates that disqualified all but the regularly employed "respectable poor."[27] Although housing only a fraction of Washington's freed population, the bureau's provision of public housing represented a most unusual venture. For all its limitations, the program stepped well outside the normal boundaries of social policy in nineteenth-century America.

The bureau endeavored to remove as many of the freed population as possible from the city. Where possible, the sick, disabled, and elderly were transferred to Freedmen's Village at Arlington, although dependent freedpeople showed a marked reluctance to forsake the congested streets of Washington for the stricter regime of the Village. Veering between competing models of a self-supporting freedmen's community and a bucolic repository for dependent freedpeople and between lax and draconian styles of management, Freedmen's Village lurched from crisis to crisis and was the subject of a number of investigations and boards of enquiry. There were disputes over the collection of rent; complaints by residents of removals, harsh punishments, and a stingy distribution of relief; complaints by bureau agents of the poor "state of police"; attempts to prevent cohabitation by men and women who were not formally married; and recurrent campaigns to prevent the inmates from "tampering with whiskey." Various efforts were made to remove able-bodied freedpeople, unless working in the camp or on the nearby government farms, and persuade them to find gainful employment elsewhere, preferably outside the District. The residents were subjected to regular purges when various categories of unauthorized persons were supposed to be removed, but without noticeably reducing the overall population, which remained at just over a thousand during the postwar years. In 1868, in a determined

---

[27] For the orders vacating the tenements, see Stuart Eldridge to O. S. B. Wall, July 24, 1868, LS, 4:836; to J. V. W. Vandenburgh, March 24, July 14, 1868, LS, 4:423, 773; S. N. Clark to Vandenburgh, January 13, 1868, LS, 4:149, Reel 2; SO, 1868, Nos. 3 (9 January), 24 (9 April), 69 (9 September), fn 160, 166, 182, Reel 13, BRFAL-DC. For an account of the removal, see C. H. Howard to O. O. Howard, October 10, 1868, LS, 4:1128, Reel 2; J. V. W. Vandenburgh to D. G. Swain, September 29, 1868, AQMR, fn 757, Reel 13, BRFAL-DC. On the origins of the Refugees and Freedmen's Fund, see Howard *Autobiography*, 2:264–68.

effort to disband the Village, dependent freedpeople were removed to the Freedmen's Hospital in Washington, but families who rented plots of land in the vicinity were allowed to retain their dwellings, and a freed community remained on the site for many years.[28]

A very different settlement was located at Barry Farm across the Eastern Branch of the Potomac, in what is now Anacostia. To help freedpeople to escape the overcrowding and high rents, not to mention the moral dangers, of central Washington, Oliver Otis Howard decided to utilize part of the Refugees and Freedmen's Fund to buy land "with a view of relieving the immediate necessities of a class of poor colored people in the District of Columbia." In 1867, a tract of 375 acres was acquired and divided into one-acre lots that could be purchased over a two-year period by freedmen. A "practical builder" was hired to supervise construction of houses, and lumber was provided at low cost. Roads were laid out and a school constructed to serve the new community. Over the next two years 266 families settled there, encouraged, said Charles Howard, by "the prospect of owning a homestead and being relieved of the all devouring demands of the rent landlords," and the community showed signs of prospering. According to Superintendent J. B. Johnson, the settlers were "good honest industrious and worthy men"; those with bad habits were discouraged from applying. Most were prompt in paying the installments on their plots. He waxed lyrical on the life-transforming character of the experience for those involved. "Men who until within five years had not owned their hands who since that time had been struggling with poverty and want, against prejudice and hatred now not only had in their possession an acre of land" but had begun to build houses on it. A man of eighty, for example, a former Lee slave, had cleared a whole lot while laboring for wages, while another of the same age had built a commodious house: "His greatest desire is to live to *pay* for his land,

---

[28] C. H. Howard to O. O. Howard, October 10, 1867, LS, III, 758a; W. W. Rogers to A. A. Lawrence, November 3, 9, 1865, LS, 1:675, 700; to P. P. Burgevin, June 7, 1866, LS, 2:185, Reel 1; Stuart Eldridge to John V. W. Vandenburgh and Charles B. Purvis, June 19, 1868, LS, 4:699; to Vandenburgh, July 14, 1867, LS, 4:775, Reel 2; S.N. Clark to C. H. Howard, May 31, 1866, LR, 1:1550, Reel 6; April 15, 1868, LR, 4:492, Reel 10; Horatio N. Howard to C. H. Howard, July 19 and October 31, 1867; to S. N. Clark, December 31, 1867; to D. G. Swain, September 30, 1868, AQMR, fn 757, Reel 13, BRFAL-DC; *National Intelligencer*, October 27, 1865; *Evening Star*, July 7 and October 2, 1865, January 1, 1866. On the history of the Village, see Joseph P. Reidy, "'Coming from the Shadow of the Past': The Transition from Slavery to Freedom at Freedmen's Village, 1863–1900," *Virginia Magazine of History and Biography*, 95 (1987), 414–28; Everly, "Freedmen's Bureau in the National Capital," 47–51, 102–4.

and leave a home for his children." Although seasonal unemployment caused financial hardships for many of its residents, the settlement survived well into the twentieth century and became the focus for a thriving black community in Anacostia.[29]

## The Problem of Relief

Among the chief responsibilities conferred on the bureau was the relief of destitute refugees and freedpeople.[30] That responsibility was intended to be temporary, lasting until the disruptive effects of war had eased, but in the District of Columbia, because of the recurrent shortage of employment, it continued throughout the life of the agency. Bureau agents and the representatives of philanthropic societies operating in the District regularly reported cases of destitution. For example, Josephine Griffing, the former antislavery and women's rights activist associated with the National Freedmen's Relief Association of the District of Columbia (NFRADC) and appointed in 1865 as a special agent of the bureau, frequently reported instances of extreme suffering. Many families, she wrote in February 1866, were suffering for want of food; in April, she noted that thousands lacked bed linen, many of them "sleeping without beds or pillows, on unventilated rugs, calculated both to invite disease and breed distemper," and in most cases sharing one room without proper facilities "to observe the laws of health, or the rules of society"; in October, she observed that general destitution was leading the freedpeople to "vice and stealing and licentiousness." At no time since 1864, she reported a year later, had so many old and destitute freedpeople applied for relief. A

---

[29] Howard, *Autobiography*, 2:420 and 416–22 passim; C. H. Howard to O. O. Howard, October 10, 1867, LS, 3:758a, Reel 1; J. B. Johnson to C. H. Howard, November 30, AQMR, fn 682, Reel 13, BRFAL-DC. See also John A. Carpenter, *Sword and Olive Branch: Oliver Otis Howard* (Pittsburgh: University of Pittsburgh Press, 1964), 185–87; Louise Hutchinson, *The Anacostia Story, 1608–1930* (Washington, DC: Smithsonian Institution Press, 1977), 81–90.

[30] On Freedmen's Bureau relief policies, see Bremner, *Public Good*, 117–21; Mary J. Farmer, "'Because They Are Women': Gender and the Virginia Freedmen's Bureau's 'War on Dependency,'" in Cimbala and Miller, eds., *Freedmen's Bureau and Reconstruction*, 165–72; Cimbala, *Under the Guardianship of the Nation*, 83–104; Martin Abbott, *The Freedmen's Bureau in South Carolina, 1865–1872* (Chapel Hill: University of North Carolina Press, 1967), 37–51; Rabinowitz, *Race Relations in the Urban South*, 128–32; Bentley, *History of the Freedmen's Bureau*, 76–79, 139–44; Ira C. Colbey, "The Freedmen's Bureau: From Social Welfare to Segregation," *Phylon* 46 (September 1985): 219–30; Victoria Olds, "The Freedmen's Bureau: A Nineteenth-Century Federal Welfare Agency," *Social Casework* 44 (May 1963): 247–54.

visiting agent noted in January 1866 that a thousand families were living "in a destitute and suffering condition" on the Island in South Washington, while, as late as January 1868, a hundred persons were discovered living in "abject conditions" in hovels near Fort Barker along the Eastern Branch of the Potomac.[31] Although Spurgin remarked in his first report as superintendent in August 1865 that conditions were not as bad as he had expected and that he had encountered "few families in a destitute and suffering condition," as winter approached, he was forced to admit that more households would require assistance.[32]

Bureau officials were generally at pains to play down the more dramatic estimates of destitution that were made, particularly by Griffing, who, in the course of a fund-raising tour of the northern states during the summer of 1865, was reported to have said that 20,000 "suffering and destitute freedmen" were living in the District and that many of them had died. When concerned individuals inquired about the accuracy of such reports, John Eaton, the District's first assistant commissioner, felt obliged to disabuse them, pointing out that only a few hundred freedpeople were in receipt of rations, most of them sick or otherwise dependent, and that the majority were self-supporting. "Many are poor," Acting Assistant Adjutant General Selden N. Clark informed the Associated Press in December, "but have managed thus far to take care of themselves – receiving now and then temporary aid."[33] It is evident that Griffing and the bureau

---

[31] Josephine Griffing to C. H. Howard, February 9, 1866, LR, 1:751; April 17, 1866, LR, 1:1180, Reel 5; October 20, 1866, LR, 2:fn 61, Reel 7; October 5, 1867, LR, 3:420, Reel 9; Joseph B. Johnson to S. N. Clark, January 16, 1868, LR, 4:959, Reel 10; Clark to Mrs. Bigelow et al., January 8, 1866, LS, 1:333, Reel 1; S. J. Bowen to O. O. Howard, January 30, 1866, LR, 1:641, Reel 5, BRFAL-DC; *Fourth Annual Report of the National Freedmen's Relief Association of the District of Columbia* (Washington, DC: 1966), 11; *Freedmen's Record*, 1:43. For a more detailed account of conditions during the winter of 1865–66, see the reports of visiting agents in AQMR, Reel 14, BRFAL-DC.

[32] W. F. Spurgin to S. N. Clark, August 4 and November 20, 1865, January 1, 1866, AQMR, fn 259, 311, 315, Reel 13, BRFAL-DC.

[33] John Eaton to George Whipple, November 15, 1865, LS, 1:234; S. N. Clark to E. Carpenter, December 5, 1865, LS, 1:265; to Associated Press, December 19, 1865, LS, 1:290; Joseph S. Fullerton to O. O. Howard, February 6, 1866, LS, 1:374, Reel 1, BRFAL-DC. See also W. F. Spurgin to Clark, January 1, 1866, AQMR, fn 315, Reel 13, BRFAL-DC; *Evening Star*, September 2, 1865; Bentley, *History of the Freedmen's Bureau*, 77–79; Keith E. Melder, "Angel of Mercy in Washington: Josephine Griffing and the Freedmen, 1864–1872," *Records of the Columbia Historical Society, 1963–65* (Washington, DC: 1967), 255–9. These letters were written in response to inquiries such as Almira E. Howard to Freedmen's Bureau, October 14, 1865, LR, 1:138, Reel 4; E. Carpenter to O. O. Howard, November 24, 1865, LR, 1:303; Arabella A. Smith to John Eaton, December 8, 1865, LR, 1:404, Reel 5, BRFAL-DC. A similar claim, this

chiefs had different agendas: the former, by sensationalizing to encourage philanthropic donations for the relief of the poor; the latter to defuse public anxiety about the results of emancipation. However, their varying estimations were also a consequence of the different meanings that they gave to terms such as "destitution" and "suffering." To bureau officers, "suffering," or "actual suffering" as they often phrased it, constituted acute physical distress caused by an insufficiency of food, fuel, clothing, or shelter. As one agent explained, those who were poor but not destitute and had some work were "not entirely objects of charity." To Griffing, "suffering" meant an inability to maintain a decent and respectable standard of living. Such differences bedeviled the relief operations of the bureau throughout its existence.[34]

Following the practice of the military authorities during the war, the bureau attempted to place permanently sick and dependent freedpeople in the Freedmen's Hospital and Freedmen's Village and to provide the able-bodied poor with temporary assistance in kind. Two soup kitchens were opened, and supplies of fuel, blankets, and clothing were made available, drawn in part from unused supplies belonging to the Army's Quartermaster Department and the U.S. Sanitary Commission. As reports of hardship increased during the winter of 1865–66, more systematic arrangements were made to ensure that assistance reached all who needed it and to avoid duplication of effort between the bureau and the various freedmen's aid societies. The cities of Washington and Georgetown were divided into thirteen subdistricts, each under the supervision of a visiting agent on whose "friendliness to the freedmen and good judgment" could be relied. The agents were responsible for investigating cases of distress and determining what assistance was required. The bureau would then honor their orders for food, fuel, clothing, and medicines. During the winter, 1,398 rations, on average, were distributed daily, along with other supplies furnished by the bureau and the various benevolent associations.[35] However,

---

time that between ten and fifteen freedpeople from the nieghboring states were "existing here in a state of almost utter destitution, inconceivable suffering, and want," was made by Senator Lot M. Morrill in appealing for a congressional relief appropriation. *CG*, 39.1:1507.

[34] Eliza Heacock to J. S. Fullerton, January 19, 1866, MRVA, fn 18, Reel 14, BRFAL-DC. See also Masur, "Reconstructing the Nation's Capital," 53–56.

[35] John Eaton to George Whipple, November 15, 1865, LS, 1:234; S. N. Clark to Sayles J. Bowen, January 8, February 1, 1866, LS, 1:332, 372; J. S. Fullerton to O. O. Howard, February 6, 1866, LS, 1:374; C. H. Howard, Circular Letter, April 13, 1866, LS, 1:567; C. H. Howard to O. O. Howard, October 22, 1866, LS, 2:152, Reel 1; W. F. Spurgin to Clark, January 1, 1866, AQMR, fn 320, Reel 13, BRFAL-DC. See also Clark to

when milder weather returned in the spring, the distribution of rations was terminated. In the expectation of a return to full employment, able-bodied freedmen were required to support their dependent relatives.[36]

Evidence of continuing destitution led Congress in April 1866 to appropriate $25,000 for the relief of suffering in the District of Columbia. This sum was entrusted to the commissioner of the Freedmen's Bureau, who appointed a Special Relief Commission, chaired by Dr. Robert Reyburn, chief medical officer for the District, to arrange for its distribution. The Commission, following the practice of the previous winter, divided the District into twenty-one subdistricts, each under the charge of a visiting agent, drawn once more, in most cases, from the various benevolent agencies engaged in freedmen's relief. The agents would, after personal investigation, issue orders for food, clothing, and fuel. The bureau's almost fanatical record keeping showed that 9,264 persons, of whom 5,107 were black, received assistance from the relief fund.[37] A further appropriation of $15,000 the following year was administered in the same fashion.[38] In 1868, another appropriation of $15,000 was made, which this time was expended on public works, under the supervision of the commissioner of public buildings and grounds, employing two hundred black and one hundred white laborers, each working for two weeks, at a dollar a day. Only laborers with destitute families, their circumstances to be determined "by actual inspection," were to be considered for employment. As Charles Howard explained, "There are so many dependent and helpless, for want of work, that there will be no harm

Spurgin, September 6, 1865, LS, 1:109, Reel 1; Spurgin to Clark, December 30, 1865, LR, 1:458, Reel 5, BRFAL-DC; *National Intelligencer*, March 5, 1866. Until it received a congressional appropriation in July 1866, the bureau was chronically short of funds. In the District of Columbia, its revenue was derived from the residue of the Contraband Fund composed of deductions from the wages of "contraband" workers during the war, as well as the rents from the small number of abandoned and confiscated properties under its control, supplemented by requisitions for rations, fuel, discarded clothes, and other equipment from the quartermaster general, and medicines from the surgeon general of the Army. See Howard, *Autobiography*, 2:225–26, 256–58, 263–65; Bentley, *History of the Freedmen's Bureau*, 76.

36 S. N. Clark to Mrs. E. M. Martin, April 4, 1866, LS, 2:21, Reel 1; W. F. Spurgin to C. H. Howard, April 9, 1866, LR, 1:1232, Reel 5, BRFAL-DC.

37 C. H. Howard to O. O. Howard, October 22, 1866, LS, 2:152, Reel 1; Robert Reyburn to C. H. Howard, July 1, 1867, Reports of Operations of Special Relief Commission, fn 607, Reel 16; J. V. W. Vandenburgh to W. W. Rogers, July 20, 1867, AQMR, fn 525, Reel 13, BRFAL-DC; Howard, *Autobiography*, 2:294–5; *Evening Star*, May 12, 1866. On the appropriation, see CG, 39.1:1507–09.

38 Special Orders 1867, No. 93 (June 10), SO, Reel 13; C. H. Howard to O. O. Howard, October 10, 1867, LS, 3:758a, Reel 1, BRFAL-DC.

in alternating with those who have not yet received assistance." In the end, more than eight hundred freedmen were given a turn. Although the objective was to encourage self-reliance by tying assistance to constructive employment, the attempt to spread the work as thinly as possible and the careful means testing that went with it marked the program off as primarily a relief rather than a public works project.[39]

As the bureau's funds were depleted during the winter of 1867–68, and in the face of continuing destitution, it came to an agreement with the local Provident Aid Society, an association composed of many of Washington's leading businessmen that was mainly concerned with relieving poverty among white families, to coordinate their activities. The bureau furnished bread, meat, and desiccated vegetables to the society's soup houses and paid the salary of some of its agents on the understanding that meals would be provided to black as well as white applicants.[40] At the end of the winter, Commissioner Howard ordered the discontinuation of supplies to the Provident Aid Society and ordered instead that "extreme want" should be prevented by issuing "through the usual channels such provisions as may be absolutely necessary." Throughout its lifetime, the bureau continued to furnish supplies of clothing, shoes, blankets, and fuel to needy freedpeople, despite its continuing efforts to shed the responsibility of relief.[41]

The bureau's relief operations closely followed the precepts of organized charity as practiced by contemporary agencies such as the New York Association for Improving the Condition of the Poor. Indeed, the military organization, the desire for system, and the attention to detail that bureau officials brought to the administration of relief anticipated the "scientific charity" of the late nineteenth century more than they

[39] O. O. Howard to C. H. Howard, March 16, 1868, LR, 4:106; to Nathaniel Michler, March 16, 1868, LR, 4:109, Reel 10; C. H. Howard to O. O. Howard, October 10, 1868, LS, 4:1128; Stuart Eldridge to Anthony Brown, February 24, 1868, LS, 4:307, Reel 2; J. V. W. Vandenburgh to David G. Swain, September 29, 1868, AQMR, fn 757, Reel 13, BRFAL-DC.

[40] C. H. Howard to Provident Aid Society, February 17, 1868, LS, 4:277; to Peter Parker, March 13, 1868, LS, 4:388; to Alexander R. Shepherd, March 25, 1868, LS, 4:427; C. H. Howard to O. O. Howard, October 10, 1868, LS, 4:1128, Reel 2; J. V. W. Vandenburgh to David G. Swain, September 29, 1868, AQMR, fn 757, Reel 13; S. H. Kauffmann to Howard, February 13, April 21, 1868, LR, 4:1204, 1241, Reel 10, BRFAL-DC; *Evening Star*, February 20, 1868. On the composition of the Provident Aid Society, see Masur, "Reconstructing the Nation's Capital," 89–92.

[41] Eliphalet Z. Whittlesey to C. H. Howard, February 19, 1868, LR, 4:B46, Reel 10; C. H. Howard to O. O. Howard, October 10, 1868, LS, 4:1128, Reel 2, BRFAL-DC.

recalled the haphazard philanthropy of the antebellum era. They typ-
ified the "new benevolence" that had emerged in response to the exi-
gencies of wartime, the watchwords of which, as Lori Ginzberg explains,
were "nationalism, discipline, centralization, and, above all, efficiency."[42]
Just as bureau officials adopted, indeed improved on, the administrative
practices of mid-nineteenth-century philanthropy, so also did they apply
similar assumptions about pauperism and poverty. Central to their purpose was the desire to disabuse the freedpeople of any notion that the
United States was "obliged to support them" and to encourage, even
compel, them to support themselves. Assistant Adjutant General Selden
N. Clark warned that indiscriminate assistance would "while relieving
the needy also foster idleness and a spirit of dependence." Hence visiting agents were required to investigate each case personally and to make
"a just discrimination," distinguishing carefully "between poverty and
actual suffering," between those able and unable to work, and between
the genuinely needy and those who sought to exploit the benevolence of
philanthropically minded citizens or the generosity of the government.
Therefore, said Eaton, "while none should suffer, the charity being from
the Government must be guarded." Even though the great majority of
recipients were aged, infirm, or widows with small children, bureau officials repeatedly warned that welfare provision, unless tightly controlled,
would "make paupers" of the freedpeople. Although it is impossible to
deny that stereotyped conceptions of African American character might
have influenced bureau policies, they were in most respects too consistent
with prevailing attitudes to pauperism and prevailing assumptions about
the behavior of the "dependent" classes to suggest that racism was the
sole, or even the primary, motivation.[43]

---

[42] Lori D. Ginzberg, *Women and the Work of Benevolence: Morality, Politics and Class
in the Nineteenth-Century United States* (New Haven, CT: Yale University Press, 1990),
133. On antebellum practice, see Bremner, *Public Good*, chap. 1; Paul Boyer, *Urban
Masses and Moral Order in America, 1820–1920* (Cambridge, MA: Harvard University
Press, 1978), 85–94, 143–55; Michael B. Katz, *In the Shadow of the Poorhouse: A
Social History of Welfare in America* (New York: Basic Books, 1986), 58–84; Walter
I. Trattner, *From Poor Law to Welfare State* (5th edn.; New York: Free Press, 1994),
chaps. 4 and 5; Carroll Smith-Rosenberg, *Religion and the Rise of the City: The New
York City Mission Movement, 1812–1870* (Ithaca, NY: Cornell University Press, 1971),
245–73. On the transformation of charity during the Civil War era, see Bremner, *Public
Good*, 113–43; Ginzberg, *Women and the Work of Benevolence*, chaps. 5 and 6; Stanley,
*From Bondage to Contract*, 128–30; and George M. Fredrickson, *The Inner Civil War:
Northern Intellectuals, and the Crisis of the Union* (New York: Harper, 1965), 211–15.
[43] J. S. Fullerton to O. O. Howard, February 6, 1866, LS,1:374, Reel 1; S. N. Clark to C.
H. Howard, January 4, 1868, LR, 4:C4, Reel 10; J. V. W. Vandenburgh to D. G. Swain,

The rigorously spartan form of benevolence advocated by the bureau was brought into focus by its long-running struggle to bring civilian agents into line. Early in the life of the agency, Spurgin found reason to condemn the efforts of two visiting agents as "productive of discontentment inasmuch as they encourage the freedmen to expect assistance from the Government, whether they make any attempt to assist themselves or not."[44] The sharpest thorn in the side of the local management was Josephine Griffing, who was appointed as a special advisor to the assistant commissioner in June 1865 but dismissed in November after raising a storm with her inflated estimates of destitution in the District.[45] Nevertheless, Griffing continued to work for the NFRADC and continued to cooperate with the bureau. From July 1866, the bureau paid the rent of her office on North Capitol Street and the salaries of two of her assistants, and in March 1867, in recognition of her work in finding employment in the North for freedpeople, not to mention her influence with several prominent Republican congressmen, it resumed the payment of her salary.[46]

Griffing persistently disobeyed instructions and flouted regulations. She was repeatedly reprimanded for handing out orders for the issue of clothing and other supplies on the statement of the applicants themselves, without the close personal investigation that bureau regulations required. In October 1867, an inspector's report recommended her removal for what he saw as insubordinate, unreliable, mendacious, and even fraudulent conduct. Among the exhibits were requests by Griffing for clothing and bedding for a number of destitute freedpeople. E. G. Townsend, the superintendent of the tenements where they resided, maintained that she had not visited the persons named and that none of them had applied to him for assistance. One of those named, Christie Allen, he said, had already been provided with a reasonable amount of bedding. Griffing, in response to these charges, claimed to have personally investigated each case before applying to the local superintendent for relief and used all

September 29, 1868, AQMR, fn 757, Reel 13; Clark to W. F. Spurgin, August 31, 1865, LS, 1:109, Reel 1; Eliza Heacock to Fullerton, 19 January 1866, MRVA, fn 19, Reel 14, BRFAL-DC; Farmer, "'Because They Are Women,'" 165–72.

44  W.F. Spurgin to S.N. Clark, December 16, 1865, LR, 1:438, Reel 5, BRFAL-DC.

45  On Griffing's career, see Melder, "Angel of Mercy in Washington"; Stanton, *History of Woman Suffrage*, 2:27–39; Faulkner, *Women's Radical Reconstruction*, 31–32, 57–60, 83–99, 117–31; McPherson, *Struggle for Equality*, 389–92; Everly, "Freedmen's Bureau in the National Capitol," 22–23.

46  W. W. Rogers to J. M. Brown, July 24, 1866, LS, 2:298, Reel 1; Special Orders, 1867, No. 46 (March 22), SO, fn 110, Reel 13, BRFAL-DC.

her means and judgment "to understand the absolute necessities of all." She had known Allen for two years and considered her to be generally destitute. As for the bedding that Allen had received from Townsend, Griffing regarded that as inadequate "to protect her and her children from exposure and suffering."[47]

In March of the following year, Griffing's principal adversary, the local superintendent John V. W. Vandenburgh, made another attempt to dislodge her. Taking a batch of requests for clothing submitted by Griffing, he claimed, on the basis of further investigation by himself and other agents, that two of the freedwomen on whose behalf the applications were made had received garments during the winter and were therefore ineligible to receive further clothing; another needed no assistance because her son was working on the streets; a fourth, although a widow, was able-bodied and at work; a fifth was "not very destitute" and owned the house she lived in; a sixth had two boys able to earn their living; a seventh was able to work and had an able-bodied husband; and an eighth claimed never to have asked for relief. Only four warranted assistance, three of whom should have properly be transferred to Freedmen's Village but refused to go. In another batch, six applicants were judged to need relief, and six were not. "Of all the foregoing cases," said Vandenburgh, "not one of 5 has been visited by Mrs. Griffing . . . not one in 10 is found at the residence stated." He accused her once more of accepting "the story of the parties" in making up her requests and failing properly to investigate their circumstances.[48]

It seems likely that Griffing was guilty of placing too much trust in the word of relief applicants and of failing to visit each family in its home. However, at the root of the ongoing controversy lay different conceptions of the function and proper allocation of relief. Vandenburgh and his colleagues were anxious to keep relief to a minimum, both to avoid unnecessary charges on the government and to prevent dependency. Therefore, they considered it appropriate to deny assistance to a family in which

[47] C. H. Howard to Griffing, November 16, 1867, LS, 3:831a, Reel 1; Willett Coulter to F. E. Town, November 6, 1867, LS, 3:722; E. G. Townsend to J. V. W. Vandenburgh, 29 November 1867; J. S. Griffing to Vandenburgh, October 28 and November 26, 1867, all in LR, 3:722; Griffing to S. N. Clark, November 18 1867, LR, 3:859; S. S. Chamberlain to Vandenburgh, October 29, 1867, LR, 3:883, Reel 9, BRFAL-DC.

[48] J. V. W. Vandenburgh to Stuart Eldridge, March 31, April 6, 7, 9, 1868, LR, 4:C115, C125, C128, C133, Reel 10, BRFAL-DC. See also S. N. Clark to Vandenburgh, April 2, 1868, LS, 4:473; Eldridge to J. S. Griffing, April 3, 7, 9, 10, 1868, LS, 4: 477, 494, 505, 508; Eldridge to Vandenburgh, April 7, 1868, LS, 4:493, Reel 2, BRFAL-DC; Melder, "Angel of Mercy," 259–62; and Faulkner, *Women's Radical Reconstruction*, 95–96.

one or more members were working; to insist on strictly categorizing the poor and relieving their needs in different ways; to refuse clothes and bedding to those that had recently received them; and to deny relief in their homes to those that refused to enter Freedmen's Village or to accept offers of work outside the District. Griffing, on the other hand, took a more open-handed attitude. The women who visited her office were, she could clearly see, destitute; they evidently possessed insufficient clothing and other necessities to maintain a decent standard of living. They were, in her view, "suffering" for want of adequate clothing, bedding, or firewood. Therefore, she was unable to deny that they warranted assistance. To Griffing, rather than an exercise in social engineering, relief was an exercise in human sympathy. Although she, too, sought, where possible, to guide freedpeople toward self-sufficiency, she believed, as a longtime abolitionist, that the devastating mental as well as physical scars inflicted by slavery would leave many, particularly the old and infirm, incapable of supporting themselves. She also believed that single mothers with young children, often separated from their husbands by the accidents of slavery and war, deserved special consideration. It was not surprising that, by the standards set by Vandenburgh and his colleagues, she often fell into error.[49]

Vandenburgh found such errors unforgivable. Griffing and other "lady visiting agents," he said, were unable "in their earnest desire to assist all who asked . . . to discriminate between poverty and actual suffering – nearly all the freedpeople were poor but many, *very many*, were not actually suffering." To Vandenburgh, female volunteers were congenitally incapable of the exact discrimination and mental toughness required to administer relief efficiently. Therefore, greater amounts of clothing and other supplies were handed out than he considered necessary. He recommended that "the system of employing female visiting agents be abrogated; and that relief be confined to the sick; and this granted only on the certificate of a medical officer, or some male parties appointed specially for such business." A smaller number of male agents could canvass the city more efficiently, relieving more suffering at less expense. Shortly thereafter, four male supervising agents were appointed at his suggestion. Vandenburgh noted with satisfaction that, whereas Griffing and the other female agents had offered assistance to nearly everyone who asked for it, only 85 of 508 applicants investigated by the male agents were found to

---

[49] See also the exchange of letters between Griffing and *New York Tribune* editor Horace Greeley, reprinted in Stanton, *History of Woman Suffrage*, 2:36–37.

be "suffering."[50] Like many of those involved in organizing relief during the Civil War era, bureau officials claimed to value the "male virtues" of efficiency and discipline more highly than "the older style of female benevolence" exemplified by Griffing. Nonetheless, the bureau was never able to dispense with the energy, as well as the expertise, of Griffing and other female agents.[51]

Assumptions regarding class and gender also affected Vandenburgh's judgments regarding the social roles of freedwomen. Whereas Griffing believed that destitute single women with children should be assisted so that they might keep their families together, the bureau superintendent recommended that they should be required to "send their children to homes where they could earn their own living, and the smaller ones to the Orphan's Home." Their mothers could then become "self-supporting." Otherwise, with young children on their hands, it would be "impossible for them to get along without assistance, and until some earnest rule is established, in such cases, and the women are learned by actual experience and suffering that they must break up their families, (hard as it may seem) and be governed by force of circumstances, as all poor people must do, – we can never get rid of, nor do away with, the many hundred cases of destitution in this city." As long as they could "run to the visiting agents and procure aid from the Bureau," the state of affairs would continue. Vandenburgh, then, took it for granted that poor black women, like all poor women, might by necessity be forced to work; that their children should be expected to work as soon as they were old enough; and that their families might have to be broken up so that family members could survive without relief. Although the bureau was at pains to impress on freedpeople the sanctity of the family unit and to impress on freedwomen the importance of their domestic responsibilities, its agents did not consider it unnatural or improper for freedwomen, and also their children, to enter the workforce.[52]

---

[50] J. V. W. Vandenburgh to D. G. Swain, September 29, 1868, AQMR, fn 757, Reel 13; to Stuart Eldridge, March 31, April 10, 1868, LR, 4:C115, C134, Reel 10, BRFAL-DC. See also C. H. Howard to O. O. Howard, October 10 1868, LS, 4:1128, Reel 2, BRFAL-DC.

[51] Ginzberg, *Women and the Work of Benevolence*, 172 and 133–213 passim. For a fuller analysis of the differences between male and female approaches to the welfare of the freedpeople, see Faulkner, *Women's Radical Reconstruction*. The Roster of Civilian Officers, Agents, and Clerks on Duty in Bureau of R., F., and A.L. for the District of Columbia, in Reel 19, BRFAL-DC, records several women as hired by the bureau. For example, the roster for July 1868 lists Griffing and five other women. Ibid., fn 468.

[52] J. V. W. Vandenburgh to Stuart Eldridge, March 31, 1868, LR, 4:C125, Reel 10, BRFAL-DC. On the contested nature of freedwomen's employment, see also Leslie A. Schwalm,

Even by mid-nineteenth-century standards, the bureau's relief program was heavy-handed and bureaucratic, often unsympathetic to the
needs of individual families. Agents such as Vandenburgh displayed a
chillingly mechanical attitude to relief. Nevertheless, the bureau had to
be sparing with its limited resources, conscious of the unpopularity of
extensive welfare programs at the expense of federal taxpayers, and sensitive to the potentially damaging political consequences of maintaining
a large number of freedpeople on relief in the national capital.[53] Harsh
though its relief policies might have seemed to Griffing and her allies,
they appeared all too generous to many white Washingtonians. On several occasions, Mayor Richard Wallach complained that the bureau was
encouraging freedpeople to subsist in idleness in Washington rather than
seeking employment on neighboring farms. "Thousands of contrabands,"
he told the City Councils, were "allured to this 'paradise of freedmen' by
the temptations to indolence offered by the gratuities of the Freedmen's
Bureau."[54] Such charges, as the Washington *Evening Star* pointed out,
were "utterly without foundation." Far from enticing freedpeople to the
city, the bureau, as we have seen, did all it could to reduce the relief rolls
and, as we shall also see, to induce them to travel elsewhere in search of
employment.[55]

## "A Vast Labor Bureau"

The bureau's principal solution to the problem of destitution and overcrowding was to seek homes for freedpeople outside the District, "giving
those now idle about this city an opportunity to support themselves,
free from the vices and diseases which are likely to arise from inhabiting
abodes of filth and spending their time in idleness, a sanitary and social
peril and an expense to the Government" and relieving the agency of the

---

A Hard Fight for We: Women's Transition from Slavery to Freedom in South Carolina
(Urbana: University of Illinois Press, 1997), 249–57; Stanley, From Bondage to Contract,
140–42, 187–90; Jacqueline Jones, Labor of Love, Labor of Sorrow: Black Women,
Work, and the Family from Slavery to the Present (New York: Basic Books, 1985), 45,
58–59; Farmer, "'Because They Are Women,'" 172–81; Masur, "Reconstructing the
Nation's Capital," 69–71; Faulkner, Women's Radical Reconstruction, 57–58.

[53] Oliver Otis Howard believed that "the relief offered by the Bureau" was "abnormal to
our system of government." Autobiography, 2:226.

[54] Message of the Mayor, June 24, 1867, Journal of the 65th Council (Washington, DC:
1868), 30. See also National Intelligencer, February 11, 1868; John B. Ellis, The Sights
and Secrets of the National Capital (Chicago: Jones, Junkins & Co., 1869), 496.

[55] Evening Star, August 23, 1867.

embarrassment of harboring a conspicuous mass of destitute freedmen at the heart of the nation's capital.[56] An Employment and Intelligence Office was established in Washington, and both unemployed freedpeople and prospective employers were invited to avail themselves of its facilities. "Work can be obtained for every man, woman, and child in the District," promised Spurgin. Freedpeople, he warned, must learn to depend on themselves; "the Government would not support them in idleness." In October 1866, in a circular letter to black ministers, Charles Howard explained that the bureau intended to make the freedpeople "self-supporting and independent of the Government, that it is not well to make paupers of them by giving them food or any aid here, provided they can be furnished with suitable work, at good wages elsewhere." Although employment had been found for 5000 freedpeople over the previous twelve months, "many others, hundreds and thousands ought to leave this District." He estimated that the African American population exceeded the employment available locally for them by as much as 7,000. The government would help them find work elsewhere, but "Government aid will not be furnished to those able to work. . . . This Bureau is established for the permanent good of the freedpeople and our plan is to make them all self-sustaining." Repeated warnings were issued that those who declined the employment offered them would be debarred from receiving assistance from the bureau.[57]

As the effort to find employment intensified during the winter of 1865–66, the bureau began to offer free transportation to workers who had received firm written guarantees of employment outside the District. The expense was justified, Howard argued, because the removal of destitute

---

[56] John Eaton to George B. Carse, June 16, 1865, LS, 1:1, Reel 1, BRFAL-DC. On the bureau's employment program, see also William Cohen, *At Freedom's Edge: Black Mobility and the Southern White Quest for Racial Control, 1861–1915* (Baton Rouge: Louisiana State University Press, 1991), 78–86, 95–96; Faulkner, *Women's Radical Reconstruction*, 117–31; Everly, "Freedmen's Bureau in the National Capital," 95–99; Horton, "Federal Social Policy," 93–100; Masur, "Reconstructing the Nation's Capital," 60–65; Bentley, *Freedmen's Bureau*, 124–25.

[57] W. F. Spurgin to S. N. Clark, November 1, 1865, AQMR, fn 305, Reel 13; C. H. Howard, Circular Letter to Colored Churches, October 15, 1866, LS, 2:146, Reel 1, BRFAL-DC. On the evolution of the employment program, see also Clark to Spurgin, 6 September 1865, LS, 1:129; Spurgin to Clark, August 4, November 20, 1865, AQMR, fn 259, 312, Reel 13, BRFAL-DC. For threats to deny assistance to those refusing offers of employment, see Clark to Perry Davis, March 20, 1867, LS, 3:18, Reel 1; to Vandenburgh, January 20, 1868, LS, 4:178, Reel 2, BRFAL-DC. The *Evening Star* welcomed the establishment of the employment office because it would "be found of much value to our citizens in quest of servants." *Evening Star*, August 2, 1865.

freedpeople to locations where they could support themselves would relieve the government of the burden of providing for their subsistence.[58] Small numbers of freedpeople were transported at government expense during the autumn of 1865 and much larger numbers during the winter and early spring of 1866. During the following spring, however, President Andrew Johnson, in his eagerness to embarrass the bureau, condemned the agency for instituting what was "little better than another form of slavery" in transporting freedpeople to work on plantations in the Deep South, while the *New York Herald* accused it of "trafficking in negroes." More crucially, the bureau's funds had run out. Therefore, in April 1866, the issue of free transportation was discontinued. As Howard told Lewis Tappan, the treasurer of the American Missionary Association, "The recent order cutting off transportation has checked the great work of relieving this District of the surplus freedpeople here."[59] It did not resume until the bureau's survival was assured by the second Freedmen's Bureau Act of July 1866 and its financial resources replenished by a congressional appropriation during the same month. The employment operations resumed in earnest and continued until October 1867, when free transportation was terminated, except for orphans and single women with small children. Thereafter, the continuing movement of adult workers depended on the willingness of employers or freedmen's aid societies to meet the cost. In consequence, the movement of freedpeople out of the District slowed markedly.[60]

In his annual report for 1866, Assistant Commissioner Charles H. Howard claimed that 5,192 freed persons from the District had found employment through the combined efforts of the bureau and the relief societies, some locally but many more outside the District. In October

[58] W. W. Rogers to J. S. Griffing, April 10, 1866, LS, 1:557; Circular Letter, December 10, 1866, LS, 2:549; S. N. Clark to E. A. Merrell, February 27, 1867, LS, 2:933, Reel 1, BRFAL-DC; *House Executive Documents*, 39.1, No. 11: *Report of the Commissioner of the Bureau of Refugees, Freedmen, and Abandoned Lands* (Serial 1255, Washington, DC, 1865), 14. On the development of the bureau's transportation policy, see also Cohen, *At Freedom's Edge*, 46–59, 79–82.

[59] *New York Herald*, quoted in the *Evening Star*, March 1, 1866; Bentley, *Freedmen's Bureau*, 125; C.H. Howard to Lewis Tappan, April 21, 1866, LS, 2:53, Reel 1, BRFAL-DC. See also W. W. Rogers to W. F. Spurgin, April 11, 1866, LS, 1:559, Reel 1; J. S. Griffing to Howard, May 30 1866, LR, 1:1533, Reel 6, BRFAL-DC.

[60] C. H. Howard to H. G. Stewart, June 22, 1866, LS, 2:100. Reel 1; C. H. Howard to O. O. Howard, October 10 1868, LS, 4:1128, Reel 2; J. V. W. Vandenburgh to W. W. Rogers, July 20, 1867, fn 525; to D.G. Swain, September 27, 1868, AQMR, fn 757, Reel 13; F.E. Town to George W. Livermore, November 7, 1867, LS, 3:778, Reel 1, BRFAL-DC; *Evening Star*, 11 October 1867.

TABLE 3.1. *Freedpeople Found Work Outside the District of Columbia*

| Period | North | South | Total |
|---|---|---|---|
| July 1865–July 1866 | 270 | 1,368 | 1,638 |
| April–October 1866 (Griffing) | 1,739 | 458 | 2,197 |
| September–November 1866 | 121 | 86 | 207 |
| November 1866–July 1867 | 2,093 | 497 | 2,590 |
| July 1867–September 1868 | 733 | 264 | 997 |
| TOTAL | 4,956 | 2,673 | 7,629 |

*Note:* This table is based on the summary figures compiled by District superintendents, supplemented when necessary by calculations made from the ten-daily returns submitted by employment offices. However, the superintendent's report for 1865–66 does not include returns from Josephine Griffing's office; Griffing reported separately until October 1866. Her report does not cover the period before April 1866, and Spurgin's does not cover July–September 1866. Therefore, the entries in the final row underestimate the total numbers.
*Sources:* July 1865–July 1866, W. F. Spurgin to W. W. Rogers, July 20, 1866, REO, Reel 14, BRFAL-DC. April–October 1866, J. S. Griffing to C. H. Howard, October 20, 1866, LR, Reel 7, BRFAL-DC. September–November 1866, calculated from ten-daily reports in REO, Reel 14, BRFAL-DC. November 1866–July 1867, J. V. W. Vandenburgh to Rogers, July 20, 1867, AQMR, BRFAL-DC. July 1867–September 1868, Vandenburgh to D. G. Swain, September 29, 1868, AQMR, Reel 13, BRFAL-DC.

1867, he put at 4,279 the number who had been found work over the past year, and, although the operations of the employment office were substantially wound down, 1,626 freedpeople were placed during the following twelve months. Hence, during the life of the agency, employment was found for around 11,000 freedpeople.[61] Because the weekly returns are incomplete, it is not possible to compile a full series of employment statistics. However, Table 3.1 provides a summary for most of the life of the agency, although it includes only freedpeople employed outside the District. In Table 3.2, the statistics are broken down by destination for those periods where evidence is available. Although the records are incomplete, a number of trends emerge. The first is that, apart from the early months, before government transportation was widely available,

[61] C. H. Howard to O. O. Howard, October 22, 1866, LS, 2:152; to O. O. Howard, October 10, 1867, LS, 3:758a, Reel 1; to O. O. Howard, October 10, 1868, LS, 4:1128, Reel 2; W. F. Spurgin to W. W. Rogers, July 20 1866, REO, fn 297, Reel 14; J. V. W. Vandenburgh to Rogers, July 20, 1867; to D. G. Swain, September 27, 1868, AQMR, fn 525, 757, Reel 13, BRFAL-DC; Horton, "Federal Social Policy," 95. Griffing, working on behalf of the NFRADC, made a separate report until October 1866. See J. S. Griffing to C. H. Howard, October 9, 1866, REO, fn 350, Reel 14, BRFAL-DC. After October 1866, her returns were consolidated with those of the other employment offices. The offices submitted reports every ten days, which may be found in Reel 14 of the microfilm edition of the Freedmen's Bureau Papers for the District of Columbia. Unfortunately, the surviving reports do not constitute a full series.

TABLE 3.2. *Destination of Freedpeople Found Work by Employment Offices*

| Destination | July 1865– July 1866 | April– October 1866 | September– November 1866 | March– June 1867 | July 1867– September 1868 |
|---|---|---|---|---|---|
| Massachusetts | 2 | 62 | 3 | 69 | 107 |
| Rhode Island | 38 | 597 | 1 | 134 | 137 |
| Connecticut | 0 | 91 | 18 | 158 | 169 |
| New York | 33 | 369 | 22 | 275 | 146 |
| Pennsylvania | 121 | 245 | 42 | 92 | 52 |
| Other Northeast | 60 | 75 | 10 | 47 | 53 |
| *Northeast* | *254* | *1,439* | *96* | *775* | *664* |
| Ohio | 7 | 163 | 3 | 100 | 30 |
| Illinois | 7 | 24 | 3 | 63 | 19 |
| Michigan | 1 | 89 | 10 | 19 | 5 |
| Other Midwest | 1 | 24 | 9 | 3 | 15 |
| *Midwest* | *16* | *300* | *25* | *185* | *69* |
| Maryland | 603 | 39 | 15 | 90 | 132 |
| Virginia | 45 | 269 | 64 | 39 | 105 |
| Other Upper S | 0 | 110 | 5 | 42 | 6 |
| *Upper South* | *648* | *418* | *84* | *171* | *243* |
| Georgia | 147 | 4 | 0 | 5 | 1 |
| Mississippi | 319 | 8 | 0 | 22 | 2 |
| Louisiana | 195 | 10 | 0 | 1 | 0 |
| Arkansas | 59 | 0 | 0 | 72 | 16 |
| Other Lower S | 0 | 18 | 2 | 6 | 2 |
| *Lower South* | *720* | *40* | *2* | *106* | *21* |
| District of Columbia | 545 | No entry | 45 | 121 | 982 |
| TOTAL | *2,183* | *2,197* | *252* | *1,358* | *1,979* |

*Note:* This table is based on the same evidence as Table 3.1, except that because the superintendent's report for July 1866–July 1867 does not provide a breakdown by destination, ten-daily returns from employment offices were used to calculate figures for that period. Unfortunately, the returns do not survive for the months between November 1866 and March 1867. For this reason and for the reasons explained in the note to Table 3.1, the series is not complete, and the figures in the final row underestimate the total numbers.

*Sources:* July 1865–July 1866, W. F. Spurgin to W. W. Rogers, July 20, 1866, REO, Reel 14, BRFAL-DC. April–October 1866, J. S. Griffing to C. H. Howard, October 20, 1866, LR, Reel 7, BRFAL-DC. September–November 1866, calculated from 10-daily reports in REO, Reel 14, BRFAL-DC. March–June 1867, calculated from 10-daily reports in REO, Reel 14, BRFAL-DC. July 1867–September 1868, J. V. W. Vandenburgh to D. G. Swain, September 29, 1868, AQMR, Reel 13, BRFAL-DC.

and the last year or so, after it had been effectively cut off, only a small proportion of placements were in the District itself. During the year ending October 1866, about a quarter of placements were local, in the year ending October 1868, nearly half; in the intervening months the proportion of finding work in the District fluctuated between 14 and 20 percent. The second notable trend is the declining importance of the South: during the first year of operation, 40 percent of non-District placements were in the Upper South, mostly in the neighboring states of Maryland and Virginia, and 44 percent in the Lower South; in the following years, only between 15 and 24 percent found employment in the neighboring states, whereas the movement to the Lower South was reduced to a trickle. On the other hand, the bureau became more successful in finding employment opportunities in the northern states, most strikingly in Pennsylvania, New York, and southern New England.[62]

At the birth of the agency, Assistant Commissioner Eaton sent an agent to visit the surrounding counties to assess the prospects for freed black workers there. The reports were optimistic, suggesting both that the demand for agricultural labor was vigorous and that freedpeople were, for the most part, fairly treated. The employment office started with the assumption that the most natural territory for the District's freed laborers would be the neighboring counties of Maryland and Virginia, which, after all, was where most of the contrabands had come from and where they had labored in the past. Local farmers were reportedly desperate for labor.[63] Bureau agents did all they could to impress on the District's freedpeople the necessity of going out into the country. The superintendent of Freedmen's Village was ordered to inform residents that "work can be obtained in the country, both in Virginia and Maryland. Every head of a family should start out at once to get a place to work for wages, and if possible make a contract for a year."[64] Although many freedpeople were persuaded to take up such opportunities, many more declined to return to their former homes. "I find that colored persons are not willing to go to that part of Maryland on account of the treatment

---

[62] Of course, many freedpeople found work in neighboring counties without recourse to the bureau's employment service, and some farmers traveled independently, or sent agents, to Washington to hire laborers. See George B. Carse to John Eaton, July 18, 1865, ULR, fn 238, Reel 12, BRFAL-DC.

[63] John Eaton to George B. Carse, June 16, 1865, LS, 1:1, Reel 1; Carse to Eaton, June 23, July 18, 1865, ULR, fn 134, 238, Reel 12, BRFAL-DC; *National Intelligencer*, September 25, 1865; *Evening Star*, August 18, 1865.

[64] S. N. Clark to J. P. Burgevin, March 6, 1866, LS, 1:459, Reel 1, BRFAL-DC. See also Clark to J. V. W. Vandenburgh, January 20, 1868, LS, 4:178, Reel 2, BRFAL-DC.

which they formerly received," observed Spurgin. Another agent observed that they were fearful of going into the country because they believed that their "old masters" were lying in wait for them. Nor did employers' treatment of free laborers suggest that they had changed their ways. As Griffing reported in May 1866, "many who have gone [to Maryland] during the past year have not been paid for their labor." The bureau received numerous allegations of brutality and nonpayment of wages, and many of the children of Washington residents were held in restrictive apprenticeship arrangements. The former contrabands already knew too much about their former masters and mistresses, and recent evidence had done little to alter their opinion.[65]

Freedpeople were hardly more willing to accept offers of employment farther south. As in the antebellum period, the newer cotton states, such as Mississippi, Louisiana, and Arkansas, suffered from severe labor shortages, which they sought to alleviate by importing workers from the older slave states. As in the antebellum period, the newer cotton states continued to evoke dark memories of exploitation and family separation. Nevertheless, Charles Howard promised applicants that if they could produce satisfactory references and assurances of good treatment and fair remuneration, the bureau would help them to find workers.[66] Those who were able to provide the necessary assurances were mostly northerners, many of them former Union army officers, who had invested in southern plantations or were acting as labor agents and that hoped to exploit their political and military contacts to procure labor. For example, a Mr. Little of Vicksburg was introduced as representing "northern men" who would treat their hands well. Bureau agents should have no hesitation in urging unemployed men to enter into contracts with him. Mr. Gifford came "by my encouragement" to procure one hundred hands for a plantation in Arkansas, Howard told Vandenburgh. "Please give [him] all the help and information you can."[67] The bureau's files contain many accounts of

---

65    W. F. Spurgin to John Eaton, September 11, 1865 ULR, fn 716, Reel 12; J. E. Wall to S. N. Clark, 20 January 1866, MRVA, fn 27, Reel 14; J. S. Griffing to C. H. Howard, May 30, 1866, LR, 1:1533, Reel 6, BRFAL-DC. On conditions in Maryland during the immediate post-emancipation period, see Fuke, *Imperfect Equality*, 25–30; Barbara Jeanne Fields, *Slavery and Freedom on the Middle Ground: Maryland during the Nineteenth Century* (New Haven, CT: Yale University Press, 1985), 137–66.

66    W. W. Rogers to S. Tyler Reade, January 23, 1867, LS, 2:708; to E. F. Malone, February 27, 1867, LS, 2:936, Reel 1, BRFAL-DC.

67    C. H. Howard to J. V. W. Vandenburgh, March 16, 1866, LS, 2:64; Howard to Vandenburgh, March 14, 1866, LS, 2:59; to W. F. Spurgin, March 26, 1866 LS, 2:75, Reel 1, BRFAL-DC. On the role of labor agents, see Cohen, *At Freedom's Edge*, 64–71, 109–37. The experience of northern planters in the South is described in Lawrence N. Powell,

orders being "filled" for Arkansas and Mississippi, of credentials received and transportation orders issued. For example, in February 1866, Griffing was ordered to send unemployed freedmen to Spurgin: "He is now engaged in filling an order for 150 families to go to Mississippi with a very reliable southern gentleman." In June, Spurgin reported that he was filling a large order for General Will of Texas. It appears that sizable numbers of freedpeople were induced, whether by offers of higher wages, the persuasive powers of bureau agents, threats to withdraw assistance, or sheer desperation, to take up offers to go south. Seven hundred and twenty were reported to have accepted employment in the Lower South, mostly in Arkansas, Louisiana, and Mississippi, between July 1865 and July 1866, but only 126 during the spring and summer of 1867.[68] The growing desperation was evident in the willingness of labor agents to make contracts with the inmates of the jail.[69]

In many respects, the most interesting aspect of the Freedmen's Bureau's employment program was the effort to find homes for freedpeople in the North. Oliver Otis Howard believed that the "demand for labor" there was "so great, that every unemployed person can be provided with a suitable situation." Of that demand there seemed to be ample evidence. When in July 1865 Griffing escorted a party of fifty men and women bound for Providence, Rhode Island, through New York City, many inquired about the possibility of bringing freedpeople there: "hundreds they say to me would find good homes and paying labor." A representative of the local freedmen's aid society reported from Boston in April 1867 that "an almost unlimited number of women accustomed to house work and of men to labor could be placed in good positions about here at once." The employment office was flooded with applications for labor from all over the Northeast and Midwest: for gardeners and cooks, for coachmen and dockworkers, for woodcutters and brick makers, for railroad construction workers, and, most commonly, for farmhands and domestic servants.[70]

*New Masters: Northern Planters during the Civil War and Reconstruction* (New Haven, CT: Yale University Press, 1980).

[68] S. N. Clark to J. S. Griffing, February 15, 1866, LS, 1:398; to James E. Rhoads, March 14, 1866, LS, 2:20, Reel 1; J. V. W. Vandenburgh to W. F. Spurgin, June 30, 1866, REO, fn 289, Reel 14; *National Intelligencer*, April 11, 19, 1866; *Evening Star*, February 21, March 30, April 10, 11, 14, 1866. Not all of these orders are reflected in the aggregate returns. For example, there are several references in the correspondence files to large orders for Texas but few traces of such orders in the periodic returns.

[69] C. H. Howard to George B. Fisher, April 15, 1867, LS, 3:101, Reel 1, BRFAL-DC.

[70] *National Intelligencer*, March 6, 1867; J. S. Griffing to O. O. Howard, July 30, 1865, ULR, fn 352, Reel 12; C. C. Jewett to C. H. Howard, April 15, 1867, LR, 2:1712,

This enterprise in many ways went against the grain of population movement in postbellum America. Black migration from the former slave states to the North was notably slight until the closing years of the century.[71] A number of factors converged to make it possible. One, of course, was the Freedmen's Bureau's search for suitable openings for freedpeople and its willingness to pay for their transportation. Another was a widely expressed dissatisfaction with Irish laborers and domestic servants. Charles L. Woodworth, the secretary of the American Missionary Association, told Oliver Otis Howard that "hundreds of colored girls" could find positions with New York's "best families" as a result of the "general disgust with Irish help." Work could be found for many freedpeople in East Bloomfield, New York, said another correspondent. It would be "the means of getting in a class of laboring people who are not Irish." Although the willingness to hire freed laborers owed something to sympathy for their plight – her neighbors were good Republicans and well disposed toward the freedpeople, said the previous witness – it also resulted from a desire to find a less troublesome labor force. Anna Lowell, one of the Bureau's New England contacts, observed tellingly that some employers might "look out for colored women as more easily imposed on."[72]

Although never explicitly acknowledged as such, this movement marked a striking reversal of federal policy. During the Civil War, as the debate over emancipation intensified, Republican spokesmen had

Reel 8, BRFAL-DC. See also S. N. Clark to George W. Pratt, December 20, 1866, LS, 2:603, Reel 1; to C. H. Howard, February 11, 1867, LR, 2:914, Reel 7; Griffing to John Eaton, November 20, 1865, LR, 1:261, Reel 4; to C. H. Howard, May 30, 1866, LR, 1:1533, Reel 6, BRFAL-DC; Cohen, *At Freedom's Edge*, 78–86; Melder, "Angel of Mercy," 256–59; Olive Gilbert, ed., *Narrative of Sojourner Truth, a Bondswoman of Olden Time* (New York: Oxford University Press, 1991), 191–99; Carleton Mabee, "Sojourner Truth Fights Dependence on Government: Moves Freed Slaves Off Welfare in Washington to Jobs in Upstate New York," *Afro-Americans in New York Life and History* 14 (January 1990): 7–25.

[71] Cohen, *At Freedom's Edge*, 87–108; Gavin Wright, *Old South, New South: Revolutions in the Southern Economy since the Civil War* (New York: Basic Books, 1986); Joshua L. Rosenbloom, *Looking for Work, Searching for Workers: American Labor Markets during Industrialization* (New York: Cambridge University Press, 2002), 33–45, 51–55.

[72] C. L. Woodworth to O. O. Howard, July 25, 1866, LR, 1:2138, Reel 6; Mary S. Sears to O. O. Howard, March 24, 1867, LR, 2:1612; Anna Lowell to C. H. Howard, December 15, 1866, LR, 2:2588; Ralph Haskins to S. N. Clark, March 28, 1867, LR, 2:1473, Reel 8, BRFAL-DC; Elizabeth H. Pleck, *Black Migration and Poverty: Boston, 1865–1900* (New York: Academic Press, 1979), 21–22. Pleck suggests that Bostonians were willing to employ black women in domestic service because young white women were attracted to manufacturing employment, and the rate of immigration was slackening. Ibid., 26.

repeatedly assured their constituents that it would not result in a large-scale migration of freed slaves to the North. Any proposed transfer of contrabands to northern locations was quite firmly stamped on. Instead of gravitating to the free states, as opponents of emancipation warned, once the disincentive of servitude was removed, "the emancipated toilsmen of the tropics" would naturally prefer to remain in warmer climes that were supposedly more congenial to their constitution and temperament. The rigorous environment of the North, said Governor John Andrew of Massachusetts, was the "worst possible place" for persons of the African race. Northern missionaries and schoolteachers working in the South actively discouraged freedpeople from going there.[73]

A few months after the end of the war, however, bureau officials were recommending the transfer north of a substantial number of freed workers not only as a way to alleviate demographic and social pressures in Washington but also as a source of "moral benefit" to the freedpeople themselves. Charles Howard believed that "the best aid the Bureau can give them" was to remove them from "this really pestilential region" to the bracing environment of New England. There they would receive "instructions to enable them to become self-supporting and independent. Everything that surrounds them there is educational and elevating," he told Anna Lowell.[74] The new policy was certainly consistent with that part of the free labor ideology that drew a distinction between a vigorous, industrious, entrepreneurial North and a lazy, degenerate South. It would be easier to direct former slaves along the paths of self-reliance in a region where the free labor system was deeply embedded than in a region where the enervating effects of slavery had been at work for centuries. Yet it is remarkable how little attention was paid to this movement, either in congressional debates or in the columns of the press, certainly in comparison with the heated controversy that had raged over similar

---

[73] Quoted in V. Jacque Voegeli, "A Rejected Alternative: Union Policy and the Relocation of Southern 'Contrabands' at the Dawn of Emancipation," *Journal of Southern History* 69 (November 2003): 776, 779. See also Leslie A. Schwalm, "'Overrun with Free Negroes': Emancipation and Wartime Migration in the Upper Midwest," *Civil War History* 50 (June 2004): 145–74; V. Jacque Voegeli, *Free but Not Equal: The Midwest and the Negro during the Civil War* (Chicago, 1967), 13–25, 105–12; Robert F. Engs, *Freedom's First Generation: Black Hampton, Virginia, 1861–1890* (Philadelphia: University of Pennsylvania Press, 1979), 27–35; Louis Gerteis, *Civil War St. Louis* (Lawrence: University Press of Kansas, 2001), 275–76.

[74] C. H. Howard to Emily Howland, n.d. November 1866, LS, 1:722; to Anna Lowell, 4 April 1867; to Committee of Industrial Schools, Cambridge, Massachusetts, LS, 3:66, 151, Reel 1, BRFAL-DC.

possibilities a few years earlier, and, indeed, in comparison with the occasional criticism of the transportation of African American laborers to plantations in the Deep South. Perhaps the fact that emancipation had now been put into effect without causing a mass migration of former slaves had eased public fears of inundation. Perhaps, also, the highly specific and localized character of the program deflected criticism. The migration originated in only a few overpopulated localities in the South and was directed toward a few largely sympathetic communities in the North that, for one reason or another, were willing to receive African American workers.

Lowell observed that "We meet with sympathy and interest among the middle classes who seem to understand that it is the right thing to do." Many northerners regarded aid to the freedmen as a natural progression from the struggle for emancipation. Freedmen's aid societies, themselves an offshoot of the antislavery movement, had sprung up all over the North during the Civil War, and some of them responded favorably to the bureau's invitation to assist in its employment project "as a legitimate branch of their relief work."[75] The bureau cooperated with the American Missionary Association and the National Freedmen's and Union Commission in New York; the Freedmen's Relief Association of Philadelphia; the African Civilization Society in Brooklyn; the Soldiers' Memorial Society in Cambridge, Massachusetts; the Hartford Freedmen's Aid Society; and the Rhode Island Association for Freedmen; as well as smaller groups in places such as Syracuse and Rochester, New York; Cleveland and Oberlin, Ohio; and Battle Creek, Michigan. The societies received parties of freedpeople, provided them with temporary board and lodging, helped them to find employment, and paid many of the incidental expenses. It is no coincidence that the cities receiving the largest number of workers from the District were those where vigorous freedmen's aid societies operated and, in particular, where black abolitionists exerted themselves on behalf of the freedpeople. The northward migration of freed laborers was greatly facilitated by the societies' willingness to cooperate in the enterprise.[76] However, not all of those involved in freedmen's aid

---

[75] Anna Lowell to C. H. Howard, December 7, 1867, LR, 2:869, Reel 7; S. N. Clark to Lyman Abbott, April 6, 1866, LS, 2:32, Reel 1, BRFAL-DC.

[76] See, for example, C. H. Howard to Lewis Tappan, April 21, 1866, LS, 2:53; to W. H. Skinner et al., January 25, 1867, LS, 2:723; S. N. Clark to N. J. Burton, March 9, 1867, LS, 2:996, Reel 1; H. G. Stewart to J. V. W. Vandenbergh, March 9, 1866, LR, 1:884, Reel 5; Anna Lowell to C. H. Howard, November 1, 1866, LR, 2:143; C. C. Jewett to C. H. Howard, January 23, 1867, LR, 2:920, Reel 7, BRFAL-DC. According to Carol

regarded this as the best use of their resources. J. M. McKim of the American Freedmen's Commission believed that trying to direct a flow of black migration to the North was like trying "to make water run up stream": "but little can be done in this way toward solving the Nation's problem or relieving your Bureau." According to Lowell, the freedmen's aid association in Cambridge, Massachusetts, considered it "foolish to bring colored people north." Like many other such organizations, it regarded the promotion of freedmen's education as a more fruitful project. In addition, public support for all such enterprises began to fall away as the war receded, making it difficult for the bureau to hand over responsibility to local agencies when its activities terminated in 1868.[77]

In cooperation with local societies, the bureau maintained employment offices in a number of northern cities. It rented rooms in Jersey City, where parties of freedpeople could stay before taking up employment around New York or traveling on to New England, and hired an agent, Mrs. Sarah Tilmon, to see to their welfare while in transit and solicit jobs for them in the locality. In Hartford, similar facilities were maintained by J. C. Cambridge, "a competent and reliable colored man," in Providence by the Reverend H. G. Stewart, and in Boston by Ralph Haskins and Mrs. H. L. Smith. The bureau provided a building and a matron's salary for the Howard Industrial School for Colored Women and Girls run by Lowell in Cambridge, Massachusetts, which was designed to provide a "training in practical housekeeping" for those intending to take up domestic service, and for the Colored Orphan's Asylum in Brooklyn, where children were cared for while their mothers took up employment in the New York area.[78] These agencies sometimes created difficulties for the Bureau: Tilmon was accused of allowing freed children to beg on the

---

Faulkner, "Abolitionist women created a network of employment agencies and personal connections" that facilitated the migration of freedpeople to the North. *Women's Radical Reconstruction*, 117.

[77] J. M. McKim to John Eaton, August 17, 1865, ULR, fn 431, Reel 12; Anna Lowell to C. H. Howard, December 7, 1867, LR, 2:869, Reel 7, BRFAL-DC. See also C. H. Howard to A. E. Butterick, October 8, 1868, LS, 4:1111, Reel 2; H. G. Stewart to C. H. Howard, October 8, 1867, LR, 3:578, Reel 9, BRFAL-DC.

[78] C. H. Howard to Anna Lowell, April 4, 1867, LS, 3:66 C. H. Howard to O. O. Howard, October 10, 1867, LS, 3:758a, Reel 1; S. N. Clark to C. H. Howard, February 11, 1867, LR, 2:914, Reel 7; Sarah Woodbury to C. H. Howard, May 24, 1867, LR, 2:2153, Reel 8, BRFAL-DC; Faulkner, "Proper Recognition of Our Manhood," 52–57; Pleck, *Black Migration and Poverty*, 25–28. The Cambridge school also received migrants from the area around Hampton, Virginia. Report of the Howard Industrial School, Cambridge, Massachusetts, August 4, 1867, Monthly Reports on Operations of Industrial Schools, fn 102, Reel 9, BRFAL-DC.

streets of New York; Stewart was reported to have lost the confidence of the local black community; and the Colored Orphans' Asylum was the subject of a number of critical investigations arising from charges of neglect, ill-treatment, and poor financial management. Nevertheless, they were critical in expediting the movement of freedpeople to New York and New England.[79]

More than five thousand freedpeople traveled north under the auspices of the Freedmen's Bureau. It is difficult to establish what happened to them after they arrived. The records of the bureau carefully document the arrangements for getting them to their destinations but provide much less information about their experience once they got there, and still less about their success in building satisfactory lives for themselves over a longer period. Griffing reported on a number of occasions that the people that she had found places for were doing well. In October 1866, she wrote that farm laborers in New England, New York, Pennsylvania, and Ohio were receiving between $20 and $25 dollars a month with board, female domestic servants between $10 and $12. "By example and instruction they are acquiring habits of personal neatness, systematic industry and practical economy," she noted. Many had opened accounts at local savings banks. A year later, she confirmed that most were still "engaged in productive labor," many in the positions to which they had originally been assigned, and most were accumulating savings. For example, a group of twenty-seven men employed on a cranberry farm in Michigan at $1 a day plus board had managed between them to save $2,000, and a couple who had been working for a shoemaker in Pennsylvania had now opened their own establishment and hired employees of their own. When the migrants returned to Washington to collect their families, they were "thoroughly changed in personal appearance, and present an air of thrift and manhood, befitting earnest Loyal Men and Christians."[80]

Others involved in the enterprise expressed similar confidence about the outcome. Stewart claimed that farmhands around Providence were

---

[79] On some of the difficulties, see W. W. Rogers to Sarah Ann Tilmon, 5, 7 February, 1867, LS, 2:778,790, Reel 1; Stuart Eldridge to A. A. Truman, 8 January 1868, LS, 4:129, Reel 2; J. A. Sladen to C. H. Howard, 21 August 1867, LR, 3:146; S. N. Clark to C. H. Howard, 22 November 1867, LR, 3:856, Reel 9; Clark to Howard, 31 December 1867, 27 April 1868, AQMR, Reel 13; and, in general, Clark to Howard, 23 July 1867, LR, 2:2423, Reel 8, BRFAL-DC. See also Everly, "Freedmen's Bureau in the District of Columbia," 111–18.

[80] J. S. Griffing to C. H. Howard, October 20, 1866, LR, 2:(unnumbered) fn 63, Reel 7; Griffing to Howard, October 5 1867, LR, 3: 420, Reel 9; Griffing to Howard, October 9, 1866, REO, fn 350, Reel 14, BRFAL-DC.

receiving more than $14 a month with board, dock hands and workers in the lumberyards in excess of $24, and female servants between $6 and $12 a month. He estimated that two-thirds had learned to read and write after one year. Clark reported that those sent to Hartford "are all in good places, and trusted and treated like men in all respects; their employers speak well of them." Lowell provided a glowing account of the success of her own protégées, illustrated by extracts from their letters. Of 267 found places, she claimed, only 7 had done badly. She was convinced that they had derived substantial "moral and physical benefit" from the move.[81] It is not clear whether such assertions were made on the basis of a thorough canvass or one or two exceptional cases, or whether, indeed, they were grounded on empirical observation or on logical derivations from the free labor ideology itself, with its inbuilt assumptions regarding the benefits of freedom and the superiority of northern institutions.[82]

A number of problems do emerge from the records. Not surprisingly, a few speculators, opportunists, and fraudsters sought to take advantage of the ignorance of the freedpeople and the generosity of the government. For example, E. A. Wadsworth, a logging contractor who had taken a large number of freedmen north to chop wood, turned out to be a thoroughly unreliable employer, taking his party of woodcutters into the Connecticut woods and abandoning them there without pay. Fortunately, all but one were found alternative employment.[83] A more general concern was that many freedmen had been contracted to take up employment, in brick making or railroad construction for example, that was temporary or seasonal in character and would require assistance when that ceased. There was also the question of who would care for freedpeople in northern communities if they should fall sick. The responsibility, Clark believed, should fall on the community where they had settled. "But the northern

---

[81] H. G. Stewart to C. H. Howard, October 4, 1866, October 31, 1867, REO, fn 347, 509, Reel 14; S. N. Clark to C. H. Howard, February 11, 1867, LR, 2:914, Reel 7 (first quotation); Anna Lowell to C. H. Howard, September 1, 1867, LR, 3:169, Reel 9 (second quotation), BRFAL-DC.

[82] S. N. Clark to W. M. Beebe, December 12, 1866, LS, 2:560; C. H. Howard to Beebe, April 29, 1867, LS, 3:139, Reel 1, BRFAL-DC; Clark to C. H. Howard, February 11, 1867, LR, 2:914, Reel 7, BRFAL-DC. Cf. Engs, *Freedom's First Generation*, 117; Pleck, *Black Migration and Poverty*, 28. Lowell repored that of seventy-six former pupils employed in the Cambridge area, only one had returned to Washington, and that was on account of her sister's death. Report of the Howard Industrial School, Cambridge, Massachusetts, August 4, 1867, Reports on Industrial Schools, fn 102, Reel 14, BRFAL-DC.

[83] Perry Davis to J. S. Griffing, January 21, 1867, LR, 2:1236; F. D. Sewall to C. H. Howard, February 26, 1867, LR, 2:1248, Reel 8; S. N. Clark to C. H. Howard, February 11, 1867, LR, 2:914, Reel 7, BRFAL-DC.

people generally according to my observation desire to have nothing to do with the freedmen unless they are well and able to take care of themselves. They are not willing to take them on the same terms that other immigrants are received."[84] It seems that a sizable number of those who were sent north returned almost immediately to the District. The bureau's records contain many irritated references to persons who returned, although there is no way of calculating how numerous they were.[85]

McKim was probably right in suggesting that the bureau's attempt to transfer the District's surplus black population to the North was like trying to get water to flow upstream. Although the agency received numerous applications for workers and enthusiastic protestations of a vigorous demand for their services, it seems that this demand was both temporary, brought on by a short-lived sympathy for the freedpeople and an antagonism for the Irish, and confined to a sizable but still restricted minority of the northern population, antislavery in its inclinations, Republican in its politics, and paternalistic in its sympathies. As it also turned out, the demand for freed laborers was heavily dependent on the government paying their transportation costs and fell away markedly once it ceased to do so. Over the longer term, the northern labor market offered little scope for African Americans. Most forms of unskilled labor remained the preserve of European immigrants; it was difficult for African Americans to establish a toehold. If anything, the range of occupations open to them contracted, rather than expanded, during the following decades.[86]

"There seems to be a great reluctance on the part of the majority to leave even the miserable homes they have established here and start forth to parts of the country new and strange to them," noted Charles Howard

---

[84] Ibid. See also Perry Davis to S. N. Clark, February 1, 1867, LR, 2:1319, BRFAL-DC, Reel 8; J. S. Griffing to O. O. Howard, October 28, 1867, LR, 3:636; petition from freedpeople of Providence, enclosed in H. G. Stewart to O. O. Howard, November 16, 1867, LR, 3:847, BRFAL-DC, Reel 9.

[85] S. N. Clark to W. M. Beebe, December 12, 1866, LS, 2:560; C. H. Howard to Beebe, April 29, 1867, LS, 3:139, Reel 1; Clark to C. H. Howard, February 11, 1867, LR, 2:914, Reel 7, BRFAL-DC.

[86] Ralph Haskins to S. N. Clark, March 28, 1867, LR, 2:1473; C. C. Jewett to C. H. Howard, April 15, 1867, LR, 2:1712, Reel 8, BRFAL-DC. On discrimination against African Americans in the employment market of northern cities, see Theodore Hershberg, ed., *Philadelphia: Work, Space, Family and Group Experience in the Nineteenth Century* (New York: Oxford University Press, 1981), 368–91, 467–73; Pleck, *Black Migration and Poverty*, 122–60; Cohen, *At Freedom's Edge*, 96–105; David M. Katzman, *Before the Ghetto: Black Detroit in the Nineteenth Century* (Urbana: University of Illinois Press, 1973), 104–34, 217; Kenneth L. Kusmer, *A Ghetto Takes Shape: Black Cleveland, 1970–1930* (Urbana: University of Illinois Press, 1976), 19–24, 66–90.

in October 1866. As Howard explained, "they are reluctant to go north. The cold is a bug bear and the fact is that they are totally ignorant of that part of the Country and its people making them prefer the hard lot here to the uncertainties and apprehend[ed] evils of going away." Griffing attributed their hesitation to a lack of confidence in northern people, a dread of the cold climate, and the "results of erroneous education" while slaves. As Griffing also pointed out, the "strong social nature of the race" made freedpeople unwilling to leave families and friends with whom they had been reunited after three or four years of wartime disruption and maybe a longer period of enforced separation during slavery. They were now gathered together in freedom, though perhaps living in "abject poverty."[87] Another attraction of Washington after January 1867, as Griffing pointed out, was that African American males would soon be able to vote there, a privilege that they prized and wished to be in a position to enjoy. Howard explained to a prospective employer in April 1867 that "just now owing to the Election excitement and for other causes, it is difficult to induce the people to go away."[88]

Too often movement north meant family separation. Sometimes children were sent away without their parents' or guardians' consent. The bureau's correspondence files contain many complaints about such separations and several paper trails resulting from the efforts to trace missing family members. For example, a freedwoman called Leanna Hughes complained that her niece Annie, whom she claimed to have cared for since infancy but on whom she had now herself become dependent, had been sent to Connecticut without her consent. For her own part, Annie, or "Laura Jones" as she now called herself, claimed that she was comfortably settled with a "respectable colored woman" and did not wish to return to her aunt. When a bureau agent came to take her back to Washington, she fled to Cambridge, where she was admitted to Miss Lowell's industrial school. Several witnesses describe "Laura" as inveterately mendacious.

---

[87] C. H. Howard to O. O. Howard, October 22, 1866, LS, 2:152 (first quotation); to Anna Lowell, December 14, 1866, LS, 2:580, Reel 1 (second quotation); J. S. Griffing to C. H. Howard, October 20, 1866, LR, 2 (unnumbered): fn 63, Reel 7 (third and fourth quotations), BRFAL-DC. See also W. F. Spurgin to S. N. Clark, November 1, 1865, AQMR, fn 305, Reel 13; L. M. E. Ricks to C. H. Howard, November 14, 1866, LR, 2:242, Reel 7, BRFAL-DC; *National Intelligencer*, September 25, 1865; Mabee, "Sojourner Truth Fights Dependence," 14–15; Masur, "Reconstructing the Nation's Capital," 64–65.

[88] J. S. Griffing to Sojourner Truth, April 14, 1867, in Gilbert, *Narrative of Sojourner Truth*, 275; C. H. Howard to Samuel C. Armstrong, April 11, 1867, LS, 3: 89, Reel 1, BRFAL-DC.

It was discovered that the employment agent who had arranged to send her north had failed to determine whether she had any family or even to establish that "Laura Jones" was her real name before applying for transportation. Although bureau regulations required careful investigation of family connections before an individual was sent away, that investigation was not always carried out, and clearly had not been in the case of "Laura Jones." Pressure was put on parents to consent to older children being sent away and younger children being placed in orphan asylums so that the parents could take up offers of work. All such instances exacerbated the freedpeople's anxieties about family separation.[89]

At the same time, the bureau's employment program illustrates the freedpeople's ability to turn its activities to their own advantage. Some, like "Laura Jones" used it to escape unsympathetic or abusive family members. When a man called Rolly Holmes protested that Griffing had sent his wife to Philadelphia without his knowledge or consent, agents discovered that the woman in question claimed to have no family and, according to neighbors, had never acknowledged her marriage to him.[90] Alternatively, husbands and fathers sought to evade their familial responsibilities.[91] Others used it as a way to obtain relief. Bureau officials complained continuously of freedpeople who had signed contracts for employment outside the District and been issued with transportation orders and a few days' rations for the journey only to disappear between the employment office and the railroad depot. They would then reappear some time later to agree to a fresh employment contract, accept the rations, and vanish again. Thus, Vandenburgh reported that, of a

---

[89] W. W. Rogers to J. V. W. Vandenburgh, June 24, 1867, LS, 3: 298; to A. K. Browne, July 13, 1867, LS, 3:335, Reel 1; Leanna Hughes to Freedmen's Bureau, June 11. 1867; M. V. Wright to Vandenburgh, July 15, 1867; O. O. Howard to J. S. Griffing, September 20, 1867; Anna Lowell to S. N. Clark, October 14, 1867; E. Sanderson to Wright, October 15, 1867 (papers relating to a board of inquiry), all in LR, 3:875, Reel 9; Rogers to Sarah A. Tilmon, May 30, 1867, LS, 3:212; Rogers to Vandenburgh, July 12, 1867, LS, III, 332, Reel 1; Rogers to John L. Roberts, March 8, 1867, LR, 2: 1276, Reel 8; Ann B. Earle to O. O. Howard, January 24, 1868, LR, 4:759, Reel 10, BRFAL-DC. For further examples of children being sent away without parents' or guardians' permission, see C. H. Howard to Sarah A. Tilmon, May 30, 1867, LS, 3:212; Rogers to Vandenburgh, July 12, 1867, LS, 3:332, Reel 1; Rogers to John L. Roberts, March 8, 1867, LR, 2:1276, Reel 8; Anna B. Earle to O. O. Howard, January 24, 1868, LR, 4:E1, Reel 10, BRFAL-DC.

[90] Eliphalet Whittlesey to C. H. Howard, October 19, 1867, LR, 3:509 (with endorsements), Reel 9, BRFALDC.

[91] See, for example, W. W. Rogers to J. G. C. Lee, December 6, 1866, LS, 2:534; to J. S. Griffing, January 28, 1867, LS, 2:734, Reel 1, BRFAL-DC.

party of 101 freedmen who had agreed to go to Cincinnati, 48 absconded between the office and the depot. He admitted to being "annoyed very much by this class of men," who, he believed, only signed on to get the rations, probably more than once. Others traveled to distant parts, returned almost immediately to Washington, and then agreed to fresh employment contracts.[92] Other irregularities included selling transportation orders and substituting one person for another. In response, the bureau introduced tighter procedures, including more elaborate record keeping and the appointment of a transportation agent to supervise the process, without ever wholly eliminating the abuses.[93]

The ten thousand freedpeople who were resettled by the local office of the Freedmen's Bureau constituted just over 30 percent of the District's 31,549 black residents in 1866. Yet the African American population of the District had grown to 43,404 by the time of the 1870 census, an increase of nearly twelve thousand.[94] That was largely because the surrounding counties of Maryland and Virginia remained inhospitable, even dangerous, for their black inhabitants for some years after Emancipation, whereas the District offered greater legal protection, a Republican government, and a developing African American community. Hence the surplus of black labor remained, and so did many of the frightful housing and sanitary conditions that had spurred the bureau to action in the first place. All that the bureau could claim was that its activity as "a vast labor bureau" and its willingness to transport thousands of idle workers to places where they might find work had prevented conditions from getting worse.[95]

---

[92] W. W. Rogers to J. V. W. Vandenburgh, 18 June 1866, LS, 2:211; C. H. Howard to W. M. Beebe, 18 February, 6 March 1867, LS, 2:880, 992; Vandenburgh to Rogers, 11 June 1866, REO, Reel 14, BRFALDC.

[93] W. W. Rogers to W. M. Beebe, January 26, 1867, LS, 2:727; C. H. Howard to O. O. Howard, October 10, 1867, LS, 3:758a, Reel 1; J. V. W. Vandenburgh to W. W. Rogers, July 20, 1867, AQMR, Reel 13, BRFALDC.

[94] Charles Howard claimed in October 1868 that more than 10,000 freedpeople had been transported out of the District since July 1865. C. H. Howard to O. O. Howard, October 10, 1868, LS, 4:1128, Reel 2, BRFAL-DC. However, this did not include those who had found work in neighboring counties or gone elsewhere without government transportation, nor did it allow for the large, but incalculable, number of returnees. A census conducted by the bureau in June 1866 put the black population at 31,549. Census of Colored Population in Washington, Georgetown, etc., Miscellaneous Reports and Lists, fn 784, Reel 21, BRFAL-DC. See also Cohen, *At Freedom's Edge*, 83–85.

[95] W. E. B. DuBois, *The Souls of Black Folk* (Henry Louis Gates, ed., New York: Norton, 1999), 28.

## The Bureau as an Urban Welfare Agency

In many respects, this account of the activities of the Freedmen's Bureau in the District of Columbia fits easily within the framework established by the New Freedmen's Bureau Historiography. It offers an example of the ways in which bureau officials applied free labor principles to the varying circumstances of the postbellum South. Free labor by definition meant labor without compulsion, but the option of not working at all was ruled out, and the bureau felt justified in employing some measure of coercion to force freedmen into the labor market. In the District of Columbia this did not extend to treating unemployed freedmen as vagrants, as it did in some parts of the bureau's domain, but it did entail a continuing "war on dependency" that sought, by denying relief to able-bodied males, and sometimes able-bodied females, to compel them to accept offers of employment outside the District.[96] Bureau agents were bedeviled by the fear that former slaves might interpret freedom as synonymous with idleness and regard any material assistance as confirming their expectation. Thus, behaviors that seemed quite logical to the freedpeople – seeking to hold families together, establishing a locus around which families and kinship groups could coalesce, resorting to irregular and opportunistic employment, using charity to tide them over difficult periods, and, above all, resisting pressures to disperse them – looked to northern officials like attempts to shirk the responsibilities of regular employment and self-reliance. Bureau agents tended to treat the formerly enslaved as a proletarian as much as a racial group. Their anxieties regarding black laborers' apparent lack of motivation to work, propensity to pauperism, and lack of self-reliance almost exactly paralleled contemporary anxieties regarding northern white laborers, and their prescriptions for dealing with lower-class dependency drew heavily on contemporary philanthropic practice and contemporary legal doctrines regarding the regulation of labor markets.[97]

---

[96] W. F. Spurgin to S. N. Clark, March 1, 1866, AQMR, fn 329, Reel 13, BRFAL-DC. On bureau policy elsewhere regarding "vagrancy," see Howard, *Autobiography*, 2: 247; Foner, *Reconstruction*, 157; Schmidt, "'Full-Fledged Government of Men,'" 238, 240, 248–49; Mary Farmer-Kaiser, "'Are They Not in Some Sorts Vagrants?': Gender and the Efforts of the Freedmen's Bureau to Combat Vagrancy in the Reconstruction South," *Georgia Historical Quarterly* 88 (Spring 2004): 25–49; Farmer, "'Because They Are Women,'" 168; Stanley, *From Bondage to Contract*, 123–25.

[97] Cf. Schmidt, "'Full-Fledged Government of Men'"; Stanley, *From Bondage to Contract*; Heather Cox Richardson, *The Death of Reconstruction: Race, Labor, and Politics in the Post-Civil War North, 1865–1901* (Cambridge, MA: Harvard University Press, 2001).

The behavior of Freedmen's Bureau officials in the nation's capital reveals important limitations on their conception of free labor. The version of the free labor ideology espoused by most bureau agents, nourished as it was by the rural and small-town society of their youth, was not easily adapted to the conditions that confronted freed African Americans in a city like Washington.[98] Convinced that the city was not a suitable site for their transition from slavery to freedom, bureau officials tried when possible to relocate them elsewhere. Like agents in other cities, they believed that the interests of the freedpeople and the nation would be best served by returning them to the countryside.[99] Even when they sent freedpeople north, it was not so that they might find a place in urban society but that they might escape from it – either in some form of rural employment or in carefully controlled working environments in small towns and cities. When freed men and women were transported to the more economically advanced regions of the Northeast and Midwest, it was to farm labor and, in the case of women, domestic service that they were mostly directed. The objective, Charles Howard explained, was to "provide homes for *families* in Country *places* and for single women with children in the cities," working as servants in middle-class households. Indeed, he and his colleagues frequently referred to black workers as "servants" who were to be provided with "homes," on the assumption that employment and home went together. Even when approaching the free labor economy of the North, they assumed a traditional world of employment, not only in terms of clearly demarcated gender roles but also in terms of a preponderance of farm and household labor.[100] Following the customary arrangements for agricultural labor in the antebellum North, bureau officials preferred that freed men and women be bound by long-term contracts that offered some protection from fraud and ill treatment but severely curtailed their economic freedoms. They sought a fixity of tenure that sat oddly in the volatile labor markets of a rapidly industrializing

---

98 On the social context in which the antebellum free labor ideology developed, see Foner, *Free Soil*, 11–39.

99 Cf. Rabinowitz, *Race Relations in the Urban South*, 20–21; Farmer, "'Because They Are Women,'" 178–79; Engs, *Freedom's First Generation*, 115–16; Tripp, *Yankee Town, Southern City*, 166; Litwack, *Been in the Storm So Long*, 318.

100 C. H. Howard to Anna Lowell, December 14, 1866, LS, 2:580, Reel 1, BRFAL-DC. See also Howard to H. C. Dunham, January 21, 1867, LS, 2:698; to Lowell, April 4, 1867; to Committee of Industrial Schools, Cambridge, Massachusetts, May 6, 1867; S. N. Clark to J. V. W. Vandenburgh, November 1, 1867, LS, 3:66, 151, 764, Reel 1, BRFAL-DC.

section.[101] According to Eric Foner, the experience of the Freedmen's Bureau in the postbellum South exposed "tensions and ambiguities in free labor thought"; its experience in the nation's capital suggests that the version of the free labor ideology subscribed to by most bureau officials was hardly more applicable to the free-flowing labor markets of the nation's cities.[102]

The circumstances under which bureau agents operated in the District, among the crowded settlements occupied by Washington's freedpeople, appeared to require assertive, sometimes coercive, actions that pushed the boundaries of contemporary notions of government power. Although their relief polices were predicated on individualistic, free labor premises, bureau officials were also influenced by environmentalist assumptions about the moral, as well as the epidemiological, dangers that confronted the inhabitants of freed communities. These assumptions validated some striking exercises in state power. Horrified at the living conditions in neighborhoods such as Murder Bay, they conducted a series of extensive sanitary operations. The bureau maintained tenements that housed more than a thousand freedpeople, harbored another thousand at Freedmen's Village, and established a model community for the more affluent and motivated members of the freed population at Barry Farm. Above all, it created a massive employment program, establishing offices in several northern cities, cooperating with freedmen's aid societies in many more, and transporting nearly ten thousand persons to employment outside the District. Rather than relying on economic forces to carry workers from points where labor was in surplus to points where it was scarce, the bureau intervened actively in the labor market. Believing freedpeople to be untrained in the disciplines of the market and fearing the social and moral consequences of leaving them to congregate in idleness, it acted as a giant intelligence office and transportation agency to expedite their quest for employment. The employment program was central to the agency's operations in the District of Columbia. Although heavily bureaucratic, regimented, and even coercive, it represented a genuine attempt to solve what its creators saw as a besetting and otherwise insoluble social problem.

The postwar era, says Foner, witnessed the growth of "a national state possessing vastly expanded authority and a new set of purposes." The

---

[101] See Stanley, *From Bondage to Contract*, 35–37; Foner, *Reconstruction*, 164–67. On practice in the antebellum North, see Schmidt, *Free to Work*, chaps. 1 and 2.
[102] Foner, *Reconstruction*, 156.

Freedmen's Bureau was central to that expanded conception of the state and to its ambitious program to remake southern society.[103] Of course, the Freedmen's Bureau was an arm of the military. Indeed, it could not have achieved what it did without the reach, resources, and administrative coherence, as well as the emergency powers, possessed by the Army. No other agency of government in the nineteenth-century United States possessed the administrative capacity to achieve such results. However, the bureau also depended on the assistance of voluntary organizations, and without their resources of manpower, and more often womanpower, it could have achieved little. Although seeming to stand outside nineteenth-century American traditions of governance, the bureau exemplified a longstanding pattern of public-private cooperation. Civilian agents, by their resistance as much as by their positive encouragement, shaped, and to a degree humanized, the bureau's relief policies; they provided important initiatives, as well as practical assistance, in setting up the bureau's employment program; and, of course, they provided a large part of the resources and an even larger part of the manpower and womanpower that were required to establish schools for African American children.[104] This last contribution has always been acknowledged, but the full extent of the symbiosis between the bureau and the freedmen's aid societies is clearly visible only in urban settings. Some aspects of the bureau's  character

---

[103] Foner, *Reconstruction*, xxvi; Richard F. Bensel, *Yankee Leviathan: The Origins of Central State Authority, 1859–1877* (Cambridge: Cambridge University Press, 1990), 14–15, 122–23; Morton Keller, *Affairs of State: Public Life in Late Nineteenth Century America* (Cambridge, MA: Harvard University Press, 1977), 85–121, 197–222. For varying interpretations of the postbellum American state, see Bensel *Yankee Leviathan*; Keller, *Affairs of State*; Stephen Skowronek, *Building a New American State: The Expansion of National Administrative Capacities, 1877–1920* (Cambridge: Cambridge University Press, 1982), esp. chap. 2; Theda Skocpol, *Protecting Soldiers and Mothers: The Political Origins of Social Policy in the United States* (Cambridge, MA: Harvard University Press, 1992), Part I.

[104] On the links between the bureau and freedmen's aid societies, see, in particular, Faulkner, *Women's Radical Reconstruction*; McPherson, *Struggle for Equality*, 393–405; Richardson, *Christian Reconstruction*; E. Allen Richardson, "Architects of a Benevolent Empire: The Relationship between the American Missionary Association and the Freedmen's Bureau in Virginia, 1865–1872," in Cimbala and Miller, eds., *Freedmen's Bureau and Reconstruction*, 119–39; and, for the District of Columbia, Everly, "Freedmen's Bureau in the National Capital," 34–37, 56–69; Melder, "Angel of Mercy." Many works deal specifically with freedmen's education: Jones, *Soldiers of Light and Love*; Butchart, *Northern Schools, Southern Blacks, and Reconstruction*; Robert C. Morris, *Reading, 'Riting, and Reconstruction: The Education of Freedmen in the South, 1861–1870* (Chicago: University of Chicago Press, 1981); James D. Anderson, *The Education of Blacks in the South, 1860–1935* (Chapel Hill: University of North Carolina Press, 1988).

and purpose are revealed only by considering its work in the cities. By incorporating the urban dimension, we gain a full sense of the range and adaptability of the bureau's programs, and therefore of the potentialities of the postwar American state.

As in the states of the former Confederacy, the Freedmen's Bureau in the District of Columbia played an important role in helping freed-people to negotiate the transition from slavery to freedom. Its officials approached the problems faced by Washington's freed population in the light of a narrow and constricted version of free labor ideology and, indeed, looked with ambivalence at its very presence there. Yet they acted vigorously not only to move as many freedpeople as possible from the city but also to ameliorate the living conditions of those who remained. The agency was handicapped by its limited financial resources, restricted legal authority, and abbreviated life span, and, of course, in the last analysis, its interventions were insufficient to transform the status and opportunities of Washington's freed citizens. Nonetheless, they alleviated overcrowd-ing, provided relief for thousands of former slaves, helped many thou-sands more find employment, promoted black schools, and defended the rights of African Americans at a time when they lacked political influence and had few friends in local government. As W. E. B. DuBois concluded more generally, the organization operated as "a vast labor bureau, – not perfect, indeed, notably defective here and there, but on the whole successful beyond the dreams of thoughtful men."[105]

[105] *Souls of Black Folk*, 28.

# 4

## Congressional Reconstruction in the District of Columbia

### An "Experimental Garden for the Propagation of Political Hybrids"

At the foot of Capitol Hill lay the United States Botanic Garden, a fruit of the largely abortive attempt during the early national period to convert the nation's capital into a center of scientific endeavor. Here exotic plants were to be collected and displayed to enhance the knowledge of the nation's nurserymen and promote the improvement of agriculture. By the eve of the Civil War, such ambitious purposes had been largely forgotten; the botanic garden served largely as a pleasant place for congressmen and their friends to take the air on summer evenings and listen to the concerts given by the naval band from the Capitol terrace. From time to time in Washington's history, it has seemed appropriate to regard the whole city as an "experimental garden" where policy initiatives designed for wider application might be tried and tested. That was especially true during and immediately after the Civil War.

The changes brought by the Civil War and Reconstruction gave congressional policy for the District of Columbia an added significance. Repeatedly, Republican congressmen tested reforms in Washington before applying them to the southern states. Washington's few slaves were emancipated in April 1862, months before the general Emancipation Proclamation and years before the Thirteenth Amendment. Black suffrage came to the District months before it was imposed, through the Military Reconstruction Acts, on the South and years before the Fifteenth Amendment ruled out racially discriminatory voting qualifications throughout the nation. Racial distinctions were eliminated from local charters and ordinances; segregation was eliminated on the city's street railroads, although less consistently in other public places; and Congress waged a relentless and ultimately successful struggle to create a system of public schools for African American children.[1] "The District of Columbia," declared Senator Charles Sumner in 1873, "is the place where all the great reforms of the war have begun. It is the experimental garden and nursery where all the generous plants have been tried." The metaphor was used as often to condemn innovative lawmaking. Thus, the chairman of the city's Board of Aldermen complained in 1868 that the District had been "specially set apart by the Government as a sort of experimental garden for the propagation of political hybrids of every conceivable description."[2] Whatever the interpretative slant, the idea that the federal District might be employed to carry out experiments in lawmaking for the benefit of the nation as a whole was part of the common currency of political discourse during the era of the Civil War and Reconstruction.

The peculiar status of the District forced Republican congressmen to consider, early and unequivocally, the implications of emancipation and the attributes of citizenship. Their deliberations led them, with surprising rapidity, to radical conclusions. Most Republicans concluded that freedom meant more than the mere absence of slavery but brought more positive entitlements, and they found it difficult to define those entitlements in terms that fell short of full citizenship rights. They found it difficult to identify an intermediate stage between emancipation and enfranchisement. In the District of Columbia, untroubled by the competing jurisdictions and political calculations that applied elsewhere, they could work through the implications of their political ideas and carry them through to their logical conclusions.[3] An analysis of congressional

---

[1] For a fuller account of Reconstruction in the District, see Howard Gillette Jr., *Between Justice and Beauty: Race, Planning, and the Failure of Urban Policy in Washington, D.C.* (Baltimore: Johns Hopkins University Press, 1995), chap. 3; Katherine Masur, "Reconstructing the Nation's Capital: The Politics of Race and Citizenship in the District of Columbia, 1862–1878" (unpublished Ph.D. diss., University of Michigan, 2001); Thomas R. Johnson, "Reconstruction Politics in Washington: 'An Experimental Garden for Radical Plants,'" *Records of the Columbia Historical Society* 50 (1980): 180–90; James H. Whyte, *Uncivil War: Washington during the Reconstruction, 1865–1878* (New York: Twayne, 1958); Constance M. Green, *Washington: Village and Capital, 1800–1878* (Princeton, NJ: Princeton University Press, 1962), 291–382; Melvin R. Williams, "A Blueprint for Change: The Black Community in Washington, D.C., 1860–1870," *Records of the Columbia Historical Society* 48 (1972): 359–93.

[2] *New National Era*, August 7, 1873; *Journal of the 65th Council* (Washington, DC, 1868), 689. See also Washington *Daily Patriot*, September 26, November 21, 1872.

[3] *New York World*, December 20, 1866.

legislation for the District during the years immediately following the
end of the Civil War therefore provides a useful illustration of the political dynamics of Reconstruction. It enables us to watch congressional
Republicans as they thought through the implications of their commitment to emancipation and equal rights. Although that commitment was
eventually pushed aside by other considerations and soon ceased to be
the guiding principle behind Republican policy making, a study of congressional policy toward the District of Columbia reminds us of just how
radical that commitment was for a few brief moments during and after
the Civil War.

### "The First Practical Triumph of Freedom"

Congressional Republicans took early action to eliminate slavery in the
District of Columbia. Although there were only a few hundred slaveholders in the District at the outbreak of the Civil War, majority opinion
among its white residents was firmly set against emancipation. When the
Senate Committee on the District of Columbia reported a bill emancipating the District's slaves in the spring of 1862, a joint resolution of the
Washington City Councils informed senators that "a large majority of the
people of this community is adverse to the unqualified abolition of slavery in this district." Such a measure was likely, the councils warned, to
convert the city, located as it was between two slaveholding states, "into
an asylum for free negroes, a population undesirable in every American
community" and a population which, they pointedly observed, several of
the nonslaveholding states had seen fit to exclude altogether from their
territory.[4] The *Evening Star*, at that time a resolutely conservative newspaper, was also fearful that the District would be overrun with fugitives
from slavery, and it accused Republican congressmen of "legislating to
deprive [slaveholders] of their property without a fair equivalent merely
that they may strengthen themselves individually with abolition sentiment
at home."[5]

---

[4] Joint Resolution of Washington City Councils, April 1862, in Ira Berlin et al., eds., *Freedom: A Documentary History, Series I. Vol. I: The Destruction of Slavery* (Cambridge:
Cambridge University Press, 1985), 178. See also Memorial from the Mayor and Aldermen in *CG*, 37.2:1496; *Evening Star*, March 25, 29, 1862; *National Intelligencer*, March
27, 1862; Wilhelmus B. Bryan, *A History of the National Capital* (2 vols., New York:
Macmillan, 1914–16), 2:513–15; Michael J. Kurtz, "Emancipation in the Federal City,"
*Civil War History* 24 (1978): 250–67.

[5] *Evening Star*, April 4, 1862.

Members of the small Democratic and Unionist minority in the Senate accepted the argument that Congress was under a moral obligation to respect the views of local residents. The emancipation proposal should be submitted to the people of the District, claimed Joseph A. Wright of Indiana, "if the people of this District have any rights at all."[6] The Virginia Unionist Waitman T. Willey offered an amendment to the emancipation bill providing for a referendum that was rejected by a vote of 13–24, every Republican but John C. Ten Eyck of New Jersey responding in the negative.[7] Republicans other than Ten Eyck were dismissive of the inhabitants' right to be heard. Was it proper, asked Lyman Trumbull of Illinois, for a few thousand voters in the District of Columbia to determine for the people of Illinois or New Jersey whether the capital of a great nation should be situated in slaveholding territory? Several Republicans questioned whether a population so riddled with disloyalty should be allowed a voice on so crucial a matter. The influential Pennsylvania congressman Thaddeus Stevens responded to a similar proposal in the House by suggesting that allowing residents of the District to vote on the abolition of slavery would be equivalent to an amendment stating "that the wicked shall be damned . . . 'provided that they consent thereto.'"[8]

The existence of slavery in the capital of the republic, Republicans argued, was an insult to the enlightened sentiment of the age. "Slavery is tolerated at the capital of no other civilized nation," noted Lot M. Morrill of Maine in presenting the bill to the Senate. "[It] is unbecoming the freest government on earth longer to allow the practice of it here." According to

---

[6] CG, 37.2:1523. See also the remarks of Senator James A. Bayard in CG, 37.2:1468; *Slavery in the District of Columbia: Minority Report*, Ho. Report 58, 37.2 (March 12, 1863), Ser. 1144. Several border state representatives, including Bayard, Anthony Kennedy (Maryland), Lazarus W. Powell (Maryland), and Waitman T. Willey (Virginia) contended that, in acquiring the ten square miles that became the District, the United States had entered into an implicit agreement that no radical change would be made in the District's institutions without the consent of the ceding states and that therefore emancipation would constitute a violation of "obligations of good faith" to Maryland and Virginia. CG, 37.2:1299–1303, 1353–56, 1523. Congress received a number of protests from residents of Maryland. Kurtz, "Emancipation in the Federal City," 257–58.

[7] CG, 37.2:1477–79, 1516, 1517. A similar amendment was defeated on a voice vote in the House. CG, 37.2:1643–44. Ten Eyck explained that during the 1860 election campaign, he had used a promise not to impose emancipation on the District without the consent of its inhabitants to meet opposition charges that Republicans, if elected, would resort to "extraordinary or ultra measures." CG, 37.2:1517.

[8] CG, 37.2:1478, 1517, 1375–76, 1471, 1473, 1643; *National Republican*, March 17, 1862.

Massachusetts Senator Henry Wilson, "For two generations, the states-
men of republican and Christian America have been surrounded by an
atmosphere tainted by the breath of the slave, and by the blinding and per-
verting influence of the social life of slaveholding society." The barbaric
laws and ordinances that went with slavery "should not be permitted to
insult the reason, pervert the moral sense, or offend the taste of the people of America." The influential Senator William Pitt Fessenden linked
abolition in the District of Columbia securely to the broader purpose of
the Republican Party, which was "to place this Government in a position
where it should not lend its aid to the support of slavery." Wherever
Congress had the power legally to weaken the institution, it had a duty
to do so. In that sense, liberation of the District's slaves formed part
of a larger emancipatory process. It would, said Massachusetts Senator
Charles Sumner, be "the first practical triumph of freedom."[9]

The debate in Congress roamed at large over questions of racial difference, the consequences of emancipation in the West Indies, the viability
of free black communities in the United States, the sanctity of property
rights in slaves, the constitutional status of the "peculiar institution," and
the universality of human rights.[10] As the *New York Times* remarked, the
debate contained "a deal of unedifying discussion on matters that have
not the slightest relation to the question in hand. . . . Each has some pet
hobby, some ethnological figment, as to the equality of races, the status

---

[9] CG, 37.2:1375, 1446. 1451, 1350, 1353, 1472; House Committee on the District of
Columbia, *Report to Accompany Bill No. 108 (Emancipation of Slaves in the District
of Columbia)*, Ho. Report 12, 37.2 (February 13, 1862), Ser. 1125. Fessenden, usually
moderate on slavery issues, was regarded as one of the most influential Republicans in the
Senate. According to the *Chicago Tribune*, when Fessenden moved, "it signified that the
whole glacier has started." Quoted in Allan G. Bogue, *The Earnest Men: Republicans
of the Civil War Senate* (Ithaca, NY: Cornell University Press, 1981), 162. For the
broader context of congressional action against slavery, see ibid., Part II; Allen Guelzo,
*Lincoln's Emancipation Proclamation: The End of Slavery in America* (New York:
Simon & Schuster, 2004); Sylvana R. Siddali, *From Property to Person: Slavery and
the Confiscation Acts, 1861–1862* (Baton Rouge: Louisiana University Press, 2004);
Michael Vorenberg, *Final Freedom: The Civil War, the Abolition of Slavery, and the
Thirteenth Amendment* (Cambridge: Cambridge University Press, 2001); Leonard P.
Curry, *Blueprint for Modern America: Nonmilitary Legislation of the First Civil War
Congress* (Knoxville: University of Tennessee Press, 1968), chaps. 2–4.

[10] The debate may be found in CG, 37.2:1191, 1266, 1285–86, 1299–1303, 1333–60,
1375–80, 1446–51, 1467–79, 1516–26, 1634–48; Henry Wilson, *A History of the Antislavery Measures of the Thirty-Seventh and Thirty-Eighth Congresses* (Boston: Walker,
Wise, 1864), 38–78. For an analysis of congressional proceedings see Bogue, *Earnest
Men*, 151–9; Guelzo, *Lincoln's Emancipation Proclamation*, 84–88; Curry, *Blueprint
for Modern America*, 36–43; Kurtz, "Emancipation in the Federal City," 252–56.

of the negro, colonization or what not, which he exploits and expands."
As the *Times* went on to say, the real question was not whether but
exactly how emancipation was to be effected: "a practical experiment
may be made in the District, over which the National Legislature exercises exclusive jurisdiction, as to the actual working of emancipation."
By setting in motion a process of gradual emancipation, rather than the
peremptory action that congressional Republicans seemed to envisage, by
allowing adequate compensation, and by providing for the colonization
of emancipated slaves, Congress might devise a procedure that would
make emancipation acceptable to the Border States. It would also be
consistent with the plans for compensated emancipation drawn up by
President Lincoln.[11]

Republicans showed no inclination to adopt a scheme of gradual emancipation. A substitute bill incorporating such a plan was defeated on a
party vote in the Senate and a similar amendment by a near party vote in
the House.[12] On the other hand, the bill contained a provision for compensation averaging $300 for each slave emancipated under the terms of
the statute. Although some radical Republicans like Samuel C. Pomeroy
of Kansas questioned the moral or legal right of even loyal slaveholders
to receive compensation for their slaves and argued that, if any compensation was in order, it should go to the victims of slavery, others like
Sumner were unwilling to jeopardize or delay emancipation by insisting
on the principle. Sumner regarded the payment as a ransom for captives
held illegally, as by the Barbary pirates sixty years earlier, rather than
as compensation.[13] Republicans gave short shrift to opposition amendments allowing for a judicial hearing in compensation cases and removing the requirement that average compensation be restricted to $300.

[11] *New York Times*, March 22, April 1, 4, 1862. Cf. *New York World*, April 2, 1862.
   Lincoln told *New York Tribune* editor Horace Greeley that he hoped the District eman-
   cipation bill would have "three main features": gradual emancipation, compensation,
   and submission to the vote of the people. Lincoln to Greeley, March 24, 1862, in Roy
   F. Basler, ed., *The Collected Works of Abraham Lincoln* (9 vols., New Brunswick, NJ:
   Rutgers University Press, 1953–55), 5:169. Lincoln also sought to incorporate some
   provision for voluntary colonization in any emancipation scheme. See his messages to
   Congress on the subject reprinted in James L. Richardson, ed., *A Compilation of the
   Messages and Papers of the Presidents, 1789–1897* (10 vols., Washington, DC: Bureau
   of National Literature and Art, 1904), 6: 68–69, 136–42.
[12] CG, 37.2:1519, 1648. Two Republicans voted for the substitute in the House. The
   substitute offered in the Senate by Wright was, in fact, the District emancipation bill
   introduced by Abraham Lincoln in the House in 1848. See CG, 37.2:1467–70.
[13] CG, 37.2:1235–36, 1446–51.

Excessive solicitude over guarantees of due process for the owners of human property was more than most Republicans could stomach.[14]

The bill was, however, amended in the Senate to provide funds for the colonization of freed slaves. The first move toward colonization came from Garrett Davis, a Kentucky Unionist, who offered an amendment requiring that all who were liberated by the bill must be colonized outside the United States and appropriating $100,000 for that purpose, on the grounds that free blacks were "the most worthless and vicious and expensive of our population to the society in which they live" and would become "a sore and a burden and a charge upon the white population." If they remained, he feared, a "war of extermination" would ensue. In its place, the Wisconsin Senator James R. Doolittle, a moderate Republican, offered a voluntary colonization scheme. He made it clear that he shared Davis's conviction that, because of "the very instincts of our nature, which are stronger and oftentime truer than reason itself," the two races could not be expected to live "side by side, on a footing of social and political equality."[15] His amendment to Davis's colonization amendment was adopted by a vote of 23–16. Both sides divided on the question, with 4 Democrats and Unionists voting for the amendment and 7 against and the Republicans supporting it by 19 votes to 9. Both the Democrats and Unionists and the mostly radical Republicans who voted against the amendment sought, for their different reasons, to make the colonization amendment as unpalatable as possible.

When the roll was called on the colonization amendment as amended, the result was a 19–19 tie, which was resolved by the negative vote of the vice president. This time, the Democrats and Unionists divided 6–4 and the Republicans 13–15. There was a close association between voting on the amendment and Republican factionalism: only three of those identified by Allan G. Bogue as radical Republicans voted for colonization, and only two of those identified as moderates voted against it. Moderates were less prepared than radicals to seek a confrontation with the president. Many of them shared Doolittle's skepticism about the prospects of racial harmony in the aftermath of emancipation, and they exhibited less confidence in the potential of freed blacks to forge successful lives in a racially mixed society.[16] Bogue argues that Republicans from western

[14] CG, 37.2:1645–46.

[15] CG, 37.2:1191, 1285, App. 83–86. See also the remarks of Orville Browning of Illinois in CG, 37.2:1520–01; and of James R. Harlan of Iowa in CG, 37.2:1357–59.

[16] CG, 37.2:1333–34, 1352, 1447, 1477. The identification of Republican factions is derived from Bogue, *Earnest Men*, 98. Some of the radicals were not immune from

states, many of which had passed laws excluding African Americans from residence, were more likely to insist on colonization, but the association is not strong. Four Democrats and Unionists voted against the amendment, and many more abstained, presumably because they wished to make the bill as obnoxious as possible to moderate Republicans.[17] A few days later, Doolittle reintroduced his amendment, which this time was adopted by a 27–10 vote. The majority of Republicans now voted to accept it. Five radicals, including Wade and Wilson, who had voted against the amendment ten days earlier, supported it this time round, clearly believing that compromise was necessary to secure passage and that voluntary colonization could do little harm. With the exception of Fessenden and Foster, the nay votes came exclusively from radical Republicans. This time the few opposition senators who answered the roll voted for the amendment.[18] The colonization section was not discussed or significantly amended in the House.

The District emancipation bill passed both houses on a strict party vote, 29–14 in the Senate and 92–38 in the House.[19] On signing the bill, Lincoln could not refrain from commenting, in a special message, "I am gratified that the two principles of compensation and colonization are both recognized and practically applied in the bill."[20] Yet the third leg of his plan for ridding the country of slavery, gradual emancipation, was not seriously considered by congressional Republicans. Although willing, to expedite emancipation in the nation's capital, to accept a measure of

racial prejudice, and some for that reason were sympathetic to Lincoln's colonization proposals. Others, like Wade, were fearful of the prospects facing freed blacks in a society where racial prejudice was so prevalent. See Hans L. Trefousse, *The Radical Republicans: Lincoln's Vanguard for Racial Justice* (New York: Knopf, 1969), 30–31, 209–10. Several Midwestern Republicans welcomed voluntary colonization as a way to ease their constituents' fears of a northward migration of freed slaves. V. Jacque Voegeli, *Free but Not Equal: The Midwest and the Negro during the Civil War* (Chicago: University of Chicago Press, 1967), 22–25; Herman Belz, *A New Birth of Freedom: The Republican Party and Freedmen's Rights, 1861 to 1866* (Westport, CT: Greenwood, 1976), 12–13.

[17] On regional factors in voting, see Bogue, *Earnest Men*, 156–58. On the strength of racial prejudice in the Midwest, see Eugene Berwanger, *The Frontier against Slavery: Western Anti-Negro Prejudice and the Slavery Extension Controversy* (Urbana: University of Illinois Press, 1967); Voegeli, *Free but Not Equal.*

[18] The other radicals to shift to support of the amendment were Foot, King, and Wilmot. CG, 37.2:1522; Curry, *Blueprint for Modern America*, 40–41. On Wilson's readiness to compromise to secure legislation against slavery, see Abbott, *Cobbler in Congress*, 143–45.

[19] CG, 37.2:1526, 1649; New York *World*, April 4, 12, 1862.

[20] Richardson, *Messages and Papers*, 6:73.

compensation for loyal slaveholders and willing, like Lincoln, to make some provision for voluntary colonization, they insisted that abolition in the District should proceed immediately. Nor were they prepared to seek the consent of local electors. Whether influenced like Fessenden by abolitionist pressure at home, like John Sherman by an awareness of the new political conditions created by the war, or by the prompting of their own consciences, Republicans took a step that not only initiated a legislative war against slavery but also marked a decisive change in the practical relationship between the national government and the capital city in which it sat. Whereas for the first sixty years of its sojourn in the city Congress had largely accepted the institutions inherited from Maryland and Virginia, which had donated the ten square miles on which it stood, now it sought to judge them and reshape them according to the precepts of the broader national conscience for which it presumed to speak.[21]

### Eradicating the Traces of Slavery

Congress moved with commendable speed to sweep away the more visible legal traces of slavery. Washington's black code was repealed in 1862, shortly after the local emancipation act. African Americans were now entitled to engage in any form of economic activity; their social life was no longer obstructed by the imposition of a curfew, and their freedom of assembly was no longer curtailed.[22] During the same year, Congress took preliminary steps towards providing educational facilities for the District's African American population. These were reinforced by supplementary legislation in 1864.[23] Charles Sumner, who was more closely associated than any other leading Republican with the cause of equal rights and the welfare of the District's black population, set out to remove every trace of discrimination from local laws. Washington's street railroads either excluded African Americans, leaving them to wait in the rain and snow for specially marked vehicles, or forced them to

---

[21] *CG*, 37.2:1338; Charles A. Jellison, *Fessenden of Maine: Civil War Senator* (Syracuse, NY: Syracuse University Press, 1962), 144–47; John Sherman, *John Sherman's Recollections: An Autobiography* (2 vols., Chicago: Werner Co., 1895), 1:310–12; Mark Krug, "The Republican Party and the Emancipation Proclamation," *Journal of Negro History* 48 (April 1963): 98–114.

[22] *CG*, 37.2:917–18, 2020; *CG*, 38.1:1995; Wilson, *History of the Antislavery Measures*, 419; Green, *Washington*, 275.

[23] See below, "The Inauguration of Biracial Education," pp. 133–37.

ride on the outside of the carriages, exposed to the elements. On several occasions, elderly women, including the renowned campaigner Sojourner Truth, and men bearing the uniform of the United States, such as the surgeon Alexander T. Augusta, were forcibly excluded from the cars. To Sumner their treatment was "a disgrace to this city, and a disgrace to our National Government, which permits it under its eyes."[24]

In 1864, Sumner persuaded the Republican majority to use Congress's power to grant charters to compel the newly established Metropolitan Railway Company to desist from discrimination as a condition of its franchise and narrowly failed to extend the ban to the older Washington and Georgetown Railroad. Democrats such as Willard Saulsbury and Reverdy Johnson, both representing border states, protested that such legislation was "a war against nature" and would be obnoxious to a "very considerable portion of the ladies and gentlemen of the capital," and they could see no objection to the provision of separate cars. Moderate Republicans such as Doolittle and Grimes were ready to agree that separate cars inconvenienced nobody and infringed on nobody's rights and were willing to leave it to the companies that operated the cars to decide how best to accommodate their passengers. Trumbull warned his fellow Republicans against passing laws that were blatantly offensive to local prejudices and would probably be unenforceable. Trumbull and Grimes also maintained that travelers excluded from the cars had every right to take their grievances to the courts. Sumner and Wilson, however, stood firm on the principle of equal rights. The Washington and Georgetown Railroad, Wilson told the Senate, "this company into which we breathed the breath of life outrages the rights of twenty-five thousand colored people in this District in our presence in defiance of our people." He told Trumbull, "I care far more for the rights of the humblest black child that treads the soil of the District of Columbia than I do for the prejudices of this corporation and its friends and patrons." Sumner insisted that the absolute right of African Americans to enter the streetcars be affirmed "because any other conclusion authorized a corporation to establish a *caste*,

---

[24] Donald, *Charles Sumner*, 154; Noah Brooks, *Washington, D.C. in Lincoln's Time* (Athens: University of Georgia Press, 1989), 191–93; Bryan, *History of the National Capital*, 2:529–32; Ingle, *Negro in the District of Columbia*, 38–40. On the campaign against discrimination, see especially Masur, "Reconstructing the Nation's Capital," 101–14; Olive Gilbert, ed., *Narrative of Sojourner Truth, a Bondswoman of Olden Time* (New York: Oxford University Press, 1991), 184–87; Carleton Mabee, *Sojourner Truth – Slave, Prophet, Legend* (New York: New York University Press, 1993), 129–38.

offensive to religion and humanity, injurious to a whole race...and bringing shame upon our country."[25]

The following session, Sumner introduced an amendment to a bill modifying the charter of the Metropolitan Railroad Company that extended the ban on excluding black citizens to all street railroad companies in the District. Although several of his colleagues objected to enacting general regulations in private bills, they relented when the company declared that it did not object to the amendment, which after all would equalize conditions in its favor.[26] Moderate Republicans on the House District Committee, however, not only removed Sumner's amendment but also the earlier ban on segregation in the Metropolitan's own cars. James W. Patterson of New Hampshire declared his opposition to special legislation for the benefit of either race and denied, in the face of the evidence (such as the signs saying "Colored Persons Admitted in this Car"), that African Americans were excluded from at least some of the carriages. "You cannot make one hair white or black by legislation, or make a black man white...Equally vain will it be to attempt to correct social prejudice by special legislation." Eventually, however, he was persuaded to withdraw his amendments and allow the bill to pass.[27]

There were no House votes on streetcar segregation, but several roll calls were taken in the Senate. These reveal a consistent scalar pattern. All Republicans but Cowan and Henderson eventually endorsed the general ban agreed to in 1865, although a number of moderates, including Doolittle, Trumbull, and Sherman, abstained on that vote; Republicans divided nearly equally in three roll calls on antidiscriminatory amendments to the bills incorporating the Metropolitan and Washington and Georgetown Railroads in 1864; and they divided 16–20 in the initial vote on Sumner's general ban. Those who voted for the specific bans but not, initially at least, for the general interdiction, were divided equally between moderates and radicals. Of those who voted with Sumner on the general ban, 7 are identified by Michael Les Benedict as radicals and 3 as moderates.[28]

[25] *CG*, 38.1:1158. See also *CG*, 37.3:1329; *CG*, 38.1:1141–42, 1156–61, 3131–35; Wilson, *History of the Antislavery Measures*, 371–76; Bogue, *Earnest Men*, 201–5; Roske, *Trumbull*, 105.

[26] *CG*, 38.2:589–90, 604.

[27] *CG*, 38.2:1026–27, 1334.

[28] *CG*, 38.1:1161, 3135, 3137; *CG*, 38.2, 590, 604; Michael Les Benedict, *A Compromise of Principle: Congressional Republicans and Reconstruction, 1863–1869* (New York: Norton, 1974), 342–44, 347–48. Cf. Bogue, *Earnest Men*, 104–5.

### "A Pillar of Fire to Illumine the Footsteps of Millions": Black Suffrage

With the elimination of slavery, Congress faced the question of how the civil and political status of the freed people should be defined, and in the District of Columbia, this was a question that Congress could not avoid facing directly. It could not avoid confronting the thorny issue of black suffrage. Radicals such as Sumner and Wilson had already attempted to remove racial qualifications for voting from the city charter during the winter of 1864, and it was certain that a suffrage bill would come before Congress when it assembled for its first postwar session in December 1865.[29] Radical Republicans were by that time strongly committed to black suffrage, believing it necessary both to protect the interests of freed people and to strengthen the forces of Unionism in the former Confederacy. It was, said Senator Jacob Howard of Michigan, "our *only* security and the only means of making emancipation effectual." Most moderate Republicans, however, considered the enfranchisement of African Americans premature, and if they supported it at all favored an "impartial suffrage" that would involve some form of educational or property qualification. They were aware that the electorates of several northern states had recently rejected black suffrage. Although closer analysis would suggest that something like three-quarters of Republican voters had supported the proposition in referenda, enough had voted against it to make the endorsement of black suffrage appear politically perilous. At this stage, the moderates were also anxious to work in harmony with President Andrew Johnson, whose plan of Reconstruction virtually excluded the possibility of black voting in the South. However, time would show, and their behavior with reference to the District would confirm, that their hesitation was engendered, in most cases, by pragmatic considerations rather than objections in principle.[30] Radical and moderate forces were

---

[29] CG, 38.1:2140–42, 2239–49, 2487, 2511–12, 2542–45; Donald, *Charles Sumner and the Rights of Man*, 181–82; Bogue, *Earnest Men*, 209–12.

[30] Patrick W. Riddleberger, *1866: The Critical Year Revisited* (Carbondale: Northern Illinois University Press, 1979), 106. On Republican attitudes to black suffrage during 1865–66, see Benedict, *Compromise of Principle*, 41–43, 103–16, 124, 130, 134–39; Eric Foner, *Reconstruction: America's Unfinished Revolution, 1863–1877* (New York: Harper, 1988), 221–24, 241–42; Trefousse, *Radical Republicans*, 310–19; Eric L. McKitrick, *Andrew Johnson and Reconstruction* (Chicago: University of Chicago Press, 1960), 55–59; Xi Wang, *The Trial of Democracy: Black Suffrage and Northern Republicans, 1860–1910* (Athens: University of Georgia Press, 1997), 28–31; Donald, *Charles Sumner and the Rights of Man*, 218–36; Richard H. Abbott, *Cobbler in Congress: The*

evenly balanced in both houses during the first session of the Thirty-ninth Congress, but the fact that radicals formed a majority of both the House and Senate District committees made it highly probable that a suffrage bill would be reported.[31]

The District's African American population held a series of meetings during the late summer and autumn of 1865, hoping to make the case for enfranchisement as much by their ability to conduct themselves in parliamentary meetings as by the substance of their arguments, and they presented Congress with a petition bearing 2,500 signatures. The petition reminded Congress that "Governments derive their just powers from the consent of the governed." Many African Americans held property, and "they pay no inconsiderable amount in taxes, but are nevertheless as slaves in its distribution. Unlike other taxpayers, they see the proceeds of their labor taken and disposed of without a single voice." Without suffrage, they had no effective protection under the law and were vulnerable to abuse; without political rights they were "but nominally free." While drawing attention to their property holdings and their tax payments, their churches and their schools, and their military service, African Americans based their claim to suffrage on the fundamental principles of American government. As the author of the petition, the educator John F. Cook Jr., explained, the ballot was "the title-deed of manhood, the bulwark against

---

*Life of Henry Wilson, 1812–1875* (Lexington: University of Kentucky Press, 1972), 173–77. On the results of referenda and other evidence of public opinion in the North, see William Gillette, *The Right to Vote: Politics and the Passage of the Fifteenth Amendment* (Baltimore: Johns Hopkins University Press, 1965), 25–29; Foner, *Reconstruction*, 222–24; Phyllis R. Field, "Republicans and Black Suffrage in New York State: The Grass Roots Response," *Civil War History*, 21 (June 1975): 136–47; Robert R. Dykstra, "Iowa: 'Bright Radical Star,'" in James E. Mohr, ed., *Radical Republicans in the North: State Politics during Reconstruction* (Baltimore: Johns Hopkins University Press, 1976), 167–93; James E. Mohr, *The Radical Republicans and Reform in New York during Reconstruction* (Ithaca, NY: Cornell University Press, 1973), 202–70; Lex Renda, "'A White Man's State in New England': Race, Party, and Suffrage in Civil War Connecticut," in Paul Cimbala and Randall M. Miller, eds., *An Uncommon Time: The Civil War and the Northern Home Front* (New York: Fordham University Press, 2002), 260–67; Michael J. McManus, *Political Abolitionism in Wisconsin, 1840–1861* (Kent, OH: Kent State University Press, 1998), 209.

[31] The House committee contained five radical Republicans, two moderate Republicans, and two Democrats; the Senate committee four radicals, two moderates, and one Democrat. For a listing of radical and moderate Republicans in the Thirty-ninth Congress, First Session, see Benedict, *Compromise of Principle*, 348–53. For a different classification, see Edward L. Gambill, "Who Were the Senate Radicals?" *Civil War History* 11 (September 1965): 237–44.

oppression and wrong, and a man's only shield from the contempt of his fellows."[32]

It was evident that an overwhelming majority of the District's white residents were horrified at the prospect. In November, the Washington Board of Common Council adopted a resolution placing its objections to black suffrage securely on the grounds of racial difference and affirming that the United States was "a white man's country and government, and not a colored one's." A substitute resolution proposing that the right of suffrage should be awarded on the basis of literacy rather than color was brushed aside, as was another trusting in the wisdom of Congress to legislate on the question, and only two votes were cast against the original resolution.[33] Among local newspapers, the *National Intelligencer*, formerly a Whig but now a Conservative journal, condemned black suffrage as "a declaration of war against existing social relations," and the *Evening Star*, which was moving toward a conservative Republican stance, was hardly less dismissive. Black suffrage, it claimed, would turn the District into "a negro Utopia" more like the capital of Dahomey than that of a civilized nation. The *National Republican*, although sympathetic in principle to impartial suffrage, at this stage hoped for the success of Johnson's Reconstruction program. Only the *Daily Morning Chronicle*, a Republican newspaper edited by the clerk of the Senate, John W. Forney, supported the measure, although it, too, expressed a preference for a restricted black suffrage. Forney was also anxious to keep on good terms with President Johnson, at least until his Freedmen's Bureau veto of February 1866.[34] Local opposition fastened on the composition of the local African American population with its large proportion of recent migrants, fugitives from slavery who had during the war taken refuge behind federal lines. Black suffrage would be an act of political madness, said the *Star*, in view of the fact that "the war has crowded Washington

[32] Petition of John Francis Cook and 2500 other Colored Citizens of the District of Columbia, December 11, 1865, Senate Papers 39A-H4 DC, RG 46, NARA; letter from Cook in Washington *Daily Morning Chronicle*, December 19, 1865. See also "A Colored Man's Plea for Suffrage," *Chronicle*, July 10, 1865; *Evening Star*, July 28, December 12, 1865, January 22, 1866; *National Intelligencer*, July 28, 1865; *New York Times*, October 25, 1865; Masur, "Reconstructing the Nation's Capital," 168–77.

[33] *Journal of the 63rd Council* (Washington, DC, 1866), 313–19, 330–31; *Evening Star*, November 14, 1865.

[34] *National Intelligencer*, November 18, December 20, 22, 25, 1865, January 13, 17, 1866; *Evening Star*, December 18, 22, 27, 1865, January 19, 1866; *National Republican*, December 16, 1865; *Chronicle*, December 16, 19, 1865; Masur, "Reconstructing the Nation's Capital," 177–86; Bryan, *History of the National Capital*, 2:546–50.

with thousands on thousands of the class of negroes ignorant and incapable of the proper discharge of the duties of citizenship." Opponents
also drew pointed reference to the fact that only five northern states permitted black suffrage and that the electorates of four states had rejected
it over the past year. They questioned the right of northern congressmen
to decide who should vote in District elections in disregard not only of
local opinion but of the professed views of their own constituents.[35]

The Washington City Councils ordered a referendum, held in December 1865, as an expression of local opinion. When the votes were counted,
the whites-only electorate had rejected the equal suffrage bill by 6,591
votes to 35. A similar vote in Georgetown produced a 712 to 1 margin. In transmitting the result of the Washington election to Congress,
Mayor Richard Wallach claimed that the vote, "the largest, with but two
exceptions, ever polled in the city, conclusively shows the unanimity of
sentiment of the people of Washington in opposition to the extension of
the right of suffrage to that class." The only exceptions, he claimed, were
African Americans and nonresident whites, who were neither part of the
community nor shared its sentiments. He hoped that Congress would
respect such an "unparalleled unanimity of sentiment" and refrain from
using its absolute power over the District to impose a policy that was so
objectionable to its citizens.[36] Such restraint was unlikely. Local Republicans challenged the result on a number of grounds. The most obvious
and the most telling, of course, was that African Americans themselves
had not been allowed to participate. Add to their number the white citizens who did not turn out, either because they anticipated malpractice or
because they considered the exercise to be pointless, said Sayles J. Bowen,
the most prominent local Republican, and the majority against equal
manhood suffrage looked less convincing. Those who voted, claimed
Bowen, were traitors, southern sympathizers, and opponents of emancipation. The *New York Times* agreed that the movement to hold a referendum "originated with the copperhead association here," and even the
*Star*, which in most respects approved of the referendum, admitted that

---

[35] *Evening Star*, December 8, 22, 1865.

[36] *Journal of the 63rd Council*, 330–31, 372, 373–80; CG, 39.1:133; *Evening Star*, Decem-
ber 18, 22, 1865; *National Intelligencer*, December 22, 1865; *National Republican*,
December 19, 1865; Ingle, *Negro in the District of Columbia*, 64–67; William Tindall,
"A Sketch of Mayor Sayles J. Bowen," *Records of the Columbia Historical Society* 15
(1915): 30–35. On the Georgetown election, see Mayor Henry Addison to Lafayette S.
Foster, president pro tempore of the Senate, January 12, 1866, Senate Committee on the
District of Columbia, SEN 39A-H4, RG46, NARA.

"The ballot box at the special election doubtless received many ballots from fingers that pulled rebel triggers."[37]

Republicans in Congress echoed many of these reasons for discounting the significance of the referendum. Some, like George W. Julian of Indiana, regarded black suffrage in the District as an act of "retributive justice to the slaveholders and rebels" that, they believed, formed a large and influential proportion of its inhabitants.[38] More important, congressional Republicans denied the validity of the whole exercise. Morrill, the chairman of the Senate Committee on the District of Columbia, considered the referendum improper. The authority of Congress over the District was plenary, and it was impertinent for its citizens to seek to instruct the national legislature on what laws to pass. The wishes of the "handful of voters who temporarily encamp under the shadow of the Capitol," said Pennsylvania Congressman M. Russell Thayer, should not stand in the way of a great national policy that involved "the justice, the good faith, and the magnanimity of the great nation."[39] Sumner insisted that black enfranchisement in the District of Columbia had a wider significance than the right to vote in municipal elections; it touched on "questions of human rights everywhere throughout this land, involving the national character and its good name forever more." It therefore formed part of a broader project. According to Morrill, "it may be said to be inaugurating a policy not only strictly for the District of Columbia, but in some sense for the country at large." There was, said the Ohio Senator Benjamin Wade, no more appropriate place to try out the experiment of impartial suffrage. Sumner closed the Senate debate in December 1866 by saying that the measure would not only bring benefits to the District but would also serve as an example to the "disorganized States." It would be "like a pillar of fire to illumine the footsteps of millions."[40]

[37] *New York Times*, October 25, 1865; *Evening Star*, December 23, 1865. Bowen, in fact, urged Republicans to boycott the election. Letter from Bowen, in *Chronicle*, December 18, 1865. See also *Chronicle*, December 16, 1865; *Evening Star*, January 1, 1866; *National Republican*, December 16, 19, 1865, January 9, 1866.

[38] CG, 39.1:259. See also the remarks of Reps. William D. Kelley (Pennsylvania), CG, 39.1:181–82; John F. Farnsworth (Illinois), CG, 39.1:205–6; Josiah B. Grinnell (Iowa), CG, 39.1:223; Sen. Lot M. Morrill (Maine), 39.2:39

[39] CG, 39.2:38–39; 39.1:281–82. See also *Chronicle*, December 22, 1865, January 11, 1866.

[40] Donald, *Charles Sumner and the Rights of Man*, 181; CG, 39.2:38, 63, 107. See also remarks of Frederick T. Frelinghuysen (New Jersey), CG, 39.2:103; John Sherman (Ohio), CG, 39.2:307–8; *Minority Report on H.R. No. 1 (Suffrage in the District of Columbia)*, Ho. Report 2, 39.1 (December 19, 1865), Ser. 1272; *Chronicle*, July 13, November 10, December 13, 1866.

Apart from rehearsing the broader arguments for black suffrage, such as the prerogatives of citizenship, the civil and political rights of men (with an important excursus on the civil and political rights of women), and the services of African Americans to the Union, Republicans insisted that ballots should be placed in the hands of black men so that they might protect themselves and their families from abuse and discrimination. It would be impracticable to secure their civil rights, said Congressman George S. Boutwell of Massachusetts, "unless fortified by the political right of voting. With the right of voting everything that man ought to enjoy or have of civil rights will come to him. Without the right to vote he is secure in nothing."[41] Although such concerns more naturally attached themselves to the welfare of freedpeople in the states of the former Confederacy, the black residents of the District also faced prejudice serious and pervasive enough for them to require the protection that the right to vote conferred. "It is because the Negro is hated in this city, and justice denied him by prejudiced officials, that his vote is necessary for his own protection," said Glenni Scofield of Pennsylvania. Then African American residents could "vote against a mayor who loads them with school taxes and deprives them of schools." If African Americans had the vote, Henry Wilson told the Senate, instead of treating them with contempt and indifference, the mayor and aldermen would come and speak at their schools and enquire after the health of their wives and children.[42] Furthermore, the extension of the suffrage would have a salutary effect on what Republicans saw as a corrupt, reactionary, and inefficient local government. Black votes would enable a reorganization and, of course, a Republicanization of municipal government.[43]

The counterarguments of Democrats, Unionists, and conservative Republicans focused on two themes. One was an insistence on the right of local communities to decide such matters for themselves. If, as Republicans claimed, the people of the District had nothing to do with the question, said Senator Edgar Cowan of Pennsylvania, then the whole

---

[41] *CG*, 39.1:310. For representative statements of the case for the bill, see the speeches by Reps. James F. Wilson (Iowa), *CG*, 39.1:173–75; Glenni Scofield (Pennsylvania), *CG*, 39.1:178–80; William D. Kelley (Pennsylvania), *CG*, 39.1:180–83; James F. Farnsworth (Illinois), *CG*, 39.1:204–7; George W. Julian (Indiana), *CG*, 39.1:255–59; George Boutwell (Massachusetts), *CG*, 39.1:308–10; Sen. Lot M. Morrill (Maine), *CG*, 39.2:38–41. See also Wang, *Trial of Democracy*, 29–33; Masur, "Reconstructing the Nation's Capital," 186–94.

[42] *CG*, 39.1:179–80; 39.2:104.

[43] *CG*, 39.1:174 (James F. Wilson), 179 (Scofield). Cf. *Chronicle*, July 4, 13, 1866.

governmental system was based on the wrong principles: "To say that the people who are to be affected by the measure ought to have no voice in the question is laying an ax to the root of the tree of liberty." Congressman Benjamin M. Boyer of Pennsylvania declared that Congress had no "moral right" to impose black suffrage in the face of the will of the people, "in violation of the fundamental principles of popular government" (he, of course, like Cowan, was referring to the *white* people).[44] The validity of this, as we have seen, Republicans simply denied. The other was an emphasis on the distinction between two races "so distant as to prevent anything like social equality." Assertions of racial equality, said Saulsbury, were contrary to Scripture. "The ordinances of nature are not to be repealed by acts of Congress," said Boyer. This was, and always should be, "a white man's Government."[45] Some Republicans met this argument with bold statements of racial equality. "I say that our fathers made this Government for men," said Representative John F. Farnsworth of Illinois, "not for black men or white men . . . but they made it for men."[46] Several cited the evidence presented in the petition of District blacks to demonstrate what African Americans could achieve, even under adverse conditions. "A community characterized by such evidence of civilization and intelligence as these is not in my opinion an unsafe depository of the right of suffrage," said Thayer.[47] However, a sizable number of Republicans, although denying the wilder claims of men like Saulsbury and Garrett Davis, firmly rooted as they were in proslavery polemics, accepted enough of their argument to question the capacity of all African American males to exercise the franchise.

Moderate Republicans argued that, in the first instance at least, suffrage should be confined to African American males who could read and write, with the addition of those who had fought for the Union and possibly also those who could meet a property qualification. Willey, who was in the course of a migration from a conservative Unionism to a hardly less

---

[44] CG, 39.1:175–6; CG, 39.2, 308. See also remarks of Reps. Andrew J. Rogers (New Jersey), CG, 39.1:201–2; John W. Chanler (New York), CG, 39.1:220–22; Sens. Thomas A. Hendricks (Indiana), CG, 39.2:106; Reverdy Johnson (Maryland), CG, 39.2: 312.

[45] CG, 39.1:176–78; CG, 39.2:85. For a particularly exhaustive review of supposed racial differences, see two speeches by Kentucky Senator Garrett Davis. CG, 39.1:245–51; CG, 39.2:78–81. For other examples, see CG, 39.1:196–204 (Rogers), 219–20 (Chanler); CG, 39.2:312–13 (Johnson); *Minority Report on H.R. No. 1.*

[46] CG, 39.1:204.

[47] CG, 39.1:282. See also CG, 39.1:174–75 (James F. Wilson), 181 (Kelley), 256 (Julian).

conservative Republicanism, claimed in June 1866 that a large proportion of the District's blacks, "but a short time taken from the worst and
lowest type of barbarism in all the world," were ignorant, debased, and
degraded: "Are such beings as these the safe repositories of the political
power of any community?" John A. Kasson of Iowa, another conservative Republican, was willing, like Lincoln, he claimed, for the "intelligent
negro" and the "fighting negro" to be enfranchised, but he believed that
to allow the thousands of freedmen to vote would admit "an alarming
infusion of ignorance" into the body politic. It would be a "burlesque on
republican government" to say that such men were fit to exercise the right
to vote, said Doolittle. Thus, Republican moderates shared Democratic
doubts about the fitness of freed African Americans for participation in
a republican polity, although they tended to regard their disability as
a temporary condition, brought on by the harrowing effects of slavery,
rather than an indelible racial inferiority.[48]

Opponents of the literacy test claimed that it was unfair to set different
criteria for black and white voters and argued strongly for unrestricted
manhood suffrage. "I want it simple and absolute, a right of human
nature," said Missouri Senator B. Gratz Brown in June 1866. It was
unfair to impose educational requirements on freedmen who had been
denied access to education. "The ballot itself is a schoolmaster," said
Julian. In any case, reading and writing were mechanical processes and no
indication of "worthiness of life or character."[49] Henry Wilson pointed
out also that to insert an educational test would give District whites an
incentive not to provide educational facilities for black children. "You
put in the power of the enemies of this race to keep them from the ballot-
box." Even more would that be the case if such a criterion were to be
applied in the South. Sumner agreed that under such restrictions there
would not be sufficient votes to protect black and white Unionists in the
South. The "controlling necessity" under which Congress was working
did not allow for an educational test.[50]

[48] *CG*, 39.1:235–40, 3438; *CG*, 39.2, 43, 83–84. See also remarks of Reps. Thomas T.
Davis, *CG*, 39.1:215; Robert S. Hale, *CG*, 39.1:279–81; Burt Van Horn (all New York),
*CG*,39.1:283–86; *Chronicle*, December 16, 1865, January 16, July 4, 1866.

[49] *CG*, 39.1:3433, 257–58. See also remarks of Rep. George S. Boutwell, *CG*, 39.1:308–9;
Sens. Henry Wilson, *CG*, 39.2:42; Samuel C. Pomeroy (Kansas), *CG*, 39.1:162; *CG*,
39.2:43–44.

[50] *CG*, 39.2:103–5, 107. Cf. *National Intelligencer*, April 21, 1866. However, Wilson had
favored an educational test in the first session of the Thirty-ninth Congress. Abbott,
*Cobbler in Congress*, 180–81.

The bill reported from the House Judiciary Committee included no literacy, property, or tax qualifications. When it came up for discussion in January 1866, a number of moderate Republicans, concerned about constituency reaction and wishing not to antagonize the president, called for a party conference. At the conference they demanded that the bill be referred back to committee with instructions to add educational or military service qualifications. Although radicals, led by Thaddeus Stevens and Judiciary Committee Chairman James F. Wilson, vigorously opposed the motion, arguing that such a test would disqualify a large proportion of the black population in the District and a still larger proportion in the South, it carried, according to newspaper reports, by a substantial majority. However, when the motion to recommit the bill with instructions to amend it so as to extend the suffrage only to those who could read the Constitution or had served in the military or naval services of the United States came before the House on January 18, Wilson and his radical allies voted against it and, with Democratic assistance, defeated it. Republican moderates then felt obliged, with a few exceptions, to vote directly for universal male suffrage, a policy that, as the *New York Times* pointed out, had never formally been adopted at a convention of the party.[51] The motion to recommit was defeated by a vote of 53–117. Voting on the literacy test probed the division between radical and moderate Republicans that was opening up in the course of the wider debate over Reconstruction. The yea votes came mostly from moderate Republicans with a smaller number of radicals and a scattering of conservatives. As we have seen, some of the moderates had doubts about the capacity of the freedmen immediately to participate intelligently in political life, and they were not yet committed to universal manhood suffrage as the centerpiece of Reconstruction. They were, however, outnumbered by what the *New York Times* called "the unnatural and unholy alliance between the radicals and the regular opposition," between radical Republicans who were ready to make such a commitment, at least in the District, and conservatives and Democrats who opposed the bill altogether.[52]

[51] *CG*, 39.1:72, 178, 279–81, 310–11; *New York Times*, January 11, 16, 20, 22, 1866; *New York World*, January 11, 12, 19, 1866; *Evening Star*, January 17, 18, 19, 1866; *National Republican*, January 19, 20, 1866; Benedict, *Compromise of Principle*, 146. Ten Republicans and five Unionists, most of whom were former Republicans, voted against the bill in the House. *CG*, 39.1:311.

[52] *CG*, 39.1:311; *New York Times*, January 20, 1866; *New York World*, January 20, 1866. Those who voted for recommittal included 42 conservative and moderate Republicans and 13 radical Republicans; those who voted against included 42 Democrats and

The bill initially reported by Morrill to the Senate in December 1865 included a literacy test, but on a motion by the radical Richard Yates of Illinois, it was recommitted and reported again from committee, this time without any qualifications. Morrill's attempt to restore the literacy test later in the session was defeated by a vote of 15–19. Again, most of the votes for the literacy test came from moderate Republicans; the nay votes came from Democrats, conservative Republicans, and radicals. A significant number of Democrats and conservative Republicans abstained.[53] Although some Democrats might have voted tactically, preferring to see the bill go forward in an "odious shape" rather than join with the moderates to improve it, others refused on principle to vote for black suffrage with any amount of education. Saulsbury, for example, whose opposition to black suffrage was grounded primarily in his racial beliefs, could not accept that a little learning would transform a field hand into an eligible voter.[54]

The District suffrage bill made no further progress during a session preoccupied with the broader politics of Reconstruction and the negotiation of the troubled relationship between Congress and president. Johnson stated his opinion in an interview with a conservative Senator in January 1866:

the agitation of the negro franchise question in the District of Columbia at this time was the mere entering-wedge to the agitation of the question throughout the States, and was ill-timed, uncalled for, and calculated to do great harm.

conservatives, 12 moderate, and 49 radical Republicans (15 were unclassified). Conservatives are defined as the members of Groups 0–2 of Michael Les Benedict's classification of Representatives in the Thirty-ninth Congress, First Session; moderates are Groups 3–4; and radicals Groups 5–6. See Benedict, *Compromise of Principle*, 348–51. If the 42 Democrats and conservatives had voted to recommit, the motion would have been carried by a vote of 93–77.

53 CG, 39.1:162, 231–32, 3434; *National Intelligencer*, February 22, 1866; *Evening Star*, January 10, 11, February 21, June 27, 28, 1866. Eleven moderates and 4 radicals voted for the amendment; 5 conservatives, 4 moderates, and 10 radicals voted against it; 7 of the 10 senators to abstain were conservatives. Conservatives are defined as the members of Groups 0–3 of Benedict's classification, moderates Groups 4–6, and radicals Groups 7–9. Benedict, *Compromise of Principle*, 351–53. If the Democrats and conservative Republicans had voted for the literacy test, the amendment would have been agreed to by a vote of 20–14.

54 CG, 39.2:45–46. Conservative newspapers were highly critical of the Democrats' strategy. *Evening Star*, January 20, 1866; *New York Times*, January 20, 1866; *National Intelligencer*, February 22, 1866. The *New York World* (January 20, 1866), the most influential Democratic journal in the nation, defended the strategy, arguing that it was not the Democrats' business to palliate the insult to the people of the District that the bill represented or to make it more palatable to moderate Republicans.

He believed that it would engender enmity, contention, and strife between the two races, and lead to a war between them, which would result in great injury to both, and the certain extermination of the negro population.

He made it clear that he would veto a bill for unqualified suffrage in the District.[55] The Senate did not take up the subject again until late June. Given that it was doubtful that the two-thirds necessary to override a veto could be obtained at this juncture, and in view of the sickness of Morrill, who was responsible for managing the bill, little progress was made.[56] Several commentators suggested also that Republican members were reluctant to press the issue in the run-up to the fall elections. Henry Wilson explained early in the next session, when pressed by the Democratic Senator Thomas A. Hendricks, that the bill had not been pushed to passage because of the pressure of other business and because of differences among Republicans over its form. Those who favored a "clean bill," without restrictive qualifications, believed that their chances of obtaining it would be better at a later date. When Allen G. Thurman suggested that the Republicans preferred not to have black suffrage as an issue during the election campaign, Wilson did not contradict him.[57] Not until Congress reassembled after the elections did the Senate pay sustained attention to the District suffrage bill. This time a literacy-test amendment received only eleven votes.[58] All but a few moderates now lined up with their Republican colleagues to force an unamended bill through the Senate on December 13 and to override a presidential veto that rehearsed familiar Johnsonian arguments about racial antagonism, local autonomy, and legislative encroachment.[59]

---

[55] Interview with James Dixon, January 28, 1866, in LeRoy P. Graf and Ralph W. Haskins, eds., *The Papers of Andrew Johnson* (16 vols., Knoxville: University of Tennessee Press, 1967–2000), 9:648; *New York World*, January 29, 30, 1866. LaWanda and John H. Cox believe that Johnson hoped to use the issue to sever the radical Republicans from the rest of the Union Party, which he hoped to lead. *Politics, Principle, and Prejudice, 1865–1866: Dilemmas of Reconstruction America* (New York: Free Press of Glencoe, 1963), 177.

[56] *CG*, 39.1:1934, 3432–44, 3453; *Evening Star*, February 21, June 27, 28, 1866; *National Intelligencer*, February 22, 1866; *New York Times*, June 28, 1866; Wang, *Trial of Democracy*, 30.

[57] *CG*, 39.2:64; *New York Times*, April 24, 1866; *National Intelligencer*, December 14, 1866; Abbott, *Cobbler in Congress*, 173–77, 180.

[58] *CG*, 39.2:107. The eleven included two moderate Republican (Anthony of Rhode Island and Fogg of New Hampshire), four conservative Republicans (Dixon, Doolittle, Foster, and Willey), and five Democrats.

[59] *CG*, 39.2:109. Six nominal Republicans voted against the bill: Cowan Dixon, Doolittle, Foster, Sherman, and Van Winkle. All were at the conservative end of the spectrum, and

A *Baltimore Sun* correspondent reported in December 1865, at the beginning of the first session of the Thirty-ninth Congress, that 14 of 17 Ohio Republicans and 7 of 11 Indiana Republicans would rather vote to repeal the city's charter than to introduce black suffrage. During the House debate, a number of Republicans expressed doubts about the wisdom of passing a suffrage bill.[60] It is not altogether clear why in the end they did so – why congressional Republicans gravitated to black suffrage for the District in January 1866, more than a year before it was adopted as a policy for the former Confederate states in the First Reconstruction Act of March 1867; why at least half of the Republican representatives voted immediately for unqualified suffrage; and why the other half receded so readily from their insistence on literacy or property qualifications. Although they would have preferred a restricted franchise, moderates in the House were prepared to vote for an unqualified suffrage rather than none at all, and it is likely that moderates in the Senate would have done the same had they not been inhibited by electoral considerations and distracted by the tortuous debates over Reconstruction policy. The break with Johnson, the results of the autumn elections, and the course of political events in the South certainly clarified the situation, but most congressional Republicans had already committed themselves during the first session.

It may be that, as Michael Les Benedict suggests, they felt free to act on principle in deciding policy for a piece of territory over which they held absolute power, in which case it would appear that the support for black suffrage was much stronger and more widespread among Republicans than we had been led to believe.[61] If they regarded it, in the words of a hostile Democratic senator, as "an experiment, a skirmish, an entering wedge to prepare the way for a similar movement in Congress to confer the right of suffrage on all the negroes of the United States," then they must have arrived at that purpose somewhat earlier than the winter of 1867, when the Reconstruction Acts were drawn up.[62] The fate of

---

three – Cowan, Dixon, and Doolittle – were so closely allied with Johnson as to have effectively severed their links with the party. For the text of the veto, see Richardson, ed., *Messages and Papers*, 6:472–83; *National Intelligencer*, January 8, 1867. See also *New York Times*, December 15, 1866; *National Intelligencer*, December 15, 1866; *Chronicle*, December 14, 1866; Cox, *Politics, Principle, and Prejudice*, 160–61.

[60] *National Intelligencer*, December 20, 1865; CG, 39.1:215–16, 235–40, 261–64.

[61] Benedict, *Compromise of Principle*, 145–46; Gillette, *Between Justice and Beauty*, 49–53; Donald, *Charles Sumner*, 281–82.

[62] CG, 39.1:246. Cf. *New York World*, December 20, 1866.

suffrage referenda in several northern states made it clear that such a stance did not enjoy majority support among their constituents. Political expediency in that sense can have played little part in their decision.[63]

Most Republicans who spoke on the bill saw enfranchisement as following naturally from emancipation. To deny the liberated slave "the rights and privileges of men," said Boutwell, was in effect, to deny him the perquisites of freedom. Freedom meant more than the mere absence of slavery but entailed more positive entitlements. Republicans found it difficult to define those entitlements in terms that fell short of full citizenship rights. The alternative to an acceptance of equal rights, believed George W. Julian, was for the nation to "re-enact its guilty compact with aristocracy and caste" and continue the policy, inspired by contempt for African Americans, that lay behind slavery and secession. Opponents' claim that this was "a white man's Government," declared Pennsylvania Congressman William D. Kelley, was "a rebel heresy entirely repudiated by the war." What the opposition case ultimately amounted to, claimed Thayer, was "but the old revolting argument in favor of slavery, and a selfish appeal to prejudice and ignorance." Disfranchisement was a historical product of slavery, and Republicans, or at least radical Republicans like Stevens and Sumner, were determined to wipe out every vestige of the institution, "wherever it shows itself, whatever form it might take." They regarded the right of man to self-government as a natural right, which was absolute and incontrovertible, rather than a conventional right conferred by the community at its discretion – as a universal attribute of manhood, rather than an accident of birth, or race, or nationality. Radical Republicans, then, concluded that emancipation entailed the conferment of not only civil but also political rights.[64]

---

[63] Hence, during the 1866 election, many Republican candidates campaigned on civil rights issues even though they knew them to be unpopular with the electorate. See LaWanda Cox and John Cox, "Negro Suffrage and Reconstruction Politics: The Problem of Motivation in Reconstruction Historiography," *Journal of Southern History* 33 (August 1967): 303–30. See also the essays in Mohr, ed., *Radical Republicans in the North*.

[64] See CG, 38.1:2486, 2543 (Sumner); CG, 39.1:180–81 (Kelley), 204–7 (Farnsworth), 255–56 (Julian), 281–82 (Thayer); CG, 39.2:76–78 (B. Gratz Brown). Of course, this line of argument left the radical Republicans open to criticism for denying women's suffrage (which some of them supported but wished, for pragmatic reasons, to separate from the enfranchisement of blacks). See CG, 39.2:46–47, 55–66, 76–84; Masur, "Reconstructing the Nation's Capital," 192–94; and, for the broader context, Ellen Carol DuBois, *Feminism and Suffrage: The Emergence of an Independent Women's Movement in America, 1848–1869* (Ithaca, NY: Cornell University Press, 1999). For a discussion of the Republicans' deliberations on the implications of emancipation and the meaning of

More conservative Republican voices argued that possession of the franchise was not an absolute right but a privilege – "citizenship is one thing and the right of suffrage is another and a different thing," said one – and that a republican government depended on the intelligence of its voters. However, the moderates' ultimate acceptance of an unqualified suffrage indicates that most of them acknowledged a substantial part of the radicals' argument.[65] "The genuine Republican standard for the suffrage is emblazoned on the bill for the District of Columbia," observed the *New York World*. "The District bill is the Republican ideal of right; the Republican standard of duty; the Republican declaration of policy." Legislating for the District allowed congressional Republicans to give voice to their political principles without worrying so much about the constitutional restrictions on their authority or the electoral costs of their actions.[66]

### The Inauguration of Biracial Education

The wartime Republican Congress took early action to provide educational facilities for the District's African American population. Although the city of Washington had set up public schools quite early in its history, they had never been adequate to provide instruction for more then a small minority of the white school-age population. Only 29 percent of the white children of school age were enrolled in 1860. No attempt was made to educate black children out of municipal funds, and the opening of colored schools depended almost entirely on the resources of the free black population itself, augmented during the Civil War by contributions from northern philanthropic societies.[67] James W. Grimes, the chairman of the

freedom, see Herman Belz, *A New Birth of Freedom: The Republican Party and Freedmen's Rights, 1861–1866* (Westport, CT: Greenwood, 1976), 138–82; Vorenberg, *Final Freedom*, 99–107, 188–91, 233–39; Jean H. Baker, "Defining Postwar Republicanism: Congressional Republicans and the Boundaries of Citizenship," in Robert F. Engs and Randall M. Miller, eds. *The Birth of the Grand Old Party: The Republicans' First Generation* (Philadelphia: University of Pennsylvania Press, 2002), 128–47; Eric Foner, *The Story of American Freedom* (New York: Norton, 1998), 100–13.

[65] See, for example, *CG*, 39.1:215 (Davis), 238 (Kasson), 3435 (Willey); *New York Times*, December 19, 1866.

[66] *New York World*, December 20, 1866.

[67] See Green, *Washington*, 42–44, 91–93, 161–62, 184–85, 212–14; James O. Wilson, "Eighty Years of the Public Schools of Washington, 1805–1885," *Records of the Columbia Historical Society*, 1 (1897), 119–70; Lillian G. Dabney, *A History of Schools for Negroes in the District of Columbia, 1807–1947* (Washington, DC: Catholic University Press, 1949); Emmett D. Preston, Jr., "The Development of Negro Education in

Senate District Committee, pointed out that black Washingtonians paid taxes worth by his estimate $36,000 a year to support public schools to which their children were denied access. Congressional Republicans believed this to be blatantly unjust, even if white Washingtonians did not. The remedying of so flagrant an injustice was clearly consistent with the broader Republican project of removing racial distinctions from the laws of the District. More specifically, the education of freed people was an obvious way of easing their transition to freedom. Despite all the efforts of benevolent associations, it was evident, as the American Missionary Association admitted, that they were "utterly inadequate to the task of caring for the thousands of children in this city." Finally, Republicans sought to apply in the District the educational philosophy of the northern states, which envisaged schools as agencies of social integration and improvement and therefore as worthy objects of public expenditure.[68]

Therefore, Congress at its first full session after the beginning of the war provided for the creation of public schools for African American children that would be financed by 10 percent of the taxes on black property, supplemented (as it would need to be) by philanthropic contributions and the provision of sites for school buildings on federal land. These schools would be administered by a federally appointed Board of Trustees of Colored Schools created under separate legislation in 1862. Thus, Congress declined to entrust management of the colored school system to the local authorities. The estimates of black tax revenues made by the city government, which, it turned out, did not keep separate records of black and white tax payments, were held to warrant so small a financial contribution, a mere $1,303 in the next three years in comparison to nearly $90,000 for the white schools, that only one schoolhouse was opened. This impelled Congress in 1864 to require instead a division of the school fund according to school-age population. The 1864 law was predicated on the assumption that education was a public responsibility and that, because African Americans constituted part of the public, the

the District of Columbia, 1800–1860," *Journal of Negro Education* 12 (1943): 189–98; M. B. Goodwin, "Schools and Education of Colored People in the District of Columbia," in U.S. Office of Education, *Special Report of the Commissioner of Education on the Condition and Improvement of Public Schools in the District of Columbia,* Ho. Exec. Doc. No. 315, 41.2 (June 13, 1871), Ser. 1427, 193–300.

[68] CG, 37.3, 1325–26; CG, 38.1, 2813–14; *National Intelligencer,* May 21, 1862; Williams, "Blueprint for Change," 375–76; Everly, "Freedman's Bureau," 67; Carolyn Collins, "Mayor Sayles J. Bowen and the Beginnings of Negro Education," *Records of the Columbia Historical Society* 42 (1956): 299–302.

city as a whole, rather than just its black residents, should be responsible for their children's education. However, as a result of ambiguities in the law and the continuing hostility of the city fathers to black education at public expense, the colored schools remained underfunded. In 1866, Congress went a step further and authorized the Board of Trustees of Colored Schools to sue the Corporation for the money that they were legally entitled to, as well as leasing former military barracks to the Board and appropriating $10,000 for school buildings. In 1867, a special census of the population of the District was ordered, which established that there were 8,401 black and 17,801 white children in the city (and 10,246 and 21,447, respectively, in the District), thereby providing firm evidence for the distribution of the school fund. Even then, bickering over the precise amount continued until all agencies of the city government were in Republican hands after the 1868 election.[69]

The city authorities during and immediately after the war, echoing the sentiment of most white Washingtonians, denied their responsibility to make proportionate provision for black children, in part at least out of prejudice. They found it difficult to regard African Americans as members of their community whose children they had a duty to educate.[70] Whereas he regarded the 1862 law as an "equitable provision," Mayor Wallach objected to the requirement laid down in 1864 that black schools should receive a proportionate share of all tax revenues, which would, he claimed, be double the whole amount of taxes paid by colored citizens. Although the city government was willing to do all that could justly be required of it, "it is reluctant to do so at so inordinate a cost to the white taxpayer." If Congress wished to inaugurate a policy of educating black

---

[69] CG, 37.2, 1544, 2020, 2037, 3117; CG, 39.1, 2719; CG, 39.2, App. 180; 40.1, 290; Wilson, *History of the Antislavery Measures*, 184–94; Ho. Misc. Doc. 48, 38.1, Ser. 1200; Daniel Breed et al. to Richard Wallach, November 29, 1864; Wallach to Breed et al., December 12, 1864, in *Journal of the 63rd Council*, 182–89; John Kimball to Charles H. Howard, January 19, 1867, U.S. Senate, Committee on the District of Columbia, SEN39A-E4, RG 42, NARA; Annual Report of Board of Trustees of Colored Schools, in *Chronicle*, November 8, 1867; *Evening Star*, July 19, 1866; Green, *Washington*, 280–83, 304–8; Bryan, *History of the National Capital*, 2:524–28; Elaine C. Everly, "The Freedmen's Bureau in the National Capital" (Ph.D. diss., George Washington University, 1972), 67–69; Allan John Johnston, "Surviving Freedom: The Black Community in Washington, D.C., 1860–1880" (Ph.D. diss., Duke University, 1980), 257–65; Carolyn Collins, "Mayor Sayles J. Bowen"; Williams, "Blueprint for Change," 375–77. For a discussion of the Washington Corporation and related aspects of civic government, see below, pp. 151ff.

[70] For example, the cantankerous William Owner objected to the demand that taxes that white citizens paid for their own schools should be given to those attended by blacks. Owner Diary, May 24, 1866.

children, it should provide the means. Conservatives in the city government repeatedly reminded Congress that a growing proportion of the black population consisted of recent migrants who had arrived as a result of federal military actions and whose welfare was properly a responsibility of the federal government. Wallach protested against "the injustice of being compelled to furnish the means for educating the thousands of contrabands forced upon them by the events of the rebellion." The city councils pointed out that about a third of the white population were also "birds of passage," attracted there for a few years by the prospect of federal employment, sending their children to the local schools, but not necessarily paying local taxes. They rightly complained that Congress, over the sixty years of its occupation of the District, had "never given a foot of public land or a dollar of money" for the support of the public schools, whereas during the same period, it had generously provided the states with large tracts of federal land for that purpose. Only the District of Columbia, with the added burden of housing the national capital, was denied this largesse. Thus, the city found it impossible to provide educational facilities for more than a fraction of the white school-age population, even without adding the "oppressive burden" of educating the black.[71]

Although racial prejudice partly accounts for the disinclination of white Conservatives to pay for the colored schools, their complaints about the financial burden on the city were well founded. During the 1870s, the Board of Trustees of Public Schools, most of the members of which were now Republicans, petitioned Congress repeatedly for pecuniary aid, citing, among other reasons, the special relationship that Congress bore toward the District and the interest that the whole nation should have in its institutions. "The schools of the capital should be models of excellence in every respect," the board declared in 1874. They referred again and again to the large number of refugees brought there by the accidents of war and government officials residing there temporarily, neither of which group paid much in the way of taxes, and to the failure of the federal government, which owned roughly half the real estate in the District, to make any financial contribution. They noted again the liberality shown

[71] *Journal of the 64th Council* (Washington, DC, 1867), 442–43; *Journal of the 65th Council* (Washington, DC, 1867), 30; Richard Wallach to James R. Harlan, secretary of the interior, in *Chronicle*, December 14, 1865; Board of Trustees of Public Schools, *Annual Report*, 1867, 13–20; *Evening Star*, January 29, 1867; Green, *Washington*, 281–83, 304–7.

to the states and territories. The District's schools, public and private, were able to accommodate no more than 18,672 of 33,115 school-age children.[72] Through the 1870s, the Trustees of Public Schools reiterated the case for congressional assistance, repeatedly reminding Congress of the sorry state of the public schools. So did the U.S. Commissioner of Education and later the District commissioners.[73]

Yet Congress consistently declined to make appropriations for local schools up until after the collapse of the territory. Democratic Congressmen in particular, but also many Republicans, demanded that the school authorities tailor their expenditures to the funds at their disposal and insisted that their constituents should not be asked to pay for the education of children in the District. "It seems to be very essential," observed Senator John James Ingalls of Kansas in 1878, "whenever any appropriation is asked for the District that every conceivable obstacle should be thrown in the way of it . . . the moment an appropriation is asked for the District of Columbia for carrying on the public schools every technicality is to be resorted to defeat it." Apart from occasional minor appropriations and loans to allow for the payment of arrears in teachers' salaries, this pattern of indifference and neglect continued until the financial relations between the U.S. government and the District of Columbia were regularized in 1878.[74]

### The Troublesome Question of Mixed Schools

The school system set up for African American children during and after the Civil War was, of course, a segregated one, and most white and some black residents wished to keep it that way. There was a certain amount of pride in the colored school system within the black community and a

---

[72] A. Hyde *et al.* to Senate Committee on the District of Columbia, January 19, 1870, SEN41A-S.2, RG42, NARA; Report of Board of Trustees of Public Schools, 1874 (p. 106), and 1875 (pp. 16–18). See also report of Board of Trustees of Colored Schools, in *Chronicle*, November 8, 1867; *Journal of 68th Council* (Washington, 1870), 304–9; *Evening Star*, January 15, February 24, November 13, 1870.

[73] Report of Commissioner of Education, in *Report of the Secretary of the Interior*, 1873, Serial 1602; *Report of the Commissioners of the District of Columbia*, 1874 (Washington, DC, 1875), 106; *Report of the Commissioners, 1875* (Washington, DC, 1876), 12; Commissioners of the District of Columbia to the House Committee on the District of Columbia, January 18, 1878, HR45A-D1, RG292, NARA; Green, *Washington*, 369–71.

[74] *CR*, 45.2:2452–57. See also *CR*, 43.1:2324, 2330–37, 2343–46; *CR*, 45.2:2849–50, 2852–58.

fear that more would be lost than gained by sacrificing its integrity to the principle of integration.[75] Nevertheless, the case for amalgamation was compelling. For all their pedagogical achievements, the colored schools undoubtedly enjoyed inferior facilities, less favorable pupil-teacher ratios, and lower rates of teachers' pay. Moreover, the very fact of separation was inconsistent with the equal rights principles embodied in the Reconstruction amendments. It could only be supported, it was argued, on the basis of the "principle of caste" embodied in slavery and was therefore fundamentally "anti-republican." The common school was meant to be both the nurturing ground and symbolic expression of a community of equal citizens; the segregation of African American children signified their exclusion from that community. Separate schooling, claimed the National Executive of the Colored People in 1870, reinforced racial distinctions and ensured their perpetuation in later generations. Proscription on the basis of color "wars with the spirit of our government" and was especially inappropriate in the capital, which should set an example to the states. Thus, a majority of the Board of Trustees of Colored Schools and many prominent black civic leaders, as well as the editors of the *New National Era*, came out in favor of integration, and the issue became something of a test of ideological purity among local black Republicans.[76]

Most Republicans in Congress would have preferred to avoid the issue altogether, trapped as they were between the prejudices of their white constituents and the insistence of their black allies. The main driving force behind the movement for school integration in Congress was Charles Sumner. To Sumner the case for school integration was incontrovertible and irresistible. It was based on the same principle as, and was therefore a logical extension of, earlier reforms; it was a stage in the progression toward equal rights that included emancipation, access to public facilities,

---

[75] For black opposition to mixed schools, see *New National Era*, February 22, 1872, June 5, July 31, October 9, 1873; *Evening Star*, August 7, 1873.

[76] *Petition of the National Executive of the Colored People*, Sen. Misc. Doc. 130, 41.2 (April 29, 1870), Ser. 1408; *Report of the Board of Trustees of Colored Schools*, Sen. Misc. Doc. 20, 41.3 (January 19, 1871), Ser. 1440; Frederick Douglass, "Schools Are a Common Platform of Nationality: An Address Delivered in Washington, D.C., on 9 May 1872," in John W. Blassingame and John R. McKivigan, eds., *The Frederick Douglass Papers. Series One: Speeches, Debates and Interviews. Volume 4: 1864–80* (New Haven, CT: Yale University Press, 1991), 300–2; *New National Era*, January 27, May 5, 1870, November 30, 1871, May 9, 16, 1872; *Chronicle*, January 8, 1870, April 25, 1874; *Evening Star*, January 12, February 17, 1871. See also Horton, "Development of Federal Social Policy," 127–34; Masur, "Reconstructing the Nation's Capital," 260–9; Johnson, "City on a Hill," 115–22, 228–34; Whyte, *Uncivil War*, 99–100.

jury service, and the right to vote and hold office. Separation was a "mark of exclusion," a "badge of inferiority," and therefore contrary to the basic principles of American government enunciated in the Declaration of Independence. It confirmed racial prejudice. After all, "the child is more impressionable than the man." How, other than by common education, could one "train the child in the way he should go"?[77] Therefore, Sumner introduced a school integration bill for the District in 1870 and every year thereafter until his death in 1874.

To Sumner, if integration was "correct in principle" it was also "correct in practice." Other Republicans were less convinced. They toyed with various expedients, including in 1869 an attempt to finesse the issue by integrating the white and black school boards but not the schools. To most black citizens, this represented the worst of both worlds – losing control over their own schools without removing racial barriers within the schools themselves. They were driven to the unwelcome recourse of petitioning President Johnson to veto the bill, which, gratified at the discomfiture of his Republican adversaries, he gladly did.[78] Two years later the chairman of the Senate Committee on the District of Columbia, James W. Patterson of New Hampshire, reported in place of Sumner's bill a proposal to combine the boards of trustees, leaving to the merged board the decision on whether to organize separate or mixed schools. Compulsory integration would, he believed, set back the development of the schools. Prejudice might be "transitory," but it was real enough and had to be recognized in legislation. So should the fact that black and white children started their education from different points and had different educational needs. It was necessary to provide the best education for all, "to lift them up, if possible, to the same level of intelligence and morality," so that prejudice would in time pass away. Only after the educational system had had an opportunity to work its magic would true integration be possible.[79]

---

[77] Letter to *New National Era*, August 7, 1873; *CG*, 41.3:1055–56; Donald, *Charles Sumner*, 422–24, 531–39, 545; Kirt H. Wilson, *The Reconstruction Desegregation Debate: The Politics of Equality and the Rhetoric of Place, 1870–1875* (East Lansing, Mich.: Michigan State University Press, 2002), 47–75.

[78] *CG*, 40.3:919, 1164; *Evening Star*, July 11, 17, 1868, February 10, 16, 1869; *National Intelligencer*, July 13, 1868; *Chronicle*, February 15–18, 1869; Johnson, "City on a Hill," 115–18; Horton, "Development of Federal Social Policy," 127–30. For Johnson's veto message, see Richardson, ed., *Messages and Papers*, 6:705.

[79] *CG*, 41.3:1053–54, 1056–57. See also *New National Era*, March 9, 1871; *Evening Star*, January 17, 23, February 4, 1871; *Chronicle*, February 6, 7, 9, 1871.

Sumner protested against such a dilution of the principle of equal rights. So did his colleague Henry Wilson. Children should not be segregated "to gratify the pride of the race that assumes to be the dominant, the superior race"; the rights of the black man should not be "subordinated to the prejudices of the white man." He believed, like Sumner, that in time "the people will be educated to the high plane of republican and Christian principle, so that they will look down on no class of their fellow-men because of race or color." The South Carolina Republican Frederick A. Sawyer warned that any equivocation on the issue would send a message to the states that the Senate was not committed to equal rights in the public schools: "It will be taken as a renunciation on the part of the Senate of their faith in the universal application of the doctrine of the equality of all men before the law." Patterson's amendment would mean "reversing the action which has been the chief glory of the Republican party." It would constitute "a betrayal of trust, a gross sacrifice of principle, an unnecessary and impolitic concession to a prejudice" originating in slavery.[80] The schools bill was shortly superseded by other legislation and was not brought up again. Meanwhile, a parallel proposal in the House was stripped in committee of all reference to racial integration.[81]

In April 1872, Sumner attempted once more to secure action on his bill. Referring colleagues to the many petitions and reports emanating from the Board of Trustees of Colored Schools, he kept his own words to a minimum. The Democratic senator Thomas F. Bayard saw the scheme as "fraught with evil to both races." Educational provision for black children in the district was, he believed, quite adequate – indeed, superior to that enjoyed by children of both races across much of the country. Integration would be "a mere act of visionary zeal" the real aim of which was not to improve education but "to break down the barriers of races," an amalgamation that Bayard believed to be "forbidden by natural law." Such a proposition had not gained favor anywhere in the United States where the people governed themselves, and it would not be adopted in the District by a popular vote. The New Jersey Democrat John P. Stockton, who generally adopted a more moderate position than Bayard on questions of race, claimed to be willing for African Americans to enjoy equal rights, "but that does not make it necessary that we shall insist upon violating the rights of white people, and force both races into the same

[80] CG, 41.3:1055–56, 1061, 1058–59.
[81] CG, 41.3:1365–66.

schools." Why should Congress "seek to overcome a natural prejudice"? Whether right or wrong, "it is not the province of the law to run counter to it in this manner." When Congress interfered with citizens' right to choose a school for their children, it was infringing on their civil liberty. Education involved matters close to everyday life, the Democratic senators argued. In proposing the integration the schools, Republicans were seeking to achieve a "social equality" and break down the boundaries of race in areas of purely private rather than public concern. Beyond that lay the prospect, rarely explicit but often implicit, of amalgamation of the races – of enforced intimacy leading to miscegenation and the breaking down of racial distinctions.[82] Radical Republicans, in contrast, regarded education as essentially a public responsibility and denied that it impinged on the private realm. "I aver, sir," said the black senator from Mississippi Hiram Revels in the debate of the previous year, "that mixed schools are very far from bringing about social equality." The response of some of his more hesitant Republican colleagues suggests that they were some way from sharing his opinion.[83]

No Republican spoke against the bill. Instead, every time the bill came up, leading Republican senators moved to proceed to other business, including a deficiency appropriation bill, a bill creating courts in the Indian Territory, and a report from the Finance Committee. Lyman Trumbull complained that "urgent public business" was postponed "morning after morning" by an effort to integrate the District's schools, while Simon Cameron described it as "a hindrance to other business." Although some of these individuals claimed to support the bill, it is evident that they did not regard it as important. The procedural wrangling was terminated on May 7, when the morning hour came to an end and the Post Office appropriation bill was in order. Sumner's motion to table the appropriation bill so that an agreement could be made on the disposition of the mixed schools bill was defeated by a substantial margin, with a majority of Republicans and all Democrats voting to proceed with the regular order. Although most Republicans had voted to prevent the schools bill from being pushed out of its place in the regular order of business, they were not prepared to give it preferential treatment. Whereas 29 Republicans had voted against a motion to table the bill, only 19 would support Sumner's motion to continue with its consideration after the end of the

---

[82] *CG*, 42.2:2539–40, App. 352–57. See also the remarks of Senator Allen G. Thurman in *CG*, 41.3:1057–58; Wilson, *Reconstruction Desegregation Debate*, 112–16.

[83] *CG*, 41.3:1060. See also Wilson, *Reconstruction Desegregation Debate*, 135–8.

morning hour. These 19 included radicals such as Sumner, Wilson, and Pomeroy and a sizable number of representatives of the reconstructed states. Twenty-one Republicans voted against the motion, as did all the Democrats present. The defeat of Sumner's motion effectively killed the prospects of the bill.[84]

The issue of school integration probed the limits of the Republican commitment to equal rights. Although congressional Republicans showed a creditable willingness to remove racial discrimination in the public sphere, they tended to shy away from any suggestion of "social equality." Moderate Republicans agreed with Democrats that the races were naturally separate in abilities and inclinations and that "promiscuous" racial mixing was undesirable. They differed mainly in where they placed the boundary between public and private interaction. Thus, most Republicans would accept integration in transport and other public facilities but were ambivalent about asking their children to share their schoolrooms with children of another race. Further, they showed a growing disinclination to intervene in private decisions about education or employment.[85]

## A Partial Reconstruction

During the years immediately following the end of the Civil War, several attempts were made to remove elements of racial discrimination from the city charter, allowing African Americans to perform jury service and stand for election as well as to vote. After legislation to that effect had twice been stalled by Johnson's pocket veto, the charter was finally amended in March 1869 to remove all reference to race and color. Thus, African Americans were admitted to the jury room and made eligible for elective office, by which time black representatives had already taken seats on the Washington City Councils.[86] But congressional Republicans showed

---

[84] *CG*, 42.2:2541, 3056–57, 3100, 3123, 3125. Of the Republicans identified by Benedict as radicals during the second session of the Fortieth Congress who voted on Sumner's motion to table the Post Office appropriation bill, 12 voted for the motion, 1 against; conservative Republicans voted 2–6 against the motion. For listings of radicals and conservatives, see Benedict, *Compromise of Principle*, 373–77. Of Republicans representing the southern states, 8 voted for, 5 against the motion.

[85] See also Masur, "Reconstruction in the Nation's Capital," 233–34, 270–73.

[86] *CG*, 40.1:677, 725–26; *CG*, 40.2:38–40, 49–51, 96, 2260–62; *CG*, 40.3:1080, 1825–26; *CG*, 41.1:30, 79; Petition of Citizens of the District of Columbia, January 16, 1866, SEN39A-H4 DC; Petition of the Republican Citizens of the 4th Ward of Washington, D.C., July 16, 1867, SEN40A-H5.1 DC, RG46, NARA; *Evening Star*, December 6, 8, 1865, February 12, 1869; *National Intelligencer*, July 20, December 10, 17, 20, 1867;

little inclination to police discrimination in the private sector, leaving it to the Councils and later the territorial legislature to pass wide-ranging, but weakly enforced, civil rights legislation. The national Civil Rights Act, passed in 1875, appears to have had little impact on race relations in the District.[87]

Nor did Congress take action to prevent trade unions and professional associations from discriminating on the grounds of race.[88] For example, the Medical Society of the District of Columbia refused to admit nonwhite physicians. In 1869, the society had refused, by a 26–10 vote, to receive a resolution offered by Dr. Robert Reyburn, a former official of the Freedmen's Bureau, that no member should be excluded on the grounds of race. In consequence, a number of black physicians, along with some sympathetic white colleagues, asked Congress to repeal the federal charter held by the old society and establish a new one which would be open to all. "A great principle is at stake," Dr. Joseph T. Johnson told Sumner.[89] In response, Sumner introduced a resolution directing the Senate District Committee to consider the expediency of repealing the charter of the Medical Society and considering whatever other legislation might be necessary "to secure for medical practitioners in the District of Columbia equal rights and opportunities, without distinction of color." Nothing having emanated from the District Committee, in March of the following year, he asked for consideration of a bill repealing the charter, arguing that "the principle of proscription and caste" that had been driven away from the ballot box and from public conveyances should also be expunged from the medical fraternity. Because it was evident from the comments of Democratic senators that they wished to debate the bill and in view of the pressure of pending business, his Republican colleagues

---

Johnson, "City on a Hill," 63–64, 98–99; Ingle, *Negro in the District of Columbia,* 38–39, 67.

[87] Whyte, *Uncivil War,* 247–48. On local civil right laws, see ibid., 73–75, 243–47; Green, *Washington,* 321–22, 371–72; Ingle, *Negro in the District of Columbia,* 40–42; Johnson, "City on a Hill," 105–8, 215–28.

[88] On patterns of discrimination, see Johnson, "City on a Hill," 128–47, 159–66, 215–25; Horton, "Development of Federal Social Policy," 188–93.

[89] For the case for federal intervention, see Memorial of National Medical Society to the House and Senate of the United States, January 20, 1870; Medical Society of the District of Columbia, An Appeal to Congress; A.W. Tucker to Charles Sumner, 15 January 1870; C. Adams Gray to Sumner, 5 February 1870; Robert Reyburn to Sumner, January 17, 1870, SEN41A-S.2 DC, RG42, NARA; Alexander T. Augusta to Sumner, 16 January 1870; Joseph T. Johnson to Sumner, n.d., Senate Committee on the District of Columbia, SEN41A-S.2, RG42, NARA. See also *Evening Star,* January 5, 13, June 17, 18, 1870; *New National Era,* January 27, March 17, 1870; Johnson, "City on a Hill," 128–34.

showed little enthusiasm for taking it up. Although those who might be identified as radical Republicans were more likely than conservatives to vote for the motion, the association was not strong. Although none of his fellow Republicans spoke against his proposal, they showed a marked disinclination to set other, apparently more pressing, business to one side to consider it. Sumner's motion therefore went down on a 21–26 vote, with 21 Republicans voting for the motion and 15 against.[90]

Still more pronounced was the failure to provide the freedpeople with more than rudimentary economic assistance. The authors of Reconstruction have been criticized – for example, by Allan Johnston – for their failure to see the need for an economic revolution to back up the revolution in social relations that they were seeking to bring about and to realize that self-reliance required a firm economic base.[91] Certainly Congress provided temporary relief for a few years after the Civil War. In 1866, Lot Morrill, chairman of the Senate Committee on the District of Columbia, told his colleagues in the Senate that between ten thousand and fifteen thousand freed people from the neighboring states were "existing here in a state of almost utter destitution, inconceivable suffering, and want." Their colonies were "literally breeding disease and death." They constituted, said Willey, a danger to the whole city: "these dens of poor creatures will be the very fountain-heads and seat of contagious pestilence and death." The city authorities did not feel bound to provide for poor blacks, unless they could prove long-term residency, which meant that they, much more than poor whites, were dependent on federal alms. Congress moved rapidly to appropriate $25,000, to be distributed by the Freedmen's Bureau, although the bill was amended to make the relief available to white, as well as black, applicants.[92]

A repeat appropriation during the following session was stalled by an argument over whether the funds should be restricted to black, or made available to black and white, paupers and whether its administration should be entrusted to the municipal authorities or the Freedmen's Bureau. However, the first session of the Fortieth Congress, which met a few weeks later, made up for the omission by appropriating $15,000 for

[90] Resolution introduced by Senator Charles Sumner, December 9, 1869, Senate Committee on the District of Columbia, SEN41A-S.2 DC, RG42, NARA; CG, 41.2:1677–78, 2905, 4307.

[91] Allan John Johnston, *Surviving Freedom: The Black Community of Washington, D.C., 1860–1880* (New York: Garland, 1993).

[92] CG, 39.1:1507–9, 1742–43, 1921.

destitute African Americans.[93] The following year, the emphasis was on providing work for jobless laborers. An appropriation of $15,000 was to be expended on public works to be administered by the Commissioner of Public Buildings and Grounds employing laborers who would be selected by the Freedmen's Bureau and the local Provident Aid Society.[94] In 1869, facing further evidence of "great destitution and suffering in the District," Congress rushed through another relief appropriation, to be administered this time by the mayors of Washington and Georgetown and the president of the Levy Court, all of whom were now reliably Republican.[95]

In 1870, the Senate passed a further relief bill, this time for $30,000 to be allocated by the mayors and Commissioner Otis O. Howard through the agency of the Association for the Improvement of the Condition of the Poor (AICP), the National Freedmen's Relief Association of the District of Columbia, and the Industrial Home School. Burton Cook Jr., the chairman of the House District Committee read a letter from the AICP reporting that its own resources, which had supported approximately 2,000 families wholly or in part, were now exhausted and that there was no alternative recourse. However, Democratic congressmen and some Midwestern Republicans objected strongly to their constituents being taxed to support of the poor of the District and warned that excessive generosity would attract black workers from the fields and plantations of surrounding states to lounge around the capital waiting for handouts, occasional government employment, and, perhaps, the opportunity to vote the Republican ticket in the next municipal election. Proctor Knott of Kentucky claimed that "able and stalwart men" reclined though the summer in Judiciary Square "like black snakes in a briar patch" while fields all round the city "were not plowed for want of laborers." Yet "the indolent vagabonds and lazzaroni of this District are to be nourished and sustained in their idleness, and fed and clothed at the public expense because they can find nothing to do. . . . They are here fattening like vampires upon the blood of the people." George W. Morgan protested at what he saw as an attempt to tax the people of Ohio and

---

93  CG, 39.2:1241–42, 1765–66; CG, 40.1:28, 75–6.

94  CG, 40.2:678, 1421; CG, 41.2:980–89, 3920–21; *Evening Star*, January 20, February 26, 1868, January 31, 1870. See also Peter Parker et al. to Senate Committee on the District of Columbia, January 16, 1868; petition of the National Freedmen's Relief Association of the District of Columbia, January 9, 1868, SEN40A-E4, RG46, NARA; *Chronicle*, January 15, 1868.

95  CG, 40.3:100, 181, 775–76; petition of the Provident Aid Society, January 22, 1869, SEN40A-H5.1, RG46, NARA; *Chronicle*, January 23, 29, 1869.

other states "to support in idleness hordes of negroes who are kept here as voters and maintained as paupers, in order to aid in keeping the Republican party in power." Republican members of the District committee managed to persuade the House that Washington's was a special problem, the result of congressional policies as well as the city's narrow tax-base, that worn-out former slaves were a special case, and that Congress could not allow people to suffer "under the very eaves of our Capitol," and the relief bill, although heavily amended, was passed. However, Sumner's attempt to secure an additional $10,000 a few months later when the initial appropriation was exhausted met with a stony reception.[96]

For the next few years, Congress left the provision of relief to the municipal authorities. However, in 1875 what the Citizens' Relief Association called the "appalling destitution now prevalent in the District" persuaded James A. Garfield to offer an amendment to the Sundry Civil bill adding an appropriation of $10,000 for emergency relief. Similar appropriations were made in later years, despite repeated objections that relief payments attracted a population of paupers and vagrants. Just as other municipalities were compelled to aid the suffering poor, victims of the depression in business and employment, argued Congressman Nathaniel Banks, so was Congress, "acting as a municipal legislature," obliged to offer relief.[97]

The agency chiefly responsible for providing economic assistance to freed people was, of course, the Freedmen's Bureau, which distributed temporary relief, provided information about employment opportunities, transported as many unemployed freedpeople out of the District as could be persuaded to go, and furnished accommodation, either in rented tenements in Washington itself or on government farms outside the city boundaries. However, the bureau was never intended to be anything but a temporary agency, and its existence was terminated in 1868, even though in Washington, as elsewhere, the social and economic problems associated with the adjustment to freedom were far from solved. Although inadequate in scope or duration, the work of the bureau demonstrated what kind of government assistance was required to alleviate at least some of the problems of destitute African Americans.

---

[96] CG, 41.2:840, 849, 980–89, 1045–46, 3920–21; petition of AICP, January 8, 1870, Senate Committee on the District of Columbia, SEN41A-H5.2, RG46 NARA; *Evening Star*, January 31, 1870.

[97] CR, 43.2:2005; CR, 44.2:1059, 1088–91, 1109–10, 1186.

"The great want is work," declared one black Republican activist, but Congress itself felt little responsibility to provide for unemployed African Americans, beyond scattered appropriations for public works projects.[98] Successive U.S. Commissioners of Buildings and Grounds were not notably sympathetic to African American demands for equal access to work on federal projects.[99] Thus, it was left to local government to provide employment for the still considerable number of jobless black workers. The Republican mayor Sayles J. Bowen, in his efforts to find work for his supporters, carried municipal finances heavily into debt. The still more ambitious projects carried out by the Board of Public Works under the territorial government led to a quadrupling of the city labor force, and, as under Bowen's regime, a considerable proportion of those hired were black.[100]

By the early 1870s, the commitment of congressional Republicans to their local Reconstruction project was wavering. Bowen's administration, elected in June 1868 and ingloriously ousted in June 1870, proved a severe disappointment. The city's continuing financial and administrative problems led Congress in 1871 to introduce a form of territorial government for the District. The new government initiated an audacious and grandiose program of improvements that went far beyond any expenditure anticipated by Congress and quadrupled the indebtedness inherited from the old regime. Mounting protests from taxpayers and property holders, charges of corruption, which were largely not substantiated, and of mismanagement, which largely were, along with the unmanageable level of debt, led Congress to wind up the territorial government in June 1874 and replace it with a presidentially appointed commission. In 1878, direct federal control of the District was made permanent, lasting, indeed, until the restoration of home rule nearly a hundred years later.[101]

In consenting to the termination of representative government in the District of Columbia, Congress brought to an end its short-lived experiment in biracial democracy. This followed in part from a growing acknowledgment in the halls of Congress that the creation of a capital city worthy of a great republic would require a substantial injection of federal money and that if the federal government were to undertake

---

[98] *Evening Star*, November 5, 1868; *Petition of Citizens of Washington*, Sen. Misc. Doc. No. 153, 41.2 (June 14, 1870), Ser. 1408.

[99] For complaints, see *Evening Star*, January 17, March 8, 1868.

[100] *Evening Star*, April 8, 1869, April 15, May 7, 14, 1870; Bryan, *History of the National Capital*, 2: 565–67, 588, 596–97. On Bowen's program, see Chapter 5.

[101] For an account of the rise and fall of the territorial government, see Chapter 8.

financial obligations on such a scale, it must also assume greater control of the way in which the money was spent. However, it was also felt that the Reconstruction project for which the District had served as a testing ground had moved beyond its experimental phase. Black suffrage in the District was no longer necessary as a model for the southern states, argued Senator William M. Stewart of Nevada in 1871, now that it had been written into the Constitution in the shape of the Fifteenth Amendment. Three years later, in contemplating the end of home rule, Republicans found it wiser to dissociate government in Washington altogether from the broader project, and in so doing, they denied much of the rationale for their earlier endeavors.[102]

In November 1866, the *Chronicle*, which had become the primary spokesman for radical Republicanism in the District, expressed the hope that "the capital of the great Republic shall be as free from political prejudices and class legislation as it is from human slavery." This was the place for Congress to try the "experiment" of creating a society based on the principle of equal rights and fulfill the obligations that had been assumed in emancipating the slaves.[103] Congress's exclusive control over the District gave Republican lawmakers the opportunity to carry out their ideals more rapidly and more completely than anywhere else. The determination, and in matters of essence the unity, with which they not only eliminated slavery but also removed racial distinctions from local charters and ordinances, enfranchised African Americans, barred discrimination in public places, and compelled the municipality to provide schools for children of both races is a measure of their radicalism. Although falling short of modern standards of racial justice, the Republican Party's commitment to the principle of equality before the law as the basis for incorporating freed African Americans into U.S. society constituted a massive advance on the *status quo ante bellum*. For that reason, we would be justified in describing the Republican Party of the war and immediate postwar years as a radical party.[104]

---

[102] *Evening Star*, January 25, 1871; Gillette, *Between Justice and Beauty*, 58–72.

[103] *Chronicle*, November 10, December 13, 1866.

[104] Cf. Belz, *New Birth of Freedom*; Eric Foner, "The Ideology of the Republican Party," in Engs and Miller, *Birth of the Grand Old Party*, 8–28; Foner, *Reconstruction*; Peyton McCrary, "The Party of Revolution: Republican Ideas about Politics and Social Change, 1862–1877," *Civil War History* 30 (1984): 330–50; James M. McPherson, *Abraham Lincoln and the Second American Revolution* (New York: Oxford University Press, 1991); Robert J. Kaczorowski, "To Begin the Nation Anew: Congress, Citizenship, and Equal Rights after the Civil War, *American Historical Review* 92 (February 1987): 45–68.

If so, it did not remain a radical party for long. If the beginning of Reconstruction came early to the District, so did its demise. After a few years, Republicans turned to other matters, and it became almost impossible for the few congressional friends of black Washingtonians to gain their colleagues' attention. On the rare occasions when they did attend to District affairs, congressmen showed more concern for the physical refurbishment of the city than the attainment of social justice or racial adjustment, more interest in creating a monumental capital for an expanding and reunited nation than a "paradise for free negroes," and they designed new frameworks of government for the District with that in view. As more generally, the Republican commitment to equal rights, although never entirely abandoned, was pushed aside by other priorities. In the District of Columbia, then, the events of Reconstruction were played out in accelerated time and in sharper outline than in the states of the former Confederacy, but with a similar outcome.

# 5

# Reconstructing the City Government

## Introduction

During the debate on black suffrage in the District of Columbia, a number of congressmen expressed the opinion, widespread among Republicans, that the government of the capital left a lot to be desired. "Is there a worse-governed city in all the Republic?" asked Representative James F. Wilson. Its manifest defects – the shabby condition of its streets, the feeble quality of its street lighting, the insufficiency of its water supply, the inadequacy of its sewers, the unwholesome state of the Washington City Canal, the lack of dedicated school buildings, and the paucity of railroad communications – could all be laid at the door of an unreconstructed city government, steeped in its lazy, unambitious, and quintessentially southern habits. What was needed was a burst of Yankee energy to haul the city out of its slough of complacency, its hopeless inertia, and the only way to achieve that was to install a Republican government that would not only protect the rights of all its citizens but also impart a new vigor to municipal affairs. "There is no remedy for the complaints and needs of the District at once so simple and so just as impartial suffrage," pronounced the *Daily Morning Chronicle* in July 1866.[1] Although the primary purpose of congressional Republicans in introducing black suffrage in the District of Columbia was to lay down a marker for their broader Reconstruction project, they were not unaware of the positive benefits that would flow from the reformation of local government in the nation's capital. During the late 1860s, congressional Republicans and

---

[1] CG, 39.1:174; *Washington Daily Morning Chronicle*, July 4, 1866.

their local allies acted to bring about such a reformation, although, as we shall see, with uneven results. Only after the apparent failure of that reconstruction project did they begin to look for other solutions to the problem of governing the capital.

As in the states of the former Confederacy, congressional leaders saw the local Republican Party as their main agent in reconstructing the District of Columbia, and they intervened on several occasions to ease its path. They anticipated that the installation of a Republican administration in City Hall, made possible by the newly enfranchised black vote, would inaugurate a system of efficient government and material improvement that would elevate Washington from its dusty dilapidation to a condition worthy of a modern capital city. As in the states of the former Confederacy, the new Republican regime faced serious problems of legitimacy, fell prey to internal divisions, and, perhaps most importantly, lacked the resources to bring its program to fruition. Its failures owed much to internal difficulties but much also, in the end, to the lack of federal support, particularly federal financial support.

## The Mayoralty of Richard Wallach: Washington's Ancien Régime

Washington had been governed since 1802 by a corporation consisting of a mayor and two boards of Aldermen and Common Council. The city was divided into seven wards, which were the centers of grassroots political activity. Several of the wards represented distinct neighborhoods with a strong sense of their own identity, such as the older residential district north of Pennsylvania Avenue (the "Old Fourth" Ward), Capitol Hill (Fifth Ward), or the area between the Potomac River and the Washington City Canal, commonly known as the "Island" (Seventh Ward). Washington shared with other cities a rambunctious political culture, especially at ward level, and a largely amateurish management of affairs.[2] It suffered

---

[2] For a description of local government in 1865, see James H. Whyte, *The Uncivil War: Washington during the Reconstruction* (New York: Twayne, 1958), 17–21. On government and politics in other cities during the antebellum period, see Amy Bridges, *A City in the Republic: Antebellum New York and the Origins of Machine Politics* (New York: Cambridge University Press, 1984); Leo Hershkowitz, *Boss Tweed's New York: Another Look* (Garden City, NY: Anchor Books, 1978), 3–75; Stephen Erie, *Rainbow's End: Irish-Americans and the Dilemmas of Machine Politics, 1840–1985* (Ithaca, NY: Cornell University Press, 1988), chap. 2; Michael H. Frisch, *Town into City: Springfield, Massachusetts, and the Meaning of Community, 1840–1880* (Cambridge, MA: Harvard University Press, 1972), chap. 2; Robin Einhorn, *Property Rules: Political Economy in Chicago, 1833–1872* (Chicago: University of Chicago Press, 1991).

from an unusually restricted tax base because the federal government, although owning roughly half the real estate in the city, paid no tax on its property and contributed only intermittently to the costs of municipal government. As a result, as a succession of visitors to Washington observed, the streets were largely unpaved, public services inadequate, and the founders' plans for an imposing capitol a long way from fulfillment. "It was called a city through courtesy," recalled a northern journalist, "because in reality it was a struggling awkward village."[3]

Washington's chief executive during the war and immediate postwar years was Richard Wallach, a lawyer who had served as marshal of the District of Columbia before winning election to the Board of Aldermen. When the incumbent mayor, James Berret, refused to take a loyalty oath in August 1861, arguing in vain that a municipal officer elected by popular vote was not covered by a law designed to test the fealty of federal employees, Wallach, who had been narrowly, and acrimoniously, defeated by Berret in the municipal election of the previous summer, was selected by the Board of Aldermen to take his place. Wallach, unlike Berret, was prepared to take the oath of loyalty. A staunch Unionist, he gladly supported the federal war effort, although not federal emancipation policies. He had an imposing personal presence and maintained close connections with the local business community – his brother was editor of the *Washington Evening Star* – but did not provide strong leadership. According to local historian Wilhelmus Bryan, "Mayor Wallach was popular, had a pleasing personality and was a man of standing in the community. His administration was dignified and respectable, but lacked force and initiative." Wallach won reelection three times, in 1862, 1864, and 1866, in each case by a substantial margin but chose not to stand again in 1868, by which time both the electorate and the political situation had been radically transformed.[4]

In contrast, with the intense political conflicts of the previous decade, when Know Nothings and their Democratic opponents exchanged insults, and frequently blows, there were no clear or consistent party divisions

[3] Emily Edson Briggs, *The Olivia Letters* (Washington, DC: Neale, 1906), 315/19. See also Mary C. Ames, *Ten Years in Washington: Life and Scenes in the National Capital, as a Woman Sees Them* (Hartford, CT: A. D. Worthington, 1875); Mark Twain and Charles Dudley Warner, *The Gilded Age* (New York: Doubleday, 1964 [1874]), 263–69.

[4] Wilhelmus B. Bryan, *A History of the National Capital* (2 vols., New York: Macmillan, 1914–16), 2:554; Green, *Washington*, 230, 248–50, 312; Whyte, *Uncivil War*, 19–20; Allen C. Clark, "Richard Wallach and the Time of His Mayoralty," *Records of the Columbia Historical Society*, 21 (1918), 195–245.

in municipal politics during the early and mid-1860s.[5] Although a Whig in his political antecedents, Wallach had run in 1860 as an independent. With many pro-Confederate citizens having departed for the South, and with the Republican Party being mostly confined to a corporal's guard of former antislavery men and federal officeholders from the North (and, of course, to African American residents who could not vote), the majority of politically active individuals characterized themselves as Unionists of one kind or another. In 1862, Wallach ran for reelection as an Unconditional Unionist. His opponents described themselves as "Union Democrats and Union Whigs and other Union voters . . . who adhere to the principles of the Constitution and the Union," although they were most commonly described as Union Democrats. The Union Democrats of the Fourth Ward condemned the abolitionists and "their efforts to elevate the negro by force of legislation," which would encourage "an indolent and worthless population from the adjoining slaveholding States" to take up residence in the city. Their nominating convention passed resolutions condemning the Unconditional Unionists, by virtue of their cooperation with the national administration and their readiness to "place the children of negroes on a footing of equality with the whites" by establishing colored schools, as "willing auxiliaries to the peculiar workings of abolition." According to one speaker, "the issues of the present contests were the peace, prosperity and dignity of the white men."[6]

The *Chronicle*, whose proprietor was the now staunchly Republican John W. Forney, believed that there were "no differences of political sentiment" between the candidates in the mayoral election; "the question was one of personal character and preference." Certainly both sides claimed to be loyal Unionists; Wallach was hardly more prepared than his opponent to see African Americans placed on terms of equality with whites or to provide equal funding for black schools. Nonetheless, he was willing to make some gestures toward black schooling by applying the miniscule tax revenue attributed to African Americans to educate their children, so as "to make them useful and prevent them from becoming common thieves and pilferers," as one of his supporters explained. The Unconditional Unionists acquiesced in the administration's moderate program of emancipation and education, as they interpreted it, whereas the Union Democrats still raged against the new directions in government policy.

[5] On the Know Nothing riots, see Constance M. Green, *Washington: Village and Capital, 1800–1878* (Princeton, NJ: Princeton University Press, 1962), 215–16.

[6] *Washington Evening Star*, May 5, 16, 22, 1862.

Although the Union Democrats, as their title suggests, were mostly former Democrats, many Democratic ward meetings endorsed Wallach, as did some Republicans. The overwhelming majority by which Wallach won reelection, 2,898 votes to 952, indicates the nonpartisan support his campaign received.[7]

Two years later, Wallach defeated John H. Semmes, again by a sizable majority, the contestant winning a majority only in the ward where he resided, the Seventh. The candidates in this election did not bear party labels.[8] In 1866, Wallach having endorsed the Reconstruction policies of President Andrew Johnson, the local Democratic Association declined to make a nomination against him. Again, the candidates wore no party labels, either in the mayoral or council elections, although Wallace's opponent, Horatio N. Easby, claimed to speak for the interests of the city's workers. His platform included such demands as the eight-hour day and direct recruitment of laborers on public works. Both, however, supported Johnson's policies; neither was objectionable, according to the *National Intelligencer*, to "the conservative and Union-loving citizens of Washington." The *Chronicle* agreed that both candidates professed "the same political creed." The election was "a quiet, cozy, one-sided affair" in which Easby fell badly behind Wallach, even in precincts with large working-class populations. Only in the Sixth Ward did he gain a majority. The overall margin was 4,087 votes to 1,688.[9]

In comparison with Washington's antebellum elections, turnout was low. The total mayoral vote in 1862, at 3,850, was sharply down from the 6,844 votes cast for Berret and Wallach in 1860. A sizable number of politically active Washingtonians, of course, had joined the Union Army, and a not insignificant number – around six hundred according to one estimate – had gone south to join their fortunes with those of the Confederacy. The low registration in 1862 was also attributed to the demand for a loyalty oath.[10] As late as 1866, when nearly everybody had returned from the war, the turnout was still a thousand down from 1860. Many residents were deterred by the poll tax imposed in 1848 to pay for

---

[7] *Evening Star*, April 11, May 2, 9, 23, 28, 1862. For Democratic support for Wallach, see *Evening Star*, May 8, 1862. For the results, see *Evening Star*, June 3, 1862.

[8] *Chronicle*, June 7, 1864; *Evening Star*, June 7, 1864.

[9] *Evening Star*, April 23, May 15, 28, June 5, 1866; *Washington National Intelligencer*, May 18, 25, June 4, 5, 6, 1866; *Chronicle*, June 4, 1866.

[10] *Chronicle*, May 3, 1862; Green, *Washington*, 162–63, 284–88; Whyte, *Uncivil War*, 19; Bryan, *History of the National Capital*, 2:555–56. Unconditional Unionists strongly supported the imposition of a loyalty oath as a qualification for voting in local elections, in the hope that it would disqualify a considerable number of their opponents. *Evening Star*, May 6, 1862.

the public schools or disqualified by the strict residential requirements. Others were put off voting by the violence that had marred local elections during the 1850s and again in 1860. Above all, perhaps, in view of the sameness of the contesting candidates and the limited powers of the corporation, prospective voters might have questioned the utility of going to the trouble of registering and turning out at all.

The city officials, said Constance M. Green, speaking of the 1850s, "were on the whole a quarrelsome and undistinguished lot." Perhaps making implicit comparisons with the caliber of municipal personnel in the early years of the capital's existence, elite Washingtonians, like their compeers in other cities, commented adversely on the low origins and social standing of some of the men elected to councils.[11] Certainly they lacked experience. The turnover on both boards was at least as high as in other nineteenth-century legislative bodies. On average, just under 40 percent of councilmen sought and secured reelection over the period bracketed by the 61st and 65th Councils (1862–68). For example, none of the 63rd Council, which sat between June 1865 and June 1866, had served in the 61st Council two years earlier. Given that their term of office was merely one year, and that the board rarely met more than one evening a week, few councilmen had the opportunity to accumulate much experience of municipal legislation. The aldermen, by virtue of their two-year terms, had more time to familiarize themselves with their duties, but there, too, the turnover was relentless. Over the whole five-year period, only nine aldermen won reelection, that is, 26 percent of the total. The enlargement of the electorate in 1867, and the consequent rise of the Republican Party, led to a dramatic wipeout of Conservative incumbents, with five aldermen and fifteen councilmen losing their seats to Republican challengers, but the turnover in that year was no greater than in 1864, when no organized political parties had entered the campaign. During the period of Republican ascendancy, between 1867 and 1871, the rate at which members gave up, or lost, their seats was no lower than it had been in the early 1860s. Thus, the frequency with which council members replaced one another had less to do with the intensity of party competition than with the limited cachet, and limited remuneration, to be gained from serving in local government.[12]

---

[11] Green, *Washington*, 208. See also Jon C. Teaford, *The Unheralded Triumph: City Government in America, 1870–1900* (Baltimore: Johns Hopkins University Press, 1984), 15–41.

[12] Lists of members are found at the beginning of successive volumes of the council journal and election results in the *Evening Star* and other local newspapers on the first Tuesday in June.

A perusal of the journals of the Washington City Councils, or of newspaper reports on their proceedings, soon makes it apparent that the greater part of the business that passed before them concerned proposals for the improvement of streets.[13] The grading or graveling of streets, the laying of sewers and water mains, the provision of lighting, and other local infrastructural concerns formed the subject of most of the legislation that they considered. Most of these proposals originated with local residents and were introduced by their representatives. As in so many other legislative arenas in the nineteenth century, the principle of localism prevailed across a large part of the councils' business. Members were jealous of their constituents' interests and demanded the right to speak for them, responding angrily when others brought forward bills for improvements in their wards. Most work was carried out by the commissioners of improvements appointed for each ward who, through their power to prioritize jobs and appoint laborers to carry them out, developed considerable political influence and became, in effect, petty ward bosses. "The ward politician must be propitiated," observed the private secretary of Sayles J. Bowen, Wallach's successor. The commissioners competed with one another for funds, the ward representatives in councils serving as their proxies. During 1864–65, $207,300 – 29 percent of corporation expenditure – was accounted for by the ward funds. During 1866–67, the figure was $340,600, 38 percent of expenditure.[14]

Washington's extraordinarily wide streets and avenues, stretching to the far horizons, presented the corporation with an almost insoluble problem. Amounting to more than half the area of the city, they would have called for the expenditure of huge amounts of time, money, and materials to get them into a passable condition. As it was, they were the subject of endless grumbling by the inhabitants and of hostile criticism by contemptuous visitors. Mostly unpaved, or paved with rough stone, giving off clouds of dust in summer and choked by mud in winter, pockmarked by holes and corrugated with bumps and ridges, "those vast, uncared-for wastes of alternate quagmire and sun-baked earth and dust" mocked the magnificent intentions of the founders. They were streets, said the *Star*, "where when it's dry you could not see where you were going, and

---

[13] All the daily newspapers published in the city printed detailed reports on council proceedings, which included summaries of speeches, as well as votes, titles of bills, committee reports, and other matters included in the journals. This chapter mostly relies on the weekly reports in the *Evening Star*.

[14] William Tindall, "Sketch of Mayor Bowen," *Records of the Columbia Historical Society* 15 (1915): 39; Whyte, *Uncivil War*, 20; Teaford, *Unheralded Triumph*, 25–32. Money spent on poor relief and medical assistance was also allocated by wards.

when it's wet you can't go." A western journalist described the "fearful condition" of Washington's streets: "They are seas or canals of liquid mud, varying in depth from one to three feet, and possessing, as geographical features, conglomerations of garbage, refuse and trash." Even Pennsylvania Avenue, the most important thoroughfare in the founders' design, according to the *New York Times*, had for eighty years "lain in the condition of a dirt road, undrained, unpaved, and unswept."[15]

Under the terms of the city charter, as it stood on the eve of the Civil War, the paving and lighting of streets or the laying of sewers required the consent of a majority of property holders in the affected area; the only improvements that the corporation was authorized to make on its own initiative were to grade and gravel streets – that is, to level out irregularities and to cover the carriageway with a thin layer of gravel. As a result, only a few miles had been paved by 1864. On the other hand, the boards passed innumerable bills for grading and graveling, which did not require the approval of property holders and could be paid for out of ward funds. These, however, provided for little more than filling a few holes or leveling a few bumps. As one Alderman complained in 1863, a great deal of money was wasted on street improvements that did not last, leaving holes as big as buckets and a "patchwork" of treated and untreated surfaces. As a result, the corporation faced repeated suits for damage to carriages, horses, and sometimes pedestrians, caused by gaping cavities in the road.[16] In 1864, Congress permitted the corporation to finance improvements out of general funds and, the following year, to assess property owners for part of the cost.[17] The corporation now had the power to order the work to be done without seeking prior

---

[15] *Evening Star*, November 4, 1869, March 23, July 2, 1870; Noah Brooks, *Washington, D.C., in Lincoln's Time* (Herbert Mitgang, ed., Athens: University of Georgia Press, 1989 [1895]), 294–95; *New York Times*, December 26, 1870. See also *Chronicle*, November 3, 1862; Benjamin B. French, *Witness to the Young Republic: A Yankee's Journal, 1828–1870* (Don B. Cole and John J. McDonough, eds., Hanover, NH: University Press of New England, 1989), 386; Alan Lessoff, *The Nation and Its City: Politics, "Corruption," and Progress in Washington, D.C., 1861–1902* (Baltimore: Johns Hopkins University Press, 1994), 4–5.

[16] *Chronicle*, July 14, August 10, 1863, April 2, 1867; Bryan, *History of the National Capital*, 2:496–98; Lessoff, *Nation and Its City*, 32–33. The role of assessments in financing mid-nineteenth-century urban improvements is explained in Einhorn, *Property Rules*; Stephen Diamond, "The Death and Transfiguration of Benefit Taxation: Special Assessments in Nineteenth-Century America," *Journal of Legal Studies* 12 (1983): 201–40.

[17] *U.S. Statutes at Large*, 38.1, chap. 12 (May 5, 1864), 68; 38.2, chap. 13 (February 23, 1865), 434; CG, 38.1:982; CG, 38.2:450; CG, 40.2:2264–67; *Evening Star*, December 6, 1865.

consent. This provided the cue for a rush of paving, lighting, and sewerage ordinances that went far beyond the capacity of the corporation, or
the willingness of the property holders, to pay for them. In June 1865,
Wallach warned councils of "the want of consideration and caution"
shown in ordering improvements: "It arises chiefly from the disposition
of individual members to please their constituents and the facility with
which bills for improvement are hurried through your Boards." The measures already approved would, if executed, "absorb the revenue of the
corporation for the next two years." It was left to the mayor to incur
the wrath of citizens by refusing to execute work that had been ordered
but for which no funds were available. Indeed, over the period 1864–71,
only about half of all the paving work ordered by councils was actually
completed.[18]

Beyond paying assessments for work on streets adjacent to government
property, Congress made no contribution to the laying out and paving of
the wide and extensive thoroughfares demanded by the L'Enfant plan. In
1863, a committee of councils appealed for federal aid, drawing attention to the "deplorable condition" of the streets caused by the passage
of government wagons during the war and reminding Congress of the
limited taxing powers possessed by the corporation. Similar petitions
were presented at regular intervals in the following years. The city fathers
pleaded in vain that the extravagant scale on which the city had been
planned imposed special burdens on local taxpayers and that therefore
the United States, the extensive property of which went untaxed, "was
bound by every principle of justice to pay a portion of the expense of
improving the federal city." Anyone "who looks around the broad streets
and broader avenues," said the *National Intelligencer*, would see at once
that it was impossible for the resident population to make the necessary
improvements. As Wallach explained in December 1865, in a letter to the
secretary of the interior,

Laid out for the permanent seat of the general government, with a view to the
growing greatness of the country upon a scale and of a magnitude unparalleled,
with streets and avenues of a width and extent greater than the necessities of its
inhabitants will, for years to come, demand, and what is more extraordinary,
and consequently burdensome, with a greatly larger area of land appropriated
for streets and avenues and reservations for public use than reserved for building

---

[18] *Journal of the 63rd Council*, 19, 23–24, 519; Bryan, *History of the National Capital*,
2:499–505; *Evening Star*, December 6, 1865, May 29, June 6, 1866. See the list of
improvements since February 1864 compiled by the mayor in July 1866, *Journal of the
64th Council*, 72–74. See also *Journal of the 65th Council*, 38–39.

purposes, this city required, and still requires, means beyond its ordinary resources of taxation to fill up so great a plan.

Congress, however, repeatedly turned a deaf ear to such pleas.[19]

In the absence of federal assistance, the improvements placed a severe burden on municipal finances. The overall tax rate rose from 60 cents in 1863 to $1.00 in 1866 and $1.80 in 1870, largely through the practice of imposing special taxes for schools, police, lighting, and debt management. Even at that rate, many congressmen considered local property seriously undertaxed, as, indeed, did the *Star*, which suggested in 1866 that the tax rate was "less than one-third of what is levied per centum in enterprising, go-ahead cities elsewhere."[20] During the twelve months ending in June 1865, the corporation raised $369,193 from taxes, $175,000 from licenses, and $40,122 from other sources – that is, $594,315 in all – whereas expenditures amounted to $713,668, of which $207,300 passed through the ward funds. The mayor attributed the $119,353 excess of expenditures over receipts to the large number of improvement bills passed by councils.[21] Two years later, the receipts were $814,315 and the expenditures $899,737, nearly two and a half times the amount spent in 1859–60. The outlays included $107,321 for schools, $70,924 for policing, $51,511 for waterworks and sewerage, $340,600 to be expended by the several wards, and $345,326 from the General Fund, out of which salaries, interest payments, and contingent expenses were paid, as well as the costs of the fire department, which amounted to $34,522. In comparison, the cost of maintaining schools in fiscal 1861 had been $27,064, of the police service $32,581, and of the fire service a mere $1,611.[22]

Largely as a result of the wave of improvement bills, the corporation debt had increased to $303,282 by June 1867, over three times the level in 1864. Municipal finances were also stretched by greater spending on schools and police, some of which was required by Congress, as well as bounties for soldiers serving in the Civil War amounting to more than

[19] Committee of the City Councils of Washington to the Senate and House of Representatives of the United States, March 2, 1863, SEN37A-H4, RG46, NARA; Memorial of the Citizens of Washington to the Congress of the United States, February 7, 1863, HR37A-G3.5, RG292, NARA; *National Intelligencer*, December 15, 1865; Richard Wallach to James Harlan, in *Chronicle*, December 14, 1865; *Journal of the 65th Council*, 20–21; Green, *Washington*, 204–07. For examples of congressional appropriations to pay assessments, see *CG*, 39.2:554–57, 559.

[20] Bryan, *History of the National Capital*, 2:511; *Evening Star*, July 10, 1866.

[21] *Journal of the 63rd Council*, 18–19.

[22] *Journal of the 65th Council*, 21–26; *Chronicle*, October 19, 1870; Green, *Washington*, 210.

$100,000. Thus, even before the more ambitious improvement schemes of Sayles J. Bowen and Alexander R. Shepherd got under way, the municipality was facing severe financial difficulties.[23] The root of the problem was the limited tax base. As noted earlier, federal property, nearly a half of all real estate, went untaxed. Thanks to the generous franchises awarded by Congress, the local street railroad companies paid nothing for the privilege of running cars along the city's streets. Potential tax revenues were also restricted by the composition of the population, 20 percent of which, said the *Star*, consisted of "untaxable negroes from the South," with "perhaps as many untaxable whites from the North." This was a problem that offered no easy or immediate solution.[24]

### The Rise of the Republican Party

What little there was of a local Republican Party before 1867 was mainly peopled by federal officeholders from the North, like Sayles J. Bowen and Frederick A. Boswell, along with a few local citizens of Free Soil or antislavery views. It enjoyed a marginal and isolated existence. Nevertheless, its numerical strength was greater than its low political profile might suggest. Some five hundred Republican Wide-Awakes paraded through the streets toward the end of the 1860 presidential campaign, braving the taunts and brickbats hurled at them along the way. A few nominal Republicans were elected to councils. Although some staunch Republicans, particularly in the Seventh Ward, already a stronghold of radicalism, argued for a "straight-out" Republican ticket in municipal elections, most local sympathizers, like Lewis Clephane and John R. Elvans, supported various Unionist candidates, only identifying themselves conclusively with the Republican Party after 1867. Others, like Bowen and Boswell, declined to participate in municipal politics until the rules of engagement had changed.[25]

---

[23] *Journal of the 64th Council*, 68; *Journal of the 65th Council*, 684; Bryan, *History of the National Capital*, 2:505.

[24] *Evening Star*, January 7, 1867; Green, *Washington*, 259–60.

[25] Stanley Harrold, *Subversives: Antislavery Community in Washington, D.C., 1828–1865* (Baton Rouge: Louisiana State University Press, 2003), 169–70; Bryan, *History of the National Capital*, 2:455–56; Ernest B. Furgurson, *Freedom Rising: Washington in the Civil War* (New York: Knopf, 2004), 6–10; Green, *Washington*, 230; William Tindall, "A Sketch of Mayor Sayles J. Bowen," *Records of the Columbia Historical Society* 15 (1915): 25–27; Whyte, *Uncivil War*, p. 34. On the "straight-out" Republicans, see *Evening Star*, May 7, 21, 1862, April 30, May 2, 1863.

With the enfranchisement of African Americans in January 1867, the party was transformed into a powerful political force with excellent prospects of power. As early as December 1866, even before the suffrage bill became law, local Republicans set about creating a citywide organization, with a central Republican Association and clubs in each ward, to contest the municipal elections of the following June.[26] Naturally, in view of the nature of its grassroots support, the advancement of civil rights, the eradication of discrimination in local employment, and the equal allocation of funds to black schools held pride of place in its platform, but the party also promised a more extensive transformation of the city government. Enfranchisement, said the *Chronicle*, by dislodging the "Conservative and reactionary Bourbons" from the local government and "throwing aside the dead weights which have retarded the progress of the city," would enthrone the ideology of "political equality and material advancement" that had inspired the progress that had "made the great cities of the North and West the wonder and admiration of the world." The Republicans would initiate a vigorous program of public works that would provide the infrastructure for economic development, as well as heading off moves to remove the capital to a more westerly location. They also promised better schools, more gas and water mains, and a solution to the perennial problem of the Washington City Canal. By installing officers "in harmony with the federal government," a Republican takeover would increase the likelihood of congressional generosity. However, above all, they promised, by ridding the city of "that Copperhead machine at the City Hall," to begin the reformation of what one local Republican described as "the worst-governed ten square miles [he had forgotten about the retrocession of Alexandria] in the world."[27]

The Republican conquest of the city government came in two stages.[28] In the first, in June 1867, the Republicans won all the citywide contests – for city collector, register, and surveyor – sixteen of the twenty-one seats on the Board of Common Council and five of the eight seats on the

[26] The earliest notice of a meeting of the Republican Association that I could find was in early December 1866, but the report implies that this was not the first. *National Intelligencer*, December 6, 1866.

[27] *Chronicle*, February 7, May 26, 27, 1867, May 9, 1868; *Evening Star*, January 24, May 15, June 3, 10, 1867, June 3, 1868; Gillette, *Between Justice and Beauty*, 53V6; Green, *Washington*, 312.

[28] Local Republicans made overtures to Congress with a view to bringing forward the date of the next mayoral election, so that all the major electoral offices could be filled with Republicans simultaneously – otherwise "the city will virtually be left in the hands of the Copperheads for another year." *Chronicle*, 22 March 1867.

Board of Aldermen that were open to election that year. Despite warn-ings against complacency from Conservative politicians and newspapers and pleas to white voters to register and vote, the habits of apathy and abstention apparent in previous local elections continued to keep white voters from the polls. "If the city is turned over to the Radicals, the white voters will only have themselves to blame for the result," warned the *National Intelligencer*. The *Intelligencer* believed that many stayed at home because they did not wish to be placed on terms of political equality with African Americans. Others, according to the *Star*, were deterred by a Conservative ticket that featured too many Democrats "of the most ultra stripe," instead of "a strong Conservative ticket of the best men available," one that was not tarnished by association with the partisan battles of the past. Black registration was high, whereas many Conser-vative whites declined to register, with the result that whites, although comprising more than two-thirds of the population, contributed just over half the names on the electoral roll.[29]

On election day, African American voters arrived at the polls early and in numbers, forcing whites either to wait for hours in the midsummer sun, losing precious time from their regular pursuits, or return later and run the risk of failing to cast a ballot before the polls closed. Rather than establishing a separate line for white voters and allowing them through in tandem, as many had expected, the Metropolitan Police chief, Major A. C. Richards, a moderate Republican by inclination, ordered the police to admit voters on a first-come, first-served basis, which worked to the advantage of the early-rising and well-organized Republican cohorts. For this he was roundly condemned by Conservatives. Despite the poten-tial for violent confrontation implicit in the situation, there was little disorder.[30] Black turnout was approximately 90 percent of eligible vot-ers, whereas white turnout was probably around 60 percent. With the aid

[29] *National Intelligencer*, March 22, 23, April 1, 6, 8, 10, 1867; *Evening Star*, April 23, May 28, 1867. For registration figures, see *Evening Star*, June 1, 1867. The names of black and white voters were recorded separately.

[30] *New York Times*, May 4, 1867; *Evening Star*, March 20, June 3, 4 1867; *National Intelligencer*, April 2, 12, 15, 1867; Bryan, *History of the National Capital*, 2:555–6; Johnson, "City on a Hill," 54–61; Melvin R. Williams, "A Blueprint for Change: The Black Community in Washington, D.C., 1860–1870." *Records of the Columbia Historical Society* 48 (1972): 380–82. For Richards's orders, see *Evening Star*, May 31, 1867; for Conservative protests, see *National Intelligencer*, June 5, 7, 1867. On the absence of serious disorder, see Charles R. Douglass to Frederick Douglass, June 6, 1867, Frederick Douglass Papers, Microfilm Edition, Reel 2, Library of Congress; *New York Times*, June 4, 1867; *Evening Star*, June 4, 1867.

of between 1,500 and 2,000 white Republicans, that was enough to carry the city and win five of seven wards. In contrast, only about 45 percent of eligible white voters cast their ballots for the Conservative candidate for collector.[31]

Conservative whites denied the legitimacy of such an outcome. They protested that the votes of longtime residents had been swamped by a "horde of ignorant Negroes lately redeemed from slavery" who had, allegedly, been marched to the polls by their new political masters and even carted in from the surrounding countryside to cast their ballots – this an allegation that would be made at every election for the next six years. Neither they nor white Republicans, argued Conservatives, could be said legitimately to represent the community. "We have had...a so-called election," said Thomas E. Lloyd, the retiring president of the Board of Alderman, "the farce has been played out, and...a class of men who never before could have been elected to any position here" had been elected to positions of trust. Old citizens who had given their lives to the welfare of the community had to give way to men elected by the massed votes of contrabands. "The men elected by the negro vote on Monday could never have been elevated to office by those white citizens who have the welfare of the city at heart." Indeed, Conservatives noted with disdain the difficulty that the Republicans had in finding candidates for elective office, even white candidates, who met the property-holding qualifications set by the city charter. That revealed, said the *National Intelligencer*, "the extreme poverty of the party.... Yet these are men who claim the right to control the wealth of the city by passing laws for the city government." To Lloyd and the editor of the *Intelligencer*, the interests of the community were synonymous with those of its white citizens. More than that, the corporation should represent the property owners, the taxpayers, and its governing body should properly be drawn from their ranks.[32]

The partial Republican takeover left the city government in dead-lock. The boards of Aldermen and Common Council, the one with a Conservative majority, the other with a Republican majority, engaged in interminable wrangling about tax and appropriation bills, about the

[31] For further analysis of black and white voting patterns, see below, chapter 6.

[32] *Journal of the 64th* Council, 704–24; *Evening Star*, June 7, 1867; *National Intelligencer*, April 16, 22, June 4, 7, 1867. On the charges of importing voters, see *National Intelligencer*, June 4, 5, 7, 1867. See also Chapter 6 of this volume. For similar views of urban government as the prerogative of property owners, see Einhorn, *Property Rules*; Masur, "Reconstructing the Nation's Capital," 5–10.

allocation of contracts, about municipal advertising, and about the credentials of some of the newly elected members.[33] The Republican register, Frederick Boswell, supported by the Board of Common Council, argued with the Mayor and Aldermen over the proportion of the school fund which, under recent congressional legislation, should be handed over to the Board of Trustees of Colored Schools. Boswell refused to authorize payment of the salaries of teachers in the white schools until the mayor paid what he regarded as the full amount owing to the black schools, yielding only when ordered to do so by the District courts. This led to the teachers going without pay for three months as the dispute dragged on through the winter and spring. Angry Conservative aldermen demanded his removal from office, and the Board of Common Council endorsed his actions by a large majority.[34]

Republicans also complained of the mayor's patronage appointments. As they were so often to do, local Republicans appealed to Congress to change the rules, transferring the power of appointment from the mayor, with the advice and consent of the aldermen, to a joint convention of the two boards, in which the Republicans would hold a majority. That, they argued, was a necessary step toward the "Reconstruction of the District." Wallach's appointees, they said, included many members of the old "City Hall Ring"; "Copperheads" like Corporation Attorney Joseph H. Bradley; and the superintendent of sewers, streets, and buildings, Thomas Forsyth, the failed Conservative candidate for surveyor whose newly created post duplicated many of the functions of the office with which the electorate had recently chosen not to entrust him. "Nearly all the officers now appointed by the mayor and confirmed by the Board of Aldermen are utterly opposed to the reconstruction policy of Congress," and "under the arrangement of such officers the most open schemes of fraud" were practiced, "to the great injury of the city and its improvements." By changing the mode of appointment, "a large number of incompetent, dishonest and disloyal persons would be removed from power and place," insisted

---

[33] On the tax bill, see *Journal of the 65th Council*, 128–29, 135–38, 150–51. On the publication of the *Journal* and ordinances, see *Journal of the 65th Council*, 96, 201–3. On contracts, see ibid., 9, 14. On the mayor's appointments, see ibid., 105–6, 146, 214, 218–20. On members' credentials, see ibid., 73, 90–91, 140–41, 157–59; *Evening Star*, July 9, 16, August 13, 20, 1867. See also *Journal of the 65th Council*, 652, 663–69; *Evening Star*, June 10, 25, July 8, 9, 16, 23, 30, August 6, 13, September 3, 21, 1867; Whyte, *Uncivil War*, 63–65.

[34] The complicated controversy may be followed in *Journal of the 65th Council*, 416–20, 438–39; *Chronicle*, October 14, November 8, 30, December 31, 1867, January 3, 4, May 14, 1868; *Evening Star*, December 28, 31, 1867, January 2, 4, 21 May, 1, 5, 7, 11, 1868; *National Intelligencer*, December 23, 24, 27, 30, 1867, January 2, 1868.

the Seventh Ward Republican Club. The charter was amended in accordance with their desires, but not until the following spring, by which time Wallach's term was nearly at an end. Several months later, with a Republican in the mayor's office, the rules were revised again to restore the appointment power to the mayor.[35]

## The Election of Sayles J. Bowen

The mayoral election of 1868 gave the Republicans the opportunity to complete their sweep of the city government. As in the previous year, Republican ward clubs organized early and met at regular intervals to prepare for the campaign. Their candidate was Sayles J. Bowen, a 54-year-old native of upstate New York who had been resident in Washington since 1845. After being dismissed from the Treasury Department for distributing Free Soil literature, he became one of the founders of the local Republican Party, for which he was rewarded, once Lincoln came to power, with the lucrative post of city postmaster, as well as membership of the Levy Court, the Board of Commissioners of Metropolitan Police, and the Board of Trustees of Colored Schools. Indeed, at one point he enjoyed the benefits of six separate federal offices, earning himself the nickname "Six-Teat Bowen." During the war, he also served as president of the National Freedmen's Relief Association of the District of Columbia, and he is credited with drafting the 1862 law mandating the creation of black schools. It was he who antagonized white residents by challenging the validity of their referendum on black suffrage in December 1865. Bowen, claimed the *National Intelligencer*, was "known as a libeller of the people of this city" who condemned them as "rebels" and "worms to be trodden on." As a result of his longstanding commitment to equal rights and his work for the promotion of black schools, as well as his close association with leading congressional figures, Bowen was the most conspicuous Republican in the city and the party's most obvious candidate for mayor. The obverse side of his steadfast commitment to equal rights was an unfortunate degree of stubbornness, self-righteousness, irascibility, and sometimes vindictiveness. He lacked a sense of humor, along with the other interpersonal skills that are such an important part of the politician's tool kit. Bowen's private secretary later commented on his

---

[35] *Journal of the 65th Council*, 97–99; *CG*, 40.1:698, 748–49; 40.2:2260–64; *Evening Star*, July 16, 18, November 29, 1867; *Chronicle*, June 11, July 8, 17, 18, November 30, 1867. For the reversal, see *CG*, 41.1:289, 508; *Evening Star*, March 22, 28, April 1, 1869.

"facility to estrange his co-workers" and his "disinclination to conciliate his enemy." In time he would reveal a surprising talent for making, and keeping, enemies. As his record for accumulating offices showed, he was also unduly fond of political power and the perquisites of office. However, he never became personally wealthy, seeing out his days in the humble post of watchman in the State Department building. Although the most obvious candidate to establish a new Republican regime in Washington, he was not in all respects the most suitable.[36]

Wallach declined to be a candidate for reelection because, as he put it, "the dignity, importance and usefulness of the office of mayor" had been diminished by the removal of the appointing power and also because he was uncomfortable with the newly established biracial politics. Instead, John T. Given, a prominent local businessman and a member of the Board of Aldermen, was the conservative nominee. The *Intelligencer* described Given as "the white man's candidate." As a native of Washington whose business interests were tied up with those of the city, he was "a candidate who will enlist the enthusiastic support of the whole population proper of Washington." Bowen, in contrast, appealed to outside interlopers, whether black contrabands or Yankee office seekers.[37]

The municipal election of 1868 was much more closely fought than that of 1867. The overwhelming majority of black voters once more registered and came to the polls to cast Republican ballots. This time, however, larger numbers of whites registered. Realizing that the fruits of apathy were a Republican city government, Conservative whites responded more vigorously to appeals from newspapers and political leaders to register and vote. The District courts permitted the enrollment of some citizens who had been debarred the previous year for alleged disloyalty, and of soldiers, mostly domiciled in the Fifth Ward, who had been stationed in Washington for several months but whose right to vote was called into question by legislation passed by Congress just before the election. As a result, whereas black registration fell slightly, from 8,212 in 1867 to 8,139 in 1868, white registration rose from 9,792 to 12,363.[38]

[36] *National Intelligencer*, May 9, 28, 1868; Tindall, "Sketch of Mayor Bowen," 37–38 and 25–43 passim; Green, *Washington*, 316–17; Johnson, "City on a Hill," 66–69; Madison Davis, *History of the Washington City Post Office, from 1795–1903* (Lancaster, PA: New Era Printing Co., 1902), 54–56.

[37] *Evening Star*, May 13, 1868; *National Intelligencer*, May 13, 14, 1868.

[38] *Chronicle*, April 28, 29, 30, 1868; *Evening Star*, May 27, 28, 1868; Memorial of Soldiers Residing in the Fifth Ward of Washington, June 23, 1868, SEN40A-H5.1, RG46, NARA; Bryan, *History of the National Capital*, 2:562–64.

After a hard-fought campaign, on election night neither candidate could claim a clear victory. Once more, it seems, the African American vote went solidly to the Republicans. Black turnout appears to have been close to 100 percent, close enough once more to fuel opposition charges of "colonization." Somewhere between 1,000 and 2,000 whites also voted Republican, including, it was charged, a large number of government clerks who customarily voted in their home states. However, Conservative support rallied considerably in comparison with 1867, carrying the Third, Fourth, and Sixth Wards and claiming a narrow majority in the Fifth. Only the refusal of Republican registrars of elections to count the ballots of a large number of soldiers in the Fifth Ward gave Bowen a narrow overall margin of 83 votes and allowed the Republicans to claim control of the councils.[39] This time, although the election itself passed off peacefully, the following night, as black Republicans took to the streets en masse to celebrate their victory, a fight broke out between some of their number and white onlookers, one of whom was shot and later died. This was "a specimen of what our city is to become under negro rule," warned the *Intelligencer*.[40]

Register Boswell used his formal authority to issue certificates of election to successful candidates to declare that the Republican nominees had been elected. For several days Wallach refused to yield up the mayoralty, which he persisted in claiming, on an ad interim basis, until the dispute might be resolved to his satisfaction (Given had given up the fight). Bowen was driven to hire a locksmith to force entry into City Hall and lay claim to the mayoral office. A few days later, the Circuit Court decided that Bowen should be recognized as the de facto incumbent, leaving it to his opponent to challenge his claim in the courts. However, for several weeks longer, Washington was treated to the spectacle of two boards of Common Council and two boards of Aldermen, who either met simultaneously in the Council Chamber, exchanging insults and squabbling over possession of the speaker's chair, or met in separate rooms or in the same room at different times, each claiming to be the rightfully elected councils. On occasion, fist fights broke out between rival members, and on one occasion between Bowen and Wallach, who still claimed to be mayor ad interim.[41]

---

[39] *National Intelligencer*, June 2, 4, 1868. For the results, see *Evening Star*, June 2, 1868.

[40] For an account of the disturbances, see *Evening Star*, June 3, 4, 1868.

[41] The dispute may be followed in the pages of all the city's newspapers. See, for example, *Evening Star*, June 4, 5, 9, 11, 12, 13, 15, 17, 1868. See also *Chronicle*, June 9, 13, 16,

The aldermanic elections were not settled until a special act of Congress resolved the issue. In February 1867, before the first election involving black voters, Congress had amended the local election laws to increase the chances of a Republican victory. The responsibility of registering voters was removed from corporation officials, whose dedication to enrolling newly enfranchised voters was questionable, and placed in the hands of a federally appointed board of registration. As the local Republican Association observed, "without a commission of loyal men the suffrage bill would become a nullity."[42] Residential requirements were eased in May of the following year in a bill renewing the city charter. Instead of living three months in the ward where they wished to vote, electors needed only be resident for fifteen days. Congressional Republicans argued that such a relaxation was necessary to enfranchise boarders and others who changed their residence frequently and claimed that it was comparable to the rules that applied in other municipalities. Democrats, perhaps rightly, identified this as a measure "to carry the coming election," which was only a few days away. They warned that it would be used to move black voters around the city and even to "colonize" voters from the surrounding plantation counties of Maryland and Virginia. In another section of the bill, military personnel were debarred from voting unless they had been resident in the city for one year.[43]

Even more questionable was the legislation passed to resolve the disputed municipal election of June 1868. The election turned on the credentials of a number of serving soldiers stationed in the District who had voted in the Fifth Ward. Members of the armed forces had been disqualified from voting a month earlier, but by that time, the registration had already been carried out. Uncertain how to proceed, the election officials had received the soldiers' votes but set them to one side. Congress cut the Gordian knot by pronouncing such voters ineligible and by declaring that the certificates of election issued by the City Register would be prima facie evidence of election unless successfully challenged in the courts. Democrats, and, indeed, some Republicans at first, demanded that the dispute be settled under existing laws, none of which gave the Register, who was essentially a returning officer, any such powers. "Congress shall

1868; *National Intelligencer*, June 8, 9, 12, 13, 17, 1868; Johnson, "City on a Hill," 70–76

[42] *CG*, 39.2:602–3, 899; *Chronicle*, February 1, 1867; *Evening Star*, January 17, February 1, 1868.

[43] *CG*, 40.2:2409–11, 2417–19; *Evening Star*, May 12, 29, 1868; *Chronicle*, May 13, 28, 1868; Bryan, *History of the National Capital*, 2:553–54.

not undertake to legislate one man into office and another out," said Senator Thomas Hendricks. However, as Republican Senator James R. Harlan pointed out, existing laws left it to the City Councils to decide contests. As things stood, two rival boards of Aldermen claimed authority. Some urgent measure was necessary to relieve a crisis that might result in violence, to provide the city with regular government, and to relieve Congress of the distraction. "We must give tranquility and peace to the city government, where we have exclusive jurisdiction," said Charles Sumner. In the end, a united Republican vote, fortified in the House by a resolution suspending the rules, forced the bill through. However, as the *Intelligencer* pointedly argued, the fact that new legislation was necessary to legalize the "outrages" could be read as confirmation that the Conservatives had been acting within the law all along.[44]

Even after Congress had summarily pronounced that the certificates issued by Register Boswell constituted the authoritative statement of who had been elected, with one rogue Republican voting with the Conservatives, the Board of Aldermen was still deadlocked and unable to organize for business. Still the two sets of Aldermen tried to meet simultaneously, with what the *Evening Star* called "the usual turbulent performances of personal altercations, gavel-snatching, table-pounding, cross-firing," and general confusion. It urged the Republicans to compromise and the Conservatives to desist from their "Chinese war tactics of gong-beating and yelling." The *Chronicle* was still more critical of the Conservatives' actions, which, it claimed were animated by the "spirit of rebellion." Not until the end of September was an agreement reached, in fact by the Republicans' conceding the election of a chairman, John Grinder, who was among their more moderate members and who had, indeed, run for election as a Conservative a few years previously – in other words, by yielding up partial control of the chamber to their opponents.[45]

Although such disputes were not uncommon in the history of American local government, the manner in which the Washington mayoral contest of 1868 was conducted, and even more the manner in which it was resolved, anticipated future political contests in the Reconstruction South. There were no doubt irregularities on both sides, but what was alarming was the willingness of Republicans to change the rules to their

---

[44] *CG*, 40.2:3116–30, 3172–74; *National Intelligencer*, June 12, 15, 17, 1868; *Evening Star*, June 13, 17, 1868; Whyte, *Uncivil War*, 68–70.

[45] *Evening Star*, August 4, 1868; *Chronicle*, June 13, 1868. See also *Evening Star*, June 23, 30, July 7, August 3, 4, September 29, October 6, 1868; *Chronicle*, June 27, 1868; *New York Times*, June 27, 1868.

own advantage, exploiting the eagerness of congressional Republicans to support the local Reconstruction project. Even more disturbing was the refusal of many Conservatives to acknowledge the validity of an election that was largely decided by the vote of African Americans, whose rights to participate in elections, or even to be recognized as citizens, they were loath to accept. "Today seventy thousand white men were admitting themselves to be crushed under the heel of a negro government," General John Tyler told the Jackson Democratic Association shortly after the election. "Great God! To what depth of degradation have you fallen?" A few months later Alderman Robert W. Fenwick told a Conservative political club of his humiliation at having to sit with an African American: "He had not yet condescended to reply to him, as he did not regard him as eligible." This was, according to the *New York World*, a "shiftless, idle, vagabond, contraband local government." Nor were Conservative whites prepared to recognize the legitimacy of an administration largely composed of newcomers to the city. It was, in their eyes, a "carpetbagger" regime brought to power by the black vote. It was composed, said the *National Intelligencer*, of "mere adventurers," of "shysters and tricksters . . . who have ridden into office upon the shoulders of the blacks." The unseemly and embarrassing wrangle that inaugurated the Bowen administration weakened its effectiveness from the start.[46]

### Improvements

Bowen promised voters upon his election that he would eliminate discrimination in municipal employment and protect the legal rights of African Americans. He promised to enforce congressional legislation on the funding of black schools and secure congressional aid for District schools but considered it "at present impracticable" to move toward integrated education. He promised, through a funding program, to eliminate the floating debt. He also promised, unlike his predecessor, to bring greater benefits to the city by working in harmony with Congress. However, his principal pledge was to initiate a substantial program of public works that would bring about significant improvements in the city's infrastructure, thereby strengthening the case for the retention of the capital on the banks of the Potomac, and, not incidentally, provide employment for many of his black supporters. "Laboring men will have employment at remunerative

[46] *New York World*, August 20, 1868; *Evening Star*, July 31, November 11, 1868; *National Intelligencer*, May 28, 1868.

wages with prompt pay," he promised his supporters the day after the election. The program would include the opening and paving of streets, the laying of gas and water mains, the initiation of a comprehensive system of sewerage, and a program of parking, by which the carriageway on many of the city's wider thoroughfares would be narrowed, leaving strips of land on either side or in the middle of the street that would be grassed over and planted with trees, thereby both reducing the area to be paved and achieving a more pleasing and relaxing aesthetic effect. This scheme, which was continued under later regimes, was one of the few lasting legacies of the Bowen era. In other words, he promised to carry out the extensive program of improvements that was necessary to make up for what he described as decades of neglect. "Probably no city government in the nation has ever been longer or more persistently misruled than this," he told the councils. Simply by ruling honestly and efficiently, Bowen seemed to believe, he could achieve the results that had escaped his predecessors.[47]

Bowen and his supporters proposed a fundamental alteration of the way in which municipal projects would be conducted. The work would be carried out on a "day's work" basis, that is, instead of public works projects being put out to tender, leaving it to the contractor to decide who should be employed and under what terms, they would be executed directly by the commissioners of improvement, who themselves would hire the necessary labor. Large sums, said Bowen, had been wasted on shoddy work by inefficient contractors, which would have to be redone year after year: "Under the system of contracts, as it has been carried out, the city has been robbed of hundreds of thousands of dollars." Indeed, he claimed, "it is a common remark that no one has seen for years a job done for the Corporation according to the terms of the contract." Whereas private contractors were likely to practice favoritism in selecting workers, municipal officials, assuming that they were loyal Republicans, would hire workers "regardless of race or color." Hence Republicans in councils regularly attached to improvement bills the requirement that they should be executed on a "day's work" basis, and Conservatives regularly voted against it. Whereas annual expenditure from the ward funds had averaged $454,507 during the last four years of Wallach's mayoralty, under Bowen spending rose to $638,636 in 1868–69 and

---

[47] *Evening Star*, June 3, 30, September 1, 1868; *Journal of the 66th Council*, 20–32, 117, 305–6. Congress approved the parking scheme in April 1870. *CG*, 41.2: 2332. See also Lessoff, *Nation and Its City*, 34, 84–86.

$1,032,393 in 1869–70. However, most of this money was applied to grading and graveling of streets, rather than to paving and sewerage, which would have required an assessment of adjacent property. Thus, 223 squares were graded and graveled during Bowen's first year in office, but only 10 were paved. Most of the work completed consisted of what might be called "dirt-jobs," pick and shovel work that required relatively small appropriations and employed relatively large numbers of men; the results were no more durable than those of the improvements made under Wallach.[48]

According to Bryan, Bowen's improvements were "largely determined by the needs of the colored voters." That is, he perceived them as a means to provide work for unemployed black laborers.[49] Certainly, large numbers of black laborers found work on the streets. In January 1869, the commissioner of improvements for the Fifth Ward rebutted charges that he had given preference to white laborers by reporting that only three of the thirty-eight men working under him were white. A year later, the Irish Republicans of the Fifth Ward complained that they had only managed to secure work for 4 of their number, whereas 160 black laborers were working on the streets. It was reported that all of the laboring jobs in the Second Ward were carried out by African Americans. Unsympathetic white residents complained that large numbers of black laborers were kept in virtual idleness on the city payroll. According to a widely circulated rumor that soon acquired something of the status of urban myth, several able-bodied men were put to work removing grass from the gutters with pen knives before the 1870 election.[50]

African Americans were not confined to temporary laboring jobs. Although the city charter confined eligibility for municipal office to

---

[48] *Journal of the 66th Council*, 25–26, 226–31; *Journal of the 67th Council*, 79; *Chronicle*, May 28, 29, 1868; *Evening Star*, June 3, 1870; Tindall, "Sketch of Mayor Bowen," 28–29; Bryan, *History of the National Capital*, 565–67; Johnson, "City on a Hill," 77–79. Conservatives argued against the abolition of the contract system, "the fairness, justice, and economy" of which had been demonstrated by "the experience of half a century in this city," whereas the "day's work" system would allow favoritism in the employment of men and purchase of materials, while adding a further layer of administration and, in addition, greatly augmenting the power of the ward commissioners. *Journal of the 65th Council*, 614–15; *Evening Star*, April 21, 1868. For "day's work" proposals, see *Journal of the 66th Council*, 207, 256, 323, 436–37, 521, 534.

[49] Bryan, *History of the National Capital*, 565.

[50] Johnson, "City on a Hill," 77–79; *Evening Star*, January 8, 1869, April 15, 1870. For charges that corporation laborers were idling, see *Evening Star*, April 19, 25, May 24, 1870.

male members of the white race, a restriction that was not removed by congressional legislation until March 1869, two African Americans were elected in June 1868, one to the Board of Common Council and one to the Board of Aldermen. Conservatives challenged the eligibility of the black representatives, but the Republican majorities on both boards, appealing to a legislative body's right to determine the credentials of its own members, defended their right to hold their seats until the charter was amended. Thereafter, larger numbers of African Americans served: one alderman and seven councilmen in the 67th Council (1869–70), and one alderman and six councilmen in the 68th (1870–71), the last before the abolition of the corporation in 1871. Although grossly underrepresented in the upper chamber, by that date the proportion of blacks on the Board of Common Council was close to the proportion of blacks in the population. In addition, John F. Cook Jr., a leading black educationalist who had been elected as an alderman from the First Ward the previous year, was elevated to the important citywide post of collector of taxes in 1869. The black invasion of local government extended to lesser posts. One year after Bowen came to power, nearly 30 percent of appointive offices were held by blacks. That included the appointment of an African American to the key post of commissioner of improvements in the Fifth Ward, despite Conservative protests that such an appointment was unfair to the many competent white men who might have done the job and degrading to the white laborers that would come under his supervision. "We hold," said Fenwick,

that while the colored man is entitled to a *part* of the labor which the city affords, he should be placed under the direction of the white race. We hold that the white man is entitled to a portion of the labor of the Corporation, and that he should under no circumstances be compelled to seek that labor at the hands of a colored man, and work under a colored overseer. We do not believe that any good will come of the mode which is now being sought, of degrading the white people of this District."[51]

Fenwick also objected to the appointment of an African American, Dr. Alexander T. Augusta, as ward physician on the grounds that he should not be placed in authority over white patients. There was resistance to the appointment of black officers from the police commissioners

---

[51] *Journal of the 66th* Council, 821–23; *National Intelligencer*, May 24, 1869; Johnson, "City on a Hill," 77–79. For a list of black members of Councils, see Bryan, *History of the National Capital*, 559 n.4.

and, in particular, the fire commissioners, with whom Bowen engaged in a protracted confrontation.[52]

However, with one or two Republicans regularly voting with the opposition to block appropriation bills, Bowen found it difficult to carry out his promises. First Ward Alderman J. Q. Larman frequently sided with the Conservatives, whereas John Grinder, representing the Seventh Ward, also sometimes broke ranks with his party. Indeed, the compromise that had resulted in the replacement of the Republicans' initial choice for chairman, Zalman Richards, by Grinder seriously undermined the Republicans' control of the upper chamber. The result was a protracted deadlock, both within the Board of Aldermen and between the two boards, which was only a little less intractable than that of the previous session. It resulted in teachers, laborers, and other corporation employees going without pay for long periods and yet another installment in the long-running dispute over the proper funding of colored schools.[53]

Bowen found it no easier than his predecessor to finance his improvement schemes. Congress provided little more assistance, beyond a small appropriation for public works allocated essentially for relief purposes. With tax revenues running at $742,355, slightly below the level for the previous year, the corporation ran further into debt. Although Bowen successfully funded $500,000 of debt at the start of his term, his expenditures eventually added over $800,000 to the floating debt of the city, and the funded debt climbed to $1,314,786. The clerk of the Senate Committee on the District of Columbia, instructed during the summer of 1870 to investigate municipal indebtedness, found corporation officials either ignorant of its extent or unwilling to acknowledge it. Thus, Bowen put the floating debt at $335,000 when it turned out to be at least $800,000 and probably not far short of $1,000,000. Municipal bonds were selling at 75 to 80 cents to the dollar. Once more, schoolteachers and municipal laborers went without pay. In January 1870, Bowen faced the indignity of having to use the furniture in his office as surety for unpaid bills. Even more embarrassing, a few months later, city property had to be sold to meet the claims for damages of a lady who had been injured by falling into an excavation on New Hampshire Avenue.[54]

[52] *Evening Star*, December 22, 1868; *Chronicle*, August 20, 1868; *National Intelligencer*, May 24, 1869.

[53] *Evening Star*, December 22, 1868, March 30, April 10, 13, June 17, 1869; *Chronicle*, June 15, 1868, April 13, 1869.

[54] *Journal of the 66th Council*, 43, 147–49, 197–99; *Journal of the 67th Council*, 179–83; Augustus S. Perham to James Harlan, July 12, 1870, SEN41A-E5, RG46, NARA;

## The Reform Republicans

The Republicans consolidated their advantage in the 1869 municipal election, in which they were opposed by a Citizens ticket that attracted a few dissident Republicans, including a small number of African Americans, who incurred considerable opprobrium for doing so, but consisted mainly of Conservatives. They were, said a Republican speaker, no more than "played-out Democrats in sheep's clothing." The Republicans carried every ward, some by massive majorities, and the city by 9,954 votes to 5,306. That left the party in complete control of the Board of Common Council and with a majority of eleven to three on the Board of Aldermen, two of the minority consisting of holdover members from the previous council. "We Radicals carried it all our own way," said Benjamin B. French, "and carried all before us. Of Copperheadism there is scarcely a grease spot left." The election was marked by a much reduced turnout and outbreaks of disorder, particularly in the Second Ward, where a group of black Republicans attacked a prominent black Citizen, who had to be rescued by the police. In the ensuing melee, the police fired on the crowd, seriously injuring two of its members. The riot, although of a kind not unknown in urban politics, confirmed Conservatives in their opposition to black suffrage and persuaded some moderate Republicans that the empowerment of African Americans might have gone too far. "It will afford the most telling argument against negro suffrage that could be placed in the hands of its opponents," said the *Star*, "that the colored people in the first city where the experiment has been tried undertake to control the exercise of the right by brute force."[55]

It was the election of 1869 that unequivocally placed control of local government in Republican hands. Despite its apparent triumph, the Bowen administration soon encountered choppy water. The first evidence came in a succession of angry confrontations between the mayor and leading Republicans. In July, George Hatton, a Union Army veteran and

*Evening Star*, May 3, 4, 7, 14, June 3, 1870; William Van Z. Cox, "Matthew Gault Emery: The Last Mayor of Washington," *Records of the Columbia Historical Society* 20 (1917): 24. On the 1868 tax bill, see *Journal of the 66th Council*, 190–200 and 245–47; *Evening Star*, August 4, October 6, 27, 1868. On the funding proposal and the legislation authorizing it, see *Journal of the 66th Council*, 21, 112–13; *Evening Star*, June 26, July 23, 27, August 25, 1868; *Chronicle*, November 18, 1868.

55 *Evening Star*, May 21, June 8, 1869; French, *Witness to the Young Republic*, 595. On the Citizens, see *Evening Star*, May 6, 12, 13, 20, 25, 1869. On the election and its aftermath, see also *National Intelligencer*, June 8, 1869; Johnson, "City on a Hill," 82–86.

an especially prominent black Republican who represented the Fourth Ward in the Board of Common Council, complained that Bowen had failed to stand up for his rights when he was refused service in a hotel restaurant while traveling to Gettysburg as part of a municipal delegation. Although Bowen insisted that he had done all he could to ensure equal treatment for Hatton, the councilman bore a deep personal grudge against the mayor for the remainder of his term. Hatton was a highly articulate individual with a large following in the Fourth Ward and a dangerous enemy.[56] Equally damaging was the opposition of John H. Crane, the commissioner of improvements for the Fourth Ward, who in August 1869 accused Bowen of "gross fraud and malfeasance" in the awarding of municipal contracts. Bowen, said Crane, had awarded a contract for grading and graveling sections of K and M Streets north of the Capitol without allowing the statutory ten days' notice to other prospective bidders. Further, he had authorized a payment to the contractor for work in progress, exceeding the whole amount of the original contract, at a time when laborers working for the corporation had not been paid for several weeks. Bowen, in reply, argued that it was customary to extend such advances, principally so that the workers might be paid. Both boards ordered an investigation, in each case by committees consisting entirely of Republicans, which, not surprisingly, exonerated Bowen, stating that his actions did not violate the law. However, the hearings allowed a great deal of bile to be directed toward the mayor, and the final reports left a great many questions unanswered. Individual members of both investigating committees refused to sign the report, and others expressed disquiet. Fourth Ward Alderman Matthew G. Emery, for example, believed that the payments in question were unauthorized and that the contract had not gone to the highest bidder, although he was willing to accept that no improper motives were involved.[57] In the general atmosphere of corruption and charges of corruption that floated around U.S. city governments in the postwar years, it was impossible for Bowen completely to shed the imputation of graft or wholly to clear his name. His enemies began to talk about a "City Hall ring" and to tar Bowen with the

---

[56] *Evening Star*, July 13, 15, 1869; *Chronicle*, July 9, 1869; Whyte, *Uncivil War*, 79–80.

[57] *Chronicle*, October 13, November 2, 1869; *Evening Star*, September 7, 21, 24, October 1, 5, 23, 25, 26, November 1, 2, 9, 30, 1869; May 17, 1870; Whyte, *Uncivil War*, 80–82. For Crane's charges, see *Evening Star*, August 31, 1869. Soon after making the charges Crane was removed from his post as commissioner of improvements, and his ally, J. H. Crossman, was discharged from the post of inspector of flour. *Evening Star*, September 21, 25, 1869.

same brush that was used to besmirch the name of William M. ["Boss"] Tweed.[58]

Much more than personal animosity was at stake, although Bowen generated plenty of that. There were a number of structural reasons for the developing opposition to Bowen within the party. In the first place, a growing number of conservative Republicans, who had originally supported Bowen as a "reform mayor" largely in the hope that he could execute the changes that were needed to improve Washington's commercial prospects and, most important, that he could attract some federal money to the city, now became critical of his failure to achieve these objectives. According to the *Evening Star*, which spoke for a large part of the business community, Bowen had made several grandiose promises before his election, none of which had been redeemed. The municipal debt had risen from $1 million to $2 million, the treasury was empty, the laborers went unpaid, and the city's bonds were depreciated in the market. The streets were full of mud holes, and there was "hardly a sign of substantial improvement." The policy of the administration seemed to be directed to garner the votes of African Americans rather than to advance the interests of the community as a whole. Congress was no more generous than it had been during the Wallach years.[59] Therefore, many business-orientated Republicans, like Shepherd and the editors of the *Evening Star*, became increasingly critical of the administration, and many of them concluded that the kind of improvements that they sought could not be achieved without more fundamental changes in the structure of the city government.[60]

During the winter of 1869–70, Reform Republican clubs were formed in each of the wards, attracting a large number of dissatisfied party members of both races. Crane and Hatton were prominent among the True Republicans of the Fourth Ward, for example, and William Andrew Freeman and Walker White took a leading part in organizing the First Ward Invincibles. They drew added strength from the blatant attempts made by Bowen supporters, led by stalwarts like First Ward Commissioner Henry Himber, to infiltrate and disrupt proceedings, which gave apparent substance to their charges that they faced a tyrannical "City Hall ring" and

---

[58] Accusations of bribery were also brought against Corporation Attorney William A. Cook, who was alleged to have accepted $500 for expediting an advance payment to another contractor. *Evening Star*, October 8, 1869, March 15, 29, 1870.

[59] *Evening Star*, May 2, 15, 26, 1870. For the paper's earlier endorsement of Bowen, see *Evening Star*, June 15, 1868.

[60] On the movement for governmental reform, see Chapter 9.

that Bowen only retained the support of those who depended on civic employment for their livelihood, on what the *Star* called "bread and butter men." It was necessary to establish an Anti-Bowen Club, dissident Third Ward Republicans declared, because "the old organization was in the hands of Bowen men, contractors, and rioters."[61]

The dissidents condemned Bowen for corruption and extravagance, his patronage policies, and his allocation of contracts. "The municipal government in Washington is a byword abroad and a scandal at home," said the *Evening Star* in May 1870. The *Star* had abandoned Bowen nearly a year earlier; now it was followed by the *National Republican* and opportunistic radicals such as Frederick Boswell. The Reform Republicans protested against "unnecessary improvements . . . to benefit a few unprincipled men . . . and to be used as a means of controlling the votes of the laboring classes." They promised to purge the party of "its festering corruptions and its incompetent, selfish leaders." Now the dissidents began to give countenance to Conservative charges that Bowen had been wrongly elected, by keeping white voters away from the polls and flooding them with temporary migrants from Maryland and Virginia, and, above all, that he had been carried into office by force majeure, through congressional edict, in the face of contrary election returns. Now they began to echo Conservative complaints that the Bowen administration was controlled by men who were alien to the city and had no real appreciation of its interests. Lewis Clephane, a businessman and newspaper proprietor who had been associated with the Republican Party in the District since its early days, suggested that men must be elected who had "some taxable interest in the city" to ensure that municipal funds were not squandered.[62]

At the same time, a growing number of black Republicans turned against Bowen. Some were disappointed officeholders or laborers disgruntled that there was not enough work on the streets and sewers to support them all; some were ward politicians dissatisfied at being excluded from power. Others were offended by Bowen's pusillanimous course in

---

[61] *Chronicle*, March 3, 1870. For the split in the Fourth Ward Republican Club, see *Evening Star*, October 20, November 10, 19, December 8, 1869, February 11, 1870; *Chronicle*, November 18, 24, 25, 1869, January 5, 6, 1870; for the First Ward, *Chronicle*, February 2, 18, April 8, 1870; *Evening Star*, January 20, 26, 1870. For the attempts to organize a central Reform Republican association, see *Evening Star*, January 20, 22, 28, 1870.

[62] *Evening Star*, May 25, 1869, February 7, March 2, April 26, May 2, 17, 1870; Gillette, *Between Justice and Beauty*, 57–59; Johnson, "City on a Hill," 88–90; Whyte, *Uncivil War*, 83–87.

relation to black schools, both his failure to ensure that the Board of Trustees of Colored Schools received its proper allocation and his reluctance to endorse the principle of school integration, which, although popular among black politicians (but not invariably among the wider black public), was guaranteed to alienate white voters.[63] Although the majority of politically active African Americans continued to support the regular ticket, including influential leaders such as the educator John F. Cook Jr., the Reverend Anthony Bowen, and the proprietors of the *New Era*, a weekly established at the beginning of 1870 by Frederick Douglass and J. Sella Martin, there were enough defectors seriously to weaken Bowen's prospects of reelection. Hundreds of black voters turned out at anti-Bowen meetings in the Seventh Ward and elsewhere. A large section of the black quasi-military organization the Boys in Blue defected to the Reform movement. Black leaders complained that they had for too long followed cravenly the edicts of the Republican Party, which had come to take their support for granted. Republican managers, said Hatton, boasted that they could drive black voters like sheep. The *Star* urged black voters to throw off their slavery to radical politicians who demanded that they act out of loyalty to their race and who sought to "betray and defraud the colored people of Washington to their own selfish ends." Reform Republicans urged African Americans not to remain loyal to an administration that had professed to promote their interests but had done nothing but "degrade and enslave them" by vicious politics. They had been "taken advantage of by artful demagogues, huckstering politicians, canting hypocrites, and selfish and mercenary adventurers of the white race, to practice upon the credulity and abuse the confidence of these people."[64]

A Reform Republican convention met in May 1870 and nominated Matthew Emery, a former stonemason and businessman currently representing the Fourth Ward in the Board of Aldermen, as its candidate for mayor. Emery, said the *Star*, was an "original Republican" whose friends included the "best men" in the local community. He was a friend of labor who had always treated his own workers fairly and supported the eight-hour day. The Reform Republicans promised to clear out corruption, eliminate multiple office holding, reduce salaries, cut taxes and ensure that they were "judiciously expended," award contracts to the

---

[63] See *Evening Star*, January 8, 26, April 21, 26 1870.

[64] *New Era*, May 19, 1870; *Chronicle*, November 26, 27, December 10, 1869, May 30, 1870; *Evening Star*, January 28, February 7, April 16, 30, May 6, 11, 12, 31, 1870.

lowest bidder, appoint honest and efficient commissioners of improvements, clean out the canal, and, once more, secure liberal appropriations
from Congress.[65] They were, of course, dismissed by Bowen's supporters as rebels, "disorganizers," and disappointed office seekers, deluded,
as one black Republican put it, "by passion, prejudice and ambition."
Charles Syphax, a black Republican from the First Ward, described the
Invincibles, the local anti-Bowen faction, as "a few disappointed men."
They represented, said the Second Ward commissioner of improvements,
the dying shrieks of the old regime. Unable to control the party, said the
ever-loyal *Chronicle*, "a few turbulent spirits" set out to ruin it. "The
contest is now an open and plain one between the instrument of a petty
faction and the regular Republican candidate."[66]

In any case, Bowen suffered a heavy defeat in the mayoral election
in June, losing every ward to his rival Emery, and the city by 10,096
to 6,877 overall. Presumably, those conservatives who voted gave their
ballots to the Reform candidate, as no doubt did a sizable number of
white Republicans, and there is evidence of substantial black voting for
Emery, as even the *Chronicle* acknowledged. However, given that black
registration stood at 7,535 and that Bowen received 6,877 votes, unless a
sizable proportion of his votes was cast by whites, which seems unlikely,
Bowen, to make up his total, must have received a substantial majority of those African American ballots. According to the *Chronicle*, "The
Democracy was reinforced by dissatisfied Republicans, and the city government passes into Democratic hands by Republican votes."[67]

## Conclusion

Bowen's term of office came to an ignominious end, yet its achievements
were not insubstantial. It initiated a program of improvements that in
some ways anticipated the more grandiose projects carried out under
the Territory. At no period, claimed the *Chronicle*, had improvements
proceeded so rapidly; more streets had been cleared and sewers laid than
in any two-year period in the city's history. Although perhaps marred by

---

[65] *Evening Star*, April 13, 21, 22, May 6, 11, June 2, 1870.
[66] *Chronicle*, November 18, 1869, May 6, 17, 19, 1870; *Evening Star*, February 23, March
10, April 15, 1870. The regulars also claimed that Emery had been a candidate for
the American party in 1857 and tried to tarnish him by association with the "Bloody
Monday" election riots of that year. *Evening Star*, April 15, May 28, 1870.
[67] *Chronicle*, June 7, 1870; *Evening Star*, June 1, 6, 1870; Williams, "Blueprint for
Change," 384–92; Whyte, *Uncivil War*, 87–89.

extravagance and not always efficiently executed, the work was necessary if the city was to pull itself out of its antebellum despond. The Bowen administration created conditions under which African Americans could play an active role in political life, and it promoted the development of black schools. Its employment program furnished work to many African American men whose families would otherwise have been brought close to starvation. It made Washington a Republican city, in tune for a while with the aspirations of the Republican Party in Congress. Washington had "quickened into life since the rebellion," suggested the *Chronicle*, and the work of Republicans in transforming the city government had gone some way to make that possible. Yet much remained to be done: most of the streets remained unpaved and poorly lit; the sewers had been unsystematically, and sometimes badly, laid; and the canal remained in its entire noisome splendor. As a *New York Times* correspondent noted in 1869, the city still gave the impression of "lying around loose as if an earthquake had shaken it."[68]

The ultimate failure of Bowen's mayoralty certainly owed much to his personal failings – his stubbornness, his propensity to make enemies, and his overall lack of political skill – but it was also a result of structural weaknesses parallel to those that would later contribute to the collapse of Reconstruction regimes in the South. As Eric Foner observes, the southern Republican governments faced a recurrent "crisis of legitimacy." They were viewed by large sections of the native white populace as "alien impositions" that relied on the leadership of northern "carpetbaggers," the electoral support of former slaves, and continuing federal intervention to prop them up. Hence, their legitimacy was contested, and they were subject to obdurate, sometimes violent, resistance. The opposition of white Washingtonians to their own Reconstruction experiment was more measured and rarely erupted into physical violence. However, theirs, too, was regarded as a "carpetbag" regime, the elected representatives of which would not have won power with the consent of the local white electorate but depended on contraband votes. Most white citizens accepted black participation only reluctantly and used it as an excuse for dismissing Republican government in the nation's capital and ultimately, as we will see, any form of self-government at all. Even some conservative Republicans began to question their acquiescence in black suffrage. Finally, the new regime was regarded as a congressional imposition, a

---

[68] *Chronicle*, May 27, 1868, May 13, 31, 1870; *New York Times*, January 15, 1869. For a more hostile view, see also *Evening Star*, June 17, 1869, March 17, 23, May 2, 1870.

dubious "experiment" foisted on the citizenry and ultimately dependent on federal power for its survival. So what we see in postbellum Washington, then, is a gentler version of the troubled politics of Reconstruction.[69]

There were further correspondences. These included a shared tendency to fall prey to factional disputes, the unwillingness of many white Republicans to accept the full implications of equal rights and of many black Republicans to accept half measures, the tensions caused by the growing insistence of the black majority on recognition in patronage and policy, and the unease felt by many white Republicans at having to work closely with African Americans. Another common feature was the exceptional strain placed on the financial resources of local government by Republican programs that sought both to expand social facilities, particularly public schools, and to improve the economic infrastructure. Republican governments sought to promote economic development, both because they wished to bring material benefits to their core supporters and, if possible, widen their electoral base and because they perceived themselves as the "party of progress," pulling the South out of its backwardness by an application of northern energy and expertise. Such programs were in the end thwarted by the region's limited tax base, imposing unacceptable burdens on taxpayers that, as J. Mills Thornton III has shown us, contributed greatly to the mounting opposition to the Republican regimes. Yet they received little financial assistance from Congress to help them meet their obligations. Southern Republicans in Congress during the 1870s found it almost impossible to persuade their colleagues to make appropriations for their states, even at a level proportionate to their population. Likewise, the financially embarrassed Bowen administration received little or no federal assistance in executing its improvement schemes and was, instead, increasingly blamed by congressmen for living beyond its means. The most obvious reason Bowen failed is because Congress failed him. The financial assistance that Bowen, and many of those who voted for him, had expected was not forthcoming, and therefore his bolder schemes could not be executed. Thus, his projects inevitably fell short.[70]

---

[69] Eric Foner, *Reconstruction: America's Unfinished Revolution, 1863–1877* (New York: Harper, 1988), 346 and 346–64 passim; Michael Perman, *Emancipation and Reconstruction, 1862–1877* (2nd edn., Wheeling, IL: Harlan Davidson, 2003), 73–75; *Abraham Lincoln, Constitutionalism, and Equal Rights in the Civil War Era* (New York: Fordham University Press, 1998), 217–46.

[70] On the failure of southern Republican regimes, see Lawrence N. Powell, "The Politics of Livelihood: Carpetbaggers in the Deep South," in J. Morgan Kousser and James M.

The story of Reconstruction in Washington, of course, did not end with the fall of Bowen. His successor found it no easier to resolve the financial and governmental difficulties that had beset the Bowen regime.[71] In any case, Emery's two-year term was cut short by the decision in 1871 to replace the miscellaneous governmental jurisdictions in the District with one overarching territorial government that would, it was hoped, manage affairs more systematically and purposefully than its predecessors. As it turned out, during its three-year life span, the new regime would initiate a program of improvements that far surpassed anything that had gone before and set in motion a train of consequences that in some ways replayed the events of the Bowen years, but in a highly exaggerated form. The outcome this time would be the end of self-government in the District of Columbia for close to a century.

McPherson, eds., *Region, Race, and Reconstruction: Essays in Honor of C. Vann Woodward* (New York: Oxford University Press, 1982), 315–48; J. Mills Thornton III, "Fiscal Policy and the Failure of Radical Reconstruction in the Lower South," in ibid., 349–94; Terry L. Seip, *The South Returns to Congress: Men, Economic Measures, and Interpersonal Relationships, 1868–1879* (Baton Rouge: Louisiana State University Press, 1983); Richard F. Bensel, *Yankee Leviathan: The Origins of Central State Authority, 1859–1877* (Cambridge: Cambridge University Press, 1990), 380–95; Foner, *Reconstruction*; Michael Perman, *The Road to Redemption: Southern Politics, 1869–1877* (Chapel Hill: University of North Carolina Press, 1984); Perman, *Emancipation and Reconstruction*, 73–102; Carl H. Moneyhon, "The Failure of Southern Republicanism, 1867–1876," in Eric Anderson and Alfred A. Moss Jr., eds., *The Facts of Reconstruction: Essays in Honor of John Hope Franklin* (Baton Rouge: Louisiana State University Press, 1991), 99–119; Otto H. Olsen, ed., *Reconstruction and Redemption in the South* (Baton Rouge: Louisiana State University Press, 1880); Michael Fitzgerald, *Urban Emancipation: Popular Politics in Reconstruction Mobile, 1860–1890* (Baton Rouge: Louisiana State University Press, 2002).

[71] Cox, "Matthew Gault Emery"; Green, *Washington*, 327–28; Johnson, "City on the Hill," 187–90; Whyte, *Uncivil War*, 96–98.

# 6

## Race, Radicalism, and Reconstruction

### Grassroots Republican Politics

### Introduction

For a few years after the Civil War, the enfranchisement of male African Americans opened up the space for an extraordinary efflorescence of political organizing, grassroots activism, and community development. It has become clear from recent studies of grassroots Reconstruction, by, for example, Steven Hahn, Michael W. Fitzgerald, Julie Saville, Rebecca J. Scott, and John C. Rodrigue, that freedpeople's political activity in the postbellum South served a much wider range of practical and psychological functions than merely the exercise of an abstract constitutional right.[1] Not only in the countryside of the South but also in cities such

---

[1] Julie Saville, *The Work of Reconstruction: From Slave to Wage Laborer in South Carolina, 1860–1870* (Cambridge: Cambridge University Press, 1994), 161 and passim; Saville, "Rites and Power: Reflections on Slavery, Freedom and Political Ritual," in Sylvia R. Frey and Betty Wood, eds., *From Slavery to Freedom in the Atlantic World* (London: Frank Cass, 1999), 81–102; Steven Hahn, *A Nation under Our Feet: Black Political Struggles in the Rural South from Slavery to the Great Migration* (Cambridge, MA: Harvard University Press, 2003); Hahn, "The Politics of Black Rural Laborers in the Postbellum American South," in Enrico Dal Lago and Rick Halpern, eds., *The American South and the Italian Mezzogiorno: Essays in Comparative History* (New York: Palgrave, 2002), 112–31; Michael W. Fitzgerald, *The Union League Movement in the Deep South: Politics and Agricultural Change during Reconstruction* (Baton Rouge: Louisiana State University Press, 1989); Rebecca J. Scott, "Stubborn and Disposed to Stand Their Ground: Black Militia, Sugar Workers and the Dynamics of Collective Action in the Louisiana Sugar Bowl, 1863–67," in Frey and Wood, eds., *From Slavery to Freedom in the Atlantic World*, 103–26; John C. Rodrigue, *Reconstruction in the Cane Fields: From Slavery to Free Labor in Louisiana's Sugar Parishes, 1862–1880* (Baton Rouge: Louisiana State University Press, 2001); Rodrigue "Labor Militancy and Black Grassroots Political Mobilization in the Louisiana Sugar Region, 1865–1868," *Journal of Southern History* 67 (February 2001):

as Charleston, Richmond, and Mobile, freedpeople organized politically, converting the newly established Republican Party to serve the social and economic needs of their communities.[2] However briefly and however imperfectly, the Republican Party acted as a force for social change. "More than a political party," says Saville, "a social movement was in the making."[3]

This chapter asks similar questions about the functions and meaning of politics for African Americans in Washington, D.C., during Reconstruction. Although there have been several studies of the black community in postbellum Washington and of local politics in the Reconstruction era, few historians have paid attention to the process of political mobilization or considered its wider significance.[4] In Washington, as in the states farther south, the enfranchisement of male African Americans initiated a surge of grassroots organizing. Republican ward clubs, with their biracial but predominately black membership, were the locus for a vibrant political culture in which newly enfranchised African Americans, many of them former slaves, played a leading role. Through participation in

115–42; Eric Foner, "Black Reconstruction Leaders at the Grass Roots," in Leon Litwack and August Meier, eds., *Black Leaders of the Nineteenth Century* (Urbana: University of Illinois Press, 1988), 219–36; Foner, *Nothing but Freedom: Emancipation and Its Legacy* (Baton Rouge: Louisiana State University Press, 1983).

[2] See, for example, Michael Fitzgerald, *Urban Emancipation: Popular Politics in Reconstruction Mobile, 1860–1890* (Baton Rouge: Louisiana State University Press, 2002); Wilbert Jenkins, *Seizing the New Day: African Americans in Post-Civil War Charleston* (Bloomington: University of Indiana Press, 1998); Fitzgerald, *Union League Movement*, 177–99; Elsa Barkley Brown, "Negotiating and Transforming the Public Sphere: African American Political Life in the Transition from Slavery to Freedom," *Public Culture* 7 (Fall 1994): 107–46; Peter J. Rachleff, *Black Labor in the South: Richmond, Virginia, 1865–1890* (Philadelphia: Temple University Press, 1984), 34–54.

[3] Saville, *Work of Reconstruction*, 161.

[4] Exceptions are Katherine Masur, "Reconstructing the Nation's Capital: The Politics of Race and Citizenship in the District of Columbia, 1862–1878" (Ph.D. diss., University of Michigan, 2001), especially 201–27; and David Taft Terry, "A Brief Moment in the Sun: The Aftermath of Emancipation in Washington, D.C., 1862–1869," in Elizabeth Clark-Lewis, ed., *First Freed: Washington, D.C., in the Emancipation Era* (Washington, DC: Howard University Press, 2002), 71–97. Studies of the black community in Washington include Constance M. Green, *The Secret City: A History of Race Relations in the Nation's Capital* (Princeton, NJ: Princeton University Press, 1967); Allan John Johnston, *Surviving Freedom: The Black Community of Washington, D.C., 1860–1880* (New York: Garland, 1993); Thomas R. Johnson, "The City on the Hill: Race Relations in Washington, D.C., 1865–1885" (Ph.D. diss., University of Maryland, 1975); James Borchert, *Alley Life in Washington: Family, Community, Religion and Folklore in the City, 1850–1970* (Urbana: University of Illinois Press, 1980); Melvin R. Williams, "A Blueprint for Change: The Black Community in Washington, D.C., 1860–1870," *Records of the Columbia Historical Society* 48 (1972): 359–93.

grassroots Republican politics, they asserted their claim to full citizenship and explored the institutional processes through which that claim might be realized. The political clubs united the diverse elements of the black population as no other social institutions could. Hence, they played a crucial role in the process of community-building. Their "multifarious activities" reflected what Eric Foner has called "the politicization of everyday life" after emancipation.[5] African Americans used the ward clubs as a forum in which they could give voice to their concerns about public education, civil rights, and, above all, employment. By organizing politically, the black working class, with its heavy dependence on public employment, put pressure on the city authorities to execute large-scale public works projects. For a while, their interests coincided with elements of the local business community who were committed to the physical refurbishment of the capital. However, the improvements initiated by the Republican Mayor Sayles J. Bowen between 1868 and 1870 strained the financial resources of local government far beyond what either taxpayers or Congress would tolerate. This set in motion a sequence of changes in the arrangements for governing the District that eventually led to the abrogation of home rule and the destruction of that particularly vital form of black politics.

### Black Voting

The subject of this chapter is that relatively brief moment of opportunity when the Republican Party offered itself as a vehicle of social justice and political empowerment for the city's black population. Here, as elsewhere in the South, it was a predominately black party. Republican leaders in 1868 estimated that they could count on between 1,500 and 2,000 white votes, an estimate that an analysis of election returns shows to have been roughly correct, but the bulk of the votes that contributed to Republican majorities during the late 1860s and early 1870s came from African Americans, both former residents of the city and recent migrants from the surrounding states.[6]

The city's election laws required prospective voters to register a few weeks in advance of Election Day; most of those who took the trouble to register also took the trouble to vote. Because separate records were kept of black and white registration in each ward, we can form a fairly

[5] Foner, "Black Reconstruction Leaders," 222.
[6] *Evening Star*, May 7, 1868.

accurate picture of the racial composition of the electorate. Before the first election in which African Americans could vote, in June 1867, 8,212 black and 9,792 white men registered to vote – that is, 18,004 in all. As Conservatives complained, a great many white voters abstained from the electoral process, whereas black participation was close to 100 percent.[7] Even though African Americans constituted only about one-third of the population, they accounted for 46 percent of registered voters. Further-more, they were present in force on Election Day. Assembled in the early hours of the morning by bugles and horns, the members of the various ward clubs marched to the polls, where, marshaled by Republican leaders, they queued patiently to vote. In the Seventh Ward, nearly a thousand black voters were standing in line by 10:30 A.M. There party officials passed among them, distributing party tickets and instructing them care-fully on how to cast their ballots. By such a strategy, Republicans ensured clear access to the polls and forced their Conservative adversaries either to wait for hours in the hot sun or return later in the day. In consequence, many white voters were prevented or dissuaded from voting, and the impact of the consolidated black vote was maximized. This contributed to the lopsided Republican victories in the citywide contests and in five of the seven wards.[8]

The 1868 election, in which white voters participated more vigorously, gives us a better opportunity to analyze the voting behavior of newly enfranchised African Americans. This requires us to make two assump-tions. The first is that the proportion of registered electors who turned out to vote was the same for both races, which introduces an important margin of error into the calculation. The second is that all but a handful of black votes went to Republican candidates, which in Washington in 1868, and, indeed, in all elections up to 1874 (with one exception) is a fairly safe assumption. There is abundant evidence of the powerful com-munity pressures that African Americans were subjected to. As one black activist warned in May 1867, "the colored man who votes a Democratic ticket will find the soles of his feet too hot for him." In 1869, when a disenchanted African American contractor called Charles Stewart led a few followers into the Citizens Party, they opened themselves up to vio-lent abuse and even physical attack, even though, as the *Evening Star* observed, "we do not believe that fifty colored people in the whole city

---

[7] For conservative complaints of apathy, see *National Intelligencer*, March 22, 23, April 1, 6, 8, 10, 1867.

[8] *Chronicle*, June 4, 1867; *Evening Star*, May 28, June 4, 1867; Whyte, *Uncivil War*, 62.

would have voted that way." Any African American who might have considered deserting the Republican camp to vote for the Democratic candidate for delegate to Congress two years later, in the first election for the territorial government, came under powerful pressure to reconsider his position. "I say shame, eternal shame on any colored voter who supports Richard T. Merrick, and withered be the black man's arm and blasted be the black man's head who casts a vote against General N.P. Chipman," thundered Frederick Douglass, with powerful echoes of the ancient Hebrew curse. Except in 1870, when the black vote split down the middle, its Republican loyalties were never in doubt.[9]

Following Allen Trelease's method for estimating the number of scalawags, we can then calculate the number of white Republican voters by subtracting the number of black voters from the aggregate Republican vote.[10] In 1868, black registration, at 8,139, was slightly down from the previous year, whereas white registration had increased by more than 2,500. In the June election, the Republican candidate, Sayles J. Bowen, won 9,170 votes, his Conservative opponent 9,087, which meant that 89 percent of registered voters had turned out at the polls. Given our operating assumptions that the conversion rate of registered to actual voters (0.89) was the same for both races and that all blacks voted Republican, we arrive at an estimate of 7,247 black and 1,923 white Republicans – a ratio of just under four to one. However, in view of the continuing practice of black voters massing at the polls and the continuing complaints of white voters that they were denied access to the polling places, it is possible that the conversion rate for African American voters may have been higher, which would have resulted in a larger number of black and fewer white voters. In the extreme case, in which the turnout of registered African American voters was 100 percent, the number of white Republicans would have stood at 1,031. The most likely estimate, then, is that

---

[9] For complaints of apathy among white voters, see *National Intelligencer*, March 22, 23, April 1, 6, 8, 10, 1867; *Evening Star*, April 23, May 28, 1867. For evidence of pressures to vote Republican, see *Evening Star*, May 15, 1867, June 8, 1869; *National Intelligencer*, May 18, 1869; *New National Era*, April 20, 1871. Cf. Hahn, *Nation under Our Feet*, 226–30; Saville, *Work of Reconstruction*, 167–70.

[10] On the procedure for estimating white Republican votes, see Allen W. Trelease, "Who Were the Scalawags?" *Journal of Southern History* 29 (November 1963): 445–68. For critical comments, see Warren Ellem, "Who Were the Mississippi Scalawags?" *Journal of Southern History* 38 (May 1972): 217–40; Lawrence N. Powell, "Correcting for Fraud: A Quantitative Assessment of the Mississippi Ratification Election of 1868," *Journal of Southern History* 55 (November 1989): 633–58.

TABLE 6.1. *Distribution of the Vote in the Municipal Election of 1868*

| Ward | 1 | 2 | 3 | 4 | 5 | 6 | 7 | City |
|---|---|---|---|---|---|---|---|---|
| Registration | | | | | | | | |
| Black | 1,739 | 1,528 | 897 | 1,122 | 721 | 386 | 1,746 | 8,139 |
| White | 1,521 | 1,697 | 1,928 | 2,432 | 1,314 | 1,462 | 2,009 | 12,363 |
| TOTAL | 3,260 | 3,225 | 2,825 | 3,554 | 2,035 | 1,848 | 3,755 | 20,502 |
| Proportion black | .533 | .474 | .318 | .316 | .354 | .209 | .465 | .397 |
| Voting | | | | | | | | |
| Republican | 1,694 | 1,508 | 1,119 | 1,337 | 953 | 696 | 1,863 | 9,170 |
| Conservative | 1,149 | 1,125 | 1,443 | 1,864 | 978 | 967 | 1,561 | 9,087 |
| TOTAL | 2,843 | 2,633 | 2,562 | 3,201 | 1,931 | 1,663 | 3,424 | 18,255 |
| Proportion Republican | .596 | .572 | .437 | .418 | .494 | .419 | .544 | .503 |
| Turnout | .872 | .816 | .907 | .901 | .949 | .900 | .912 | .890 |
| Estimates | | | | | | | | |
| Black voters* | 1,517 | 1,247 | 813 | 1,011 | 684 | 347 | 1,592 | 7,247 |
| White voters* | 1,326 | 1,385 | 1,749 | 2,190 | 1,247 | 1,316 | 1,832 | 11,008 |
| White Republicans[†] | 177 | 260 | 306 | 326 | 269 | 349 | 271 | 1,923 |

* Estimates of black and white voters are arrived at by multiplying the number of registered voters by turnout.
† Estimates of white Republicans are arrived at by subtracting the estimated number of black voters from the number of Republican voters.
*Sources:* Registration: *Evening Star*, June 1868. Voting returns: *Evening Star*, June 2, 1868.

somewhere around 1,500 whites voted Republican and around 7,700 blacks. Table 6.1 shows registration figures and election results for the whole city and also for individual wards. This reveals that the areas of greatest Republican strength were the First, Second, and Seventh Wards, the wards that also contained the largest black populations.[11]

By the time of the first elections for the new territorial government in April 1871, we find, using the same estimation procedures, that more than a third of Republican voters were white – that is, a total of 5,265 white compared with 9,930 black Republicans in the election for the District's delegate to Congress, which the Republican candidate won by 15,196 votes to 11,104. In those legislative districts that were located within the former boundaries of the city of Washington, the Republican Party attracted an estimated 4,727 white and 8,108 black votes. Nevertheless, even though a growing number of white Washingtonians gravitated to the

[11] The *Evening Star* for June 3, 1868, estimated the black vote at 8200. For accounts of the election, see *Evening Star*, June 1, 2, 1868; *Chronicle*, June 2, 1868.

Republican Party, throughout the period of Reconstruction, the party's electoral base remained predominately black.[12]

Let us stay with the election statistics a little longer. On comparing the number of registered black voters in 1868 with population estimates, it appears at first sight that black registration actually exceeded the number of black males of voting age. Applying the age and sex ratios suggested for the national black population by the 1870 U.S. Census to the African American population of Washington, which the special census conducted in November 1867 in connection with the allocation of revenues for public schools put at 31,937, gives us an estimate of 7,026 adult males, whereas 8,139 were registered to vote. Likewise, in 1871, 10,772 black voters were registered – in this case, in the District of Columbia as a whole – whereas the estimated adult male population, based on the 1870 census, stood at 9,050.[13]

Conservatives made free with accusations that trainloads, even boatloads, of black laborers from the plantation counties of Maryland and Virginia were imported a few weeks before the election, registered, and then marched in "squads" to vote the Republican ticket before, presumably, being spirited away. In 1868, said Wilhelmus Bryan, an early historian of the District, "began the custom of bringing negroes to the city at election time." The Republicans, declared the *National Intelligencer*, with the assistance of the Freedmen's Bureau, imported blacks from the surrounding counties, "whom they drove to the places of registration and voting like sheep to the shambles," on promises of employment. Two years later, the *Evening Star* took up the theme, accusing Mayor Bowen of squandering money on laborers from Maryland and Virginia that should have gone to unpaid municipal employees and of flooding the surrounding counties with offers of work. In April 1871, such charges were given added substance when Tom Bowie, a notorious ward heeler,

---

[12] For registration and voting returns, see *Evening Star*, April 17, 21, 1871. An ecological regression analysis was carried out for the twenty-two legislative districts (using the SPSS-7 software package). This produced estimates of 103.7 percent of blacks and 29.6 percent of whites voting Republican, proportions that, despite the errors introduced by the small number of cases, are fairly close to those generated by the subtraction method, that is, 100 percent and 32 percent, respectively.

[13] U.S. Office of Education, *Special Report of the Commissioner of Education on the Condition and Improvement of Public Schools in the District of Columbia*, HED 315, 41.2, Series 1427 (June 13, 1871), 28–38; U.S. Bureau of the Census, *Historical Statistics of the United States, Colonial Times to 1957* (Washington, DC: Government Printing Office, 1960), 11.

was drowned while ferrying "a choice assortment of potential negro voters" to participate in the District elections.[14] Even if charges of "colonization" might hold true for later elections, and there is little more than circumstantial evidence to support them, they could hardly apply to 1867 and 1868, when most of the city government was in Conservative hands. As for the Freedmen's Bureau, as we have seen, its determined objective was to accelerate the dispersal of the freed population rather than encourage additional persons from Maryland and Virginia to enter the city. Republican politicians regularly complained of its policies, particularly at election times. Rather than by systematic fraud, the discrepancy is more likely caused by an underestimation of the African American population, which included a great many recent migrants, many of whom lived in places that the census enumerators were unable or disinclined to reach. In addition, there was perhaps a further underestimation of the proportion of adult males within that population, which, again as a largely migrant population, had a skewed age and sex distribution.[15]

However one reads the evidence, it is clear that African American registration was close to 100 percent and electoral participation close to 90 percent. White turnout, in contrast, was around 60 percent of white male citizens of voting age. Voting for black Washingtonians evidently held a special significance, as it did for freedpeople across the South.[16] As a group of District blacks declared in a petition to Congress in December 1865, without political rights, they could be "but nominally free." Voting was a civic ritual "full of symbolic meaning": it signified membership of a community of self-governing male citizens and the assertion of those very manhood rights that, whether slave or free, African American men

[14] On charges of colonization of voters, see Bryan, *History of the National Capital*, 2:563–64, 596–97; *National Intelligencer*, May 14, 1869; *Evening Star*, May 24, 28, 1870; Tindall, "Sketch of Mayor Bowen," 38–40; Whyte, *The Uncivil War*, 108–9; Johnson, "Reconstruction Politics in Washington," 185–88, 280–83.

[15] For examples, see *Evening Star*, March 1, 15, October 11, 1867.

[16] Lawrence N. Powell estimates that 95 percent of the potential black electorate in Mississippi was registered to vote in 1868. "Correcting for Fraud," 653–55. Saville's estimate for South Carolina is just under 90 percent, and Williamson's is 85 percent. *Work of Reconstruction*, 166–67; Joel Williamson, *After Slavery: The Negro in South Carolina, 1861–1877* (Charlotte: University of North Carolina Press, 1865), 343. Richard Lowe estimates that 88 percent of registered black voters voted in 1867 and 81 percent in 1869. *Republicans and Reconstruction in Virginia, 1856–1870* (Charlottesville: University of Virginia Press, 1991), 176–77. See also Eric Foner, *Reconstruction: America's Unfinished Revolution, 1863–1877* (New York: Harper, 1988), 288–91; Hahn, *Nation under Our Feet*, 198.

had long been denied. That is why they exercised their newly attained prerogative with such vigor.[17]

   That commitment was strongly reinforced by the manner in which black Republicans organized for elections and the manner in which they conducted themselves at the polls. Rather than approaching the ballot box and exercising their right to vote as individuals, African Americans typically proceeded to and from the polling places in large groups, sometimes in military formation. They massed in large numbers both for tactical reasons and as a demonstration of their collective strength. As Steven Hahn and others suggest, the purpose of this military-style organization of voters was not only, as it might be in the states of the former Confederacy, to prevent intimidation and to give anxious freedmen the confidence to approach the polling booths despite the presence of hostile whites; it was also a way to compel apathetic, lazy, or disloyal members of their own race to abide by the collective judgment of the community and march with their fellow African Americans to the polls. Its function was as much disciplinary as defensive. Therefore, the manner in which Republicans marshaled the vote was one of the principal reasons for the high levels of turnout among black voters in Reconstruction elections, in Washington and elsewhere. It was a triumph as much of organization as of ideology.[18]

### The Style of Grassroots Republican Politics

The most striking feature of black political activity in postbellum Washington was the high level and intensity of participation, which was most obviously manifest in the impressive rates of electoral registration and turnout. It was evident also in the attendance at Republican ward clubs, which met weekly in the months before elections and intermittently at other times. The *Evening Star*, which published full reports of such

---

[17] Petition of John Francis Cook and 2,500 other Colored Citizens of the District of Columbia, December 11, 1865, Senate Papers 39A-H4, RG46, National Archives. Cf. Foner, *Reconstruction*, 291; Jean H. Baker, *Affairs of Party: The Political Culture of Northern Democrats in the Mid-Nineteenth Century* (Ithaca, NY: Cornell University Press, 1983), 267–79; Baker, "The Ceremonies of Politics: Nineteenth-Century Rituals of National Affirmation," in William J. Cooper Jr., Michael F. Holt, and John McCardell, eds., *A Master's Due: Essays in Honor of David Herbert Donald* (Baton Rouge: Louisiana State University Press, 1985), 161–78.

[18] Cf. Hahn, *Nation under Our Feet*, 205, 223–26; Saville, *Work of Reconstruction*, 175–76.

meetings, frequently recorded attendances in hundreds. For instance, four hundred were present at the meeting of the Second Ward Republican Club on April 27, 1867, six hundred at the First Ward Club the following week (which was over a third of the Republican voters in the ward). Other meetings were reported as "packed," "densely crowded," or "filled to overflowing."[19] Although in the early years, several of the clubs' executive officers, and a majority of those nominated for elective office, were white, blacks usually outnumbered whites in the body of the hall by a ratio of five to one, even eight to one. At an early meeting of the First Ward Club, for example, twenty-five whites were present and an uncounted number of blacks; almost all the speakers were black, as were twelve of the fifteen delegates sent to the city nominating convention. At a meeting of the Seventh Ward Radical Republican Association in April 1867, in the words of the Conservative *National Intelligencer*, "About four-fifths of those present were negroes, most of whom attended from curiosity more than aught else."[20]

Bryan claimed that African Americans were "not assertive" at the early meetings of the clubs but instead "fell into a humble place," sitting at the rear and demurely voting for candidates and resolutions proposed by white members.[21] That is not the impression that emerges from contemporary newspaper reports. Theirs was evidently more than a token presence. Rather than sitting passively and following a program laid out by more experienced figures, members repeatedly intervened from the floor, raising points of order, sometimes to excess, presenting resolutions in alarming profusion, and challenging the presumptions of club officials. Although most of the African Americans who were elected to positions of responsibility were "old residents," many of those who spoke from the floor were former "contrabands" whose unfamiliarity with parliamentary etiquette did not deter them from speaking their mind. "I speak as a soldier and one who has been a slave," proclaimed one especially vocal member of the Second Ward Club, expressing the pride and

---

[19] See, for example, *Evening Star*, April 19, 27, May 11, 16, 1867, May 23, 1868, April 29, 1869; *Washington Daily Morning Chronicle*, March 5, April 20, 1867; *National Intelligencer*, April 20, May 16, 1867. It must be stressed that, in the absence of minutes or other manuscript records of the conduct of these meetings, the following discussion is based primarily on the reports published by newspapers, especially the *Evening Star*.

[20] *National Intelligencer*, April 11, 1867; *Evening Star*, April 18, 24, 1867.

[21] Bryan, *History of the National Capital*, 2:558. The *Star*, at least during 1867 and 1868, identified participants by race on the grounds that readers would be interested in the political performance of newly enfranchised citizens. See *Evening Star*, April 19, 1867.

self-confidence that many newly enfranchised African Americans felt in their new roles as political actors.[22]

Republican meetings, according to the *National Intelligencer*, were "remarkable for nothing but abuse and blasphemy."[23] Some ward meetings, commented a *Star* editorial, were "entirely given over to personalities." The black newspaper the *New National Era* admitted that rowdy meetings were embarrassing to the party, and Carter Stewart, a leading black Republican, criticized his people for the "disorderly manner" in which meetings were conducted. Chairing a meeting of the First Ward Club in 1868, he reprimanded members for their disorderly and argumentative behavior. "Don't disgrace yourselves," he urged them; there were white people present. "We don't care" was the response from the floor.[24] Ward meetings were often decidedly unruly affairs, characterized by a great deal of shouting, "boisterous interruptions," some imaginative and distractingly subversive heckling, angry personal confrontations, and even violent scuffles, which led on occasions to the smashing of windows, tables, and chairs and the summoning of police officers to restore order. Procedural arguments frequently became personal; factional contests dissolved into aggressive confrontations and even violence. In one such instance, a heated meeting of the Fourth Ward Club was brought to boiling point when the volatile Marcellus West interrupted George W. Hatton, who was engaged in a tirade against "weak-kneed-Republicans," by telling the speaker, "You are as weak-kneed as any of them." In response, Hatton accused West of admitting openly that he intended to support the Democratic Party, whereupon his antagonist, shaking his fist under Hatton's chin, called him "a d – d liar." A crowd gathered round in expectation of a more violent confrontation, but, as the *Star* reporter noted, the protagonists did not have "much fight in them," and order was soon restored. At a Fifth Ward meeting, intemperate criticism of the club chairman by another black Republican led to an exchange of personal accusations of mounting severity, until the two main protagonists, each surrounded by his friends, angrily confronted one another, while neutrals made their escape through the windows or hid under tables. The arrival of a detachment of police finally restored order. At a meeting in the First Ward, said the *Star* reporter, the excitement was "indescribable," as the

---

[22] *Evening Star*, May 4, 1867.

[23] *National Intelligencer*, May 8, 1869.

[24] *Evening Star*, May 10, 1867, April 24, 1868, May 20, 1869, March 25, 1870; *New National Era*, January 27, 1870. See also *Evening Star*, April 24, 1868.

nomination, for the first time, of a black candidate for alderman was carried "amid the most deafening applause," with one elderly freedman reportedly performing "an Indian war dance on his hat."[25]

Much of this boisterousness constituted the normal stuff of American grassroots politics, which was rarely decorous. Indeed, black Republicans often blamed white politicians, in pursuit of power and preferment, for fomenting discord. Divisions, it was said, were "caused by a few white men who go into the organization for the purpose of looking for the loaves and fishes." It was white men who "brought personalities in." They seemed to "come to the meeting with bowie knife in hand."[26] Fractiousness sometimes resulted from a suspicion that small groups of wire-pullers, mostly white, were manipulating proceedings so as to deny rank-and-file members, mostly black, an equal voice. Participants regularly protested at the manner in which club officials appeared to railroad business through meetings by moving the appointment of committees to make nominations or draft resolutions that were then put before the meeting for ratification. "It seems that parties have everything cut and dried," observed one Fifth Ward activist. They did not need a select committee to make nominations, rank-and-file members protested. Believing that there was "intelligence enough on the floor" to make a decision, they expressed a preference for a mass meeting as the forum for making club policy and nominating candidates, a forum in which they, and not party managers, might have more influence.[27]

Outraged members protested in the conventional language of reform politics, but on occasion they drew on analogies with slavery to describe the condition of powerlessness that they struggled to avoid. "The relation of the colored men to Mayor Bowen," proclaimed Marcellus West, an especially outspoken black Republican, "was the most abject slavery." Another insisted that "colored men should act like men and not be driven."[28] Individual freedmen exhibited a prickliness about matters of personal honor that derived in part from their recently emancipated status. The uneasy tranquility of the Fourth Ward Club was broken when Marcellus West (again) accused John H. Crane, a prominent white

[25] *Evening Star*, May 22, 23, 1868, May 20, 1869. See also *Evening Star*, May 4, 1867, March 19, April 24, May 14, 1868; May 25, 1869; *Chronicle*, May 2, 1867, May 20, 26, 1869.

[26] *Evening Star*, May 9, 1867, March 26, 1868.

[27] *Evening Star*, April 13, May 4, 10, 1867, May 22, 23, 1868; *National Intelligencer*, April 10, 1867.

[28] *Evening Star*, January 28, 1870; May 14, 1867.

Republican, of having remarked while serving on a jury that "colored women generally were not virtuous" – inflammatory enough in itself. To West's fury, Crane refused to listen to charges made "by men of no character." The story, he insisted, was false, "told outside the jury box by a poltroon and added to by scamps." "Who do you call scamps?" asked several voices at once, and, in the words of the *Star* reporter, "Considerable commotion ensued."[29] Whether Crane had used the language attributed to him remains unclear, but any such aspersions on black womanhood would certainly have been provocative. In the eyes of his accusers, in responding so dismissively to their accusations, Crane was also guilty of showing disrespect to themselves and their race. Neither he nor his interlocutors may have been familiar with the niceties of the language of honor employed by southern whites, but it is not surprising that African Americans, on the cusp of emancipation, should have responded angrily to words that described them as worthless and devoid of character.[30]

Perhaps the most important reason for the disorderly character of Republican meetings, however, was simply that politics mattered deeply to these newly enfranchised voters. This was definitely not, in their eyes, politics as usual. They looked to the Republican Party not only to pass legislation in their favor or to facilitate their acquisition of jobs but also as a medium of personal expression and civic education. They regarded political participation as a way of acclimatizing themselves to the procedures of democracy and, in a broader sense, to the culture of freedom. His members desired regular meetings, explained the secretary of the Second Ward Club, because they recognized their need for political education. Like the Union Leagues, the clubs "served as crucial political schools, educating newly enfranchised blacks in the ways of the official political culture."[31] Glenn C. Altschuler and Stuart M. Blumin have raised questions about the depth and intensity of nineteenth-century Americans' engagement with politics, citing the paltry attendance at caucuses and primary elections as some of their most telling evidence, but there can be no doubt about the depth and intensity of black Washingtonians' engagement with politics

---

[29] *Evening Star*, April 29, 1869; *Chronicle*, April 24, 1867.

[30] On the language of honor, see Kenneth Greenberg, *Honor and Slavery* (Princeton, NJ: Princeton University Press, 1996).

[31] *Evening Star*, April 13, 1867; *Chronicle*, April 18, 1867; Hahn, *Nation under Our Feet*, 183. Cf. Masur, "Reconstructing the Nation's Capital," 207–19; Fitzgerald, *Union League Movement*; Saville, *Work of Reconstruction*, 160–70; Robert H. Wiebe, *Self-Rule: A Cultural History of American Democracy* (Chicago: University of Chicago Press, 1995), 71–75.

during Reconstruction and their relish for the excitement of local party meetings.[32]

Republican meetings sometimes took place in black schoolhouses, sometimes in rooms acquired through the good graces of the Freedmen's Bureau, but most often they were held in black churches. The First Ward Republicans met in the 19th Street Baptist Church and Union Bethel Church, the Second Ward in the 15th Street Presbyterian Church, the Fourth Ward in the Reverend Isaac Bouldin's Baptist Church, the Fifth Ward in Ebenezer Church, and the Seventh Ward for a while in St. Paul's Chapel. Black churches, as the central institutions among Washington's African Americans, offered natural meeting places. Ministers not only offered the use of their buildings; they played an active role in proceedings as well, regarding political leadership as a necessary extension of their responsibility as community spokesmen. Possessing an independent power base and personal qualities, such as literacy, organizational skills, verbal fluency, and sometimes personal charisma, that especially fitted them for political leadership, churchmen found it natural to participate actively in local Republican organizations. In the Seventh Ward, in South Washington, the Reverend Anthony Bowen, who officiated at St. Paul's Chapel, was the most prominent and influential black Republican; the Reverend A. M. Green's facility at formulating political statements won him the epithet "Resolutions" Green; Bouldin offered not only his church but his opinions to the Republican Party of the Fourth Ward; and the Reverend D. W. Anderson of 19th Street Baptist Church played an active part in the affairs of the First Ward Club.[33]

More than any other institutions, church organizations bound African Americans together and formed a network of solidarity and communication on which the nascent party could build. They were especially well

---

[32] Glenn C. Altschuler and Stuart M. Blumin, *Rude Republic: Americans and Their Politics in the Nineteenth Century* (Princeton, NJ: Princeton University Press, 2000), especially 228–35.

[33] *Evening Star*, March 2, 6, April 11, 18, 25, 27, May 2, 23, 1867; Etta V. Moran, "Anthony Bowen," *Negro History Bulletin* 7 (1944): 5–6, 18–21; John W. Cromwell, "The First Negro Churches in the District of Columbia," *Journal of Negro History* 7 (January 1922): 64–106. Cf. Foner, *Reconstruction*, 93, 282–83; Saville, *Work of Reconstruction*, 163–6; Jenkins, *Seize the New Day*, 127–32; Hahn, *Nation under Our Feet*, 130–34; William E. Montgomery, *Under Their Own Fig and Vine Tree: The African-American Church in the South, 1865–1900* (Baton Rouge: Louisiana State University Press, 1993); Larry Eugene Rivers and Canter Brown Jr., *Laborers in the Vineyard of the Lord: The Beginnings of the AME Church in Florida, 1865–1895* (Gainesville: University Press of Florida, 2001).

situated to mobilize the sentiment of African American communities.[34] At an early meeting of the Second Ward Club, poorly attended because of inadequate publicity, it was pointed out that newspaper advertisements provided insufficient notice of meetings, because many members could not read them, and that the best way to spread news was to have announcements made in the churches or circulated by "leading colored men." The Republicans of the Fourth Ward asked ministers to instruct their congregations where and when to register to vote. In the Seventh Ward Club, it was proposed in 1867 that pastors should be invited to nominate suitable candidates for delegates to the city nominating convention and that auxiliary Republican clubs should be created in association with the churches.[35] So intensely was politics entwined with church affairs that several ministers got into serious trouble with their congregations for supporting the Reform Republican candidate Matthew Emery against Sayles J. Bowen in the mayoral election of 1870, and several members were expelled for voting the wrong way.[36]

The style of black political culture owed much to the church. Republican meetings usually opened with a prayer, and it was not uncommon for members to sing hymns at intervals in proceedings.[37] The behavior and emotional intensity of those present and their close identification with the Republican Party, their sense that the party belonged to them and expressed the needs and values of their community, suggest a religious congregation rather than a political caucus. The language, too, of many speakers drew heavily on the Bible, describing in millennial terms the mission of the Republican Party in the restoration of the Union and the liberation of the race. Religious analogies are often used, sometimes inappropriately, to characterize the party allegiances of nineteenth-century Americans. It does seem, however, that, newly enfranchised African Americans believed their spiritual and political identities to be closely entwined and drew important lessons from their religious experience on how to organize

---

[34] However, in a city like Washington, where the African American community was divided along class lines, the churches varied greatly in the nature of their congregations. Union Bethel, for example, served a largely elite clientele, as did the 15th Street Presbyterian Church. Jacqueline M. Moore, *Leading the Race: The Transformation of the Black Elite in the Nation's Capital, 1880–1920* (Charlottesville: University of Virginia Press, 1999), 16–21.

[35] *Evening Star*, March 18, April 13, 18, 1867; *Chronicle*, February 15, April 2, 1867.

[36] *Evening Star*, June 20, July 16, 1870.

[37] See, for example, *Chronicle*, March 5, 1867; *Evening Star*, March 6, May 4, 1867, April 21, May 23, 1868, May 7, 1869.

politically and on what the purpose and significance of political organization should be.

## Taking It to the Streets

Black Republicans' engagement with politics frequently took them into public places. Like other Americans of the period, black Washingtonians showed a relish for political parades. The District's Republicans, most of them black, assembled to serenade national dignitaries and local Republican candidates, or to celebrate events such as the ratification of the Fifteenth Amendment and Emancipation Day (which in the District was April 16). These parades involved elaborate organization and advance planning, which was largely carried out by members of Republican ward clubs or by ancillary organizations such as the Boys in Blue. For example, on Emancipation Day in 1868, more than ten thousand African American men assembled near Franklin Square before following a complicated route that took in most of the city's public monuments. Marshal-in-Chief John T. Johnson led the way, seated on Old Abe, a "magnificent white charger" formerly belonging to President Lincoln, and accompanied by his deputy marshals. He was followed by a number of black militia companies with marching bands, including the Lincoln Zouaves from Baltimore, the Washington City Guard, the Independent Blues, and the Georgetown Liberty Guards, each resplendent in their colorful uniforms; a chariot from Georgetown decorated with the national colors, containing a "light-complexioned colored girl" dressed entirely in white representing Liberty; a wagon bearing a printing press "in full operation" churning out copies of the District Emancipation Act; another bearing the inscription "First Ward Union League and Workingmen" on which blacksmiths, a painter, a carpenter, and a wheelwright busily plied their trades. Then came the delegations from Georgetown and the several wards, wearing brightly colored sashes and badges, carrying banners, and accompanied by bands.[38]

[38] This and the following paragraph are based on the accounts in *Chronicle*, April 17, 1868; *Evening Star*, April 16, 1868; Mitch Kachun, *Festivals of Freedom: Memory and Meaning in African American Emancipation Celebrations, 1808–1915* (Amherst: University of Massachusetts Press, 2003), 207–32; Masur, "Reconstructing the Nation's Capital," 148–60; Craig A. Schiffert, "Stepping toward Freedom: An Historical Analysis of the District of Columbia Emancipation Day Parades," in Clark Lewis, ed., *First Freed*, 111–34; Terry, "Brief Moment in the Sun," 92–96. For accounts of earlier and later Emancipation Day parades, see *Chronicle*, April 19, 1866; April 17, 1867; April 17, 1869.

Other African American citizens, including many women, lined the streets and applauded the marchers as they strode past. A festive atmosphere pervaded the occasion, accentuated by the presence of large numbers of schoolchildren, released from their studies for the day. However, it carried an important message. The banners borne by the marchers, along with the numerous portraits of Lincoln, reminded onlookers of the significance of emancipation and of the need to preserve the memory of the struggle against slavery, but they also pointed to the further reforms that were necessary to achieve full citizenship rights. The Emancipation Day parade had something of the character of a Republican rally. Republican ward clubs were prominent among the marchers, Republican politicians addressed the crowds at various points along the way, and the messages conveyed on most of the banners were essentially Republican slogans. As Craig A. Schiffert points out, the parades "must have been perceived widely as an expression of unilateral and unqualified support for the GOP."[39]

The various elements of Republican parades in Washington – the marshals, the militia companies, the floats carrying female figures symbolic of republican virtue, the symbols of labor, the meticulously orchestrated sequences of militia companies and ward delegations, the Pioneer companies with their axes and capes, the emblems of nationality, the torches and transparencies carried in nighttime processions – were the common currency of spectacular campaigning in nineteenth-century America.[40] Here, however, the faces in the parade, and many of the faces along the sidewalks, were black. For a few hours, African Americans took possession of the public spaces of the city and made a point of marching past the most important public buildings – the White House, the Capitol, and City Hall. By parading so openly in public spaces, by engaging in the "vital democratic theater" of political campaigning, African Americans were laying claim to recognition as American citizens in the fullest sense.

---

[39] Schiffert, "Stepping toward Freedom," 120.

[40] For other examples of parades, see *Chronicle*, September 23, 1868; *Evening Star*, November 12, December 11, 1869, April 16, 1870. Cf. Michael McGerr, *The Decline of Popular Politics: The American North, 1865–1928* (New York: Oxford University Press, 1986), 22–41; Baker, *Affairs of Party*, 292–97; Susan G. Davis, *Parades and Power: Street Theater in Nineteenth-Century Philadelphia* (Philadelphia: University of Pennsylvania Press, 1986); Mary F. Ryan, "The American Parade: Representations of the Nineteenth-Century Social Order," in Lynn Hunt, ed., *The New Cultural History* (Berkeley: University of California Press, 1989), 131–53; Ryan, *Civic Wars: Democracy and Public Life in the American City during the Nineteenth Century* (Berkeley: University of California Press, 1997), 223–58. On the symbolic role of "apparitions of femininity" see ibid., 245–47.

They were making the clearest possible statement of their newfound status and marking their entry into public life.[41]

Veterans' organizations, such as the Boys in Blue, were present in force at such events; so were the many black militia companies that had been organized in the District. By October 1867, according to the *Chronicle*, two black regiments were in existence, and a later investigation found three military organizations in the city. Like black militia companies elsewhere in the South, they mostly wore their Civil War uniforms and carried their Civil War weapons or weapons acquired from the War Department by purchase.[42] So troubled were Conservatives by the "large number of armed organizations formed without authority of law" that they asked President Johnson to suppress them. Republicans, said the *National Intelligencer*, had become reckless and menacing, insolent in the exercise of power. Many blacks were armed and were "carrying matters with a high hand." In November 1867, in response to such fears, Johnson asked General Grant to order the disbandment of such organizations, but Grant, maintaining that because martial law was not in force in the District, they were not illegal and, well aware of the wider political repercussions of such a ban, declined to take action.[43]

Obviously such organizations, like their white equivalents, were an expression of the pride that Civil War veterans took in their service and in the collective memories that bound them together, as well as serving a variety of social and recreational purposes. However, they held additional meaning for African Americans, who had been prevented from carrying weapons in the past. Individually, by bearing arms, black men asserted their claim to full manhood; collectively, they asserted their claim to public space and public recognition. By parading in uniform, they demanded respect and recognition as soldiers of the Republic.

[41] McGerr, *Decline of Popular Politics*, 6. The growing significance of parades in African American communities earlier in the century is explored in Shane White, "'It Was a Proud Day': African American Festivals and Parades in the North, 1741–1834," *Journal of American History* 81 (June 1994): 13–50.

[42] *Chronicle*, October 22, November 9, 1867; *National Intelligencer*, November 9, 1867; Masur, "Reconstructing the Nation's Capital," 137–48; Martin R. Gordon, "The Black Militia in the District of Columbia, 1867–98," *Records of the Columbia Historical Society* 48 (1972): 411–20.

[43] *National Intelligencer*, November 9, 1867, August 31, September 24, October 9, 1868; *Evening Star*, October 21, 1868; Andrew Johnson to Ulysses S. Grant, November 4, 1867, in Leroy P. Graf and Ralph W. Haskins, eds., *The Papers of Andrew Johnson* (16 vols., Knoxville: University of Tennessee Press, 1967–2000), 13:209; John S. Gallagher to Johnson, October 21, 1868, in ibid., 15:162.

"Drilling and marching," says Saville, "became a form of political practice, as ex-slave men took the lead in fashioning an organization that
would express their burgeoning claims to social authority." Although
rather less obviously than in a state such as South Carolina, military organizations offered a measure of protection to freedmen who still lacked
full confidence in the exercise of their democratic privileges, and they
represented a clear assertion of social and political power.[44]

### "The Great Want Is Work"

Why did African Americans commit themselves so heavily to Republican
politics in Reconstruction Washington? In their eyes, first of all, the party
stood for equal rights. They regularly extolled the Republican Party for
its part in the emancipation of the slaves and the suppression of the
Confederacy. They looked to it to go further by removing discriminatory
provisions from the statutes and ordinances of the city and by enacting
and enforcing civil rights legislation. They looked to it to ensure equal and
adequate provision for the colored schools, which the city government,
until the Republican takeover in 1868, stubbornly refused to do, and to
keep management of those schools as far as possible in their own hands.
Like black Republicans further south, they held to an almost millennial
view of the party's purpose. According to G. H. Brooks of the Seventh
Ward, "The Republican party had been used, through the providence of
God, to deliver the race, and if they showed ingratitude to the party they
would show ingratitude to God." For all its faults, the Republican Party
was the party of freedom. The opposition Conservative or Democratic
Party, on the other hand, consisted of "white rebels" who "wanted to
reduce them to a condition next door to slavery." "If the Republicans
were defeated," Walker White warned his fellow black Republicans, "the
Democrats would drive them from their homes... and they and their
children would be compelled to sit on the sidewalk."[45]

---

[44] Cf. Saville, "Rites and Power," 89–90; Saville, *Work of Reconstruction*, 143–51, 170–
75; Fitzgerald, *Union League in the Deep South*, 66–71; Scott, "Stubborn and Disposed
to Stand their Ground," 119–20; Hahn, *Nation under Our Feet*, 173–76; Elsa Barkley
Brown and Gregg D. Kimball, "Mapping the Terrain of Black Richmond," *Journal of
Urban History* 21 (March 1995), 305–8; Richard Paul Fuke, *Imperfect Equality: African
Americans and the Confines of White Racial Attitudes in Post-Emancipation Maryland*
(New York: Fordham University Press, 1999), 185–88.
[45] *Evening Star*, April 23, 14, May 27, 1868. For local Republican platforms, see *Evening
Star*, June 3, 1867, May 9, 1868.

As Michael Fitzgerald found in the Deep South, newly enfranchised blacks, many of them newly emancipated, saw politics as a way of improving their economic prospects.[46] One thing that emerges strongly from Republican politics at the grass roots is an obsessive interest in jobs. A First Ward Republican put it bluntly: "No man should get his vote unless he had a chance at the spoils."[47] Of course, nineteenth-century politics was largely concerned with the distribution of patronage, but this went far beyond the usual fascination with office holding as a means of personal advancement and group recognition. For a large number of poor black Washingtonians, government employment was almost their sole means of subsistence. If work was not provided, said a black preacher, three-quarters of his friends would have nothing to do. Thus, black Republican politics in Washington at the grassroots was fueled by a mass of raw discontent that led to recurrent challenges to the party leadership and occasional outbursts of insurgency. A persistent undercurrent of need ran through the decision-making processes and added a note of desperate urgency to the discussion of policy.[48] In the absence of other suitable employment, male contrabands were heavily dependent on municipal labor – grading and paving streets, dredging the canal, digging sewers. Thus, political participation had, for them, a direct and immediate significance. Blacks appreciated, says Howard Gillette Jr., "that the fruits of victory would be political jobs." "The great want is work," declared Anthony Bowen; and he hoped that whatever men were sent to the Councils would be "good, true and honest and provide work for the laboring man."[49]

Ward meetings pressed the corporation to spend more money on improving the streets, if necessary anticipating future revenues to expedite

---

[46] Fitzgerald, *Union League Movement in the Deep South*, 177–89; Foner, *Reconstruction*, 289–90. The importance of patronage in Republican politics during Reconstruction and its often divisive impact are explored in Michael W. Fitzgerald, "Republican Factionalism and Black Empowerment: The Spencer-Warner Controversy and Alabama Reconstruction, 1868–1880," *Journal of Southern History* 64 (August 1998): 473–94; and, most influentially, in Lawrence N. Powell, "The Politics of Livelihood: Carpetbaggers in the Deep South," in J. Morgan Kousser and James M. McPherson, eds., *Region, Race, and Reconstruction: Essays in Honor of C. Vann Woodward* (New York: Oxford University Press, 1982), 315–48.

[47] *Evening Star*, January 31, 1867, January 18, 1870.

[48] *Evening Star*, December 4, 1868. According to one estimate, about half the black population was destitute. Green, *Secret City*, 93. See also Johnston, "Surviving Freedom," 233–42. Cf. Fitzgerald, *Urban Emancipation*, 24–25, 121–22, and passim.

[49] Gillette, *Between Justice and Beauty*, 56; *Evening Star*, March 1, 1867, November 5, 1868, May 7, 1869.

construction. Rather than handing out work on the streets to private
contractors, they demanded that the city carry it out on a "day's work"
basis, which black laborers rightly suspected would provide them with
more work for longer. Meetings were called at various times in the year,
but particularly in the winter, when most forms of pick-and-shovel labor
came to a standstill, to urge the city government and Congress to set
about dredging, or in some other way improving, the Washington City
Canal, which would provide employment for hundred of workers who
would otherwise be idle. At party meetings in the Seventh Ward, which
abutted the canal, resolutions were passed demanding that the city carry
out dredging operations using the unexpended part of an appropriation
made two years earlier or, as Anthony Bowen put it, to follow "any plan
whereby his brethren could get work." His son J. N. L. Bowen "wanted
the work to go on, for it would prevent the necessity of men going to the
soup-house." Indeed, the Seventh Ward Republicans passed resolutions
binding members to vote against any candidate for councils who opposed
cleaning the canal and condemning ward representatives who refused to
carry out their constituents' wishes.[50]

African American laborers' overwhelming desire for municipal employment, regardless of the fiscal consequences, had radically redistribu-
tive implications. Members called on Republican officials to take action
against public and private employers who discriminated against African
American workers. They called on Mayor Bowen to remove the commissioner of improvements in the Fifth Ward because of his failure to employ
a sufficient number of black workers; they demanded the removal of a
master workman in the Navy Yard who refused to appoint blacks; they
condemned the boards of police commissioners and fire commissioners for similar discriminatory practices; and they criticized the federal
commissioner of public buildings and grounds for refusing to appoint
Republicans as long as "unrepentant rebels could be found."[51] Bowen, in
his efforts to find work for his supporters, opened and graded the streets
right out to the city boundaries, employing black laborers on a day's work
basis, and, in doing so, carried municipal finances heavily into debt. As we
have seen, a large proportion of those employed were black. Shepherd's

---

[50] *Evening Star*, November 5, December 11, 1868. See also *Evening Star*, February 6, October 23, November 11, December 4, 17, 1868, April 15, September 3, 1869; *Chronicle*,
November 5, 1868, September 3, 1869; *National Intelligencer*, March 1, 1867.

[51] *National Intelligencer*, May 23, 24, 1869; *Evening Star*, March 8, 1867, January 18,
1868, January 12, February 18, 1869; *Chronicle*, April 23, May 21, December 10, 1867,
August 21, 1868, April 28, 1869.

still more ambitious projects led to a quadrupling of the city labor force, and, again, a large proportion of those hired were black.[52]

Through their ward meetings, black Republicans maintained a continuing scrutiny of the city government. Councilmen were regularly summoned to appear before ward meetings and held to account for their official actions, particularly in relation to the allocation of work and appropriations for the black schools. Interrogation was rigorous, sometimes acrimonious, and in no way deferential. First Ward Alderman George Larman was accused of contributing to a stalemate on councils that had resulted in appropriations not being made and corporation employees not being paid. Larman was forced to appear before the club to explain his actions to the membership. A meeting of the Seventh Ward Republican Club was called to allow councilmen to explain their votes. "Here are councilmen of the ward who are supposed to represent the ward," said H. G. Johnson, an African American member; "and Republicans who had elected them have a right to call them to account."[53] A mass meeting was called in the First Ward to consider nominations for the crucial post of commissioner of improvements, responsible for supervising work on streets and sewers. The incumbent, it was alleged, was neither humane nor respectful in his treatment of black laborers.[54] Ward meetings were called "for the purpose of advising suitable persons for office," and council representatives were expected to vote for the appointment of those named. The Fourth Ward Republicans passed a resolution demanding that their representatives disregard applications for appointment from the ward without the recommendation by majority vote of the club, "on the grounds," explained its author, George W. Hatton, "that candidates for office nowadays need harnessing up in order to keep them in the traces." Candidates, said Hatton, were generous with promises while running for office but tended to leave blacks out when jobs were to be distributed.[55]

[52] *Evening Star*, April 8, 1869, April 15, May 7, 14, 1870; Bryan, *History of the National Capital*, 2:565–67, 588, 596–97. On Bowen's program, see also Green, *Washington*, 317–19; Johnson, "City on the Hill," 64–65, 77–79; Whyte, *Uncivil War*, 71–89; and Chapter 5, this volume.

[53] *Evening Star*, August 14, October 23, 1868, February 18, 1869. See also *Evening Star*, May 27, 1868; *Chronicle*, August 15, 1867.

[54] *Evening Star*, July 20, 23, 1869. In some wards, the commissioner of improvements chaired the club, indicating how close the link was between municipal improvements and Republican politics. *Evening Star*, April 15, October 21, 1869.

[55] *Evening Star*, May 16, 1867, April 23, 24, 1868, July 24, 1869; *National Intelligencer*, May 16, 1867; *Chronicle*, April 9, 23, 1868. Similar resolutions were passed in the First and Second Ward Clubs. *Evening Star*, April 24, 25, 1868.

Of course, most of the candidates in question were white, and most of the club members were black. Although forced to accept, for the time being at least, that most of the key positions in the party and the government would be held by white men, black Republicans attempted to use the ward clubs as a mechanism to influence those who held formal power. As Anthony Bowen explained in March 1867, "All the race wanted is work; they did not want office yet, but would vote white men in who would give them work and a chance to compete with the white men."[56] Yet as time went on, African Americans began to demand a larger share of the offices, insisting on the nomination of black candidates for council and other city offices, the appointment of blacks to the important post of commissioner of improvements, and the election of blacks to positions of leadership in the ward organizations. Over time, the Republican Party in the nation's capital began to take on more and more of the complexion of a black organization, just as it would in some of the states of the former Confederacy.[57]

### "To Become a People"

Recent studies of black political culture in the Reconstruction South have explored its roots in the institutional fabric of local communities and, ultimately, in the shared experience of slavery. Union Leagues and Republican clubs were linked to a dense network of associations, which included churches, lodges, philanthropic societies, military companies, and schools.[58] However, it would be difficult to describe Republican political organizations in Washington as growing out of a set of shared institutions because, strictly speaking, there was none. Rather than a settled plantation community formerly held in place by the constraints of

---

[56] *Evening Star*, March 1, 1867.

[57] *Evening Star*, May 22, 1868, January 15, 29, 1869; Masur, "Reconstructing the Nation's Capital," 224–25; Terry, "Place in the Sun," 91–92.

[58] Fitzgerald, *Union League in the Deep South*, 26–36; Saville, *Work of Reconstruction*, 143–95; Steven Hahn, *Nation under Our Feet*, 165–76; Hahn, "'Extravagant Expectations of Freedom': Rumor, Political Struggle, and the Christmas Insurrection Scare of 1865 in the American South," *Past and Present* no. 157 (November 1997): 122–58; Hahn, "Politics of Black Rural Laborers"; Brown, "Negotiating and Transforming the Public Sphere"; Leon F. Litwack, *Been in the Storm So Long: The Aftermath of Slavery* (New York: Knopf, 1979), chaps. 9–10. Armstead Robinson, on the other hand, sees a clear division between blacks' political organization and their religious and benevolent associations. "Plans Dat Comed from God: Institution Building and the Emergence of Black Leadership in Reconstruction Memphis," in Orville Burton and Robert McMath, eds., *Toward a New South?* (Westport, Conn.: Greenwood, 1982), 71–102.

slavery or an older free black community that had formed by a process of gradual accretion, black Washington contained diverse elements: old and new, free and freed, native and migrant. As Fitzgerald says of Mobile, "in social terms it makes little sense to talk of a single population, so diverse were the backgrounds of people of African descent."[59]

Washington's African American population consisted in part of old residents, most of them either born free or freed long before the Civil War. As in other cities with sizable free black populations, although the majority existed on or below the margins of poverty and earned their scanty wages in various unskilled manual occupations, a small but significant minority had attained a measure of economic security. Washington's antebellum black community maintained several schools, churches, and philanthropic institutions. Prominent figures in that community, such as the caterer James T. Wormley, the barber Carter Stewart, and the educationalists John F. Cook Jr. and William Syphax, provided important leadership for the Republican Party after 1867.[60] However, a majority, perhaps two-thirds, of Washington's blacks had arrived during or immediately after the Civil War. Irregularly employed and dependent for much of the year on public or private charity, these former contrabands lived in conditions of extreme destitution, inhabiting overcrowded tenements and dilapidated shanties on the fringes of the city or in areas such as Murder Bay between Pennsylvania Avenue and the Washington City Canal, located in a neighborhood that during the war had, for notorious reasons, been called "Hooker's Division" but that is now more familiar as the Federal Triangle.[61]

[59] Fitzgerald, *Urban Emancipation*, 9–10. See also Bernard E. Powers Jr., *Black Charlestonians: A Social History, 1822–1885* (Fayetteville: University of Arkansas Press, 1994); Jenkins, *Seizing the New Day*; Dylan C. Penningroth Jr., *The Claims of Kinfolk: African American Property and Community in the Nineteenth-Century South* (Chapel Hill: University of North Carolina Press, 2003).

[60] Green, *Secret City*, 13–54, 65–66; Dorothy Provine, "The Economic Position of Free Blacks in the District of Columbia, 1800–1860," *Journal of Negro History* 58 (January 1973): 61–72; Melvin R. Williams, "A Statistical Study of Blacks in Washington, D.C. in 1860," *Records of the Columbia Historical Society* 50 (1980): 172–79; Williams, "Blueprint for Change," 360–66.

[61] Green, *Secret City*, 58–65; Lois E. Horton, "The Day of Jubilee: Black Migration during the Civil War and Reconstruction," in Francine C. Cary, ed., *Urban Odyssey: A Multicultural History of Washington, D.C.* (Washington, DC: Smithsonian Institution Press, 1996), 65–78; Ira Berlin et al., eds., *Freedom: A Documentary History of Emancipation, 1861–1867. Series I, Vol. I. The Destruction of Slavery* (Cambridge: Cambridge University Press 1985), 159–67; idem, *Series I, Vol. II. The Wartime Genesis of Free Labor: The Upper South* (Cambridge: Cambridge University Press, 1993), 243–62; Leech, *Reveille*

The division between what the *National Intelligencer* called "lazy contrabands" and "old residents" occasionally came to the fore in the heat of debate in ward meetings, or when a black onlooker at the 1869 Emancipation Day parade caused a brief disturbance by calling the marchers "contraband niggers," but it manifested itself less often in overt confrontation than in a divergence of experience and interests.[62] Rather than expressing the values and interests of a settled black community, therefore, the Republican ward clubs and marching companies, like the churches and the schools, played an important part in creating one, in binding together the disparate elements of a heterogeneous black population. Republican politics gave community leaders, most of them older residents, a positive incentive to seek out, communicate with, and influence the behavior of the poor migrants in the shantytowns of Fredericksburg and Murder Bay. The removal of that incentive with the ending of self-government perhaps contributed to the widening gap between the respectable and the disreputable, between the black middle class and the larger population of laborers and domestics, that had become apparent by the 1880s.[63]

"Wee have, for the past four yars been studing with justis and the best of our ability what step wee should take to become a people," a group of South Carolina freedpeople wrote to President Andrew Johnson in October 1865.[64] In that process of self-emancipation, participation in grass-roots Republican politics played an important role. Like the Union Leagues farther south, the ward clubs were "hybrid organizations," carrying out the functions of employment agency, civic education class, and citizens' advice bureau, as well as political caucus. Like the Union Leagues, they provided "forums for collective decision-making in black communities." Political mobilization was therefore intrinsic to community formation.[65] In joining Republican clubs, in sitting there and speaking and arguing, in learning the rules of parliamentary behavior, in learning to interact peacefully and productively with others, African

---

in *Washington*, 236–52; Johnson, "City on the Hill," 152–81; Johnston, *Surviving Freedom*; Borchert, *Alley Life in Washington*; Donald E. Press, "South of the Avenue: From Murder Bay to the Federal Triangle," *Records of the Columbia Historical Society* 51 (1984): 51–70.

[62] *National Intelligencer*, May 25, 1867; *Evening Star*, April 18, 1867, April 24, 1868, April 16, 1869; John B. Ellis, *Sights and Secrets of the National Capital* (Chicago: Jones, Junkin, 1869), 494–97.

[63] See Moore, *Leading the Race*; Green, *Segregated City*, 138–44.

[64] Quoted in Saville, "Rites and Power," 83.

[65] Fitzgerald, *Union League Movement in the Deep South*, 57.

Americans developed some of the skills and gained some of the self-confidence that, if the process of political Reconstruction in Washington had not so rapidly gone into reverse, would have prepared them for a full and active citizenship. As it was, the outcome disturbed the more conservative Washingtonians, like the former U.S. Commissioner of Public Buildings and Grounds Benjamin B. French, himself a Republican of long standing. "I am almost convinced," said French, commenting on the jubilant, and sometimes aggressive, demeanor of African American voters following their election victory in June 1868, "that giving them freedom has given them so exalted an estimate of themselves that it will be hard to keep them in their proper places."[66] Republican politics played a critical role in the passage to freedom. For a brief moment in time, it offered a forum in which African Americans could feel themselves to be free men in the fullest sense. For a brief moment also, it provided a forum in which the disparate elements of Washington's black community could come together and "become a people." It is a pity that that opportunity was so abruptly cut short.

According to Charles Joyner, enslaved African Americans "did not so much adapt to Christianity . . . as adapt Christianity to themselves."[67] Similarly, black Washingtonians after slavery attempted to convert the local Republican Party organization to their own brand of enthusiastic political religion, to their own economic agenda, to their own aspirations for citizenship and civic education, and to their own community-building project. The Republican Party played a central role in the narrative of emancipation and enfranchisement that described their passage from slavery to citizenship. Yet there were other elements within that party, much closer to the centers of power on Capitol Hill and much better situated to shape events, who had a very different agenda and a very different sense of the party's purpose. In their eyes, the untidy democracy of grassroots Republicanism was at worst a destabilizing element in local politics, at best a subject of derision. The *Star*, a newspaper close to the modernizing elite that had earlier adopted an attitude of amused tolerance toward black political organization, engaged after 1870 in a campaign of systematic ridicule and condemnation of the "Murder Bay politicians" who supposedly exploited the votes of the "floating population" of contrabands

[66] Benjamin B. French, *Witness to the Young Republic: A Yankee's Journal, 1828–1870* (Don B. Cole and John J. McDonough, eds., Hanover, NH: University Press of New England, 1989), 569.

[67] Charles Joyner, *Down by the Riverside: A South Carolina Slave Community* (Urbana: University of Illinois Press, 1984), 141.

and "the whole narrow-minded tribe of corner-grocery politicians" who flourished in the rowdy atmosphere of petty ward politics. The whole purpose of reforming the District government was to bury them and their kind. No new framework of government for the District, declared the *New York Times* in 1874, should allow "the disgraceful system of ward politics" to continue.[68] Whether by intent or as an incidental by-product of their developmental project, the modernizers ensured that, for later generations of Washingtonians, the short-lived experiment in interracial democracy would be no more than a memory and that, for African Americans, an incipient tradition of activist politics would be cruelly nipped in the bud.

[68] *Evening Star*, January 24, 25, February 25, 1871, January 29, 1878; *New York Times*, June 26, 1874.

# 7

# A City and a State

## *Governing the District of Columbia*

### "A Badly Governed City"

Congress, according to the Constitution, possesses an "exclusive" legislative power over the District of Columbia. However, for most of the nineteenth century, the national government was willing to permit local authorities in the cities of the District and the surrounding Washington County to exercise many of the powers of municipal government, and, within certain broad but ill-defined limits, it was willing to leave them to their own devices. Chiefly preoccupied with the construction and maintenance of federal buildings and federal spaces, it paid only intermittent attention to the governance of the capital city that grew up around them. The city governments of Washington and Georgetown and the Levy Court that managed the affairs of the county were allowed to pass municipal ordinances, to raise taxes and set budgets, to improve streets and construct sewers, and to make provisions for the health and safety of their citizens.[1] They stood in the same constitutional relation to the federal government as cities elsewhere did to the states. As municipal corporations, those cities possessed no powers that were not derived from the superior authority of the state, but, in practice, state legislatures were usually

---

[1] For a historical review of the relationship between the federal government and the District of Columbia, see Steven J. Diner, "Statehood and the Governance of the District of Columbia: An Historical Analysis of Policy Issues," *Journal of Policy History* 4 (1992), 389–417; Donald C. Rowat, "Ways of Governing Capital Cities," in John Taylor, Jean G. Lengellé, and Caroline Andrew, eds., *Capital Cities – Les Capitales: Perspectives Internationales – International Perspectives* (Ottawa, Canada: Carleton University Press, 1993), 149–71.

prepared to acknowledge the peculiarly local elements that entered into the governance of cities and to defer often to the wishes of their representatives in passing laws that concerned them. Washington differed from other cities in that it enjoyed no representation in the national legislature, whereas the nation's legislators were much less inclined to take account of local opinion when making decisions concerning the District.[2]

There were considerable limitations on the discretionary authority of the Washington Corporation. In the first place, any of its decisions might be overridden or countermanded by federal legislation. Alternatively, Congress might, quite independently, initiate a completely new line of policy. Second, the power to issue charters to business corporations or educational and philanthropic associations lay with Congress. Third, being chronically strapped for cash, the corporation relied heavily on the pathetically few grants for municipal purposes that Congress was prepared to make. The city continuously required assistance from the nation's lawmakers, and that assistance the nation's lawmakers provided fitfully and begrudgingly. The later president James A. Garfield, who served in the House of Representatives for much of this period, admitted that "For more than fifty years the behavior of Congress toward the city of Washington has been like a whimsical step-mother. The course of Congress has been capricious, fitful, and uncertain." There had been, he said, "no regular plan, no steady permanent policy on the part of the government." As a result of congressional neglect, declared the *National Intelligencer*, Washington was "A Badly Governed City."[3]

This and the following chapter investigate the tangled relationship between Congress and its stepchildren in the District of Columbia in relation to a variety of aspects of local government. After a general examination of the manner in which the national legislature handled District matters, and in particular at the haphazard and often mean-spirited way in which it doled out appropriations for local projects, we consider the provision for social welfare that emerged from this process. The strange career of the District Board of Health, in many ways successful in combating disease but peculiarly vulnerable to attack from its political enemies, displays many of the difficulties and inconsistencies that this bipartite

---

[2] On the relationship between cities and state governments, see, in particular, Jon C. Teaford, *The Unheralded Triumph: City Government in America, 1870–1900* (Baltimore: Johns Hopkins University Press, 1984), 83–102; Ballard C. Campbell, *Representative Democracy: Public Policy and Midwestern Legislatures in the Late Nineteenth Century* (Cambridge, MA: Harvard University Press, 1980).

[3] CR, 42.3:230–31; *National Intelligencer*, February 17, 1869.

system of governance engendered. We then go on to consider the interaction of congressional and local policy making in relation to the troubled efforts to solve the problem posed by the "great ditch," Washington's malodorous, unsanitary, and only occasionally navigable canal and the energetic, sometimes frantic, campaign by local business and civic leaders after the Civil War to improve the city's restricted railroad communications. Finally, we seek to place the governance of the nation's capital in the context of broader trends in state and municipal government during the central decades of the nineteenth century.

### Congress as a City Council

That Congress had the last word on questions of District governance was unfortunate because its members devoted little attention to the task. Any municipal regulation, any institutional development, any franchise or charter, any item of spending required legislation, which had to go through the same legislative stages as any other bill and compete for congressional time and attention with a host of other business, ranging from individual claims and pension bills to questions of national importance. Time, therefore, was at a premium. Whenever District legislation came before either house, the members responsible for managing tax bills, appropriation bills, bills reorganizing the judiciary, and, especially pressing in this period, legislation dealing with the issues of Reconstruction, would repeatedly move that District business be set aside in their favor. Any District bill that took more than a few minutes to deal with, that faced serious opposition, or that gave rise to protracted debate was liable to be tabled. A single objection was often enough to condemn it to oblivion.[4] District legislation was, at best, treated with a mixture of frustration and impatience. According to Senator Samuel C. Pomeroy, "that legislation which respects the District is anything but agreeable to the Senate or to the House of Representatives. Gentlemen are anxious to get on with the legislation that pertains to the whole country; and when they are asked for a day or two to legislate especially for the

---

[4] DeAlva S. Alexander, *History and Procedures of the House of Representatives* (New York, 1916), 213–25. As Susan Margaret Thompson has shown, Congress in this period was seriously overextended and inefficient in the use of its time. The trouble was that, the business before Congress had greatly increased, but its decision-making procedures were largely unchanged. *The "Spider Web": Congress and Lobbying in the Age of Grant* (Ithaca, NY: Cornell University Press, 1985), 41–51.

District, it is given grudgingly and generally with a great deal of opposition." Therefore, much worthy and well-supported District legislation
languished helplessly on the calendar. For example, noted the *Evening
Star*, during the final session of the Forty-first Congress, only four District bills "of the most trifling and inconsequential character" had got
through, but then not much could be expected in view of the "infinites-
imal amount of time" allowed.[5] Decisions by both houses to set aside a
few hours a month for District business did provide more space for the
passage of local legislation, but even this supposedly sacred period was
often diverted to other matters when members discovered more urgent
priorities. The chairman of the House District committee noted in 1871
that his committee had only been allowed parts of nine afternoons over
the previous two years.[6]

Most members showed a lack of interest in District affairs that was
either lamentable or inevitable, depending on one's point of view. Congressmen, said Garfield, "looked upon their duties to this city as incidental." How could it be otherwise when so many were "utter strangers
here," passing a few brief years in Washington in the midst of political
careers that were conducted almost wholly elsewhere? In many important
respects, they were quite ignorant of conditions in the District. Erroneous
statements about District affairs went uncorrected, noted the *Star*, concerning, for example, the location of bridges over the Potomac or the
responsibilities of the Metropolitan Police. New Jersey Senator Frederick
T. Frelinghuysen admitted in 1868 that "we cannot do it properly for
want of local knowledge."[7] What passion members did show in District

[5] CG, 39.1:1239–40; CG, 40.2:3717; *Evening Star*, March 8, 1866, June 5, 1868, February
16, March 24, 1869, January 17, 21, February 28, March 2, 3 1870; Wilhelmus B. Bryan,
*A History of the National Capital* (2 vols., New York: Macmillan, 1914–16), 2:572.

[6] CG, 41.3:642; *Chronicle*, February 13, 15, 16, 1869, March 19, 1870, January 24, 1874;
*National Intelligencer*, February 13, 1869; *Evening Star*, February 16, 1869, February
12, March 7, 11, 18 1870, January 24, 1874; Lawrence Schmeckebeier, *The District
of Columbia: Its Government and Administration* (Baltimore: Johns Hopkins University
Press, 1928), 3–6; Alexander, *History and Procedures of the House of Representatives*,
213–25.

[7] CG, 40.2:3717; CG, 42.3:230; CR, 43.2:2214; CR, 44.1:4137; *National Intelligencer*,
March 12, 1869; *Evening Star*, February 28, March 2, 1868, January 18, 1875; Lessoff,
*Nation and Its City*, 149–50. On the high rate of turnover, see Thompson, *Spider Web*, 71–
79; Nelson Polsby, "The Institutionalization of the U.S. House of Representatives," *Amer-
ican Political Science Review* 62 (March 1968): 146–47; H. Douglas Price, "Careers and
Committees in the American Congress: The Problem of Structural Change," in William
O. Aydelotte, ed., *The History of Parliamentary Behavior* (Princeton, NJ: Princeton University Press, 1977), 36–39; H. Douglas Price, "Congress and the Evolution of Legislative

debates was liable to be an expression of their own, or their constituents', prejudices rather than the product of serious reflection on local circumstances. Some of those prejudices were directed against District residents themselves: against the southern orientation and supposed disloyalty of its white inhabitants by Republicans during and immediately after the Civil War; against the assertiveness of the District's African American population by Democrats during Reconstruction; and against the apparent irresponsibility, fecklessness, and dependency of citizens of both races by congressmen of both parties.

In such a sea of indifference and ignorance, the District relied heavily on those few individuals whose duty, and in rare cases inclination, involved them particularly in its affairs. Most prominent, of course, were the members of the House and Senate Committees on the District of Columbia. They were by no means equally attentive to the laborious duties of a committee service on which brought neither public recognition nor political advantage and counted for nothing with their constituents in Missouri or Maine. Turnover was therefore high. Of the members of the House District Committee in the Thirty-ninth Congress, noted the *National Intelligencer*, only one had served on the committee before. Committee members were discouraged by the difficulty of getting action on the floor. As the *Star* noted, "the desks of the District Committee are loaded down with important District business that there was no possibility of getting action upon." Indeed, the clerk of the House District Committee admitted in December 1869 that its members had met only twice during the previous session because they had grown weary of reporting bills that never passed and were sometimes not even considered.[8]

The citizens of the capital, lamented the *Star*, were "an oppressed people in need of prayer." As a result of congressional neglect, "the people of Washington are unable to get authority from Congress to build a railroad, pave a street, or carry out at their own expense any one of the

'Professionalism,'" in Norman W. Ornstein, ed., *Congress in Change* (New York: Praeger, 1975), 4–12; H. Douglas Price, "The Congressional Career Then and Now," in Nelson Polsby, ed., *Congressional Behavior* (New York: Random House, 1971), 14–27; Morris Fiorina et al., "Historical Change in House Turnover," in Ornstein, ed., *Congress in Change*, 24–57; Thomas R. Witmer, "The Aging of the House," *Political Science Quarterly* 79 (December 1964): 526–41.

[8] *Evening Star*, February 16, December 29, 1869, February 28, 1870; *National Intelligencer*, December 15, 1865; Lessoff, *The Nation and Its City*, 150–2; Thompson, *Spider Web*, 94–106.

improvement measures they have asked the right to make." The municipal government depended on Congress to move a muscle, yet Congress rarely found the time to pass the necessary legislation. Thus, action to replace the Centre Market and improve the canal was repeatedly delayed, corporate charters trod water, and only belatedly was decisive action taken to improve Washington's railroad communications. "The District gets no show in Congress at all," observed the New York *Herald*.[9]

Congressional neglect of the District was most obvious in matters of finance. Members showed a marked reluctance to appropriate money to defray municipal expenses. For example, in 1862, an appropriation for a new jail was struck out on the grounds, as Charles Delano of Ohio explained,

that the Government had been long enough making appropriations for the District of Columbia, and that the time had come when that policy should cease . . . and that the District of Columbia is a parasite and mendicant feeding on the charity of the Government, and that is high time a new system should be adopted, and the seventy-five thousand inhabitants of the District taught that it is their business and their duty to take care of themselves and to provide and foster their public institutions at their own expense.

Several members echoed the sentiment, and the appropriation was voted down by an overwhelming majority. The following year a similar appropriation was stymied by complaints against "the grasping disposition of the people of this District to get everything they can out of the Government."[10]

In 1868, hostile attention focused on an appropriation for the Metropolitan Police, a force set up by the federal government in 1861 as a result of doubts about the loyalty of the municipal force. An Ohio Republican listed the "enormous appropriations" for the District over the past six years, not realizing how small federal expenditures had been over the previous sixty, and argued that "there is no city in the United States where the taxes are so light as they are in this." He told the House, in blithe contradiction of the facts, that the people of the United States were pouring funds into the District and were expected "to grade the streets, light the avenues, support the poor, pay the police force, and pay a large

[9] *National Intelligencer*, February 17, 1869, *Evening Star*, March 8, 1866, May 26, June 5, 1868, April 10, September 20, 1869, April 5, 1870; CG, 42.3:230–31; CR, 43.2:1214. See also the complaints by J. Russell Barr, president of the Board of Aldermen, in May 1868. *Journal of the 65th Council* (Washington, DC, 1867), 688–89.
[10] CG, 37.2:2687–90; CG, 38.1:1491–94.

proportion of all the local expenses of the city." Ingersoll, on behalf of the District Committee, was forced to remind him yet again that the police force was set up to protect federal property, that the United States paid no local taxes, nor did the thousands of government employees who lived there and consumed municipal services. Although this item was not cut, many others were, and almost every District appropriation had to be defended in the face of hostile criticism that was often as uninformed and misplaced as this.[11]

Appropriations for the improvement of Pennsylvania Avenue, which had always been regarded as a federal responsibility, were persistently objected to. Gustavus Finkelnburg, a liberal Republican from Missouri, complained in 1871 that such grants "for the most ordinary munici-pal expenses of the city of Washington" were farcical and unjust, and, although members of the District committee reminded colleagues that the avenues belonged to the government and that it was unfair to expect local residents to keep "these enormous streets and avenues in repair," a sum of $10,000 to repair the avenue was struck out of the Sundry Civil Appropriation bill, along with several other appropriations for street improvements. The United States had already spent $422,693 on the avenue, said John Coburn, an Indiana Republican. "It seems to me that that is enough for the people of the United States to spend on one avenue in this city." Why should the United States "be responsi-ble for building bridges and aqueducts for the city of Washington?" asked Senator John A. Logan of Illinois, and $20,000 designated for that purpose was removed.[12] In the course of discussion, William Lawrence of Ohio presented the House with a table of expenditures on the Dis-trict over the last four years amounting to $5,686,570, although it was vitiated by the inclusion of a sum of $3.35 million for the aqueduct, which had been authorized in 1853, and $660,000 for bridges over the Potomac, improvements as necessary to the survival of the government as the citizenry. In fact, the District Board of Public Works reported a year later that the United States had paid only $1,321,288 for street improvements since 1802, during which period the city had expended $13,921,767.[13]

[11] CG, 40.2:1482–85; *Evening Star*, February 28, 1868.

[12] CG, 41.2:1656–60, 1660–62, 4536; CG, 41.3:1656–57.

[13] CG, 41.2:1616; Report of the Board of Public Works of the District of Columbia from its Organization until November 1, 1872, Ho. Exec. Doc. 1, 42.3 (1872). See also CG, 41.2:4536; CG, 42.3:201; letter from Mayor Richard Wallach to the Secretary of the

As we shall see, Congress showed a marked reluctance to contribute to the expense of improvements initiated by the Board of Public Works. After 1874, with the imposition of direct rule, Congress was forced to reach into the Treasury to bail out the District, the bankruptcy of which would now undermine the credit of the federal government itself, but it did so with reluctance and over numerous objections. The people of the United States should not be taxed to build up "a great splendid, idle, profligate capital," said John Q. Smith of Ohio. The citizens of the District must learn to live within their means, as others did. "It is evident to any who has been in these halls, that whatever can be wrung out of the Treasury of the Government of the United States is wrung by the citizens of this District," complained Clinton Merriam of New York.[14] After handing over $1.2 million in 1874, which was close to half the total cost of governing the District, Congress made appropriations of $500,000 in succeeding years and advanced smaller sums for interest payments and teachers' salaries but always kept the commissioners on a tight rein. "This government has declined to assume its fair share of responsibility," suggested the Republican Senator William Windom in 1878. "It has shirked its obligations because it had the power to do so."[15]

Although Democrats were less likely than Republicans to condone a higher level of appropriations and although western and southern members of both houses were especially prone to criticize extravagance in local expenditures, the variations between members in their generosity toward the District were far less significant than their overall unwillingness, as long as a measure of home rule survived, to fund District projects at an adequate or equitable level.[16] The decision finally arrived at in the Organic Act of 1878 that the costs of government should be borne in equal proportions by the U.S. Treasury and local taxpayers constituted a retrospective, if reluctant, admission by Congress that its contributions had been unduly stingy in the past.

---

Interior, reprinted in the *Washington Daily Morning Chronicle*, December 14, 1865; *Evening Star*, May 22, 1868; *New York Times*, December 4, 1872; Lessoff, *Nation and Its City*, 34–35; Constance M. Green, *Washington: Village and Capital, 1800–1878* (Princeton, NJ: Princeton University Press, 1962), 326–27.

[14] CR, 43.2:1610. Cf. CR, 43.2:1213, 2212

[15] CR, 45.2:2854.

[16] For illustrative roll calls on District appropriations, see CG, 42.2:4348; CG, 42.3:330–31, 2023, 2092; CR, 43.2:2151; CR, 44.1:858, 1142, 1201, 1254, 2541, 4273; CR, 44.2:1593, 1595; CR, 45.3:2361.

## The Charities of the District

Care of the destitute, the sick, the insane, and the otherwise dependent had long been accepted as a responsibility of state and local government. Social policy, such as it was, clearly lay within the parameters of the "police power" of the states.[17] The District of Columbia in the Civil War era can scarcely be said to have had a social policy in the sense of a coherent and comprehensive program of services for the needy. Instead, it offered a heterogeneous array of provisions, public and private, federal and local, that were initiated and maintained in a thoroughly ad hoc fashion in response to individual initiatives by groups of citizens or individual members of Congress (and in some cases, their wives). Those programs, both public and private, expanded markedly during the 1860s and 1870s, yet at the end of the period social provision in the District of Columbia remained, even by nineteenth-century American standards, something of a hodgepodge.

"We are woefully deficient in charitable and reformatory institutions," Mayor Richard Wallach told the councils in June 1865.[18] Indeed, the only institution supported by the municipality before and immediately after the Civil War was the Washington Asylum, which incorporated an almshouse, a workhouse, and a smallpox hospital. Besides that, the corporation provided medicines and paid for medical attendance for the poor. The municipality made no systematic allowance for outdoor relief. For most of the year, relief for the destitute could only be found within the walls of the asylum. However, seasonal unemployment led the corporation to appropriate greater or lesser sums for emergency relief nearly every winter. This was all the more likely when Republicans, highly sensitive to the newly enfranchised black vote, were in control.[19]

---

[17] For an explanation of the "police power," see William Novak, *The People's Welfare: Law and Regulation in Nineteenth-Century America* (Chapel Hill: University of North Carolina Press, 1996).

[18] Message of the Mayor, in *Journal of the 63rd Council* (Washington, DC, 1866), 21.

[19] See, for example, *National Intelligencer*, January 16, February 4, March 29, 1865; *Journal of the 66th Council* (Washington, DC, 1869), 421, 425, 442–44, 458, 486, 491; *Journal of the 67th Council* (Washington, DC, 1870), 337–41, 440–41; *Evening Star*, December 18, 1867, November 23, 30, December 11, 1869, March 15, April 26, 1870. See also Teaford, *Unheralded Triumph*, 268–75. On the hostility to outdoor relief, see Michael B. Katz, *In the Shadow of the Poorhouse: A Social History of Welfare in America* (New York: Basic Books, 1986) 37–50; Walter I. Trattner, *From Poor Law to Welfare State: A History of Social Welfare in America* (5th edn., New York: Free Press, 1994), 89–90; Robert Bremner, *The Public Good: Philanthropy and Welfare in the Civil War Era* (New York: Knopf, 1980), 198–201.

The Washington Asylum was an imposing red-brick structure set on a 58-acre site close to the Eastern Branch of the Potomac, a mile east of the Capitol. Four wooden buildings 250 yards away served as an isolation hospital for smallpox patients. Like many public institutions, the asylum was seriously overcrowded. A building designed in 1843 to accommodate 100 inmates regularly housed 200 during the immediate postwar years, and on one occasion as many as 308. In August 1865, according to the local Freedmen's Bureau superintendent, the almshouse contained 109 women and 27 men, and the workhouse contained 51 women and 40 men. Wallach told him that, although room would be found for permanent residents, "it is impossible for the Corporation of Washington to care for all the indigent who have come here during the war." That distinction overlooked the fact that temporary residents had always formed a large part of the poorhouse population. What he really meant is that the city was unwilling to care for the large population of so-called contrabands that the war had brought to Washington. A proposal to build a new wing to accommodate what Wallach called "the great influx of destitute persons into the city in consequence of the rebellion" – that is, to build segregated accommodation for African Americans – was not followed up. Despite the fact, often bruited by city officials, that a majority of the male inmates were not long-term residents of the city, Congress did not respond to their appeals for assistance.[20]

The managers of the asylum appeared to be stricter in applying residency requirements to black than white applicants to keep at bay the large number of impoverished contrabands brought to Washington by the war. In October 1866, the *Chronicle* reported that an elderly African American, sick and destitute, had been refused entry by the intendant of the asylum, who claimed that there was "no room for niggers" and that there were "no niggers here to attend to them." The applicant was referred to the bureau and placed in the Freedmen's Hospital even though he was

[20] *Daily Morning Chronicle*, August 26, 1867; *Journal of the 63rd Council*, 21; William F. Spurgin to Selden N. Clark, August 31, 1865, AQMR, Reel 13; Robert Reyburn to Charles H. Howard, July 9, 1866, Letters Received, 1:1775, Reel 6, BRFAL-DC. The central role played by the poorhouse in the theory, if not always the practice, of contemporary poor relief is explained in Katz, *In the Shadow of the Poorhouse*, 13–35; Trattner, *From Poor Law to Welfare State*, 59–64; David Rothman, *The Discovery of the Asylum: Social Order and Disorder in the New Republic* (Boston: Little, Brown, 1971), 155–205.

a long-time resident of Washington.[21] In fact, the asylum always contained a few black inmates. In November 1865, the Freedmen's Bureau superintendent reported that there were fourteen adult black females and five males, old and infirm, in the almshouse and that they were "well provided for." In July 1866, Robert Reyburn, the surgeon-in-chief of the local Freedmen's Bureau, found 13 African Americans among 134 inmates. The authorities told him that destitute freedpeople could not be admitted without the provision of further accommodation, because the existing buildings were always filled to capacity. African American inmates were segregated from the others, and the black section, especially of the Asylum hospital, was seriously overcrowded.[22]

The asylum included an almshouse, where paupers and the indigent aged were cared for, and a workhouse, where persons convicted of petty offenses were sent to work off their fines. Thus, the "unfortunate poor" lived "in close proximity to convicted vagrants, prostitutes, and drunkards." Although some effort was made to keep them apart, as the District commissioners remarked in 1874, "the very nature and construction of things as they now are tends toward a commingling." This state of affairs, they pointed out, was not "creditable to the District." However, the building could not be turned over to the exclusive use of the poor until a new jail had been constructed in the District, a project that was repeatedly stalled over the better part of a decade. Although the Washington Almshouse does not seem to have suffered from the mismanagement, and ill treatment reported in some state poorhouses, its regime of regularity and discipline, offering basic accommodation and unpalatable food, combined the same principles of cheapness and deterrence that were applied in similar institutions across the nation.[23]

During the generation or so preceding the Civil War, considerable efforts were made to remove children from what one reformer called

---

[21] John V.W. Vandenburgh to William F. Spurgin, November 22, 1865, LR 1:263, Reel 4; William W. Rogers to Spurgin, October 9, 1866, LS 2:423, Reel 1, BRFAL-DC; *Chronicle*, October 11, 1866.

[22] William F. Spurgin to Selden N. Clark, November 6, 1865, fn 779, ULR, Reel 12; Robert Reyburn to Charles H. Howard, July 9, 1866, LR 1:1775, Reel 6, BRFAL-DC; Horton, "Development of Federal Social Policy," 111–12.

[23] Green, *Washington*, 218; *Report of the District Commissioners, 1874* (Washington, DC, 1874), 108–11; *Report of the District Commissioners, 1875* (Washington, DC, 1875), 15. Cf. Katz, *Shadow of the Poorhouse*, 22–25, 29–30, 85–99; Rothman, *Discovery of the Asylum*, 237–40, 287–95; W. R. Brock, *Investigation and Responsibility: Public Responsibility in the United States, 1865–1900* (Cambridge: Cambridge University Press, 1984), 103, 112–13.

"the loathsome moral corruption so common in our poorhouses" and place them in more appropriate institutions. In consequence, a variety of orphanages and reformatories sprang up across the country.[24] In 1860, four orphanages operated in Washington: the Washington Orphan Asylum, St. Vincent's Orphanage, St. Joseph's Orphanage for boys, and St. Ann's Infant Asylum. All were private institutions, the last two being wholly and the second partially supported by Catholic charities. In 1866, Congress passed a bill incorporating the National Soldiers' and Sailors' Orphans' Home, which was funded partly by the transfer of the fathers' pensions and partly by regular appropriations from the federal government. In addition, an Industrial Home School, founded in 1867, furnished meals, shelter, and industrial training to destitute children, which its founders believed to be the best way "to prevent crime and pauperism." Its emphasis on order and obedience, rigid schedules, and practical work experience was typical of children's homes across the United States. That institution, too, being mostly dependent on private contributions and "only aided slightly" by the corporation, applied to Congress for assistance.[25] From 1869, Congress also made regular grants for the Colored Orphans' Home, which had formerly been supported by the Freedmen's Bureau.[26]

Although dependent children had mostly been removed from the almshouse, there was no facility in the District for the confinement of juvenile offenders, with the result that they were either discharged or committed to the workhouse alongside adults. "The establishment of at least a house of refuge and reformation for vicious and depraved youth in our midst is imperatively demanded by the ordinary claims of philanthropy," declared Mayor Wallach in 1865. Citizens therefore petitioned Congress for legislation chartering a reform school and for

---

[24] Bremner, *Public Good*, 159. See also ibid., 30–31, 85–89, 158–64, 171–73; Katz, *Shadow of the Poorhouse*, 103–9; Rothman, *Discovery of the Asylum*, 206–36, 237–40, 257–64.

[25] CG, 37.3: 1330; CG, 39.1:2376–77; CG, 40.1:4270–71; CR, 43.1:4919–20; Sayles J. Bowen et al., petition to Senate Committee on the District of Columbia, February 10, 1869, SEN40A-H5.1; H. W. Blackford et al. to Senate Committee on the District of Columbia, n.d., SEN41A-H5.2, RG46, NARA; Green, *Washington*, 219; Trattner, *From Poor Law to Welfare State*, 112–16; Bremner, *Public Good*, 148–50.

[26] Managers of Colored Orphans' Home to Senate Committee on the District of Columbia, February 13, 1869, SEN40A-H5.1, RG46, NARA; *Evening Star*, January 11, 1870, June 5, 1874; *Chronicle* January 11, 1871; Masur, "Reconstructing the Nation's Capital," 71–73.

financial assistance.[27] After an attempt to construct a House of Industry in conjunction with the so-called Guardian Society to Reform Juvenile Offenders in the District of Columbia had failed to get off the ground, Congress decided in 1866 to "take it out of private hands" and establish a public House of Correction with a government-appointed board of trustees.[28] The act creating the House of Correction appropriated $12,000, which enabled a building to be erected on a farm four miles above Georgetown. The school finally opened its doors in December 1869. However, it could accommodate only sixty boys and was chronically overcrowded, and the site was unhealthy, being chronically prone to malaria. In 1872, Congress agreed to appropriate $100,000 for the acquisition of a new site and the construction of a building sufficient to accommodate three hundred boys. Thereafter, the Reform School, as it was now called, received $10,000 annually in the Sundry Civil Appropriation bills.[29]

The *Daily Morning Chronicle* welcomed Congress's liberality toward the Reform School, claiming that it enjoyed great success in turning boys away from lives of idleness and crime and preparing them for useful careers. Yet, like many other institutions responsible for the care of dependent or difficult children, its reformatory purpose was carried out with a firm hand. It sought to instill moral values and influence the formation of character by combining manual work and education. The managers were anxious that juvenile offenders should be committed to the care of the Reform School for long terms, the duration of which should be determined by the school authorities according to their evaluation of the

---

[27] *Journal of the 63rd Council*, 21; Catherine L. B. Spears to Senate Committee on the District of Columbia, December 22, 1864; petition of citizens for incorporation of a Reform School, February 24, 1865, SEN38A-H4, RG46, NARA.

[28] CG, 37.2:2157, 2846, 2906; CG, 38.1:1762–63, 3129–30, 3406; 39.1, 2675–76, 4020–21. On the government's dealings with the Guardian Society, see Trustees of the Guardian Society to House Committee on the District of Columbia, n.d., HR39A-H6.1; Correspondence Relating to Opposition of Trustees of Guardian Society to House of Correction for Juveniles, HR39A-F6.2, RG292, NARA; A. K. Browne to Charles H. Howard, March 20, 1867 (and enclosures); John V. W. Vandenburgh to William W. Rogers, April 20, 1867, LR, 2:1616, 1760, Reel 8, BRFAL-DC.

[29] CG, 42.2:2528, 3243, 3277, 3399; CR, 43.2:1998; CR, 44.1:4039, 4283–84; CR, 44.2:1778; CR, 45.2:4802; *Chronicle*, April 8, 1872; Report of the Board of Trustees of the Reform School of the District of Columbia, in *Report of the Secretary of the Interior*, 1871, Sen. Misc. Doc. 34, 42.2, Ser. 1505, 1179; Report of Board of Trustees, in *Report of the Secretary of the Interior*, Sen. Misc. Doc., 42.3, Ser. 1560; *District of Columbia Reform School*, Ho. Report 39, 42.2, Ser. 1528; *Report of the District Commissioners*, 1874, 109–11.

pupils' progress, rather than sentenced for short periods, which made it impossible for these objectives to be achieved. Indeed, the trustees believed that not only boys convicted of a specific offense but all difficult and ungovernable boys that were in need of "proper correction" should, when necessary, be taken from their home environment and committed to the care of the institution. As a further extension of their quasi-parental authority, the trustees wished, like the managers of other institutions caring for the young, for the power to bind their charges out to suitable employers.[30]

Congress also supported a number of hospitals. The government gave $1,000 a month for the treatment of up to sixty transient paupers at the Providence Hospital, chartered in 1864 and maintained by the Roman Catholic Sisters of Mercy, as well as providing half the cost of a new and larger building. According to the *National Intelligencer*, "The poor are always received, none being refused."[31] A congressional grant made possible the establishment of the Columbia Hospital for Women and Lying-in Asylum in 1865, which received regular appropriations of from $15,000 to $28,000 a year, "it being peculiarly a Government institution," as the *Chronicle* observed. The hospital provided treatment for females "suffering from diseases peculiar to their sex" and facilities for women "lying in" during pregnancy. Fifty of the beds were free and forty private; twenty were set aside for the wives of soldiers and sailors. When questioned as to the reasons for federal support, a member of the House Appropriations Committee explained that the institution was established by Congress for the people of the District and those visiting the capital; a majority of patients were nonresident. Garfield described it as "one of the noblest of the charities this Congress has been assisting in the District of Columbia."[32]

The Freedmen's Hospital, the only one of the hospitals operated by the Freedmen's Bureau to survive the agency's demise, also received a regular

[30] *Chronicle*, April 8, 1872; Katherine Masur, "Reconstructing the Nation's Capital: The Politics of Race and Citizenship in the District of Columbia, 1862–1878" (Ph.D. diss., University of Michigan, 2005), 75–76.

[31] CG, 38.1:727, 1464; Petition of Lucy Gwynn et al., January 27, 1864, SEN38A-H4; Joseph K. Barnes to Senate Committee on the District of Columbia, December 6, 1869, SEN41A-E5, RG46, NARA; *National Intelligencer*, August 27, 1867, September 23, 1868.

[32] CG, 41.2:4848; CG, 41.3:1615–17; CG, 42.3:1468–69; CR, 43.1:4919; CR, 44.2:2093–94; CR, 45.3:2100–1; *Report of the Secretary of the Interior, 1867*, in CG, 40.2:49; *Report of the Secretary of the Interior, 1868*, in CG, 40.3:43; *Evening Star*, October 29, 1868, August 3, 1869; *Chronicle*, January 16, 1868; March 18, 1870.

grant from Congress. Located on a site just north of the city boundary, the hospital had 150 beds and cared for a total of 9,517 patients between September 1867 and September 1868.[33] As the bureau wound up its operations in the District, its chief medical officer, Dr. Robert Reyburn, wrote to the secretary of the interior, calling attention to the "absolute necessity" of congressional support to keep the hospital open. It contained 350 patients, 200 of whom were "so utterly disabled by old age or disease that they will require to be supported during the remainder of their lives." In most cases, there was nowhere else for them to go. Mayor Bowen warned that its discontinuation would throw a large number of refugees and paupers on the charitable resources of the corporation that should be supported by the government, and he urged that provisions should be made for the hospital to remain open.[34] In response, Congress began to appropriate regular sums for the Freedmen's Hospital, amounting to $78,000 in 1871. Further annual appropriations were made, although at a reduced level during the period of Democratic control of the House in the late 1870s. The Freedmen's Hospital remained in existence well into the next century, having gone a long way to securing its survival by establishing itself as a teaching hospital and relocating itself on the campus of Howard University.[35]

While wrestling with the sectional conflict during the 1850s, Congress found time to charter the Government Hospital for the Insane. Set in a handsome building beyond the Eastern Branch, it embodied contemporary approaches to the care of the insane, setting its complement of local residents and distressed members of the armed forces to labor in the household and on the farm, in the hope that regular habits would overcome the mental disorders that had caused them to be committed.[36] In 1865, the hospital housed 866 inmates, 645 of whom were military

[33] Charles H. Howard to O. O. Howard, October 10, 1867, LS 3:758a, Reel 1; Robert Reyburn to C. H. Howard, September 1, 1865, October 12, 1866, fn 279, 345, AQMR, Reel 13, BRFAL-DC; Horton, "Development of Federal Social Policy," 107–10.

[34] Robert Reyburn to James Harlan, February 15, 1869, HR40A-F7.6, RG292; Sayles J. Bowen to Harlan, February 16, 1868, SEN40A-E4, RG46, NARA; Reyburn to C. H. Howard, October 1, 1867, LR 3:441, Reel 9, BRFAL-DC; CR, 44.2:2094; Horton, "Development of Federal Social Policy," 106–10; Thomas C. Holt, Cassandra Smith-Parker and Rosalyn Tuborg-Penn, A Special Mission: The Story of the Freedmen's Hospital, 1862–1962 (Washington, DC: Academic Affairs Division, Howard University, 1975), 2–17.

[35] CG, 41.3:1665–66; CR, 43.2:2005; CR, 44.2:2094; CR, 45.2:4386; Holt et al., Special Mission, 8–17.

[36] Green, Washington, 300–2; Rothman, Discovery of the Asylum, 109–54. After the war, mental hospitals tended to become glorified warehouses for the confinement of the

or naval personnel.[37] Although regular appropriations were made for the support of the hospital, their propriety was persistently challenged. In 1871, an Illinois Congressman asked why Congress should support the insane asylum to the tune of $125,000 a year, more than was appropriated for all the insane asylums in Illinois, when other states supported their own sick and insane with their own tax revenues. Henry Dawes and Ben Butler reminded him that many of the inmates were veterans of the Union Army and Navy unhinged by their wartime experiences. It was wrong, said Butler, to economize at the expense of the defenders of the Union.[38]

A characteristic product of the idiosyncratic, although sometimes creative, manner in which charities were created in the District of Columbia was the Columbian Institution for the Deaf, Dumb and Blind, later known as Gallaudet College. It grew out of an individual initiative by Andrew Jackson's former advisor and political fixer Amos Kendall, who, taking pity on a group of deaf children living in squalor near to his home, pressed Congress to furnish funds for their instruction. Incorporated in 1857 and receiving $150 a year from the Treasury for every deaf, dumb, or blind pupil from the District whose parents could not afford to pay for their tuition and smaller sums from the corporation, the Columbian Institution was founded on land just north of the city donated by Kendall himself. The school was managed by Edward M. Gallaudet, an experienced teacher of the deaf whose father had pioneered in the introduction of sign language in America. The intake of pupils rapidly expanded to include children from neighboring states, as well as the children of government employees, an enlargement that was made possible by increasing federal appropriations, as well as private funds.[39] By 1862, the institution provided instruction for thirty-eight pupils. It

---

mentally ill, increasingly acting as custodial rather than therapeutic institutions. Ibid., 265–87; Katz, *Shadow of the Poorhouse*, 99–103.

[37] *Report of the Secretary of the Interior, 1863*, Ho. Exec. Doc. 1, 39.1, Ser. 1248, xxiii–xxiv. Cf. Benjamin B. French, *Witness to the Young Republic: A Yankee's Journal, 1828–1870* (Don B. Cole and John J. McDonough, eds., Hanover, NH: University Press of New England, 1989), 397; *Evening Star*, October 21, 1868, November 27, 1869, November 27, 1870.

[38] CG, 40.2:4270–71, 4453; CG, 41.3:1614–15; CR, 43.2:2002–5, 2127; CR, 44.1:4037–38; *Report of the Secretary of the Interior, 1867*, in CG, 40.2:49; *Report of the Secretary of the Interior, 1868*, in CG, 40.3:43; *Patriot*, February 26, 1871.

[39] Green, *Washington*, 219–21; Edward M. Gallaudet, "A History for the Columbia Institution for the Deaf and Dumb," *Records of the Columbia Historical Society*, 15 (1911): 1–22.

had received in all $18,925 from private donations and was in receipt of a regular allowance of $4,500 from Congress. It had already begun to distinguish itself from state schools for the deaf by offering not only manual instruction and a common school education but a higher education that would develop the pupils' facilities to the highest extent and train them as teachers. In 1864, the institution was authorized to confer degrees.[40]

In later years, regular appropriations were made for the Columbian Institution, although not always without objection. The Civil Appropriations Bill for 1870 included $40,775 for regular expenses and an additional $90,000 for the completion of new buildings. Some congressmen objected to the running costs of the institution, as well as its capital expenditure, far in excess of the amounts spent on equivalent, if not larger, facilities elsewhere. William Mungen of Ohio claimed that most northern states had ample facilities for the care of the deaf, and he could see no reason why the people of the United States should be asked "to feed a lot of lazy, idle teachers, and give a collegiate education to the deaf and dumb." Dawes explained that it was desirable for the District to have an institution for the education of the deaf and dumb, as all the states had, and argued that at least some of these unfortunate people would benefit from a higher education, which only the Columbian Institution could provide. The appropriation was agreed to and repeated in succeeding years, along with further grants for capital expenditures.[41]

Although this was rarely mentioned on the floor of Congress as a requirement for federal aid, most of the agencies in receipt of appropriations did admit some African Americans, as many private charities did not. The Columbia Hospital for Women treated black patients, who in 1869 constituted 32 percent of the total. The Government Hospital for the Insane, being managed by government directors and supported by government money, also admitted African Americans, although only if

---

[40] Report of the Columbia Institution for the Deaf, Dumb, and Blind, in *Report of the Secretary of the Interior, 1862,* 37.3, Ho. Exec. Doc. 1, Ser. 1157, 629–36; *Report of the Secretary of the Interior, 1863,* Ho. Exec. Doc. 1, 38.1, Ser. 1182, xvi–xvii, 716–39; *Report of the Secretary of the Interior, 1865,* Ho. Exec. Doc. 1, 39.1, Ser. 1248, xxiv–xxvi, 831–41; CG, 38.1:1108–9, 1468.

[41] CG, 40.2:4270–71, 4453; CG, 41.2:4682–84, 4847–48; CG, 41.3:1615; CG, 42.2:4247; CR, 44.2:2093–94; *Report of the Secretary of the Interior, 1867,* in CG, 40.2:49; *Report of the Secretary of the Interior, 1868,* in CG, 40.3:43; *Evening Star,* February 10, 1870; January 30, 1871.

they could produce affidavits proving their long-term residency in the District. However, there were allegations that black patients were isolated from other patients and that they were not so well cared for. The Reform School had roughly equal numbers of black and white inmates, but they, too, were segregated.[42]

At the start of the Civil War the federal government supported the Columbian Institution for the Deaf, Dumb and Blind and the Government Hospital for the Insane. After the war, it began to allocate increasing sums to Providence Hospital, the Columbia Hospital for Women, the House of Correction (later the Reform School), the National Soldiers' and Sailors' Orphans' Home, and the Colored Orphans' Home. Whereas during the early 1860s, the federal government appropriated just over $60,000 a year for charities, by the latter part of the decade the aggregate sum had risen to nearly $250,000 a year, with between $110,000 and $150,000 going to the Insane Asylum and between $43,000 and $85,000 to the Columbian Institution; the other institutions received between $10,000 and $15,000 a year each.[43] During the 1870s, the Freedmen's Hospital (between $45,000 and $75,000 a year), the Colored Orphans' Home ($10,000), the Soldiers' and Sailors' Orphans' Home (between $10,000 and $12,000), and the Children's Hospital ($5000) were added to the list of regular beneficiaries. The total expenditure ranged around $350,000 a year.[44]

During the 1870s Congress began to show a greater reluctance to take on new obligations. "It is utterly impracticable for the Government of the United States to sustain all of the so-called eleemosynary institutions of the country, or even of this city or District," said Senator Cornelius Cole of California in 1871. "I think that we have already gone about as far as Congress ought to go in donating to these institutions as far as their number is concerned." Increasingly, proposed grants to charitable institutions, like the Little Sisters of the Poor in 1875 and the Industrial Home School in 1876, were struck out on points of order because they had no

[42] Petition of Colored Citizens, n.d., SEN41A-H5.2, RG46, NARA; Charles H. Howard to James Harlan, June 6, 1866; to Charles Nichols, January 16, 1867; to Benjamin Wade, January 16, 1867, LS 2:204, 674, 677, Reel 1; W. J. Otto to Howard, June 6, 1866, LR 1:[137], Reel 6, BRFAL-DC; *New National Era*, March 20, 1873; Thomas R. Johnson, "The City on the Hill: Race Relations in Washington, D.C., 1865–1885" (Ph.D. diss., University of Maryland, 1975), 144.

[43] See the tables in CG, 39.2:1482–83; CG, 41.3:1616.

[44] See CR, 43.1:5260; CR, 44.1:4774–75; CR, 44.2:4038–39, 4723–4; CR, 45.1:2210–11; CR, 45.2:4326–27.

warrant in prior legislation. Members were fearful that a new appropriation would form the basis of a claim that would be repeated every year. "It is well known," said Windom, "that whenever the Government takes one of these benevolent institutions in the District of Columbia under its charge it has continued to appropriate for it."[45] Members of Congress, particularly Democrats and Midwestern Republicans, objected to the "enormous expenditures to support these institutions" and demanded that local citizens should no longer be treated as "wards of the nation." Such attitudes contributed to a growing reluctance to make new grants and, toward the end of the decade, an overall reduction in federal appropriations for District charities.[46]

Nearly all the institutions that were assisted by Congress were private charities run by their own boards of trustees and setting their own policies for admission and the management of their resources. In 1871, the newly appointed governor of the District of Columbia suggested that a Board of Charities and Correction should be established to monitor the activities of the numerous charitable agencies operating in the District. A few years later, the District commissioners recommended that all charities in receipt of public funds should be placed under the supervision of a commission appointed by the District government: "Under such a system Congress and the citizens of the District will be annually informed of the exact amount expended, and how expended, and improved methods of economy and discipline will be introduced in their management." Such proposals were spurned by Congress, on the grounds that, because these institutions were supported by the federal government, they should be controlled by the federal government. In addition, individual members jealously guarded congressional control of charities in which they held a strong personal interest. Whereas several state governments established state boards to cope with precisely this problem of coordination and information, not until 1900 did Congress create a Board of Charities to lay down regulations for the delivery of federal money.[47]

---

[45] *CG*, 41.2:1892; *CR*, 43.1:4920–23; *CR*, 43.2:2005; *CR*, 44.1:4276.

[46] *CG*, 41.2:4683, 4848; *CG*, 41.3:1614, 1615.

[47] *CR*, 44.2:2093; *Evening Star*, May 15, 1871; *Report of the District Commissioners, 1876*, 10. On state boards of charities, see Brock, *Investigation and Responsibility*, 88–115; Bremner, *Public Good*, 152–58. On congressional policy in the early twentieth century, see Robert Harrison, *Congress, Progressive Reform, and the New American State* (New York: Cambridge University Press); Robert Bremner, *The Public Good: Philanthropy and Welfare in the Civil War Era* (New York: Oxford University Press, 1980), 2004), 143–44.

Such an approach to welfare was typical of social policy in postbellum Washington, as, indeed, in postbellum urban America. A series of initiatives, sometimes public, sometimes private, but more often an amalgam of the two, were taken to address a variety of specific problems and specific categories of need. Each of the agencies concerned had its own particular emphasis, its own particular clients, its own particular supporters, its own particular history, and its own particular relationship with the federal government. There was something fundamentally illogical about the selection of charities for federal assistance. "The argument in favor of them is that they are supported now by a sort of law, the law of custom," said Cole.[48] In some cases, influential citizens like Amos Kendall successfully persuaded Congress to support their favorite institution. In others, members of Congress, or, in the case of the Colored Orphans' Home, their wives, took on a particular philanthropic cause. There was no guiding hand to shape social provision for the District as a whole and to ensure that it met the needs of all its citizens equally. Provision for women and children was more generous than for men, for whites more generous than for African Americans; groups like alcoholics, the chronically ill, and the "mildly insane" could find little or no assistance outside the walls of the asylum. Congress made no effort to coordinate welfare policy in the District of Columbia but merely reacted to a series of private initiatives. Social policy in the District of Columbia, then, was very much a product of its history rather than of systematic thinking about social need.[49]

## The District Board of Health

Hidden among the provisions of the Territorial Act of 1871, barely noticed by press or public, was a section creating a Board of Health for the District of Columbia. The protection of public health had long been regarded in U.S. law as a necessary implementation of the "police power" of the states. Indeed, it was primarily in the field of public health that legal concepts of the "police power" were first articulated. During the early nineteenth century, several cities, including Washington itself, had appointed boards of health that sometimes wielded extraordinary

---

[48] CG, 41.3:1892.

[49] On charitable provision in late nineteenth-century Washington, see Constance M. Green, *Washington: Capital City, 1879–1950* (Princeton, NJ: Princeton University Press, 1962), 61–76. On the relationship between public and private sectors, see Bremner, *Public Good*, 181–85.

power during periods of medical emergency, like the cholera epidemics that intermittently terrorized American cities between the 1830s and the 1860s but that were normally quiescent and frequently moribund. For example, Washington's board had a budget of $15 in 1848. After 1865, these agencies were progressively replaced by municipal health departments with professional rather than lay membership, which in turn came under the authority of state boards of health created to investigate, advise, and coordinate the activities of local health officers. The new boards did not necessarily have more extensive statutory powers than their predecessors, but they had larger budgets, more effective powers of enforcement, more professional staff, and, in time, the authority provided by a greater scientific expertise. They exemplified the trend toward a greater centralization, uniformity, and professionalism in the provision of government services in the late nineteenth century. Indeed, says William Novak, "public health was at the center of a legal and political revolution that culminated in the creation of modern constitutional law and a positive administrative state." The District Board of Health established in February 1871 was an example, although, as so often in District affairs, a peculiar example, of this trend.[50]

Washington's municipal board of health had fallen into desuetude by 1860, but the disruptive impact of the Civil War, the explosive increase in population, and the consequent health hazards led to demands for more effective sanitary regulation. Residents complained of the overcrowded and dilapidated alley dwellings that clustered behind the main avenues, the filthy streets and gutters, the poor drainage that left pools of stagnant water in close proximity to private dwellings, the livestock that roamed everywhere through the city, the carcasses of dead animals that lay unattended for weeks, the infrequent collection and unsatisfactory disposal

[50] Novak, *People's Welfare*, 194. On trends in public health, see John Duffy, *The Sanitarians: A History of American Public Health* (Urbana: University of Illinois Press, 1990); and, more specifically, Duffy, *A History of Public Health in New York City* (2 vols.; New York: Russell Sage Foundation, 1968–74); Charles Rosenberg, *The Cholera Years: The United States in 1832, 1849, and 1866* (Chicago: University of Chicago Press, 1962); Barbara G. Rosenkrantz, *Public Health and the State: Changing Views in Massachusetts, 1842–1936* (Cambridge, MA: Harvard University Press, 1972); Trattner, *From Poor Law to Welfare State*, 140–62. Novak, *People's Welfare*, 191–233 demonstrates the extent of public health regulation during the first half of the century. See also, Duffy, *Sanitarians*, 35–51, 57–62, 84–85. Brock, *Investigation and Responsibility*, 116–47, analyzes the development of state boards of health after 1865. On municipal departments of health, see Teaford, *Unheralded Triumph*, 245–50. On Washington's early board of health, see Betty L. Plummer, "A History of Public Health in Washington, D.C., 1800–1890" (Ph.D. diss., University of Maryland, 1984), 27–32, 62–63.

of "night soil," the unfiltered water supply "impregnated with organic matter," the inadequate sewerage, and, above all, the malodorous Washington Canal, which received, but did not always release, much of the city's waste matter, forming, in consequence, as the *National Intelligencer* described it, a "monstrous pool of pollution and putrefaction." Washington, complained the *Chronicle*, was a "city of stinks," and it badly needed a properly constituted board of health. These were regarded as more than aesthetic flaws. It was widely believed before the discovery of microbes that disease was caused by miasmas rising from decomposing organic material. Its prevention therefore required rigorous cleaning of homes and streets, the removal of stagnant water, and the elimination of garbage, night soil, and other "nuisances" that might endanger public health. That was why efficient sanitation was considered essential to combat epidemic disease.[51] Added urgency was imparted by the approach of Asiatic cholera, which reached the shores of North America late in 1865 and promised to devastate the cities of the East Coast during the following summer. "In a word," warned the *National Intelligencer* in April 1866, "the condition of the city is powerful inviting to the pestilence that stalketh at noonday."[52]

The functions of the former board of health were transferred in 1861 to the Metropolitan Police. The Superintendent of Police detailed sanitary officers to patrol the city and "provide for the removal of nuisances, noxious and deleterious substances." To supplement their activities, a newly-constituted board of health was created by the Corporation in November 1865, with a view to combating the anticipated cholera epidemic, and the number of policemen on sanitary duty was doubled.[53]

---

[51] See, for example, the reports of the Board of Health in *Evening Star*, September 22, 1869, July 1, 1870; of the Committee on Health of the Board of Common Council, July 10, 1865, in *Journal of the 63rd Council*, 55; *National Intelligencer*, August 7, 1865; *Chronicle*, August 10, 1863. See also Thomas Antisell to House Committee on the District of Columbia, June 24, 1864, HR38A-G4.1, RG292, NARA; Robert Reyburn to John Eaton, September 8, 1865, fn 708, ULR, Reel 12, BRFAL-DC; *Chronicle*, March 28, July 19, December 18, 1865, June 6, 1866; *Evening Star*, May 12, 1866; *National Intelligencer*, November 11, 1865; Duffy, *Sanitarians*, 79–92; Rosenberg, *Cholera Years*. On contemporary theories regarding the spread and prevention of disease, see ibid., 1–100; Duffy, *Sanitarians*, 20–22, 102–8.

[52] *National Intelligencer*, April 21, 1866; Richard Wallach to Board of Aldermen, November 6, 1865, in *Journal of the 63rd Council*, 304–5. See also *National Intelligencer*, October 13, 1865; *Chronicle*, June 6, 1866; *Evening Star*, October 16, 1866; Rosenberg, *Cholera Years*; Duffy, *Sanitarians*, 79–92.

[53] Richard Wallach to Board of Aldermen, November 6, 1865, in *Journal of the 63rd Council*, 304–5; *Evening Star*, November 3, 7, 1865.

The increased activity of the sanitary police apparently brought about an improvement in conditions and the removal of many egregious nuisances. Its effectiveness may be judged by the frequency with which householders complained of its inquisitorial behavior, and the strict enforcement of sanitary regulations led to many arrests. In August 1867, the board claimed that Washington was "extremely healthy" and that a serious epidemic had been averted. Reyburn, recently appointed president of the board, reported in September 1869 that the sanitary condition of Washington compared favorably with that of any city in the United States. However, he then went on to list a series of problems that needed to be tackled and asked for increased powers to deal with them. The board could do nothing about that elongated municipal cesspool the Washington Canal; it was powerless to round up the hogs and other domestic animals that roamed freely through the city; it could not order the removal of slaughterhouses and other "noxious trades" beyond the city limits; it did not have the power to demolish dilapidated and unsanitary buildings; and it could not compel the vaccination of citizens in the event of a smallpox epidemic. Although able to remove a great many so-called nuisances, the board was unable under existing law to deal with the most recalcitrant culprits.[54]

In 1870, the councils finally gave the board more effective powers to direct the removal of nuisances. Using its new authority, the board took action against the poudrette factories operating within the city limits and proceeded to round up the hogs and other domestic animals roaming at large. When a serious attempt was made to enforce the law, those who kept dairy cattle in the District or maintained hog pens appealed to council members, who responded to the hubbub of protest by repealing the 1870 public health law. This reduced the Board of Health once more to the status of "a mere nullity."[55]

It was evident that a municipal board lacked the authority to impose its will on recalcitrant citizens and hostile councilmen. The only answer, believed the *Evening Star*, was to create a metropolitan board of health that would be beyond the control of local politicians and immune from the influence of local property holders. The experience of other cities

[54] *Evening Star*, May 12, June 25, August 15, 1866, February 14, July 1, 11, August 12, 1867, September 21, 22, 1869, July 1, August 18, 25, 1870; *National Intelligencer*, November 9, 1865. For an example of the difficulty that the board faced in enforcing its orders, see *National Intelligencer*, October 30, November 6, 1866; *Evening Star*, May 12, 1866.

[55] *Evening Star*, January 6, 10, 14, 1871.

had shown the need to vest all sanitary powers in one body and to give it the authority to protect the public against the causes of disease.[56] It is notable that one of the four aldermen to vote against the emasculation of the board was Alexander R. Shepherd, the prime mover of the legislation creating the Territory of the District of Columbia that was going through Congress at that time. It is not clear how the Board of Health found its way into the Territorial Act as it was redrafted in conference or who was responsible for the insertion. The language of the section was surprisingly terse. It established a board, to be appointed by the president, with the responsibility "to declare what shall be deemed nuisances injurious to health, and to provide for the removal thereof." The only specific duties imposed upon it were "to make and enforce regulations to prevent domestic animals from running at large in the cities of Washington and Georgetown" and "to prevent the sale of unwholesome food in said cities."[57] Rather than setting out its responsibilities in great detail, Congress relied on common law understandings of what constituted "nuisances" and on the accumulated precedents of over half a century of sanitary regulation.[58]

The board's first major test came with the smallpox epidemic that attacked eastern cities during the early 1870s, arriving in Washington in December 1871. The board sought to combat the disease by means of a combination of isolation and vaccination. It divided the territory into ten districts, each under the supervision of a medical practitioner who would canvass his district, seeing to the vaccination of persons who required it and the proper isolation of those who had been infected. Every effort was made to isolate those who were suffering from the disease and to remove them from contact with others. Those who could not be safely isolated in their homes were transferred to the smallpox hospitals that

---

[56] *Evening Star*, January 14, 1871. The same argument had a few years earlier warranted the establishment of the Metropolitan Board of Health in New York. The success of that body in containing the 1866–67 cholera epidemic encouraged other municipalities to follow its example. See Duffy, *Sanitarians*, 118–21; Duffy, *History of Public Health in New York City*, 1:540–71, 2:1–47; Rosenberg, *Cholera Years*, 175–212. There is also a useful account of the origins and early history of the Metropolitan Board of Health in Mitchell Okun, *Fair Play in the Marketplace: The First Battle for Pure Food and Drugs* (DeKalb: Northern Illinois University Press, 1986), 32–48, 54–62.

[57] *U.S. Statutes at Large*, 41.3, chap. 62 (February 16, 1871), 424–25. Cf. Novak, *People's Welfare*, 228–33. The terms of reference of the New York Metropolitan Board of Health and the Massachusetts Board of Health, created a few years earlier, were also very broad. Duffy, *Sanitarians*, 120; Brock, *Investigation and Responsibility*, 118.

[58] Novak, *People's Welfare*, 191–98.

were established in the grounds of the asylum and in temporary quarters elsewhere. However, the health officers were handicapped by their lack of authority to compel the removal of infected persons from their homes and thereby to "separate the diseased from the healthy." At the same time, a general program of vaccination was initiated that treated 40,292 District residents between November 1871 and May 1873 at an overall cost of $27,817. Here, too, complete coverage was prevented by the lack of authority to compel citizens to submit to vaccination, a power that during the late nineteenth century neither legislatures nor courts were prepared to confer. The week ending June 1873 was the first since January 1872 in which no new cases were reported, and the following month the board was able to announce that the epidemic was over.[59]

The second function of the Board of Health was to remove what were broadly termed "nuisances." The board prided itself on its success in abating nuisances. The health officer reported in 1876 that 20,261 nuisances "of greater or lesser degree" had been reported and dealt with during the previous year. These included the removal of garbage, stable manure, dead animals, and other offensive materials; the filling in of sunken lots where stagnant water might collect; and, more controversially, the removal of slaughterhouses, soap and glue factories, and other "noxious trades" from residential areas.[60] The abatement of other nuisances was achieved with the cooperation of the Board of Public Works, which, by filling in the canal, at the urging of the Board of Health, draining marshes along the Potomac riverfront, paving and cleaning streets, laying sewers, and improving drainage, had done a great deal to improve

[59] Reports of the Board of Health, in *Evening Star*, May 13, 1873; *Report of the Commissioners, 1876*, 8–9. The progress of the epidemic and the board's response can be traced in *Evening Star*, July 2, 1872, October 16, 18, December 18, 26, 1872, January 1, 22, February 15, May 13, July 23, 26, August 1, 1873. The breakdown of those infected by race was not always recorded, but, according to the *Star*, in January 1873, of 275 new cases, 194 were black and 81 white; *Evening Star*, February 15, 1873. On the program of vaccination, see *Evening Star*, October 31, November 22, 1871, January 2, 18, 23, July 2, October 16, 1872. On the broader application of quarantine, see Novak, *People's Welfare*, 204–17; Brock, *Investigation and Responsibility*, 138–46; Duffy, *Sanitarians*, 24–26, 58–62, 100–8.

[60] Report of the Board of Health, in *Report of the Commissioners of the District of Columbia for the Year 1874* (Washington, DC, 1874), 287; *Report of the Commissioners, 1876*, 13; *Evening Star*, May 13, 1873; T. S. Verdi to Christopher C. Cox, October 25 1876, Senate Committee on the District of Columbia, SEN44A-E4, RG46, NARA. On the treatment of nuisances, see Novak, *People's Welfare*, 217–27. In contrast, the sanitary police claimed to have dealt with 3,875 nuisances in the nine months ending April 1870. *Evening Star*, July 1, 1870.

the sanitary condition of the District by the time of its abolition in June 1874.[61]

The board was responsible for ensuring the regular and efficient collection of garbage. It declared in 1874 that, "owing to the strict discipline to which the garbage masters have been subjected, the service has been much more satisfactorily and effectively performed than ever before" and proudly enumerated the 16,000 loads of garbage that had been collected over the previous year. However, newspaper reports suggest that the garbage was not always conclusively disposed of. Because the collection was carried out on a contract basis, it was difficult to ensure regular and efficient performance. The deficiencies of the contract system caused the board to experiment with a force paid and hired by itself, but this, it seems, proved no more satisfactory in its operation.[62] Similar problems attended the collection of night soil. In the absence in most homes of water closets connected to the main sewers, human waste was collected in privy vaults that were, in theory, emptied nightly by a corps of municipal scavengers and their contents, estimated at forty tons a day, transported to a point far beyond the city boundaries where they could be safely deposited or converted into fertilizer. The board contracted with a private company for the removal of night soil to "a remote location on the river," although not remote enough, it seems, to prevent the operation of the tide from returning much of it to Washington's waterfront.[63]

The board also moved to eliminate the noisome alley dwellings that clustered behind the main streets and avenues, harboring poverty, disease, and a good deal of human misery. However, paving and draining the alleys and disposing of "the squalid shanties that line them" were not a primary concern of the Board of Public Works or other municipal agencies, and landlords could rarely be persuaded to improve their properties. Hence, the agency took it upon itself in 1874 to condemn 389 unsanitary dwellings, and 985 dwellings in all between 1874 and 1877, of which 300 were demolished, a peremptory approach that seemed all the more appropriate in the immediate aftermath of a smallpox epidemic that had hit alley communities especially severely. The abolition of the board in

[61] See *Chronicle*, June 11, 1874; *Evening Star*, December 18, 1872, June 15, 1874.

[62] *Report of the Commissioners*, 1874, 117, 287; *Chronicle*, June 28, 1874; *Evening Star*, February 17, 1872, May 13, August 5, 1873, June 20, 1874.

[63] Reports of the Board of Health in *Evening Star*, December 18, 1872, April 15, May 13, August 30, 1873; *Report of the Commissioners*, 1874, 292–95. See also *Evening Star*, September 15, 1871.

1878 left no municipal authority with the power to condemn and remove unsanitary dwellings.[64]

A longstanding nuisance, frequently remarked on by residents and visitors alike, was the large number of domestic animals (in excess of twenty thousand according to an 1868 estimate), hogs, sheep, goats, and cattle, as well as cats and dogs, which roamed freely across the city, wreaking destruction upon newly planted trees and even garden plants, as well as leaving traces of their passing in the form of piles of excrement and, at the last, decaying corpses. Vermont Senator George F. Edmunds, during debate on the territorial bill, gave vent to his rage at "the infinite, abominable nuisance of cows, and horses, and sheep and goats, running through all the streets of this city, and whenever we appropriate money to set up a shade tree, there comes along a cow or a horse or a goat, and tears it down the next day." Only two trees in a hundred did not display "the marks of ill-treatment by horned animals or by pigs or by some animals that are running at large." It was not unusual for citizens to encounter hogs and other animals grazing on their lawns, rooting around in their flower beds, or even slumbering happily on their front porch. The city was also, according to the *Chronicle*, cursed with a "legion of worthless curs" that evaded the dog catchers by day and roamed the streets at night, keeping the citizens awake with their barking and squabbling.[65]

Earlier attempts to capture and impound the errant beasts had failed, either because of political opposition or a perceived lack of legal authority. Municipal legislation that gave the old board of health greater powers to deal with the problem was soon reversed.[66] The District Board of Health, however, was given explicit authority to impound livestock, one of the few responsibilities explicitly conferred by the enabling legislation. One of its first actions was to establish a pound, appoint a poundmaster, and order the apprehension of animals wandering at

---

[64] Reports of the Board of Health in *Evening Star*, December 18, 1872, May 13, 1873; *Report of the Commissioners, 1874*, 287–88; *Report of the Commissioners for the Year 1877* (Washington, DC, 1878), 67; Green, *Washington*, 367–8; James Borchert, *Alley Life in Washington: Family, Community, Religion and Folklore in the City, 1850–1970* (Urbana: University of Illinois Press, 1980), 45. On the development and character of alley dwellings, see ibid., 1–47; Allan John Johnston, "Surviving Freedom: The Black Community in Washington, D.C., 1860–1880" (Ph.D. diss., Duke University, 1980), 17–35, 132–42, 242–53.

[65] CG, 41.2:844; *Chronicle*, July 1, 1874; Duffy, *Sanitarians*, 87–88.

[66] *Evening Star*, March 10, 16, 1868, August 12, 1870, January 6, 10, 14, 1871.

large on the city streets. The *Star* welcomed the order, triumphantly proclaiming:

From and after tomorrow ... the cities of Washington and Georgetown will cease to be common pasture and browsing ground for vagrant animals. Roaming droves of porkers will no longer be permitted to ravage our yards, root up our grass-plots, and carry destruction to our flower and kitchen gardens. No longer will they be allowed to make a hog wash of every gutter, and afterwards to paint our palings with mud. No longer will the exuberant cows have the run of our shrubberies and parked streets. No longer will the musical geese contest with the pigs for the possession of the puddles and the sidewalks. No longer will the frisky goats carry on their pugnacious frays on the footways, or make lively butting raids on the juveniles. None of these things will be after to-morrow. Thus pass away time-honored institutions under the ruthless hand of modern innovation.[67]

In 1876, the board reported that 11,747 animals had been impounded since the agency had come into existence: "No animals are now allowed to run at large; and although this nuisance baffled the efforts of the police for many years, it is now entirely abated." In addition, 7,327 stray dogs, "another source of evil and danger to the community," had been captured and put down.[68] However, the fact that as late as the winter of 1878 the Senate passed a bill augmenting the Board's powers to prevent animals from roaming at large suggests that the problem was far from solved.[69]

The Board of Health was also responsible for the inspection of food. It instituted a daily inspection of markets, groceries, and fish wharves to monitor the comestibles on sale to the public. It supervised the care and transportation of animals prior to slaughter not only to prevent "unjustifiable cruelty" but also "overcrowding, heating, bruising, and irregularities in feeding and watering" that might render them unfit for slaughter and their meat unfit for consumption.[70] The board assumed responsibility for public hospitals and for the distribution of medicines to the poor.[71] Not the least of its achievements was the more efficient

---

[67] *Evening Star*, June 14, 1871. See also *Evening Star*, June 15, July 3, November 13, 1871.

[68] Reports of the Board of Health in *Evening Star*, December 18, 1872; *Report of the Commissioners, 1874*, 287; *Report of the Commissioners, 1876*, 10. See also *Evening Star*, March 18, April 8, July 1, 1874.

[69] *CR*, 45.2:1299.

[70] Reports of the Board of Health in *Evening Star*, December 18, 1872; *Report of the Commissioners, 1874*, 287; *Report of the Commissioners, 1876*, 8, 10, 13–14. See also *Evening Star*, January 9, 1873, June 10, 1874; Brock, *Investigation and Responsibility*, 137–8; Okun, *Fair Play in the Marketplace*, 37–43, 54–58.

[71] Report of the Board of Health in *Report of the Commissioners, 1874*, 117, 287; Horton, "Development of Federal Social Policy," 110–14.

collection of vital statistics. A more complete registration of deaths and the early notification of disease permitted the board to ascertain the causes of death more accurately and made possible an analysis of the distribution of disease and, in theory at least, its more efficient prevention.[72]

"The wisdom of this law creating a board independent of all local and political influence was early apparent," said the board in 1876, "for the legislature of the District, affected by the prejudice of the ignorant and the interests of political tricksters, became openly inimical to the board.... The local legislators had interests at variance with the board of health; they had votes to secure and preferred to listen to the complaints of their prejudiced and ignorant constituents, rather than to the appeals of the board of health." Throughout its life, the Legislative Assembly, particular its lower chamber, was jealous of the independent authority of the board and frequently denied it the funds and additional powers that it asked for. Its members argued against a further grant of power before the House District Committee, complaining that their own authority would be curtailed. It would, said one, give the board arbitrary powers without reference to the people's elective representatives, leaving the people "totally subservient to the Board of Health." Members frequently challenged the board's authority, for example, over the collection of night soil or the impounding of livestock, and held back funds for its operations. The legislature refused to supply the means, said the *Chronicle*, "because the voters who are now, for the first time, compelled to watch cows, shut up pigs, cleanse alleys, &c., are sworn and swearing enemies of the Board.... The work of the Board naturally makes them unpopular. They ought not, therefore, to be dependent on the popular branch of the Legislature for the means to do their work."[73]

Despite the broad grant of authority in the organic act, the board appealed to Congress for additional powers. In 1872, the Senate passed a bill further defining the duties of the Board of Health to make and enforce regulations for the prevention of contagious or infectious diseases; the disinfection and removal of night soil, garbage, offal, and manure, the

---

[72] Report of the Board of Health in *Report of the Commissioners, 1876*, 9–10; *Evening Star*, May 13, 1873. A preoccupation with the collection of statistics, and a confidence in their utility, was characteristic of all late-nineteenth-century boards of health. See Brock, *Investigation and Responsibility*, 127–28.

[73] Report of the Board of Health in *Report of the Commissioners, 1876*, 7, 9; *Journal of the House of Delegates of the District of Columbia, Annual Session, 1871* (Washington, DC, 1871), 502–3, 589–90; *Evening Star*, June 27, July 31, August 2, 10, November 13, 1871, January 18, 1872; *Chronicle*, January 26, May 2, 7, 1872.

sale of poisons, and the making of medicines. Strongly opposed by local druggists and by members of the Legislative Assembly, the bill made no progress in the House.[74] Two years later, the board's request for a law empowering it "to make and enforce regulations to secure a full and correct record of vital statistics, including the registration of births and deaths," was granted by Congress. It also sought, but failed to secure, legislation that would give it the authority to require the draining and filling in, at the owner's expense, of lots containing stagnant water, to enter and search premises, to make and enforce quarantine regulations, and to inspect and supervise hospitals relying wholly or in part on public funds.[75]

Much of the time, Congress was generous with appropriations to finance the board's activities (part of its expenses were met from federal and part from local funds).[76] However, congressional support for the board was by no means certain. In 1873, the House Committee on the District of Columbia reported a bill appropriating $39,300 to recompense the board for expenses incurred in the course of combating the smallpox epidemic. John F. Farnsworth, a liberal Republican from Illinois often critical of District expenditures, protested that the act creating the board, along with the other agencies of territorial government, was intended to relieve Congress of the bother of legislating for the District. Why should the people of Illinois be asked to pay to remove dead animals belonging to residents of Washington, clean out their privies, or prevent the sale of bad meat? Enough members agreed with him to defeat the bill by a vote of 84–87, largely along party lines.[77] Two years later, an appropriation of $36,994 for the Board of Health was criticized as wildly extravagant by senators such as Edmunds and the South

[74] CG, 42.2:2484, 2526; CG, 42.3:850; *Chronicle*, May 2, 7, 1872; *Evening Star*, January 1, 10, 1873.

[75] Report of the Board of Health in *Report of the Commissioners, 1874*, 282–84, 289; *Chronicle*, March 20, 1874; copy of HR 2440, March 1, 1876, SEN44A-E4, RG46, NARA.

[76] However, the commissioners complained of inadequate appropriations in 1876, insufficient in particular to pay for medicines and physicians for the poor. *Report of the Commissioners, 1876*, 11. Senator William Windom later complained that "the unreasonable reduction of the sanitary force" – a consequence of the "inadequate appropriation made by Congress" – had resulted in an increased incidence of diphtheria and scarlet fever over the past few years. *CR*, 45.2:3787–88.

[77] CG, 42.3:888–90. Republicans voted in favor of the appropriation by a margin of 74–23, the Democrats by 10–61, and liberal Republicans by 0–3. The appropriation was restored in conference. *U.S. Statutes at Large*, 42.3, chap. 172 (1873), 540.

Carolina Republican Thomas J. Robertson. This time, Republican Senator Joseph R. West defended the board's record in reducing mortality at "quite as reasonable and quite as economical an expenditure as attends the administration of health in any other city of the same population." There was "no better conducted sanitary service in the United States," said John J. Ingalls of Kansas. On this occasion, the Senate agreed by 21 votes to 16 to accept the amount proposed by the Appropriations Committee.[78]

The Board of Health was the only agency of the territorial government to survive the municipal counterrevolution of June 1874. When Congress finally set about devising a permanent framework of government in 1878, a separate board of health was not included. The bill drawn up by the House Committee on the District of Columbia eliminated the independent boards of health, fire, police, and public schools. The Board of Health, said a Democratic member, should have been abolished long ago.[79] The Senate District Committee, with its Republican majority, took a different view. It restored the Board of Health, which Ingalls described as "one of the most valuable adjuncts of the District government" and, indeed, gave it additional powers to regulate hospital admissions and to require the filling in of lots.[80] Edmunds believed that the board was "a very useful body, but an enormously expensive one" and argued that it was invidious to retain the Board of Health when other independent boards had been removed. Democratic senators eagerly picked up on his suggestion and launched into a series of bitter assaults on the agency. Augustus S. Merrimon of North Carolina described the Board of Health as "a sort of practical despotism . . . invested with powers that no body in a free country ought to be allowed to exercise." Others complained of "its unnecessary expense and cumbersomeness." It was, said Maryland Senator William P. Whyte, "a useless and unnecessary ornament to the government of the District of Columbia," costing $50,000 a year.[81] Ingalls observed, in reply, that he had so far heard "no just cause of complaint" against the board and could see no good reason for its abolition. It was admittedly efficient, protecting the citizens from pestilence, collecting vital statistics,

[78] *CR*, 44.1:4271–73. Republicans voted in favor by 20–7, Democrats by 1–9. The appropriation for the Board was reduced to a slightly lower level in conference. *CR*, 44.1:4723. See also *CR*, 43.2, 115–16.

[79] *CR*, 45.2:1922, 1926. For discussion of the role of the Board of Health in an earlier plan of government, see *CR*, 43.2:100, 124–26.

[80] *CR*, 45.2:3604–6, 3608.

[81] *CR*, 45.2:3780–1, 3785–87, 3819–21, and 3780–91, 3817–24 passim.

and reducing the death rate, all this at a per capita cost lower than in equivalent cities. Public health, in any case, should not be seen in terms of "parsimonious economy." Several Republicans spoke up in defense of the board, referring to the "wonderful change" in health and sanitation that it had brought about, at a cost that compared favorably with that of health departments in cities such as Philadelphia and Baltimore. Congress would be "tampering with a serious matter" if it denied the city "proper sanitary supervision." Stanley Matthews of Ohio believed that its abolition would be an "injurious step." There was no city of that size that did not possess an independent board of health staffed by persons with special expertise in the field of preventive medicine and invested with quasi-legislative powers that enabled them "to define the occasions and contingencies of their executive actions." Ordinary municipal officers were not competent to handle such matters. Washington, he said, ought to be "a model and example for all other cities in every element of good government."[82] When the Democratic Senator Allen G. Thurman offered an amendment, taken from the House bill, which replaced the board with a health officer and sanitary inspectors appointed by the commissioners, Edmunds and two other Republicans voted with the Democrats to ensure its passage by a narrow 24–23 vote. Thus, the Board of Health ended its short but eventful existence.[83]

The Board of Health of the District of Columbia was one of a number of similar agencies established during the decades after the Civil War. In the first place, it involved a centralization of authority, supplanting earlier, more local boards of health. Second, it represented a model of professional authority that, in principle, challenged the prerogatives of elected officials. In its 1876 report, the board criticized the selfish and ignorant opposition of local legislators and argued that, in the capital city, "the board of health should be responsible only to Congress, and entirely free from local influences. Hygiene is the art by which health is preserved, and the hygienist, like the physician, should not be deterred by religion, politics, or self-interest from performing his sacred duty, and he should be sustained by the strong arm of the Government. Laws of health, physiologically speaking, are immutable." They existed independent of any political authority. Strictly speaking, therefore, the constraints on interference by local legislators should apply to Congress as well. Congressmen were also moved by prejudice and ignorance, influenced by

[82] CR, 45.2:3784, 3789–90, 3822–23.
[83] CR, 45.2:3824.

hostile lobbyists, responsive to popular feeling, and motivated by considerations of party and ideology. Their support, as it turned out, could not
be depended on either.[84]

Members of the Board of Health attributed public resistance to ignorance and self-interest. They blamed both the greed of one class of the population, which, possessing "more property than heart," rented unsanitary
hovels and carried on "filthy trades or manufacturing, such as fat boiling,
crushing bones and the like," and on another class, which was "indifferent
to habits of cleanliness" and resentful toward "sanitary interference."[85]
Yet they failed to acknowledge the biases incorporated within their own
decisions and procedures. For example, their campaign against wandering
domestic animals embodied a middle-class love of order and cleanliness
and a disregard for the means through which many poorer Washingtonians were compelled to make their living. It penalized and, insofar as it was
effective, extinguished a mode of existence founded on casual labor and
small-scale husbandry. Although a nuisance to some residents, animals
roaming at large were an important source of income for others who kept
cattle for milk and hogs and sheep for slaughter, allowing them to graze
on the extensive public reservations that formed so large a proportion
of the capital's area, as well as undeveloped land on the outskirts. When
attempts were made to eradicate the practice, local legislators complained
of the injustice that would be inflicted on the poor man. As in rural areas
in the early and mid-nineteenth century, grazing on unfenced common
lands formed an important part of the livelihood of many smallholders,
and the attempt to suppress it, although perhaps justified on grounds of
public health and public convenience, formed part of a wider movement
to control the use of public property and to force elements of the urban,
as well as the rural, poor into more regular forms of economic activity.
It was, Michael W. Fitzgerald suggests, equivalent to the closing of the
open range in the rural South, and it generated a similar kind of class
politics.[86]

---

[84] Report of the Board of Health in *Report of the Commissioners, 1876*, 15.

[85] Report of the Board of Health in *Report of the Commissioners, 1876*, 14–15.

[86] In similar vein, a New York City alderman in 1831 had objected to a ban on the grounds
that keeping cows was "the entire support of some of the poorer classes in the upper
wards." Duffy, *Sanitarians*, 87; *Evening Star*, January 14, 1871; Michael Fitzgerald,
*Urban Emancipation: Popular Politics in Reconstruction Mobile, 1860–1890* (Baton
Rouge: Louisiana State University Press, 2002), 255–56. On the political significance
of fencing laws in the postbellum South, see also Steven Hahn, *The Roots of Southern
Populism: Yeoman Farmers and the Transformation of the Georgia Upcountry, 1850–
1890* (New York: Oxford University Press, 1983), 59–63, 239–68; Charles L. Flynn

Quarantine regulations, although presented as measures to protect the community against the intrusion of epidemic disease, operated in practice as restrictions on the movement and attempts to modify the behavior of poorer citizens, especially African Americans, who bore the brunt of the smallpox epidemic. The board took pride in the fact that, of 1,738 cases of smallpox, "not a dozen cases occurred among that intelligent class of citizens who observed the orders and regulations of the board" and that, although "the small-pox was raging while Congress was in session ... its members were scarcely aware of its presence." It was in alley dwellings and in other poorer neighborhoods, populated largely by freed families, that the regulations were most rigorously applied. It was "poverty, ignorance, and vice," as much as infectious disease, that threatened the health of the community. Like other nineteenth-century sanitary reformers, the members of the board saw close links between cleanliness and morality. Health regulations were presented as a way of protecting the healthy part of the community from the unhealthy, the clean from the unclean, the responsible from the irresponsible, and the informed from the ignorant. They therefore reflected "hierarchies of social difference."[87]

"Under the intelligent administration of the Board of Health," the commissioners observed in 1876, "the sanitary condition of the District is excellent and compares creditably with that of the most favored cities of the country." Nevertheless, the board met with disapproval from many of those who were directly affected by its actions and from the newspapers and politicians who responded to their complaints.[88] As Alan Lessoff notes, the progress that the board achieved came "at a high cost in terms of public ill-will." Its intrusions into private concerns and the sometimes peremptory exercise of its powers left it vulnerable to political attack. The approach to policy formation and enforcement that it adopted, in William Novak's words, "displaced the common law understandings of

---

Jr., *White Land, Black Labor: Caste and Class in Nineteenth-Century Georgia* (Baton Rouge: Louisiana State University Press, 1986), chap. 5; J. Crawford King Jr., "The Closing of the Southern Range: An Exploratory Study," *Journal of Southern History* 43 (February 1982): 53–70; Shawn Everett Kantor and J. Morgan Kousser, "Common Sense or Commonwealth? The Fence Law and Institutional Change in the Postbellum South," *Journal of Southern History* 59 (May 1993): 199–242.

[87] Report of the Board of Health in *Report of the Commissioners, 1876*, 9; Novak, *People's Welfare*, 214–17; Duffy, *Sanitarians*, 81–82, 99.

[88] Report of the Board of Health in *Report of the Commissioners, 1876*, 279, 298–99; *Report of the Commissioners, 1876*, 15; *Evening Star*, June 15, 20, 1874.

self-regulating communities." It generated precisely the kind of sectional-ized but well-focused opposition that had the greatest influence on local legislators and even on the national Congress. It might have been expected that its potential immunity from local legislative authority and its ability to appeal to the higher authority of Congress would protect it from such attacks, but this turned out not to be so. Hence, the federal territory's Board of Health provided a model for the nation for only a short while.[89]

### The "Great Ditch": The Washington Canal

One of the less successful features of the founders' design for the nation's capital was the plan for a canal to run through the heart of the city. Roughly following the line of the grandly named Tiber Creek, it passed along the northern edge of the Mall from 17th to 7th Street before nego-tiating a series of right-angle turns around Capitol Hill and proceeding in a southerly direction until it made contact with the Eastern Branch of the Potomac a little below the Navy Yard. The Washington City Canal was designed to allow supplies to be shipped to markets in the center of the city and, more generally, to provide a connection with the interior by way of the Chesapeake and Ohio Canal. It provided a clear illustration of the founders' vision of Washington as a center of commercial as well as political activity. Only occasionally, in fact, did vessels manage to get from the 17th Street entrance to Centre Market, between 7th and 9th Street, or from the Eastern Branch as far as the Botanic Garden; still less often did they manage to traverse the full length of the canal. The prob-lem was that because the water level at the two ends of the canal differed by only a few inches, nobody could find a way to maintain a sufficiently vigorous flow of water to prevent it from silting up. Thus, for much of its life, the canal was not navigable, and the sporadic attempts to make it so by dredging were successful in clearing it only for a few years before new layers of sediment deposited by the Potomac tides undid the work of improvement.[90]

[89] Lessoff, *Nation and Its City*, 131; Novak, *People's Welfare*, 229.

[90] Cornelius W. Heinze, "The Washington City Canal," *Records of the Columbia Historical Society, 1953–1954* (Washington, DC, 1959): 1–23; Green, *Washington*, 72, 128, 147, 193–94, 255; Lessoff, *The Nation and Its City*, 21–22; Bryan, *History of the National Capital*, 2:107–13, 122–32. On the founders' faith in the city's commercial potential, see Carl Abbott, *Political Terrain: Washington, D.C. from Tidewater Town to Global Metropolis* (Chapel Hill: University of North Carolina Press, 1999), 28–38.

To make things worse, many of the city's sewers emptied into the canal. Any hope that it would perform the functions of a mains culvert, admitting waste matter from various parts of the city and releasing it into the Potomac, were also defeated by the action of the tides. Even when a current flowed through the channel, much of the refuse washed into the river at low tide was washed back again at the next high tide. When accumulations of sediment obstructed the flow, as they frequently did, filth accumulated unchecked. Hence, the canal accepted, but did not always succeed in releasing, a great deal of sewage, as well as other unwanted items ranging from dead cats to old clothes. According to a report made by a board of U.S. Army engineers in April 1866, the bottom of the canal was "covered with a mass of decaying animal and vegetable matter and earth, forming a soft, slimy and offensive compound" that was exposed to the air "a great portion of the time." The U.S. Commissioner of Public Buildings and Grounds described it as "nothing more than an open sewer." The "putrid, fetid, poisonous, pestilential canal," as the *National Intelligencer* described it, was an eyesore, an offence to the olfactory glands, and, in the light of contemporary ideas of sanitation, a serious danger to public health. The city's Board of Health warned in April 1867 that if no action were taken to secure a flow of clean water through the canal, "much sickness would result from the miasmatic vapors arising therefrom." Furthermore, its banks were occupied by unsightly wharves and warehouses and by the cabins and shanties of those who could not easily find space elsewhere in the city, in neighborhoods such as the notorious Murder Bay. Thus, its presence blighted the sections adjoining it and hampered the development of the Mall.[91]

In any listing of improvements designed to render the capital more habitable, not to mention achieving the aesthetic grandeur that its planners had envisaged, cleaning out the canal almost always came close to the top. "No other thing," said the *Chronicle* in July 1870, "nor any two, three or half dozen other such nuisances has so injured Washington in the estimation of everybody, citizens or strangers, as the great ditch or

---

[91] *Journal of the 63rd Council,* 547; *Chronicle,* April 17, August 26, 1869; *National Intelligencer,* September 5, November 11, December 16, 1865; Green, *Washington,* 134–35, 212. See also *Evening Star,* December 2, 1867, July 7, 1868; *National Intelligencer,* August 7, October 13, 1865; P. J. Staudenraus, ed., *Mr. Lincoln's Washington: Selections from the Writings of Noah Brooks, Civil War Correspondent* (South Brunswick, NJ: Rutgers University Press, 1967), 186–87; Donald E. Press, "South of the Avenue: From Murder Bay to the Federal Triangle," *Records of the Columbia Historical Society* 51 (1984): 51–70.

canal nuisance."[92] Yet the three-mile open sewer that residents so regularly complained of had resisted improvement for over half a century and would resist improvement for several years more before the Board of Public Works finally resolved the long-standing problem by filling it in once and for all. The delay was partially explicable in terms of the technical problems that it posed and the many competing solutions proffered by hydraulic engineers. However, it also resulted from intractable flaws in the structure of local government, in particular the division of responsibility between Congress and the municipality. Indeed, nothing illustrates the deficiencies of that structure more effectively than the sorry saga of the Washington City Canal.

The standard response to the buildup of sediment in the canal was to clean it out and dredge it in the hope of returning it to something like its pristine condition. Earth was repeatedly removed from the channel, to be deposited on areas of marsh land below the White House and around the Washington Monument, in the vain hope that a sufficient current of clear water could be introduced, whether by building floodgates to control the tidal flow or by diverting freshwater from Rock Creek or from higher up the Potomac, to keep it open for navigation. The chief advocate of dredging and the chief apostle of a commercial canal was Benjamin Severson, a hydraulic engineer appointed by the city to supervise work on the canal. A further refinement was the proposal that the canal should be narrowed from its extravagant dimensions of 145 feet along the central sections to something like 75 feet, thereby improving the flow of water, facilitating future dredging, and reclaiming land for other uses. There was no need for so wide a canal, argued the *National Intelligencer*, "even for the delusive purpose of an imaginary commerce." There were others who believed that the experiment of maintaining a channel for waterborne commerce was doomed to failure and, furthermore, that combining the functions of navigation and sewerage was disastrous. For raw sewage to be introduced into an open channel, they argued, was a serious danger to public health. An increasing number of voices called for the canal to be filled in and replaced by a covered sewer that would receive effluent from the city's other sewers and deposit it in the Potomac. This solution received its most authoritative statement in a report written by a former chief of the Bureau of Engineers at the behest of the board of directors of the Smithsonian Institution. Severson did his best to ridicule the Smithsonian

[92] *Chronicle*, July 6, 1870. See also *National Intelligencer*, December 15, 1865, February 13, 1869.

report, arguing that accumulated "sewer gas" would pose a still greater menace to public health and warning that a closed sewer that also served as a drainage channel for surface water would result in serious floods at times of exceptional rainfall – a prediction that was, in fact, borne out by later experience. Many civic leaders, including Severson, were reluctant to abandon the idea that the canal might be commercially profitable and shared the hope that the next improvement might be thorough enough and effective enough finally to realize their aspirations.[93]

By the war's end, the condition of the canal was the subject of regular comment and, indeed, of an indictment brought against the city author- ities by a grand jury.[94] The City Councils considered various proposals for the improvement of the canal and finally accepted the conclusions of a report made at the request of Congress by members of the Bureau of Engineers in April 1866, which recommended a full-scale cleaning of the canal. It would be kept clear by a regular current of freshwater con- trolled by floodgates at both entrances alternately opening and shutting in rhythm with the tides. The engineers estimated that the work would involve the removal of 143,000 cubic feet of sediment and cost approx- imately $75,000. In recommending the scheme to the City Councils, Mayor Richard Wallach stated that it "combines much that is material and absolutely necessary for the purposes of commerce and sewerage," and he urged them to provide the financial means for the prosecution of the work. He also expressed the hope that Congress would contribute to the expenditure, specifically because it ran through government reserva- tions and drained government buildings and more generally because the

[93] *National Intelligencer*, April 10, 1866. Alternative proposals for the improvement of the canal are set out in *Report of the Board of Engineers on the Improvement of the Washington Canal*, Ho. Exec. Doc. 35, 39.1; Benjamin Severson's *Report on the Washington City Canal*, Ho. Misc. Doc. 103, 40.2; report of the committee appointed by the Regents of the Smithsonian Institution, *Evening Star*, June 16, 1868; report of S. R. Seibert to Board of Common Council Committee on Canals, *Evening Star*, June 18, 1869; report of the Architect of the Capitol Extension, the Superintendent of Sewers in Washington, and the Secretary of the Smithsonian Institution on the improvement of the Canal, Senate Committee on the District of Columbia, May 20, 1870, SEN41A-E5; letter from Benjamin Severson, September 14, 1868, in *Journal of the 66th Council*, 133– 41. See also *Chronicle*, April 5, 1866, November 20, 1868, January 22, 1869; *Evening Star*, September 8, 1865, April 5, 1866, August 27, December 2, 1867, April 6, July 29, September 15, 1868, January 9, September 4, 1869, January 25, 1870; *National Intelligencer*, August 7, 11, September 11, December 16, 1865, December 18, 1866; Lessoff, *The Nation and Its City*, 89–91; Heinze, "Washington City Canal," 23–27; Press, "South of the Avenue," 56.

[94] *Evening Star*, November 9, 1865. For earlier improvement plans, see *Journal of the 61st Council* (Washington, DC, 1864), 201, 219, 343–44.

United States owned half the property in the city but paid no taxes. In the event, Congress made no such gesture. The councils promptly passed a bill putting the plan into effect, authorizing the mayor to anticipate revenues by $75,000, imposing a special tax to make up the deficit, and establishing the Canal Board to supervise the work.[95]

Work on the canal proceeded rapidly. Soon a flow was restored over part of its length, and in September, Severson, the engineer in charge of the improvements, reported that "a strong current of comparatively pure water constantly flowed in one direction through its entire length, and with sufficient force to carry off all the drainage of the city and all floating matter that finds its way into the canal." By October, he could claim that some sections were already navigable. Severson proposed further measures to deepen the canal for purposes of navigation, to alter its course in the central section to eliminate the bends that both slowed shipping and obstructed the removal of sediment by running water, and to make a connection with the Chesapeake and Ohio Canal, improvements that he estimated would cost in excess of $200,000 and would therefore require a congressional appropriation. In the absence of any such grant, the work petered out during the following winter without even expending all of the funds allocated for it.[96]

Severson's improvements having failed to resolve the problem, the councils returned to the subject the following summer. There were proposals to arch the canal and turn it into a sewer, to dredge it again at the cost of $170,000, raised by yet another special tax, and to lease it to a private company. Despite counterarguments that the Severson plan had failed and that it would be foolish to appropriate another large sum for its continuation, the Board of Aldermen passed a dredging bill in November 1867, on the grounds, as Crosby Noyes argued, that something had to be done to abate the nuisance posed by the canal, and that could only be achieved by repeated dredging. The measure did not pass the Board

[95] Letters from Benjamin Severson, November 20, 1865, and January 29, 1866, in *Journal of the 63rd Council*, 334–42, 425–35; messages from the mayor, in ibid., 546–52, and *Journal of the 64th Council*, 74–75; Richard Wallach to the Senate and House of Representatives, April 7, 1866, in *Evening Star*, April 10, 1866; *Evening Star*, January 23, April 5, 10, 17, 1866; *Chronicle*, April 5, 1866; Green, *Washington*, 309.

[96] Message of the Mayor, July 16, 1866, *Journal of the 64th Council*, 74–75; *Journal of the 65th Council*, 36; Benjamin Severson to Richard Wallach, September 1, 1866, in *Evening Star*, September 12, 1866; *Chronicle*, June 7, October 20, 1866; *Evening Star*, June 6, September 12, October 20, 1866; *National Intelligencer*, April 30, October 18, December 18, 1866.

of Common Council, which refused to accept the scheme unless Severson was employed as engineer.[97]

In December 1868, the Board of Aldermen, for the first time under Republican control, passed yet another version of the Severson plan, despite warnings that any such measure would be inoperative without congressional assistance. Once more the Board of Common Council stalled, with many members favoring measures to transfer the rights of the Corporation to the United States or to a private company.[98] The following summer, the Committee on Canals of the Board of Common Council recommended a $100,000 appropriation to dredge and clean the canal to a depth of four feet below low tide. To lease the canal to a private company, said the committee's report, would be an admission of failure, and to arch it would be prohibitively expensive, leaving dredging as the only practical recourse. There was some support in the board for a project that would not only improve the canal but also furnish employment. As Councilman John McKnight observed, "the winter is likely to be a hard one, and by giving work to many needy people want would be kept from their doors." Nonetheless, eventually the bill was defeated by 5 votes to 14. Critics pointed to the expense of the proposed improvements, an expense that the corporation in its current financial circumstances would have been unable to bear, and reminded members of the discouraging result of earlier efforts.[99] The Committee on Canals of the Board of Aldermen also recommended the appointment of a commission to dredge the canal and the appropriation of $150,000 to execute its plan. However, after some discussion, action was postponed.[100]

One reason for hesitation was the fact that newly elected Mayor Bowen had declared himself firmly in favor of arching the canal. Despite all the expenditure over the past decades, he told the councils, it was "worthless as a means of transportation, and so long as it remains open, it will be a plague spot and a means of engendering disease all over the city." Therefore, it was suggested that it should be contracted and covered to

---

[97] *Evening Star,* July 23, 30, October 22, November 19, 26, December 2, 18, 1867; *Journal of the 65th Council,* 101–4.

[98] *Journal of the 66th Council,* 302, 434–6; *Evening Star,* September 15, December 29, 1868, February 3, April 20, 27, 1869.

[99] *Chronicle,* August 26, 1869; *Evening Star,* August 25, September 7, 16, 22, 28, October 5, 1869. Three of the five votes in favor of the bill came from representatives of the Seventh Ward, who were under particular pressure from rank-and-file Republicans, who frequently discussed the subject in ward meetings. See *Evening Star,* October 23, November 5, December 4, 11, 17, 1868, May 7, 1869.

[100] *Evening Star,* January 18, 25, February 8, 1870.

form a sewer, which could be kept clean by a flow of water from a bulkhead at 17th Street. The expense of the operation would be offset by the value of the reclaimed land. "In my opinion, the time has arrived when measures should be taken for arching and hiding from view this pestilential eye-sore."[101]

Thus, during the immediate postbellum years as during its earlier history, the corporation showed itself incapable of resolving the problems posed by the canal. It lacked the financial resources. It could not impose a special tax in excess of three-quarters of a percent without permission from Congress, and the funds that it could raise without doing so were clearly less than a comprehensive plan of improvements would require. The councils were left to devise elaborate schemes and then abandon them when it became apparent that Congress was not going to contribute to their cost. The city lacked clear authority over the canal. Because for much of its length it ran alongside federal reservations, the corporation was restricted in its weight to change the course of the canal or to open and close sewer outlets that passed through government land. Indeed, some questioned whether the city had not forfeited its title on account of its failure to carry out the terms of the initial grant – namely, that the channel should be maintained to a depth of four feet below low tide, a commitment that the corporation had not come close to meeting. A resolution presented to the Board of Common Council in February 1869 suggested that the city's title was probably void, that the city was in debt and could afford to spend no more on the canal, and that therefore control should be allowed to pass over to Congress. The resolution only narrowly failed on a tied vote.[102]

Congress was no more decisive in resolving the fate of the canal. Over a period of years, it toyed with various alternatives but gave little extended consideration to any of them. Immediately after the Civil War, the House and Senate Committees on the District of Columbia showed some inclination to attend to the subject. In January 1866, members of the House committee, accompanied by Secretary of the Interior James Harlan and a

---

[101] *Journal of the 66th Council*, 24–5, 352–3; *Evening Star*, November 24, 1868, May 5, 1869. The *Evening Star* agreed that the canal was not fit for navigation, sewerage, or drainage in its current form and that it was dangerous to use it as a sewer unless it was filled in; *Evening Star*, July 7, 29, 1868.

[102] *Journal of the 66th Council*, 544. See also *Chronicle*, May 1, 14, 1866, April 27, 1870; *National Intelligencer*, December 16, 1865. For a counterargument, see the letters of Richard Wallach to the Councils and to Congress, in *Evening Star*, April 10, 26, 1866.

number of city officials, visited the site and examined the improvements suggested by Wallach, expressing general approval of his plan. A few weeks later, the Senate passed a resolution directing the secretary of war to appoint a board of engineers to investigate the Canal and report on improvements that would secure the health of the inhabitants. The board recommended a program of dredging, which was taken up by the municipal authorities.[103] Influential members of the Senate District Committee, it transpired, had become attracted to an alternative way of disposing of the malodorous ditch. In April 1866, the Senate passed a bill chartering the District of Columbia Canal and Sewerage Corporation and transferring to it all rights in the canal or at least all rights belonging to the U.S. government, in the hope that private capital and private initiative would be more effective in converting it into a navigable and commercially viable waterway.[104] Only intensive lobbying by Wallach prevented the bill's passage in the House.[105]

Congress gave little further attention to the subject until the summer of 1870. Near the end of the session, a section of the Sundry Civil Appropriation Bill not only set aside money for the improvement of the canal but also appointed a commission to determine how the work was to be done. The commission, which would include the mayor of Washington, the secretary of the interior, the commissioner of public buildings and grounds, the architect of the capitol extension, and two further members to be appointed by the mayor, was instructed to "cause the Washington city canal, either in whole or in part, to be dredged, or, if deemed best, dredged and narrowed." To pay for the improvement, the corporation was authorized and directed to levy a tax of $100,000, and Congress would contribute an appropriation of $50,000. An additional clause was inserted in the Senate that rounded off the list of possible solutions by allowing the commission to consider the option that the canal might be "arched and converted into a sewer."[106] In fact, the choices before

---

[103] House Committee on the District of Columbia, 39th Congress, Minutes, January 10, 1866, RG262, NARA; CG, 39.1:1221; *Chronicle*, March 8, 1866; *Evening Star*, January 15, March 15, April 5, 10, 1866.

[104] CG, 39.1:1707, 1730–6, 1965–68; *Chronicle*, March 8. 1866; *Evening Star*, April 2, 3, 1866; Heinze, "Washington City Canal," 23–27. The *Star* alleged that the bill was backed by speculators who had spent lavishly to get it through. *Evening Star*, July 21, 1866.

[105] CG, 39.1:2822–24, 3115–22, 3907–8, 3934; *Evening Star*, April 30, May 24, June 12, 13, July 21, 1866; *Chronicle*, July 23, 1866.

[106] CG, 41.2:4943–44, 5477; *U.S. Statutes at Large*, 41.2, ch. 292 (1870), 309; *Chronicle*, June 18, July 6, 1870; *Evening Star*, June 16, 17, July 22, 1870.

the commission were narrower than the terms of the bill allowed. The $150,000 allocated was clearly insufficient to pay for arching the canal, and it would not allow for a great deal of narrowing or straightening. While it considered its options, the commission decided, as a short-term measure, on the first solution, that of dredging the canal. Tenders were put out in October 1870, and work began early in December.[107]

As it happened, the Canal Commission, along with other agencies of the city government, ceased to function in June 1871. Its successors took a very different view of the canal's future. The Board of Health created by the Territorial Act was strongly of the view that it was a serious nuisance to health and that it should be eliminated altogether by constructing an enormous sewer along its bed and filling in the rest. With the assistance of Joseph Henry of the Smithsonian, Commissioner of Public Buildings and Grounds Orville E. Babcock, and Alfred B. Mullett, the supervising architect of the Treasury Building, its members persuaded Alexander Shepherd and the Board of Public Works to cooperate in transforming the canal into a sewer. Shepherd was told that its commercial possibilities were purely fictional, that its presence blighted the development of the center of the city, and that removing it would release more than 600,000 square feet for other purposes. Regardless of the contracts recently made to clear and deepen the canal and the $50,000 already spent, in August 1871, the Board of Public Works decided to fill it in. By December, the section between 3rd and 14th Street, W, had been completed; by November 1873, the whole of B Street, along the route of the former canal, had been paved and parked. At the same time, the southern section along James Creek was narrowed, although not for many years would it finally be filled in.[108]

As Alan Lessoff has shown, the filling in of the canal and its replacement with a main sewer resolved one problem but created another. The expansion of the city's sewerage system, and the growing number of households connected to it, along with the unfortunate decision to drain surface water and domestic waste through the same channels, left

---

[107] *Evening Star*, July 22, October 28, December 1, 1870; *Chronicle*, March 8, April 21, June 23, August 9, 1871; Green, *Washington*, 328; Bryan, *History of the National Capital*, 509.

[108] U.S. House of Representatives, Committee on the District of Columbia, *Affairs in the District of Columbia*, Ho. Rep. 72, 42.2 (1872), 117, 138–50, 571–75, 598; *Evening Star*, May 6, August 9, October 10, 1871, March 8, April 9, 10, 1872; Lessoff, *Nation and Its City*, 90–91; Maury, *Alexander "Boss" Shepherd*, 14, 30–32; Heinze, "History of the Washington Canal," 23–27.

the system dangerously liable to overload, especially at times of exceptional rainfall or when the Potomac was in flood. On several occasions,
parts of downtown Washington lay under several feet of water. Not
for many decades was a more effective drainage and sewerage system
constructed.[109] Nevertheless, the removal of that long-standing source
of vile odors, along with the wharves, warehouses, and other unsightly
edifices that had lined its banks, left downtown areas of the city more
habitable and made possible the later development of the Mall. That
it took so long was largely a consequence of the diametrically opposed
opinions that were set before policy makers. It was also a reflection of
the almost willful persistence of Washingtonians' faith in the commercial possibilities of a navigable canal. However, it also resulted from
the diffuse character of the policy-making process itself, which left the
municipality unable to muster the resources to improve the canal and
Congress unwilling to expend either time or money on what it mostly
regarded as a local matter. As in so many aspects of local government,
divided authority hindered decisive action. The creation of the territory
and its most active agency the Board of Public Works appeared to alter
the situation. For a brief honeymoon period, Shepherd's assumption of
authority short-circuited the complexities of local power and permitted
an apparent resolution of a long-standing engineering problem that had
resisted solution for decades. However, as in other respects, the peremptory mode of decision making adopted by the Board of Public Works,
although avoiding the diffusion of authority that had paralyzed action in
the past, led to hasty decisions that ignored both the engineering and the
political constraints under which it operated.

### Washington and the B. & O. Monopoly

When in the early days of the Civil War pro-secessionist mobs obstructed
the passage of federal troops across Baltimore and the governor of Maryland ordered the burning of railroad bridges north of that city, it became
all too apparent, to those who were not already well aware of the fact,
that the capital was dangerously dependent for its communication with
the rest of the Union on one, single-track railroad.[110] In 1861, all traffic

---

[109] Lessof, *Nation and Its City*, 91–94.
[110] For an account, see Ernest B. Furgurson, *Freedom Rising: Washington in the Civil War*
(New York: Knopf), 76–81; Allan Nevins, *The War for the Union: The Improvised
War, 1861–1862* (New York: Charles Scribner's Sons, 1959), 80–83.

from the north and northwest had to proceed through Baltimore along the Washington branch of the Baltimore and Ohio, or B. & O. Although the strategic danger posed by Washington's restricted transport links was only temporary, the resulting logistical problems bedeviled the Union war effort for the duration of the conflict and hampered the economic development of the city for several years thereafter. After the war, citizens of Washington continued to complain of their inadequate railroad facilities, which, they said, added about fifty miles to journeys from the west, put a premium of something like 25 percent on the price of food and other supplies, and nipped enterprise in the bud. Railroads, declared the *Evening Star*, were crucial to the building of a great city, and Washington could not hope to realize its potential as a commercial center without improved transportation links.[111]

Through the Board of Trade and various ad hoc associations, citizens came together to promote railroad schemes linking Washington with points north, south, east, and west; newspaper editorials urged more energetic action; and city officials regularly expounded on the need for better railroads.[112] Hopes were invested in a number of projects. To the west, there were plans to build the so-called Metropolitan Railroad, which would connect the city with the main westward line of the Baltimore and Ohio at Point of Rocks, about thirty-five miles northwest of Washington, affording a more direct passage to the Ohio Valley 48 miles shorter than the existing route by way of Baltimore. Across the Potomac, the Alexandria, Loudoun and Hampshire Railroad slowly wound its way through the northern counties of Virginia, offering a connection to the fertile farmlands of the Shenandoah Valley, the coalfields of West Virginia and, ultimately, the Ohio River. Under its revised name of the Washington and Ohio, it raised grand visions of an alternative trunk line across the Appalachians, competing with the Baltimore and Ohio for the western trade. To the south, the Washington and Point Lookout, later the Southern Maryland Railroad, promised to open up the agricultural lands of southern Maryland to the markets of the capital.[113]

---

[111] *Chronicle*, January 1866 15, April 1, 1870; *National Intelligencer*, December 17, 1866; *Evening Star*, December 10, 1867, December 16, 1868, May 18, 1869; CG, 42.2:1904.

[112] *Chronicle*, October 1, 1867, December 4, 1868, February 12, November 12, 24, 1869; *National Intelligencer*, March 19, 1869; *Evening Star*, May 18, 1869.

[113] On the Metropolitan, see *Evening Star*, October 31, 1862; *National Intelligencer*, December 17, 1866. On the southern Maryland projects, see *Chronicle*, January 27,

Above all, the city vested its hopes in the Baltimore and Potomac, a railroad chartered before the Civil War to connect Baltimore with the farming counties to the south. Although the route was surveyed, no advance in financing or constructing the road was made before war broke out. After the Civil War, the Pennsylvania Railroad acquired an interest in the company and, despite stalling tactics by Baltimore and Ohio representatives at Annapolis, commenced construction in 1868. It soon became evident why the Pennsylvania was interested in this bucolic railway when it claimed that the company's charter gave it the right to build a branch line to Washington. This branch line, when it was completed in 1872, gave Washingtonians an alternative route to Baltimore, and from there to the cities of the northeastern seaboard, freeing them at last from the constrictions imposed by the Baltimore and Ohio monopoly.[114]

It had long seemed to Washingtonians that the Baltimore and Ohio, favored daughter of the Monument City and favored ward of the Maryland state legislature, exploited its control of their northern trade to extract monopoly profits and to advance the economic interests of its mother city at their expense. "That railroad has never done anything to benefit the city," said a member of the Board of Aldermen in 1862.[115] The company used its influence at Annapolis to delay competing projects such as the Baltimore and Potomac or the Southern Maryland.[116] In particular, the Baltimore and Ohio seemed determined to delay construction of the Metropolitan Railroad. When citizens of Washington offered to build the line between Washington and Point of Rocks themselves, B. & O. representatives managed to persuade the state legislature, as well as Congress, that it would complete the connection itself within five years. For two years or more, not a shovel was placed in the earth. It is true that, after coming to an agreement with the city government about the route and a number of other points at issue, some progress was made. However, local newspapers continued to report delays in completing the

1866. On the Alexandria, Loudoun and Hampshire/Washington and Ohio, see *Chronicle*, October 1, 1867; *Evening Star*, December 10, 1867; *Journal of the House of Delegates, 1872*, 312–13. On the Piedmont and Potomac, see *CG*, 42.2:2122, 3644.

[114] *National Intelligencer*, December 10, 1866, April 1, 1867, September 9, 1868; *Evening Star*, July 7, 21, 1866.

[115] *Evening Star*, May 6, 1862, November 17, December 14, 1865.

[116] *Chronicle*, August 21, 1866, February 13, 1867; *National Intelligencer*, October 12, 1866; *New National Era*, March 7, 1872; *Evening Star*, July 21, 1866, February 19, 1867.

road, which did not commence operation over its full distance until the summer of 1873.[117]

The immediate postbellum years saw a brief revival of the mania for railroad subsidies that had marked the industry's early years. Towns and cities across the country subscribed to the stock of railroad companies, lent them money, and endorsed their bonds.[118] After some initial hesitation, Washingtonians committed themselves with some enthusiasm to the promotion of railroads. The *Chronicle* impressed on its readers the need for energetic action if they wanted improved transportation facilities: "It is in the power of the people of Washington to transform this city from the dull, inanimate place it has heretofore been into a thriving commercial and even manufacturing city." With increasing vigor after 1868, with local newspaper editors acting as cheerleaders, groups of citizens petitioned the councils to pledge money to various projects and petitioned Congress to authorize the transactions.[119]

Early in 1865, the councils considered purchasing $500,000 worth of bonds of the Metropolitan Railroad in the vain hope of expediting construction but decided that they could not raise the funds. In 1867, they passed a resolution asking Congress to authorize a subscription to the stock of the Alexandria, Loudoun and Hampshire. Although one or two aldermen wondered why, if the line were likely to be profitable, it could not attract sufficient private investment, others pointed to the advantages that railroads brought in building up a city and the urgency of breaking

[117] *Evening Star*, February 14, 1869, June 23, 1870, September 7, 1872; *National Intelligencer*, June 6, 7, October 18, December 17, 1866, June 7, 1867; *Chronicle*, April 14, 1871; CG, 39.1:1535, 3126, 3135, 3605, 3969, 4025.

[118] See, for example, Carter Goodrich, *Government Promotion of American Canals and Railroads* (New York: Columbia University Press, 1960), 207–62; Edward Kirkland, *Industry Comes of Age: Business, Labor and Public Policy, 1860–1897* (New York: Holt, Rhinehart and Watson, 1961), 57–68; Kirkland, *Men, Cities and Transportation: A Study in New England History* (2 vols., Cambridge, MA: Harvard University Press, 1948); Morton Keller, *Affairs of State: Public Life in Late Nineteenth-Century America* (Cambridge, MA: Harvard University Press, 1977), 165–67; Harry H. Pierce, *Railroads of New York: A Study of Government Aid, 1826–1875* (Cambridge, MA: Harvard University Press, 1953); Carter Goodrich and Harvey H. Segal, "Baltimore's Aid to Railroads: A Study in the Municipal Planning of Internal Improvements," *Journal of Economic History* 13 (1953): 2–35; Earl S. Beard, "Local Aid to Railroads in Iowa," *Iowa Journal of History* 50 (1951): 1–34; Mark W. Summers, *Railroads, Reconstruction, and the Gospel of Prosperity: Aid under the Radical Republicans, 1865–1877* (Princeton, NJ: Princeton University Press, 1984); Robert A. Lively, "The American System: A Review Article," *Business History Review* 29 (March 1955): 81–96.

[119] *Chronicle*, October 1, 1867, December 4, 1868, February 12, 1869; *National Intelligencer*, March 26, 1866, September 9, 1868; *Evening Star*, May 18, 1869.

the Baltimore and Ohio monopoly. In 1869, Mayor Bowen transmitted to the councils a petition urging subscriptions of $1 million each to the Alexandria, Loudoun and Hampshire and Southern Maryland railroads, signed by "a large number of our wealthiest and most public spirited citizens." The councils responded positively to the request. Two years later, Alexander R. Shepherd and others called for a municipal investment in the stock of what had become the Washington and Ohio, a demand that was reiterated later in the year by the newly formed territorial legislature. The House of Delegates also passed resolutions asking Congress for authority to subscribe to the stock of a shadowy enterprise known as the Piedmont and Potomac Railroad Company.[120]

Among the railroads soliciting subscriptions from the District was the Baltimore and Potomac. The city had a compelling interest in the project, said the *Intelligencer*; the credit of the city and its citizens should be used to further its completion. In April 1870, the railroad's general manager asked the corporation for a subscription of $500,000 to enable the company to begin extending its track into the city and to push the work toward an early completion. Bowen, in forwarding his request to the councils, pointed out that the railroad, when completed, would be "of immense importance to the city," opening new lines of communication and freeing it from the "extortions and presumptions" of the Baltimore and Ohio. The councils responded with a resolution asking Congress for permission to issue bonds to finance the subscription. The *Star*, although generally supportive of railroad subsidies, questioned the wisdom of giving money to one of the country's wealthiest corporations to complete a line that would be built anyway and in return for which the city was likely to get no real influence over its construction and management. Instead, the city should invest in struggling lines that otherwise might not be built. Presumably feeling the same, Congress took no action on the bill authorizing the municipal subscription.[121]

---

[120] Green, *Washington*, 296; *Chronicle*, January 27, 1866, February 12, March 26, 1869; *Evening Star*, December 10, 17, 24, 1867, March 23, 29, 30, November 13, 20, 1869, December 12, 1870, January 21, 1871; *National Intelligencer*, March 19, 1869; petition of citizens of Washington for passage of House bill authorizing the Corporation to subscribe to the stock of the Washington and Ohio Railroad, January 4, 1871, SEN 41A-H5.2, RG46, NARA; *Journal of the House of Delegates*, 1871, 307, 312–13, 415–16, 496.

[121] Thomas Seabrook to mayor and councils, March 14, 1870; Sayles J. Bowen to Board of Aldermen, March 14, 1870; joint resolution of Board of Aldermen, April 9, 1870, SEN 41A-E5, RG46, NARA; *National Intelligencer*, September 9, 1868; *Evening Star*, March 15, 18, 22, 29, 1870. S.795, authorizing the corporation to subscribe $500,000

Without the approval of Congress, the local authorities were not permitted to extend their credit to railroad enterprises, and members of congress were generally unsympathetic to such proposals.[122] However, in 1872, Congress surprisingly relented and authorized the recently established District government to subscribe to the stock of the Piedmont and Potomac Railroad. This largely hypothetical line was supposed to extend from a point on the Potomac opposite Washington to the Shenandoah Valley, where it would link up with other railroads, as yet unbuilt, and eventually provide access over the lines of the Chesapeake and Ohio Railroad, still under construction, to the Ohio River. It would, it was claimed, give Washington a long-needed outlet to the west. The subscription was approved by the Board of Trade, the Merchants' Exchange, and many other civic organizations. It was endorsed by the House of Delegates by 17 votes to 2 and by the electorate of the District by 12,039 votes to 665. Morrill, Edmunds and other senators objected to the subsidy on principle. "I have never recently known a county or township that subscribed to railroad stock that was not the loser by it," said Frelinghuysen. If the stock was desirable it would attract private capital; the fact that the company sought government assistance suggested that it was not. Edmunds, too, considered it inappropriate for the District to invest in a private company, especially in view of the enormous indebtedness that had been accumulated for other purposes. Ultimately, said Morrill, Congress was responsible for the District and would have to pay its debts, or be "disgraced before the world." Congress, not the people of the District, should have the final word.[123] Despite these objections, which had been sufficient to convince senators on other occasions, the bill was passed by 28 votes to 19. It was then rushed through the House of Representatives, under suspension of rules, without a debate.[124]

It is not clear why. The beneficiary, said Edmunds, was "an unknown railroad corporation with a charter as vague as the wind...with a road

to the stock of the Baltimore and Potomac, was referred to the Senate Committee on the District of Columbia and not heard of again. CG, 41.2:2707.

[122] The House passed the bill authorizing the Alexandria, Loudoun and Hampshire subsidy in 1870, but the Senate took no action on the bill. CG, 41.2:2735; CG, 41.3:593, 1885; Journal of the House of Delegates, 1871, 312–13. The Senate also rejected a request by the councils for permission to subscribe to the stock of the Southern Maryland Railroad. CG, 41.2:2273–74, 4567–68, 5205; Chronicle, April 1, 1870.

[123] CG, 42.2:2130, 2123, 2134, 2156, and 2122–36, 2155–67 passim. For the result of the local referendum, see Evening Star, November 23, 1871.

[124] CG, 42.2:2135, 2166–67, 3654. A majority of both parties voted for the bill in the Senate.

that may go anywhere they please to make it go." No track had been laid; no right-of-way had been surveyed. All there was, according to the railroad's Virginia charter, was a vague intention to build a line from Washington to the Shenandoah Valley and ultimately to make a connection with the Ohio River. Even these grand intentions duplicated other railroad projects. They certainly did not open up exciting new commercial possibilities for the District sufficient to warrant a municipal subsidy.[125] According to William M. Maury, the company numbered among its incorporators some prominent local businessmen, including George W. Corcoran and Wilmer S. Shepherd, brother of Alexander Shepherd, but that does not explain how they were able to bend so many U.S. senators to their will. However influential its progenitors, the Piedmont and Potomac disappeared from view almost immediately, and the subscription was never taken up.[126]

For much of the nineteenth century, American governments, municipal, state, and, in some cases federal, had committed themselves to policies that were designed to promote investment in the infrastructure for economic growth.[127] Railroads during the middle decades of the century were the greatest beneficiaries of this largesse. Washington, finding itself stuck on the end of a branch line of the B. & O., had powerful incentives to join in the post–Civil War enthusiasm for railroad subsidies. However, the nation's capital was less generous than other equivalent cities in extending financial aid to transportation companies. It was not so much that Washington's business community was uninterested in using municipal credit to attract railroads or that the councils were unwilling to devote the city's tax revenues or lend its credit to promising railroad ventures. The problem was, first, that Washington, with its slender tax base, lacked the financial capacity to make as many investments as its citizens would have desired and, second, that Congress frequently blocked them. Congressional reluctance stemmed

---

[125] CG, 42.2:2127–28. Cf. *Evening Star*, November 21, 25, 1871.

[126] William M. Maury, *Alexander "Boss" Shepherd and the Board of Public Works* (Washington, DC: George Washington University Press, 1975), 23. For a list of incorporators, see CG, 42.2:23, 25. There was a later attempt to transfer the subsidy to the Southern Maryland. CG, 43.2:558–61.

[127] The clearest statement of this argument is Richard L. McCormick, "The Party Period and Public Policy: An Exploratory Hypothesis," *Journal of American History* 66 (September 1979): 279–98. See also James Willard Hurst, *Law and the Condition of Freedom in the Nineteenth-Century United States* (Madison: University of Wisconsin Press, 1956), 3–70; Goodrich, *Government Promotion of American Canals and Railroads*; Lively, "American System."

partly from a desire to defend the national credit from risky specula-
tions and partly from a growing ideological antipathy to government
subsidy, especially on the part of Democrats and some New England
Republicans.[128]

The railroads on which Washingtonians depended to connect them to
the outside world were chartered by their states of origin. However, their
entry into the District required decisions by the municipal authorities
and, more important, by Congress. In the past, both Congress and the
corporation had been injudicious in monitoring the laying of track and the
location of depots. In 1855, for example, the Alexandria and Washington
Railroad, which provided Washington's sole southerly connection, was
permitted by the city government but not by Congress, which was then in
recess, to run its track across the Long Bridge, up Maryland Avenue, and
round the front of the Capitol to the Baltimore and Ohio depot. When it
reassembled, Congress forbade the use of the tracks, but relented, in the
face of military necessity, during the war.[129] The governing authorities
in the District had still greater difficulty in keeping a check on the Baltimore and Ohio Railroad, which remorselessly exploited local desires for
a western route to extract concessions from the city. In 1866, Congress
authorized the Metropolitan branch of the B. & O. to enter the District
along a route to be determined by negotiation between the company and
the local authorities. In return for an agreement to bring the line into the
city along New Jersey Avenue to meet the main line around Delaware
and H Street, which was the route preferred by Washington residents,
the councils dropped their earlier demand for the payment of back taxes
and granted the company continued use of its depot on Delaware Avenue
until 1910. The implied threat to delay construction overcame their inhi-
bitions about granting privileges to an already powerful corporation.[130]
So generous was the grant that Congress moved immediately to amend

[128] On the anti-subsidy movement, see Carter Goodrich, "The Revulsion against Internal
Improvements," *Journal of Economic History* 10 (November 1950): 145–69.

[129] CG, 37.3:819–20, 1327–30, 1435; *Evening Star*, March 3, 1863; Green, *Washington*,
195–97, 262–63. The railroad was also authorized to use steam locomotives, a concession which aroused fierce opposition from residents of South Washington. See *Journal of
the 63rd Council*, 196–97, 289–91; *National Intelligencer*, October 27, 28, November
28, 1865; *Evening Star*, August 22, September 12, October 26, 28, 31, November 16,
1865, April 3, 4, 13, July 21, 1866; CG, 39.1:2719–23; Bryan, *History of the National
Capital*, 2:543–44.

[130] *Journal of the 63th Council*, 196; *Journal of the 64th Council*, 360; CG, 39.1:3114,
3969; *Evening Star*, December 1, 7, 1866, January 8, 12, 15, 1867; *National Intelligencer*, January 18, 1867; Lessoff, *Nation and Its City*, 32.

its earlier legislation by stipulating that Congress, not the corporation, should decide on the route.[131]

The Baltimore and Ohio, on locating its depot at C Street and New Jersey Avenue before the war, had unilaterally taken possession of a substantial portion of Delaware Avenue and neighboring streets for storing freight cars. Its track and sidings not only blighted a large section of northeastern Washington but prevented the establishment of regular grades on several blocks east of New Jersey Avenue, thereby hampering the further development of that part of the city and leaving it, according to the *Star*, with the appearance of a locality struck by pestilence. For years the railroad refused to raise its tracks to match those of the adjacent streets.[132] When Bowen set out upon his regrading program, he inevitably came into collision with the B. & O. After an angry exchange of letters with Garrett, he secured a court order requiring that the offending tracks be made to conform to grade. The company proceeded to ignore this, as it had ignored past orders, and the Baltimore and Ohio grades remained a source of annoyance for many years to come.[133]

Just as the city authorities inveighed against the Baltimore and Ohio monopoly, they welcomed into their midst a still more potent force in the transportation marketplace, the Pennsylvania Railroad, which had acquired a controlling interest in the Baltimore and Potomac. Despite the efforts of Maryland senators and other friends of the B. & O. to delay its consideration, a bill authorizing the Baltimore and Potomac to extend its tracks into the city was passed by Congress in 1867.[134] Over the next few years, a route was agreed that would bring the railroad into the city over the Eastern Branch and along M Street and Virginia Avenue to the intersection with Maryland Avenue, where its terminus was to be located.[135] However, in March 1871, the city councils, citing

[131]  *CG*, 39.2:483–84, 516, 776, 878; *Evening Star*, January 16, 1867.

[132]  James Crutchett to House Committee on the District of Columbia, April 18, 1871, HR42A-F7.8, RG233, NARA; Sayles J. Bowen, Message to Councils, *Journal of the 66th Council* (Washington, 1969), 28–29; *Evening Star*, November 13, December 13, 1869; Lessoff, *Nation and Its City*, 31–32.

[133]  *Evening Star*, December 28, 1869, January 5, 22, 1870; *Chronicle*, December 29, 30, 31, 1869, January 6, February 2, 1870. In 1876 and 1879, legislation was introduced into Congress to compel removal of the tracks. *CR*, 44.1:5028, 5261; 45.2:1684.

[134]  *CG*, 39.1:2386; 39.2:540–41, 585–86, 764; *Chronicle*, July 4, August 21, December 12, 1866; *National Intelligencer*, October 12, December 10, 1866; *Evening Star*, January 8, 1867.

[135]  *CG* 40.3:1441–42; *CG*, 41.1:21, 79–80; *CG*, 41.3:1369, 1964. The Baltimore and Potomac was also allowed to run trains along Maryland Avenue and over the Long

as the reason the presence of a new school, rejected the Maryland Avenue location and decided instead in favor of a site on 6th and B Street, just behind Pennsylvania Avenue, which, it was claimed, would bring the railway closer to the central business district. As the *Star* pointed out, it was odd that, having struggled for many years to compel the Baltimore and Ohio to move its tracks and its depot from the city center, the councils should, during the last hours of their existence, rush through legislation allowing the Baltimore and Potomac to run its tracks across the city and locate its depot on Pennsylvania Avenue, close to the point from which, many years earlier, the Baltimore and Ohio had been forcibly driven.[136] Legislation to that effect was introduced in the next session of Congress and, unusually for a District bill, occupied the members of both houses for several days.

There were essentially two points at issue. The first was whether the Baltimore and Ohio should also be allowed a depot in the center of the city. B. & O. president John W. Garrett told the House District Committee that to give one railroad a site close to the center "interferes with the rights of the people." He asked for equal facilities for all lines and offered a proposal for a central depot, which the B. & O. would approach through a tunnel under Capitol Hill, or, alternatively, a depot for his railroad on the opposite side of the avenue. Many local residents, and evidently a majority of the committee, were skeptical of Garrett's pleas for equal treatment, noting that he had done little to improve facilities for the public for thirty years or more, coming up with a plan for a central depot only when forced to do so by the arrival of a competitor. They suspected that his talk of a union station was no more than talk. If his plans were approved, he would be no more likely to carry them out than his other projects involving Washington. Garrett had failed for years to provide the facilities Washington needed; he should not be allowed to stand in the way now.[137] Friends of the Baltimore and Ohio attempted to offer amendments on the floor of the House to provide it with equivalent facilities, but the bill's sponsor, District Committee chairman Henry H. Starkweather, arguing that such amendments were really "in direct

---

Bridge, connecting with the Virginia network. CG, 41.2:4531–33, 4567; *Evening Star*, June 16, 17, 1870.

[136] *Evening Star*, March 7, 29, 1871. A letter was filed from the chairman of the Board of Trustees of Public Schools objecting to the Maryland Avenue site. CG, 42.2:1904.

[137] *Chronicle*, March 1, 16, 23, 27, April 23, May 2, 1872; *Evening Star*, March 1, 4, 14, 1872; *New National Era*, March 7, 1872. Scott claimed that the site on 6th and B Street was too small to accommodate both railroads. *Chronicle*, March 1, 1872.

antagonism with the bill," insisted on the previous question and forced the measure through to passage without amendment. Nine-tenths of the opposition, he claimed, came from the B. & O. "It seems to me," said Glenni Scofield of Pennsylvania, "looking over the contradictory arguments and amendments, that the resulting purpose of the warfare made upon this bill is to preserve to the Baltimore and Ohio Railroad, in some modified degree, its old and hateful monopoly of the trade and travel to the capital of the country."[138]

The second objection to this bill, as Dawes explained, "is not only that they want another railroad depot at this place, but it goes further, whether we shall have any at all upon the public grounds."[139] Lot Morrill told the Senate that he was unwilling to give a private corporation 120,000 square feet of public land at the heart of the city, surrendering "one of its choicest parts to the grasp of a selfish corporation" and allowing it to run tracks across a public park. "It is taking the park by the throat and throttling it," said his namesake, the Vermont Senator Justin S. Morrill. To allow a railroad to be built across the Mall, said Thurman, would be to abandon "the most beautiful feature in the whole city to commerce."[140] The bill's supporters, of course, reiterated the commercial imperative of securing better railroad connections. According to Simon Cameron, a close political ally of the Pennsylvania Railroad and the bill's sponsor in the Senate, the Baltimore and Potomac would break the existing monopoly of transportation, and its connections to other elements of the Pennsylvania system would "make Washington a very important point on the great highway of commerce between the Pacific and the Atlantic." Such advantages were worth far more than "a little bit of a park." The Mall, said John P. Stockton of New Jersey, should not be preserved at the expense of leaving Washington a "desolate city" immured in "the eternal stillness and silence that hangs to-day over Rome."[141]

When it came to voting, friends of the Baltimore and Potomac carried the day by a wide margin. In the House of Representatives, the bill went

---

[138] CG, 42.2:1980, 2048; *Chronicle*, March 27, 1872; *Evening Star*, March 22, 1872. The House debate can be found in CG, 42.2:1901–9, 1957–58, 1980–84, 2006–9, 2046–50, 2075–76. For the pro-Baltimore and Ohio amendments, see CG, 42.2:1902–3, 1906.

[139] CG, 42.2:2046.

[140] CG, 42.2:2279–80, 2284, 3483, 3491, 3498, 3499. The Senate debate can be found in CG, 42.2:2279–85, 3478–506, 3534–38.

[141] CG, 42.2:1903, 2281–82, 2285, 3481, 3484–85. See also CG, 42.2:1902, 2285. In any case, said Stewart, the site of the depot, located alongside the old canal, was "the most loathsome part of Washington" and could only be improved by the coming of the railroad. CG, 42.2:3483.

through by 115 votes to 56, narrowly achieving the two-thirds majority needed for passage under suspension of the rules. In the Senate, it passed by a clear margin of 39 votes to 18. It enjoyed nearly overwhelming support from Republicans in both houses, with the exception of a number of representatives from New England. The Democratic Party was more evenly divided, although with a majority voting against the bill. The division of opinion on the issue reflected a complex interplay between sectional interest and ideology. Many opponents of the bill, including some New England Republicans and Democrats from all regions, objected in principle to a measure, which appeared to award "special privileges" to a powerful corporation, whereas others, drawn from a broad geographic band running on either side of the Ohio River, in close proximity to the Baltimore and Ohio's main line and its western extensions, defended the interests of the trunk road that served their communities. It is no surprise to find the entire Maryland delegation voting against the bill. Likewise, it is no surprise to find that 22 of 23 Pennsylvania representatives voted to advance the interests of their state's largest carrier.[142]

Before the Civil War, the city government and Congress had been remiss in allowing the Baltimore and Ohio to locate its tracks and sidings so as to obstruct the development of a substantial portion of the city and to maintain a depot in a valuable central location. After the war, the city government and Congress were equally remiss in allowing the Baltimore and Potomac to lay its track across the Mall, blocking the completion of a continuous park linking the Capitol Grounds with the Executive Mansion for a full generation and ruling out for a generation the possibility of a consolidated depot that would bring all the city's steam railroads together on one site. That this opportunity for rational planning of the capital's transport links was lost was partly a result of the primacy of the promotional impulse in Gilded Age politics. However, it also flowed from the policy-making process itself. On one hand, the division of authority between local and federal agencies made it harder to arrive at sensible decisions about Washington's future development. On the other hand, although Congress claimed ultimate authority over all but the most routine aspects of transportation policy, its own mechanisms precluded a systematic approach to policy formation. As in so many other aspects of District governance, railroad policy was made on an ad hoc, reactive basis, lacking both continuity and planning and all too open

[142] CG, 42.2:1958, 2076, 3538.

to political pressures from a variety of sources. Furthermore, it did not always provide for the best interests of the District and its citizens.

## A City and a State

American local government in the nineteenth century carried out a wide variety of functions. These included the maintenance of law and order, protection from fire, public health, education, the provision of public welfare, the regulation of markets and supervision of food products, the regulation of banking and insurance, chartering voluntary associations formed for business or other purposes, the licensing of professions and various forms of business, the maintenance of public highways, the provision of public utilities, the regulation of taverns and other places of amusement, the suppression of immorality, and much else. Far from practicing the virtues of limited government and subscribing to the principles of laissez-faire, as a number of historians have shown, state and municipal governments interfered in the affairs of their citizens persistently and unashamedly. Earlier Anglo-American notions of the "well-ordered society" merged into newer conceptions of the regulatory state to produce a continuous tradition of government intervention. Such intervention was justified by the Anglo-American tradition of taking private property for public use, by the well-established practice of regulating markets, by the concept of the "police power" that required the state to intervene to protect the health, safety, and welfare of the public, by the long-standing obligation to abate "nuisances," and by the age-old responsibility to provide assistance to those unable to support themselves. Such exercises of public authority were usually approved and only occasionally rejected by the courts.[143] The constraints on American public policy during the nineteenth century were not so much conceptual as practical. Political structures militated against a systematic and consistent approach to policy making. Policy depended in most cases on individual initiatives and responses to particular events or outside pressures, rather than a consecutive and progressive accumulation of legislative experience. Only later in the century did administrative agencies, such as boards of charities and correction or railroad

[143] Ballard C. Campbell, "Public Policy and State Government," in Charles W. Calhoun, ed., *The Gilded Age: Essays on the Origins of Modern America* (Wilmington: University of Delaware Press, 1996), 309–29; Novak, *People's Welfare*; Brock, *Investigation and Responsibility*; Campbell, *Representative Democracy*; Keller, *Affairs of State*, Part One.

commissions, provide a locus for gathering information and expertise that would provide a basis for formulating policy in a sustained and systematic fashion.[144]

The governance of the District of Columbia exemplifies, in an exaggerated form, many of the tendencies in late nineteenth-century public policy. As we have seen, Congress failed to articulate a coherent social policy, responding instead on an ad hoc basis to a variety of initiatives emanating from groups of citizens with their own peculiar purposes and priorities. Such a set of responses did not constitute a coherent array of social provision. The municipality, for its part, did little more than cater to the most urgent forms of need within the walls of the Almshouse and, sporadically, through the provision of outdoor relief. The Board of Health, in contrast, represented a more systematic and professional approach to problems of public health. It enjoyed some success in coping with serious epidemics and in removing a variety of "nuisances" from public spaces. However, the antagonism aroused by its interventions, leading to its eventual abolition, illustrates the difficulties involved in applying such an approach to the diverse and heterogeneous social world of the nineteenth-century American city. It points to a lack of fit between the mode of administrative governance exemplified by the Board of Health and the prevailing structures of mid-nineteenth-century American politics.

The failure of either the city or the federal government to deal with the Washington City Canal exemplified the difficulties of governance under the old regime. The municipality lacked the financial resources or the statutory power to carry out more than occasional, and, as it turned out, temporary, dredging of that troublesome waterway; Congress lacked the inclination or the knowledge to act decisively on the subject, which is one reason several members were ready to accept the offer of a private company to take it over. Eventually, the territorial Board of Public Works took peremptory and decisive action to fill it in, an action that was based on an exaggerated notion of its statutory powers and a limited appreciation of the hydrological consequences. In its railroad policy, Congress failed to act decisively to help the city secure alternative railroad connections. At the same time, it gave in too readily to the demands of powerful corporations such as the Baltimore and Ohio and the Baltimore and Potomac for free use of the public streets and access to terminal sites in the heart of the city. Here, too, Congress appeared to respond to outside pressures, rather than setting out a policy in the public

[144] On this, see in particular Brock, *Investigation and Responsibility*.

interest. Congress was also remiss in granting franchises to street railroads and other public utilities that imposed few burdens in return for the privileges conferred on them.[145] The decision to construct the new Center Market to replace the dilapidated structures formerly occupying the site provides further illustration of the manner in which collisions between federal and municipal authority obstructed policy making, leading in the end to a decision to hand the problem over to an outside company.[146]

These case studies point to a number of features of governance in the nation's capital between 1860 and the introduction of direct federal rule in 1878. The first is the division of authority between federal and municipal governments. In general, the Corporation of Washington lacked authority to carry out many of its functions without congressional assent, and it certainly lacked the financial resources. The formation of the territory did not enlarge the legislative autonomy of the local government, although it did create, in the shape of the Board of Public Works, an agency that was prepared to assume a discretionary authority that it did not definitely possess, and it certainly did not fundamentally alter the terms of the financial impasse. For its part, Congress proved unwilling to devote sufficient time to local matters, except when they meshed with the concerns of national legislators, as in the early years of Reconstruction, or when they reached a crisis point, as at the close of the territory. Congressional scrutiny of local business was marked, for the most part, by inattention and ignorance. Even the District committees, although largely peopled by conscientious and interested individuals, experienced too rapid a turnover of personnel and were too often discouraged by the indifference of the wider membership to develop sustained lines of policy.

Constituted as they were, the structures of decision making in local affairs were all too easily influenced by groups of people who wanted something very much. These included the men and women involved in private charities, who were often members of Congress and their wives. Alexander R. Shepherd, the guiding spirit behind the territory, was a

---

[145] Lessoff, *Nation and Its City*, 29–30, 226; William Tindall, "Beginnings of Street Railways in the National Capital," *Records of the Columbia Historical Society* 21 (1918): 27–28, 35–36; Bryan, *History of the National Capital*, 491–94; Green, *Washington*, 263, 293–96; Leroy O. King Jr., *One Hundred Years of Capitol Traction* (n.p., 1972), 3–9.

[146] Helen Tangires, *Public Markets and Civic Culture in Nineteenth Century America* (Baltimore: Johns Hopkins University Press, 2003), 174–80; Tangires, "Contested Space: The Life and Death of Center Market," *Washington History* 7 (Spring–Summer 1995), 46–67; Green, *Washington*, 326, 353; Lessoff, *Nation and Its City*, 50–51; Bryan, *History of the National Capital*, 2:508–9; Green, *Washington*, 207.

forceful personality who enjoyed friendships with President Grant and with a great many congressmen, many of whom, judging by their correspondence with Shepherd, were obliged to him in one way or another.[147] Railroad corporations such as the Baltimore and Ohio and the Pennsylvania, through its proxy the Baltimore and Potomac, as well as the promoters of the Piedmont and Potomac, engaged in massive lobbying campaigns to secure their objectives, which help account for the exceptional amount of time and effort that Congress devoted to these measures. On a smaller scale, the Washington Market Company exerted similar influence.

Most seriously, Congress was, until 1878, unwilling to provide the resources that its real estate holdings or its role in the life of the capital warranted. That meant that local governments were continuously starved of funds and unable to initiate or bring to completion the projects that were necessary to create a modern capital for the nation. The creation of the territory did not alter the dynamics of the financial problem but only brought it to a critical point, forcing Congress to reconsider the terms of the financial relationship between the federal government and the District and, along with that, to contemplate a fundamental reorganization of the structures of local government. However, the outcome of that process reflected the particular circumstances of national as well as local politics during the 1870s as much as the logical implications of the constitutional status of the capital territory.

[147] See, for example, James A. Garfield to Alexander R. Shepherd, June 18, 1872; William Windom to Shepherd, April 13, 1873; Aaron Sargent to Shepherd, May 12, 1873; Roscoe Conkling to Shepherd, May 21, 1873, Shepherd MSS, Library of Congress.

# 8

## From Biracial Democracy to Direct Rule

### *The End of Self-Government in the Nation's Capital*

### "Worthy of the Nation"

It is often said that a capital city should serve as an expression of a nation's "self-image" and convey a strong sense of its character and destiny.[1] After the Civil War, many Americans believed that their nation's character and destiny had changed irrevocably. On one hand, with the extirpation of slavery, it had taken on a new commitment to civil rights and a new responsibility for the welfare of the men and women that it had recently emancipated. Thus, during Reconstruction, congressional Republicans used the District of Columbia as a "proving ground" for their policies of black suffrage and equal rights. On the other hand, the nation entered the postwar era with a new sense of the possibilities of federal power and a new awareness of its own strength and importance, forged in the fires of internecine conflict. A victorious and powerful national government required a capital city commensurate with its stature, which Washington evidently was not. Demands such as that made by *Harper's Monthly* in 1859 for a program of improvements "to render the seat of government worthy of the nation" carried still greater force after the triumph of the Union.[2] Such demands focused on the physical beautification of the capital rather than the attainment of racial justice. When the *New York Times*

---

[1] See Alan Lessoff, *The Nation and Its City: Politics, "Corruption," and Progress in Washington, D.C., 1861–1902* (Baltimore: Johns Hopkins University Press, 1994), 1–2.

[2] Mary C. Ames, *Ten Years in Washington: Life and Scenes in the National Capital, as a Woman Sees Them* (Hartford, CT: A.D. Worthington, 1875), 67–69; *Harper's Monthly*, quoted in Lessoff, *Nation and Its City*, 3. On the growth of federal power after 1865,

suggested in 1870 that Washington should be "a fitting representation of what is best in our national character," it went on to explain that it should be made into "a model city, not only as regards architecture, but also as regards cleanliness, paving, police, lighting, sewerage and transportation"; it said nothing about civil rights or social justice. Competing visions of Washington's future reflected competing conceptions of national purpose.[3]

Although Republican leaders had envisaged the District of Columbia as a showplace for their Reconstruction policies, in 1871, Congress replaced the local municipalities with a territorial government in which the influence of the electorate, black and white, was severely curtailed; three years later, it invested a three-man commission with governmental authority over the District and eliminated local democracy altogether; in 1878, the commission form of government was made permanent and home rule extinguished for close to a century. "In this District," noted the *Washington National Republican* in 1874, "the experiment was first made of giving the black man the suffrage. Has it come to this, that the Republican party admits and acknowledges its failure?"[4]

This abrupt *volte face* in congressional policy toward the District has been explained in a number of ways. It was clearly precipitated by the activities of a group of local businessmen and speculators, led by "Boss" Alexander Robey Shepherd, who first persuaded Congress to install a territorial form of government in the District and then launched into a comprehensive program of improvements – extravagant, badly managed,

---

see Richard F. Bensel, *Yankee Leviathan: The Origins of Central State Authority, 1859–1877* (Cambridge: Cambridge University Press, 1990); Morton Keller, *Affairs of State: Public Life in Late Nineteenth-Century America* (Cambridge, MA: Harvard University Press, 1977), Part One. On the impact of the war on American nationalism, see ibid., 38–46; Melinda Lawson, *Patriotic Fires: Forging a New Nationalism in the Civil War North* (Lawrence: University Press of Kansas, 2002); Cecilia O'Leary, *To Die For: The Paradox of American Patriotism* (Princeton, NJ: Princeton University Press, 1999); Susan-Mary Grant, "From Union to Nation? The Civil War and the Development of American Nationalism," in Susan-Mary Grant and Brian Holden Reid, eds., *The American Civil War: Explorations and Reconsiderations* (Harlow, England: Longman, 2000), 333–57. For descriptions of the physical condition of antebellum and Civil War Washington, see Lessoff, *Nation and Its City*, 3–4, 15–26.

[3] *New York Times*, December 26, 1870. For an interpretation of Washington's history based on the continuing tension between these ideals, see Howard Gillette Jr., *Between Justice and Beauty: Race, Planning, and the Failure of Urban Policy in Washington, D.C.* (Baltimore: Johns Hopkins University Press, 1995).

[4] *Washington National Republican*, December 18, 1874.

and open to charges of malpractice – that caused Congress to abolish the territory and impose direct federal rule.[5] Yet the regime's administrative failings and financial excesses could easily have been corrected by a reorganization of responsibilities and a tightening of financial restraints. It was not strictly necessary to throw the baby out with the bathwater. The end of representative government in the District is clearly related to the waning of Reconstruction over the course of the 1870s, that is, to the Republican Party's lessening commitment to equal rights and the gathering strength of the Democratic opposition. "When congressional enthusiasm for black rights diminished in the late 1870s," notes Steven J. Diner, suffrage rights were removed from the District. As Katherine Masur points out, the eradication of representative government would have been far more difficult if one-third of the electorate had not been African American.[6] The rise and fall of the territory have also been described, especially by Alan Lessoff, as episodes in a continuing search for political structures that would enable the physical reconstruction of the capital to proceed more efficiently and create a framework for "a modern business orientated city." What it signified, according to Howard Gillette Jr., was that a "commitment to physical development [had] triumphed over social advancement."[7]

The transition from biracial democracy to direct federal rule in the District of Columbia cannot be fully understood without giving careful consideration to the actions and motivations of the congressmen whose decisions shaped and reshaped the structures of government in the capital. Detailed analysis of congressional deliberations on the government of the District reveals members struggling with a number of fundamental

[5] For accounts of the rise and fall of the territorial government, see William M. Maury, *Alexander "Boss" Shepherd and the Board of Public Works* (Washington, DC: George Washington University Press, 1975); Lessoff, *Nation and Its City*, 44–129; Mark W. Summers, *The Era of Good Stealings* (New York: Oxford University Press, 1993), 137–47; James H. Whyte, *Uncivil War: Washington during the Reconstruction, 1865–1878* (New York: Twayne, 1958), 90–177, 203–36, 267–84; Wilhelmus B. Bryan, *A History of the National Capital* (2 vols., New York: Macmillan, 1914–16), 2:574–642; Constance M. Green, *Washington: Village and Capital, 1800–1878* (Princeton, NJ: Princeton University Press, 1962), 332–62, 386–95; Franklin H. Howe, "The Board of Public Works," *Records of the Columbia Historical Society*, 3 (1900), 257–78.

[6] Steven J. Diner, "Statehood and the Governance of the District of Columbia: An Historical Analysis of the Policy Issues," *Journal of Policy History*, 4 (1992), 397; Katherine Masur, "Reconstructing the Nation's Capital: The Politics of Race and Citizenship in the District of Columbia, 1862–1878" (Ph.D. diss., University of Michigan, 2001), 338–89. See also Maury, *Alexander "Boss" Shepherd*, 49–50; Whyte, *Uncivil War*, 279–80.

[7] Carl Abbott, *Political Terrain: Washington, D.C. from Tidewater Town to Global Metropolis* (Chapel Hill: University of North Carolina Press, 1999), 71; Gillette, *From Justice to Beauty*, 45. See also ibid., 58–72; Lessoff, *Nation and Its City*.

dilemmas arising from the constitutional relationship between Congress and the District, the dynamics of congressional decision making, and the requirements of constructing a capital for a reinvigorated postbellum Union. However, their decisions also reflected the particular political conditions that obtained in the 1870s. They need to be located within the complex process of federal disengagement from Reconstruction, the often covert dialectics of racial politics, the dynamics of party competition, and a contemporary discourse about the government of cities. An analysis of the factors influencing congressional policy toward the District of Columbia not only sheds light on the reasons for disfranchisement there but also illustrates the complexity of the process through which the federal government withdrew its support for Reconstruction in the South.

## Reform of the Municipal Government

Republican congressmen had anticipated that the installation of a Republican administration in City Hall, made possible by the newly enfranchised black vote, would inaugurate a system of efficient government and material improvement that would elevate Washington from its dusty dilapidation to a condition befitting a modern capital.[8] However, the efforts made by the Republican Mayor Sayles J. Bowen to initiate a comprehensive plan of clearing and grading the streets landed the municipality heavily in debt without many visible signs of improvement. Bowen's difficult personality, his peculiar talent for making enemies, and his tendency to retreat under pressure into a crude form of machine politics alienated many of his supporters. In the mayoral election of 1870, substantial numbers of black and white voters deserted him to vote for the Reform Republican candidate Matthew G. Emery. The fact that Emery, when elected, was no more successful in solving the financial and governmental problems that had bedeviled his predecessor reveals that they were more structural than personal in character.

They stemmed largely from the lack of congressional support for the local reconstruction project. Most damaging of all was the refusal of Congress to make any substantial financial contribution either to the day-to-day running of the city government or to the large-scale improvements that were necessary to make Washington livable, never mind raise it to the level that its status demanded. The city fathers pleaded in vain

---

[8] See, for example, *CG*, 39.1:174, 179; *Washington Daily Morning Chronicle*, September 16, 1865, July 4, 13, 1866.

that the extravagant scale on which the city had been planned imposed special burdens on local taxpayers and that therefore the United States, the extensive property of which went untaxed, "was bound by every principle of justice to pay a portion of the expense of improving the federal city."[9] The territorial Board of Public Works estimated in 1872 that the United States had paid only $1,321,288 for street improvements since 1802, during which period the city had expended $13,921,767. In 1878, it was calculated that the federal government had expended $9 million on District projects ($6 million since 1871), during which period the people of the District had spent $34 million. Even projects such as the paving of Pennsylvania Avenue, for which the United States had long accepted financial responsibility, had to be pushed through over loud objections to appropriations for what one congressman called "the most ordinary expenses of the city of Washington."[10] Such attitudes delayed the repaving of the avenue for several years and obstructed other developments altogether. The overall result was that the city looked much as it had before the war. "Washington remains to-day the worst paved, worst cleansed, and, in many respects, worst managed city in the Union," remarked the *New York Tribune* in 1869.[11]

As early as December 1865, while Congress was pondering the intro-duction of black suffrage, Lot M. Morrill, the chairman of the Senate Committee on the District of Columbia, presented a proposal for a three-man commission to govern the District, modeled on the body to which Congress had entrusted the organization of the capital territory at its birth. "If there is anything like bad government, shameless government anywhere, it is in this District," he told his fellow Senators. The Founding Fathers had never intended that jurisdiction over the District should lie with three small municipal corporations. The capital was never designed

---

[9] Mayor Richard Wallach to Secretary of the Interior James Harlan, in *Washington Daily Morning Chronicle*, December 14, 1865. See also memorial of Mayor and Councils to Congress, December 7, 1863, House Committee on the District of Columbia, HR37-G3.5, RG292, NARA; *Journal of the 65th Council* (Washington, DC, 1868), 687–91.

[10] Report of the Board of Public Works of the District of Columbia from its Organization until November 1, 1872, Ho. Exec. Doc. 1, 42.3 (1872); CG, 41.2:4536; CG, 42.3:201; CR, 45.2: 1923; *Evening Star*, May 22, 1868; *New York Times*, December 4, 1872; Lessoff, *Nation and Its City*, 34–5; Green, *Washington*, 325–27. For objections to federal appropriations for the paving of Pennsylvania Avenue, see CG, 41.2:4535–36, Appendix 361–65; 41.3:1656–62.

[11] Quoted in *Evening Star*, June 17, 1869. See also *National Intelligencer*, February 17, March 12, 1869, *Evening Star*, June 5, 1868; *New York Times*, January 15, 1869.

to be a municipality: "It is a seat of government of the United States." Neither Democrats, who were reluctant to abandon the ideal of "popular government" in the nation's capital, nor Republicans, who hoped that black suffrage and the creation of a viable local Republican Party would revolutionize the city government, responded favorably to Morrill's proposal for commission government.[12]

Although there was little apparent enthusiasm on Capitol Hill, influential groups of citizens took up the scheme. They included a great many "substantial citizens," local businessmen such as the bankers W. W. Corcoran and George W. Riggs; Henry D. Cooke, the brother of the financier Jay Cooke; and the proprietors of the *Evening Star*. A petition to Congress in favor of a new form of government was signed, it was claimed, by men representing two-thirds of the property interests of the District. According to the estimate of Republican alderman John R. Elvans, the eighty signatories of a petition against renewal of the city charter were large property holders with more than $10 million worth of assets between them. The leading figure in the movement for governmental reform was Alexander R. Shepherd, an energetic and ambitious building contractor and real estate developer who had served during the war as president of the Board of Common Council and had been instrumental in organizing the Washington Board of Trade. As Alan Lessoff has demonstrated, the reformers believed that the primary purpose of municipal government was to carry out improvements that would stimulate the local economy – in particular, enhance the value of real estate – and that a simplified structure of authority and an infusion of federal money were necessary to achieve those ends.[13] Over the next few years, various plans were discussed in meetings of the Board of Trade, committees were

[12] *CG*, 39.1:2481, 3191–93; *Evening Star*, May 9, 11, 1866, January 7, 1867; *Chronicle*, December 20, 1865, May 15, 1866; Bryan, *History of the National Capital*, 2:550–53, 569–72. What Republican support there was for commission government was because Conservatives, "a preponderantly disloyal element" according to the *Chronicle*, were then in possession of the city government. See, for example, *Chronicle*, November 23, 1865, December 6, 1866. Such a rationale was undercut by the suffrage bill passed early in 1867.

[13] Petition dated February 17, 1871, Container 5, Shepherd MSS, Library of Congress; *Journal of the 65th Council* (Washington, DC, 1868), 475–76; *Evening Star*, January 28, March 12, 1868. See Lessoff, *Nation and City*, 44–71 for an analysis of the "improvers" and ibid., 10–12 on "promotional governance." On Shepherd's career, see Maury, *Alexander "Boss" Shepherd*; Lessoff, *Nation and Its City*, 47–51; William Tindall, "A Sketch of Alexander Robey Shepherd." *Records of the Columbia Historical Society* 14 (1911): 49–66.

appointed to examine the alternatives, and the arguments for commission government were thoroughly rehearsed.[14]

One of the most compelling arguments for reform was the need to rationalize the District's complex system of government. Local government was divided between five agencies – including the corporations of Washington and Georgetown; the Levy Court, which administered the affairs of the rural parts of the District, known as Washington County; as well as the federally appointed boards of Metropolitan Police Commissioners and Trustees of Colored Schools – which made coordinated decision making all but impossible. It was necessary, said the *Star*, "to substitute for the present conflicting and necessarily impotent jurisdictions in the two District cities and the county one efficient government, clothed by Congress with sufficient powers to deal with all the important matters of District interest which are now hung up in Congressional committee rooms." A former Council member told the Senate Committee on the District of Columbia that consolidation was "absolutely required by the public interest and a large majority of the intelligent and respectable citizens."[15]

Even more detrimental to coordinated government was the division between municipal and federal authority. In theory, congressional power was absolute; in practice, Congress showed little interest in local affairs. Yet, while disdaining to make decisions for the District, it showed an equal disinclination to give the municipal authorities much freedom of action, and a still greater disinclination to give them money. The result, as local newspapers regularly lamented, was that the most urgent problems facing the city were not tackled and the most important steps toward making Washington into a worthy capital for the nation were not taken.[16]

---

[14] Petition of Citizens of the District of Columbia for the Organization of a Single Local Government for the District, Sen. Misc. Doc. 24, 41.1 (March 1869), Ser. 1399; *Evening Star*, February 26, March 5, 1867; *Chronicle*, January 18, 1868; Green, *Washington*, 332–34; Bryan, *History of the National Capital*, 2:569–72. For accounts of meetings see *Evening Star*, October 22, 1867, January 18, March 12, May 18, 1868; *National Intelligencer*, January 18, 1868.

[15] *Evening Star*, January 13, 1870; D. M. Kelsey to Hannibal Hamlin, January 24, 1870, SEN 41A-S2, RG46, NARA.

[16] *Evening Star*, January 13, 1870. See also *Evening Star*, November 23, December 8, 1865, May 18, 1866, October 22, 26, 1867, January 18, 1868, January 17, 1870; *National Intelligencer*, March 12, 1869; letters from "HK" in *Chronicle*, January 20, 27, 1868. The editor of the *Chronicle*, John W. Forney, whose allegiance was to the radical wing of the Republican Party, pointed out that the replacement of the city councils by a commission would make little difference, since the District was unlikely to receive any more attention from Congress. *Chronicle*, February 3, 1868.

Although it was hoped for a while that Congress would be more coop-
erative, and more generous, toward a Republican city government, this
turned out not to be the case, and the movement for reform of local
government gathered momentum during the course of Bowen's troubled
term.[17]

Civic leaders such as Shepherd hoped that Congress might be persuaded to make a substantial financial contribution to the District but
recognized that it was unlikely to do so without exercising a greater control. However, they were willing to trade some degree of autonomy for a
federal contribution to the costs of government.[18] If this meant the curtailment of democratic government in the District, then this was a price that
they were ready to pay. A large and supposedly "representative" meeting
of local citizens declared in January 1868 that presidentially appointed
commissioners would govern better than "broken down political demagogues." They would give weight to the "deliberately expressed opinion
of the citizens," rather than pandering to the wishes of the mass electorate like the "low politicians" that currently ran affairs. Commission
government, said a correspondent to the *Chronicle*, would eliminate the
"intolerable nuisance" of election contests, the only object of which was
the distribution of spoils, whereas the *Star* declared that one of the chief
objectives of governmental reform was to do away with what it called
"this miserable petty ward club business" and dispense with "the whole
narrow-minded tribe of corner-grocery politicians." In other words, what
the reformers wished to escape from was the very practice of popular
politics, newly invigorated by the enfranchisement of African Americans.
Masur points out that reformers employed the language of "public interest" as a way of validating the removal of political power from the body
of electors, who were described as too "cliquish and small-minded" to
perceive the general good, and vesting it in the hands of a public-spirited
elite of businessmen and professionals.[19]

In the context of Washington in the aftermath of the Civil War, their
antidemocratic rhetoric carried a significant racial subtext. The reformers
were mostly conservatives who were hostile, like Riggs, or at best ambivalent, like Shepherd and the proprietors of the *Star*, toward the biracial
democracy that had arisen in the nation's capital. Many "old citizens"

---

[17] *Evening Star*, May 26, 30, June 2, 1868, January 17, 1870.

[18] *Evening Star*, January 18, 28, 1870.

[19] *Evening Star*, January 18, 1868, January 24, 25, February 25, 1871; *Chronicle*, January 27, 1868; *National Intelligencer*, October 22, 1867; Masur, "Reconstructing the
Nation's Capital," 296–97.

had never come to terms with black suffrage; finding that they could not destroy it, they now sought to diminish its influence. However, the reformers also included many Republicans, drawn from the "improving strand" in the party. They were men who placed the physical and material improvement of the capital before its role as an exemplar of racial justice and were prepared to sacrifice universal suffrage to the cause of improvement. More accustomed to working through personal connections and lobbying influential figures in government than appealing to a mass electorate, they were confident of their ability to operate the new structures of power.[20]

"Excepting General Howard," said the *New National Era*, "there is not a Radical Republican on the list of names favorable to the change." No "Radical Republican" was identified with the scheme, agreed the black churchman J. Sella Martin, nor any who had "stood by the negro."[21] This was not strictly true; a few former Radicals, disenchanted with the Bowen regime, had come to support the reform movement, and so temporarily, during the mayoral campaign of 1870, did a number of black Republicans hostile to Bowen. Most, however, were suspicious of its motives. The adversaries of reform were mostly Republicans, and especially black Republicans, who were committed to the continuation of the Reconstruction project. The city councils, with their Republican majorities, and meetings of Republican ward clubs repeatedly passed resolutions condemning the proposed governmental reform. Predictably, they condemned it as a direct assault on black voting rights. The African American ward leader George Hatton warned of the consequences: "the country... will hear that negro suffrage has proved a failure in the District of Columbia; this will re-echo through the country from ocean to ocean, and be heard in every palace and hamlet in the land." Others feared the loss of the rights and opportunities so recently gained. "There is not a colored man who could get a place on Corporation work," warned one member of the First Ward Republican Club. Predictably, too, they condemned the reform as "anti-republican," as a betrayal of self-government, "in direct antagonism to the elective principles on which our government is based." As Martin told the Senate District Committee, the scheme had "assumed an aristocratic shape." The reform movement was

---

[20] *New National Era*, January 27, 1870; *Chronicle*, February 3, 1868; Masur, "Reconstructing the Nation's Capital," 294–97; Lessoff, *Nation and Its City*, 52–54.
[21] *New National Era*, March 10, 1870; *Evening Star*, March 7, 1870.

identified with a former privileged class that had not come to terms with the enfranchisement of blacks.[22]

## The Origins of the Territory

Some time in 1869, realizing that Congress was not ready to authorize a cessation of democratic representation in the District and go back so blatantly on its commitment to black voting, Shepherd and his circle abandoned the model of direct rule by a federal commission in favor of a form of territorial government that would retain elements of local democracy while also, it was hoped, rationalizing authority within the District and establishing clearer lines of decision making. The reformers anticipated that a territorial legislature would have the authority to push forward the necessary improvements that Congress lacked the time to consider. Because Congress, it was believed, was unlikely to delegate substantial authority to a local government that was wholly elective, important elements, certainly the governor, possibly also the upper house of the legislature, would have to be federal appointees, acting as a check on the elected House of Delegates.[23]

A bill incorporating the main features of their plan was passed by the Senate in May 1870 after only a brief discussion. This created a consolidated territorial government in which not only both houses of the legislature but also the governor would be popularly elected, and it allowed for the assessment of federal property for taxation.[24] The House took no action until the following winter. It was evident that members

[22] *Chronicle*, March 4, 1871; *Evening Star*, February 11, 1868, January 18, 1870. See also *Evening Star*, January 11, 18, 30, February 3, March 7, 1870, January 25, 1871; *Chronicle*, February 3, 1868, January 19, 27, February 22, 23, March 8, 1870, January 23, 1871; *New National Era*, January 27, February 10, 1870; Resolutions of the Board of Common Council, February 17, 1868, SEN 40A-H5.1, RG46, NARA; Masur, "Reconstructing the Nation's Capital," 297–312. It may be significant that some of Bowen's Republican opponents attached themselves to the cause of governmental reorganization during the winter and spring of 1870, giving members of the House and Senate District Committees an impression of substantial bipartisan support for the territorial plan just at the moment when they were giving serious consideration to the matter. Several, like Mayor Matthew Emery, later reverted to opposing the scheme. See *Evening Star*, January 13, 1871; Cox, "Matthew Gault Emery," 43.

[23] *Evening Star*, January 13, 15, 18, 26, 28, 31, February 12, 21, 28, March 4, 1870; Lessoff, *Nation and Its City*, 52–54.

[24] CG, 41.2:3912–14; *Evening Star*, March 21, May 28, 1870; *Chronicle*, March 22, 1870; Whyte, *Uncivil War*, 91.

of the House Committee on the District of Columbia were unhappy with certain features of the Senate bill. They demanded greater federal control over the District government and were concerned about the potentially uncontrollable demands on the U.S. Treasury that the assessment of federal property might allow. Some, evidently fearing the potential influence of black voters, wished to curtail the elective component. In January 1871, the committee reported its own bill, which left only the lower house of the Legislative Assembly and the District's nonvoting delegate to Congress to be elected by popular vote, whereas the governor and council were to be appointed by the president. Any requirement for a regular financial contribution from the federal government was removed: federal property could be assessed for improvements but not taxed directly. The text explicitly confirmed that "nothing shall be construed to deprive Congress of its power of legislation over said District in as ample manner as if this law had not been enacted." In other words, any legislative powers that might be delegated to the territory were wholly provisional. The bill now included a Board of Public Works, appointed by the president, which was given a loosely defined responsibility for coordinating and directing improvements.[25] The House passed the revised bill after a short debate, and so, a few days later, did the Senate. Debate in both houses focused almost exclusively on the curtailment of popular representation and ignored in particular the insertion of the Board of Public Works. Thus, the city charter was annulled, and the capital began its brief experience of territorial government.[26]

Why did Congress decide so radically to transform a system of government that had survived, more or less intact, since 1820? One reason was that the residents that members of Congress were most likely to listen to, and encounter socially, were the influential businessmen of the Board of Trade and the Citizens' Reform Association rather than the African American laborers whose voice was heard in Republican ward meetings. Shepherd, by all accounts an immensely persuasive individual who

---

[25] It seems that Shepherd was responsible, in association with Burton Cook, the chairman of the House District Committee, for the transformation of the bill, a shadowy process that is virtually undocumented. *Evening Star*, January 21, 1871; Green, *Washington*, 335; Whyte, *Uncivil War*, 103.

[26] CG, 41.3:641–47, 685–88; *Evening Star*, January 20, 21, 23, 1871; Whyte, *Uncivil War*, 91, 100–4; Maury, *Alexander "Boss" Shepherd*, 3–4; Green, *Washington*, 335–38. Important amendments, particularly concerning the Board of Public Works, were added in conference. See *Chronicle*, February 14, 1871, *Evening Star*, January 31, February 2, 13, 16, 1871. The final text can be found in *U.S. Statutes at Large*, 41.3, ch. 62 (February 16, 1871): 419–29.

counted President Grant and other prominent Republican officeholders among his personal friends, had orchestrated a lobbying campaign over a period of years, with repeated meetings, thoroughly reported in the columns of the local press, regular representations before congressional committees, personal consultations with key members, and, at appropriate moments, lavish entertainments. During the winter of 1871, while the territorial bill was pending, influential members were invited to "a steamboat excursion down the Potomac, and other functions," where, according to Shepherd's private secretary, "the gustatory proclivities of Congressmen were amply gratified, accompanied by the alluring influences of genial companionship."[27]

The *Star*, reporting earlier on another local bill, noted that "nearly every Senator who spoke expressed the opinion that the present mode of Government for the District is wretchedly defective and needs a speedy change."[28] A dissatisfaction with, indeed an embarrassment at, the physical condition of the city's streets and marketplaces, not to mention the noisome Washington City Canal, may have influenced members who themselves were forced to confront the evidence each and every day. Many considered the root of the problem to be the excessive influence that the people of the District enjoyed over their government. "I do not believe that it was intended originally that the District of Columbia should be entirely under the control of the people who might live here," said Senator William M. Stewart of Nevada, a substantial investor in Washington real estate who maintained a close interest in local affairs. Because Congress lacked the time "to sit here as a board of supervisors or as a common council to manage the affairs of the city of Washington," it might delegate some powers to a local authority, but the United States must retain a controlling influence. The new framework, said Representative John Bingham of Ohio, recognized that congressional authority was paramount and offered "simply a method of allowing the people primarily to express their feelings subject to the controlling power of Congress." Therefore, talk of self-government for the District was misplaced. For the past fifty years, agreed the Democratic congressman Fernando Wood, a former mayor of New York, the city had had "a contradictory, heterogeneous, unsatisfactory form of government" in which the republican principle of self-rule had been wrongly applied when, in fact, Congress should have taken on the responsibility of ruling directly. The events of

[27] Tindall, "Sketch of Alexander Shepherd," 54.
[28] *Evening Star*, January 31, 1870.

the past ten years, by introducing a "different class" of voters, "a mass of persons with no interests here and really disqualified to appreciate and comprehend properly the interests of others," had made things worse.[29]

Indeed, some members had come to believe that any talk of self-government for the District was misplaced. In the view of George Frisbie Hoar of Massachusetts, legislative power could not be delegated under the Constitution, which granted it exclusively to Congress. It was therefore not appropriate for the residents of the District to enjoy "republican representation" at all. Vermont senator George F. Edmunds agreed that the Constitution did not allow for the residents of the District to enjoy "republican representation." On the other hand, George W. Woodward, a former chief justice of the Pennsylvania Supreme Court, maintained that congressional authority over the District was "exclusive" only in the sense that it debarred any exercise of sovereignty there by the states; it did not preclude the delegation of power to agencies of local government. The *Federalist* and other contemporary texts were cited to demonstrate that this was also the view of the authors of the Constitution. That a majority of members at this stage supported the territorial plan implies that they did not accept the full implications of Hoar's interpretation.[30]

Of course, at this juncture in the nation's history the issue was inextricably linked with the political participation of African Americans. Democrats, a hopeless minority in both houses, clearly regretted their enfranchisement and regarded territorial government as a way of minimizing its impact. Indiana congressman William E. Niblack spoke for many: "the failure of the District government is due to a very great measure to that extraordinary infliction which we placed upon the people of the District some years ago by making the District the experimental garden for indiscriminate, vagabond, uneducated, carpetbag, and non-taxpaying suffrage, black and white."[31] However, Republicans like

---

[29] *CG*, 41.3:686, 642–44. On Stewart's career, see John A. Garraty and Mark C. Carnes, eds., *American National Biography* (24 vols., New York: Oxford University Press, 1999), 20:755–57; Russell B. Elliot, *Servant of Power: A Political Biography of Senator William M. Stewart* (Reno: University of Nevada Press, 1983). On his links with Washington real estate interests, see Lessoff, *Nation and Its City*, 41 and 159–60.

[30] See the debate in *CG*, 41.3:643–45, 686–88. See also Diner, "Statehood and Governance," 391–93.

[31] *CG*, 41.3:1612. The editor of a short-lived Democratic newspaper, the *Washington Daily Patriot*, later told a congressional investigating committee that, as he understood it, when the Territory was established, "The idea was that the objection to the importation of negroes to override the taxpayers was to be obviated by this new government." U.S. House of Representatives, Committee on the District of Columbia, *Affairs in the District of Columbia*, Ho. Report 72, 42.2 (1872), 337. See also remarks of Charles A. Eldredge in *CR*, 43.2:505.

Burton Cook of Illinois, the chairman of the House Committee on the District of Columbia and one of the bill's principal authors, also pointed to elements in the population whose presence worked against a satisfactory application of the democratic process to the nation's capital. Recent migrants (unspecified but presumably African American) rhetorically elided into federal officeholders and other temporary residents with "no earthly interest in the District" to form an image of a dangerously unstable and unreliable electorate. That meant that "a municipal government for the District, elected by universal suffrage, should be a worse government for the District than the municipal government of other cities, if that be possible." In face of such a population, the "conservative element" – that is, the federal government – should be given greater weight.[32]

Nevertheless, a substantial number of Republicans regarded presidential appointment of the governor and the upper house of the legislature as a serious departure from republican principles and regretted that those who had so recently been given the franchise should be allowed so little opportunity to exercise it. The Republican representative Jacob H. Ela moved to amend the bill by providing for an elected governor and an elected council. To restrict representation to the lower house of the legislature, he argued, struck "at the very foundation principle of free government."[33] Both amendments were defeated on a voice vote (apparently Ela's proposal for an elective governor received only 13 votes), and the bill passed by 97 votes to 57. Although Democrats approved of the new form of government more consistently than Republicans, both parties were, in fact, divided: the Democrats voted 29–13 in favor of the bill, the Republicans 68–44.[34] When the bill reached the Senate, several members argued, not unreasonably, that it was so different from the version passed earlier by the upper house and contained so much "new matter" that it should be sent back to the Committee on the District of Columbia for further consideration. A motion to recommit was defeated by 25 votes to 32.[35]

Most of the Republican senators who had compiled records for radical voting in the preceding Congress supported the motion to delay consideration; most moderates voted against it. In other words, those who had been less committed to the party's broader Reconstruction project were more likely to consent to the termination of its local manifestation, at

[32] *CG*, 41.3:642; *Evening Star*, January 23, 1871.
[33] *CG*, 41.3:642, 644–46.
[34] *CG*, 41.3:647; *Evening Star*, January 20, 1871. George W. Julian attempted to insert a women's suffrage amendment, which failed by 55 votes to 117. *CG*, 41.3:646.
[35] *CG*, 41.3:688.

least in its current form. There was a less pronounced association between Republican voting on the territorial bill and on Reconstruction issues in the same Congress – including the reconstruction of Georgia, the setting of fundamental conditions for the admission of Virginia and Georgia to representation in Congress, and the enforcement of voting rights – which indicates that senators' voting on District government was more than a simple reflection of their views on Reconstruction generally.[36] A stronger association between opposition to territorial government and support for a stricter southern policy was evident in the House, but it was neither strong enough nor consistent enough to suggest that Republican Congressmen regarded the governance of the District as no more than an aspect of Reconstruction.[37]

"There is a general disposition on the part of Congress...to grant to the people of the District the privilege of regulating their own affairs in their own way, subject only to the Constitution," declared the *Star*, with unwarranted optimism, early in the bill's progress. Some members did, indeed, regard the measure as a means of getting the District off their backs. The bill's sponsor, Senator Hannibal Hamlin of Maine, believed that territorial government would relieve Congress of the need to enact

[36] To take a crude measure, if those Republican senators who had voted for a stricter enforcement policy more often than not in those roll calls on Reconstruction in which the party was divided (that is, 10 or more Republicans voted against the majority of the party) are termed radicals and those who more often voted against stricter enforcement are termed moderates, 13 radicals and 12 moderates later voted to refer the bill to committee, whereas 10 radicals and 13 moderates voted against the motion. If we look more closely at individual roll calls, we find associations with the territorial vote (using Yule's Q) of .49 (reconstruction of Georgia: test oath), .28 (admission of Virginia: right to vote), .21 and 0 (admission of Georgia: delay legislative elections, suspend habeas corpus), .17 (enforcement of Fifteenth Amendment). CG, 41.2:228, 643, 2821, 2829, 3682. In a comparison with Republican voting patterns in the Fortieth Congress, those survivors from the earlier Congress who are identified by Michael Les Benedict as Conservatives voted 2–10 in favor of the motion, Radicals 13–6. *Compromise of Principle: Congressional Republicans and Reconstruction, 1863–1869* (New York: Norton, 1974), 360–62, 365–70, 373–75.

[37] Voting on Reconstruction issues more often followed party lines in the House than in the Senate, but there were significant intraparty divisions among Republicans (with a minority amounting to forty or more) in the following roll calls (association with voting on the territorial bill in brackets): admission of Virginia (.61); removal of political disabilities (.59); reconstruction of Georgia (.05); removal of political disabilities (.49). CG, 41.2:503, 1468, 4796; 41.3:151. If Republican representatives who voted for a stricter enforcement policy more often than they did not in those roll calls are termed radicals and those who more often voted against stricter enforcement are termed moderates, 18 radicals and 46 moderates voted for the territorial bill, and 24 radicals and 17 moderates voted against.

local legislation, for which it did not have the time. Indeed, members' remarks betray a distinct note of irritation with the whole business of governing the District. They wished to divest themselves of the irksome task yet betrayed little trust in its residents' capacity to govern themselves. Most congressmen perceived the territorial plan as a means of establishing a more rigorous scrutiny over the municipal authorities, whereas many citizens perceived it as a cession of substantive power to a stronger District government. These differing understandings of the meaning of territorial government were to be the source of much difficulty in the future.[38]

### The Meteoric Career of the Board of Public Works

In fact, many local Republicans who had been suspicious of the territorial regime soon learned to live with it. The new system of government left many of the postwar innovations in politics and social relations unaltered, and an active form of grassroots politics continued, if somewhat diminished in vigor. Republican meetings in many of the legislative districts continued to be well attended, argumentative, and often volatile.[39] African American voters were gratified when the Legislative Assembly tightened up the local civil rights law. Nor could they be disappointed with the large proportion of black laborers employed on the streets and sewers and the other improvements authorized by the Board of Public Works. The historian Thomas R. Johnson estimates that about a third of municipal employees were African American.[40]

The many black Republicans who depended on municipal work projects for their living continued to use local party meetings to voice their demands for employment and, when disappointed, to express their

---

[38] *Evening Star*, February 9, 1870; *CG*, 41.3: 685. See also *CG*, 41.3:642 (Cook), 686 (Stewart).

[39] See, for example, the reports of meetings in the *Evening Star*, March 29, October 14, 17, 1871, August 28, 1872. Increasingly, though, the *Star* in its reports adopted a detached and increasingly dismissive tone, not seeking to hide its disquiet with this kind of grassroots politics.

[40] Thomas R. Johnson, "The City on the Hill: Race Relations in Washington, D.C., 1865–1885" (Ph.D. diss., University of Maryland, 1975), 186–237; Whyte, *Uncivil War*, 242–47. The *New National Era* sometimes complained that "the colored man is being made to take a back seat in office holding in the District of Columbia" and that the new government marginalized black voters. *New National Era*, June 26, 1873, August 3, 1871; Masur, "Reconstructing the Nation's Capital," 322–23. However, it also praised the Board of Public Works for the breadth of its ambitions. See, for example, *New National Era*, December 12, 1872, February 20, 1873.

grievances against the Board of Public Works and its contractors.[41] The link between the material concerns of the African American working class and grassroots Republican politics manifested itself in a strike by black laborers on public works projects in June 1871, early in the life of the territorial regime. The strike was sparked by a dispute over wages – in particular, the refusal of contractors to pay black laborers the same rate as white laborers and to pay either of them the $2 a day laid down as a standard by a municipal ordinance during Bowen's mayoralty. After a deal brokered by Governor Cooke had collapsed and as incidents of violence became more frequent, the governor provided police protection for the public works projects, and after a while, most of the strikers returned to work. The strike leaders were largely drawn from the ranks of Republican Party activists, many of whom, like George Hatton, Walker White, and the outspoken Marcellus West, had worked for years to promote the interests of wage laborers within the party organization. Hence, the strike continued into the territorial period the pronounced streak of labor insurgency that had animated local Republican politics since 1867. Most of the city's newspapers responded to the dispute with horror. The *Evening Star* compared the rhetoric of the strike leaders to "the most bloodthirsty and incendiary utterances of the Paris Commune" and welcomed the firm response of the District authorities. To conservative Republicans like the editor of the *Star*, the incident provided telling evidence of the dangerous currents that continued to feed popular politics in the District of Columbia.[42]

The most visible difference between the territorial government and that which preceded it lay in the colossal scope of the improvements that were initiated by the board, under the inspiration of its vice president and guiding spirit Alexander Shepherd. Shepherd immediately set about a comprehensive program of public works that involved grading and paving virtually all the city's streets simultaneously and installing sewers across the city, as well as filling in the old Washington City Canal and erecting new market buildings. Fortified by a $4 million improvement loan, ratified by the electorate in November 1871, he ignored the

---

[41] See, for example, *Evening Star*, February 13, March 5, 20, 1872.

[42] *Evening Star*, June 1, 3, 6, 7, 1871; Thomas R. Johnson, "The City on the Hill: Race Relations in Washington, D.C., 1865–1885" (Ph.D. diss., University of Maryland, 1975), 201–6; Masur, "Reconstructing the Nation's Capital," 323–36; Heather Cox Richardson, *The Death of Reconstruction: Race, Labor, and Politics in the Post-Civil War North, 1865–1901* (Cambridge, MA: Harvard University Press, 2001), 100. The events of the strike may be traced in the reports printed in the *Evening Star* and *Chronicle* for June 1–9, 1871.

restraints imposed by current municipal revenues. He also did not seek specific authorization for individual projects from the territorial legislature, as the law required. These hastily planned and executed projects cause massive disruption, with streets all over the city rendered impassable for months on end, and residents, including prominent members of Congress like Senators Edmunds and Bayard, suddenly finding their property as much as 20 feet above or below street level. The projects also went far beyond any expenditure anticipated by Congress and virtually quadrupled the indebtedness inherited from the old corporation.[43]

Shepherd later told a congressional investigating committee that he had acted on the understanding that Congress would meet a substantial part of the costs of improvement. He laid the financial problems of the District squarely on the failure of Congress to meet its obligations. There was, indeed, a widespread expectation, as Norton P. Chipman, the District's delegate to Congress, remarked, "that the general government shall take upon itself a just share of expenditure in making the capital a type and exponent of American ideas and institutions." The fact that President Grant urged liberality to the District in repeated messages to Congress encouraged such expectations. Under the system of improvements inaugurated since the formation of the territory, he told Congress in December 1871, "Washington is rapidly becoming a city worthy of the nation's capital . . . I recommend liberal appropriations on the part of Congress, in order that the Government may bear its just share of the expense if carrying out a judicious system of improvements."[44]

---

[43] On the scale and scope of the improvements, see the summary in U.S. Senate, *Report of the Joint Select Committee of Congress Appointed to Inquire into the Affairs of the District of Columbia*, Sen. Report 453, 43.1 (1874), xv–xvi; District of Columbia, Board of Public Works, *Second Annual Report* (Washington, DC, 1873). See also *New York Times*, December 4, 1872; *Evening Star*, July 29, 1873; Lessoff, *Nation and Its City*, chap. 3; Maury, *Alexander "Boss" Shepherd*. The reliance on large-scale borrowing to finance urban development during this period was, of course, not confined to Washington. Cf. Scobey, *Empire City*; Robin L. Einhorn, *Property Rules: Political Economy in Chicago, 1833–1872* (Chicago: University of Chicago Press, 1991); and, more generally, Jon C. Teaford, *The Unheralded Triumph: City Government in America, 1870–1900* (Baltimore: Johns Hopkins University Press, 1984), 285–93; Eric Monkonnen, *America Becomes Urban: The Development of U.S. Cities and Towns, 1780–1980* (Berkeley: University of California Press, 1988), 138–44.

[44] *Affairs in the District of Columbia* (1872), 586–87; *Evening Star*, March 2, 1874; Chipman quoted in Bryan, *History of the National Capital*, 2:607; James L. Richardson, ed., *A Compilation of the Messages and Papers of the Presidents, 1789–1897* (10 vols., Washington, DC: Bureau of National Literature and Art, 1904), 7:154, 254; Maury, *Alexander "Boss" Shepherd*, 8, 47–48; Lessoff, *Nation and Its City*, 116–17; Green, *Washington*, 348–49.

As it turned out, Congress proved reluctant even to pay its share of the assessed value of improvements adjacent to federal property, for which it was liable like any other possessor of urban real estate. Appropriations for that purpose were made belatedly and under protest. Many congressmen could not get used to the idea that an agency like the Board of Works could be permitted to enter into contracts that would impose a financial obligation on the United States, and many declined to honor any such commitment. John F. Farnsworth, an Illinois liberal Republican, told the House that he had no idea that the Board of Public Works could "incur obligations which my constituents could be called upon to pay." If the United States were to pay the expenses of "these assumed improvements," said another congressman, it should have more control over them. "I hope the Government of the United States will not make haste to put itself body and soul into the hands of the Board of Public Works of this District," said Edmunds in the Senate in response to a proposal to recompense the Board for the expense of filling in the Canal. It was an "irresponsible board" prone to "reckless extravagance," said Senator John W. Stevenson of Kentucky, and Congress should not allow it to place the Government in debt without authority of law. A House amendment to a Deficiency Appropriation Bill in December 1872 prohibited the board from entering into any obligation that imposed liability on the United States without a prior appropriation, and the Senate required approval of the prices charged for work by the federal superintendent of public buildings and grounds (who happened to be Major Orville E. Babcock, a Shepherd crony).[45]

Nevertheless, Congress did appropriate $260,000 for District improvements in the spring of 1872, another $1.24 million in January and $2.21 million in March 1873. The $3.5 million appropriated in 1872–73 was, in fact, more than had been expended on the District over the previous seventy years. House Appropriations Committee chairman James A. Garfield was persuaded that the improvements made by the Board of Public Works served to advance "the convenience and glory of the nation" and agreed to report the appropriations. Majorities in both houses eventually conceded that this was a federal city, built on a grand scale to glorify the nation, and that "a rigid parsimonious economy" was inappropriate. "The Government is able and ought to be willing to make liberal appropriations for the ornamentation of the avenues," said Senator Joshua Hill, a Republican

[45] CG, 42.2:3657, 3658, 4347–48; CG, 42.3, 230–34, 280–87, 307–9, 328–33, 1973.

from Georgia.[46] However, although Congress did compensate the District for work adjacent to federal property, though with no great grace, it felt no responsibility to contribute to the overall cost of improvements. Of the $20 million or more expended by the Board of Public Works during its short history, just over $3.5 million came from federal appropriations. In other words, despite radical changes in the structure of government, one of the basic problems confronting the District authorities remained: they were expected to build a capital worthy of a great nation without any substantial federal contribution and without the federal government paying taxes on the extensive property that it held there. The *New National Era* had warned in February 1871, even before the new government was in place, that it could not see how the territory could meet its expenses any better than the Washington Corporation had unless the United States was willing to pay taxes on its property, in which case a new system of government would not be necessary. The only difference was that, by massively increasing the scale of reconstruction, Shepherd turned a chronic problem into a critical one.[47]

Local resistance to the improvement plan soon appeared. Many of those who petitioned against the government, claimed the *Star*, a newspaper close to the territorial government, were "obstructionists . . . willing to sacrifice the interest of the whole community" to attain their political ends. They included "red-hot Democrats" along with disgruntled Republicans such as Sayles J. Bowen and John H. Crane, formerly such bitter rivals. Democrats, who had looked to the territory to minimize the African American influence in local affairs, now turned away in disappointment that it did not.[48] Nevertheless, there were genuine grounds for complaint from property holders who suffered from the immense inconvenience of large-scale improvements as well as the sometimes crippling

---

[46] *CG*, 42.3:199–202, 1973–4, 1975, 2011–12, 2022–23; U.S. House of Representatives, Committee on the Judiciary, *Legal Relations of the United States and the District of Columbia*, 43.1 (1874), Ho. Report 627; Alan Lessoff, "The Federal Government and the National Capital: Washington, 1861–1902" (Ph.D. diss., Johns Hopkins University, 1990), 211–12.

[47] *New National Era*, February 10, 1870. See also the testimony of J. Sella Martin before the Senate District Committee, in *Evening Star*, March 7, 1870.

[48] *Evening Star*, February 26, 1874; *Chronicle*, January 28, May 16, 1874; Johnson, "City on a Hill," 238–44. Democrats did have grounds for complaining about their exclusion from patronage. Rather than creating a bipartisan regime, President Grant appointed only Republicans, and Governor Henry D. Cooke announced that it was his intention to run the territorial government in the interest of the Republican Party. Green, *Washington*, 340–41.

costs. Taxpayers complained of the arbitrary manner in which contracts were awarded and costs allowed to escalate, with the result that
projects with estimated costs of $6 million ended up costing in excess of
$20 million.[49]

Memorials to Congress by opponents of the regime forced the House
of Representatives to take action in January 1872. According to Clarkson
Potter, "its mismanagement is so great and its abuses so extravagant that
they ought to be investigated." Democrats such as Potter and Eldredge
took pleasure in holding Republicans responsible for "this miserable car-
icature of government," the rottenness of which was "equal to that of
Tammany." (It was obviously in their interests to direct attention toward
a "Republican Tammany.") Although several congressmen from both
parties favored the appointment of a special committee, believing the
Committee on the District of Columbia to be too compromised by association with Shepherd to conduct a rigorous investigation, most members
were reluctant to impinge on the committee's prerogatives.[50] Chaired by
Henry H. Starkweather, a close friend of Shepherd, the investigation was
never likely to be hostile. Attributing the mistakes made by the Board
of Public Works to innocent enthusiasm, the report praised its members
for their public-spiritedness and the ambitious scope of their plans and
urged Congress to make "generous appropriations" to assist them. There
was no direct criticism of the manner in which the Board had initiated
projects for which appropriations had not been made by the Legislative
Assembly and entered into contracts beyond the estimates submitted, of
its chaotic methods of bookkeeping, or of the manner in which prices
were set for work done. The one specific criticism was of the territory's
lavish expenditure on advertising. Although accepting the committee's

---

[49] Lessoff, *Nation and Its City,* 73–6. For examples of complaints, see Emily E. Briggs
("Olivia") to Alexander R. Shepherd, April 29, 1873; Lucy R. Freeman to Shepherd,
August 15, 1873, Shepherd MSS, Library of Congress.

[50] CG, 42.2:504–6; *Washington Daily Patriot,* January 25, 1872; *Chronicle,* January 22,
1872. The memorials that prompted the investigation are reprinted in *Affairs in the
District of Columbia* (1872), 1–11. The main points are listed in Maury, *Alexander
"Boss" Shepherd,* 39. See also the condemnation of the Board of Public Works by
Robert Roosevelt, a New York City congressman recently involved in the attack on
the Tweed Ring. CG, 42.2:App. 428–37; CR, 43.3:App. 74; *New York Times,* January
25, 1873. On the functions of accusations of corruption and the broader context in
which they were made, see Susan Margaret Thompson, *The "Spider Web": Congress
and Lobbying in the Age of Grant* (Ithaca, NY: Cornell University Press, 1985), 58–69;
Summers, *Era of Good Stealings.*

report, the House recommended that the board's indebtedness should be restricted to $10 million.[51]

Ignoring this gentle rebuke, Shepherd continued to implement his grandiose plans. By 1874, the Board of Public Works had entered into contracts that would take indebtedness way beyond the stipulated margin. Allegations of extravagance, overambition, favoritism, and careless accounting practices were augmented by charges of corruption. Criticism now extended beyond the original memorialists to embrace a wide cross-section of District opinion and beyond the local press to include national newspapers like the *New York Sun* and *New York Tribune*. Republican Congressmen were coming to find the Shepherd "Ring" a political embarrassment at a time when their party, facing a worsening economic situation, bedeviled by dissensions over civil rights and southern policy, and mired in what looked like an interminable series of political scandals, felt increasingly vulnerable.[52] Alarmed at the spiraling debt, Congress ordered a second investigation in February 1874, carried out this time by a joint committee drawn from both houses. The committee's report accused the Board of Public Works of initiating projects for which appropriations had not been made by the Legislative Assembly and entering into contracts beyond the estimates submitted; of setting excessively generous rates of compensation; of awarding contracts to persons who did not intend to execute them but to sell them on at a profit; of neglecting to verify their accounts; of holding irregular meetings and fabricating the records; and of making up an account against the United States of $4,170,427 founded on unreliable estimates and "without warrant of law." "From what has already been said we think it clear that the Board of Public Works as now organized has exercised powers that ought not to be committed to any body or board." Highly critical of the cavalier fashion in which the board had exceeded its legal authority and flouted congressional restrictions, although falling short of accusing Shepherd himself of malpractice, the joint committee recommended abolition of

---

[51] *Affairs in the District of Columbia* (1872), i–xii; Green, *Washington*, 349–51; Whyte, *Uncivil War*, 129–41; *Alexander "Boss" Shepherd*, 39–40; Ingle, *Negro in the District of Columbia*, 67–75.

[52] "How Shall We Govern the National Capital?" *Nation* 18 (June 11, 1874): 375–76; "The District Investigation," *Nation* 18 (June 25, 1874): 407–8; *Chronicle*, January 28, 1874; Whyte, *Uncivil War*, 144–64, 173–77, 205–33; Green, *Washington*, 357–60; Gillette, *Between Justice and Beauty*, 63–65. On the relationship between the District government and the press, see Mark W. Summers, *The Press Gang: Newspapers and Politics, 1865–1878* (Chapel Hill: University of North Carolina Press, 1994), 257–59.

the territorial government and its replacement, as a temporary stopgap, by a presidentially appointed commission.[53]

Although it pondered a more permanent settlement of the District's affairs, Congress adopted this expedient. Congress installed the temporary commission with little discussion. A member of the Corps of Engineers was detailed by the president to take charge of the program of public works initiated under the territory, and a tax of 3 percent was imposed on real property in the city for one year to reimburse the United States for money owing. The United States would pay the balance necessary to meet the necessary expenditures, including, of course, managing the debt inherited from the territory, a debt that loomed larger with every recalculation. The territory expired with remarkably little debate or ceremony. There was some discussion of the tax rate to be levied and some of the allocation of responsibility between the three commissioners, but, as the Chairman of the House District Committee, Jeremiah Wilson of Indiana, observed, nearly every member agreed on the need for a change in government. Nobody responded to Chipman's plea that one of the commissioners be elected. Only 22 votes, coming from both parties, were cast against the bill in the House; there was no roll call on passage in the Senate.[54]

Thus, Congress tentatively and provisionally accepted the judgment of the investigating committee: that, under the Constitution, there could be no autonomous local government; that any local government, however constituted, could be, in effect, only "an agency of the federal government"; and that the federal government must accept some responsibility for its running costs. Such also were the conclusions of the House Judiciary Committee, instructed to investigate the legal relations between the United States and the District of Columbia, which recommended that

---

[53] *Affairs of the District of Columbia* (1874), i–xxix; *New York Times*, June 17, 1864; *Evening Star*, June 16, 1874; *Chronicle*, June 9, 17, 1874; Lessoff, *Nation and Its City*, 97–98. For a summary of the evidence, see Summers, *Era of Good Stealings*, 139–45; Whyte, *Uncivil War*, 207–33. Why did the committee not recommend the indictment of Shepherd for his management of affairs? It seems that many Republicans believed the plan of improvements to have been worthwhile, although hastily executed and poorly managed. They also feared, as the Democrats hoped, that the incriminating evidence might come dangerously close to Grant himself. Also crucial, as Senator Allen Thurman, a Democratic member of the committee, admitted, was the desire to present a unanimous report. See the discussion in *CR*, 43.2:1207–8.

[54] *CR*, 43.1:5116–24, 5154–56; *New York Times*, June 9, 10, 18, 1874; *Evening Star*, June 9, 18, 19, 1874; *Chronicle*, June 18, 1874; Whyte, *Uncivil War*, 225–27, 230–31; Bryan, *History of the National Capital*, 2:627–28. For the final text, see *U.S. Statutes at Large*, chap. 337 (June 20, 1874).

some regular and predictable basis should be defined for allocating the cost of governing and improving the capital and concluded, in view of the fact that this was a federal city, designed on a grand scale for the benefit of the nation, that the federal contribution should be in the order of 50 percent.[55] When the joint committee set up to draft a new framework of government reported in December, it broadly endorsed these findings. It concluded that the government of the capital was "not local, but essentially and necessarily national." The resources needed to create and maintain a capital suitable for a great nation went far beyond what could be provided by the resident population. Therefore the federal government must provide financial support as well as administrative attention to the District.[56]

Such a conclusion was widely echoed in the national press during the inquest over the collapse of the territory. The *New York Times*, for example, in an editorial titled "How to Govern Washington," affirmed that the city's status as a capital must be the paramount consideration in devising a new form of government. The city must be clean and well run, managed by the federal government with federal financial support. "It is puerile to undertake to submit the management of the District to local representatives, and it is unjust, while refusing to do this, to throw the greatest part of the burden on local property-holders." There was therefore no question of creating a legislative assembly for the District, in view of recent experience, or of allowing "the disgraceful system of ward politics" to continue. The question of how the District should be governed was of more than local concern, for, if successful, the system adopted could serve as a model for the government of other large cities.[57]

## The Imposition of Direct Rule

It was several years before the temporary arrangements for governing the capital were made permanent. This was partly because of the claims of other business but also because congressmen of both parties were embarrassed to accept their implications. Members of both parties were uneasy

---

[55] *Legal Relations of the United States and the District of Columbia*; *New York Times*, January 27, 1874; *Evening Star*, June 5, 1874; *Chronicle*, June 6, 9, 1874; Lessoff, *Nation and Its City*, 102–3, 117–18; Whyte, *Uncivil War*, 223–24; Bryan, *History of the National Capital*, 2:625–27.

[56] *Senate Report* 479, 43.2 (December 1874).

[57] *New York Times*, June 26, 27, 1874. Cf. "The Condition of the District of Columbia," *Nation* 20 (January 7, 1875): 5–6.

about the denial of representation to local citizens, although for different reasons. In December 1874, Morrill, a former chairman of the Senate Committee on the District of Columbia who was still closely involved in District affairs and mostly followed a moderate course on Reconstruction issues, laid before the Senate the fruit of the deliberations of the joint committee entrusted with drafting a permanent framework of government. This entrusted local government to a board of regents (later renamed commissioners) appointed by the president and responsible for making rules and regulations, but not laws, governing the District. The bill imposed a 2 percent tax rate, with the expectation that the U.S. Treasury would fill the gap between revenues and expenditures. "In effect," said Morrill, "it restores to Congress the entire jurisdictional right and authority which belong to it." That authority "excluded the idea of local representation," which had no "legitimate function" under the Constitution, a view that was more widely expressed during this round of debate on the District's future. In any case, past experience of elected government was not encouraging. Did anybody want to go back to the Levy Court or the old city government of Washington, not to mention the territory? He believed that suffrage was neither necessary nor desirable for good government in Washington, where elections were controlled by what Stewart described as "the floating population who had not permanent interests in the city."[58] Edmunds made explicit many of the assumptions that underlay congressional thinking on the subject when he suggested that popular suffrage was not necessary in the District because Congress regularly received representations from citizens and could easily access local opinion. That was, of course, the problem: the voices that were heard before congressional committees or in the salons where members met local citizens were by no means representative of the local population.[59]

Morrill and Stewart insisted that the issue of black suffrage was irrelevant to the issue of good government, but their tendency to question the right of the "floating population" to be heard in the government of the city suggests that they did not consider it to be wholly so. As Masur

[58] *CR*, 43.2:98–100, 121–22, 1104–7, 1165–66, 1171–72; *Evening Star*, December 8, 17, 19, 1874; *Chronicle*, December 8, 22, 1874; *National Republican*, December 9, 11, 1874; *New York Times*, February 8, 1875. Later in the session, Congress decided on a 1.5 percent tax rate, implying that the United States would provide half of the expenses. *CR*, 43.2:2065–66, 2077–80. On Morrill's career, see *American National Biography*, 15:884–85. For an elaboration of the constitutional argument, see especially *CR*, 43.2:128–29 and 1110–11 (Thurman), 188–94 and 1166–69 (Merrimon).

[59] *CR*, 43.2:1169–70. See also *CR*, 43.2:1170–71 (Thurman).

observes, most of those who spoke took a stand on the issue of black suffrage. Even as they "disavowed the significance of race," they made it clear that it stood "at the forefront of their thinking."[60] Democrats such as Allen G. Thurman of Ohio were less equivocal. "My impression is that the old municipalities did very well," said Thurman. "There was never any complaint against them until Negro suffrage came." Thomas F. Bayard of Delaware made explicit what many of his colleagues felt: "I . . . have not the least doubt, as a question of fact, that negro suffrage has been a very sickening business to the unhappy people of this District and to those who brought it here; and I have no doubt that as a matter of fact this bill seeks to accomplish the complete abandonment of that most absurd attempt to govern this District through the instrumentality of its most ignorant and degraded classes." The evils that afflicted the District were mostly due to "the exercise of the suffrage by those who are unfit to exercise it. I believe that negro suffrage in the District of Columbia has been the largest contributing cause to the present debt and the bad government of the community." The current state of affairs would not have arisen, he commented in a later debate on the government of the District, "in any place where the people were allowed to govern themselves with intelligence." Like many Democrats, he wished for the "people" of the District to manage their own affairs, but his view of the "people" was decidedly restricted in terms of residency and, more important, race.[61]

To a Stalwart Republican like Oliver P. Morton, a former governor of Indiana who had moved from the conservative to the radical end of the Republican spectrum on issues of African American rights and who was not above some aggressive flourishing of the "bloody shirt," this denial of the right of self-government violated "the spirit of our institutions." The exclusive power of Congress over the District, as over the western territories, need not rule out the delegation of some authority to elected representatives, as indeed it had not for more than fifty years. Morton reminded his colleagues that the agencies most responsible for bankrupting the District had not been elected. Would a presidentially appointed

---

[60] Masur, "Reconstructing the Nation's Capital," 385–91.

[61] *CR*, 43.2:122, 126–9, 166–67; 45.2:3606. See also Bayard's remarks in *CR*, 44.1:788. Bayard was an extreme racist even by Democratic standards. See Jean H. Baker, *Affairs of Party: The Political Culture of Northern Democrats in the Mid-Nineteenth Century* (Ithaca, NY: Cornell University Press, 1983), 205–10. On changing party strategies on the issue of black suffrage, see Lawrence Grossman, *The Democratic Party and the Negro: Northern and National Politics 1868–1892* (Urbana: University of Illinois Press, 1976), 15–59.

commission govern any better than a presidentially appointed Board of Public Works? "There is no safety in that form of government. The principle of it is wrong." Furthermore, the proposal had wider implications for federal policy: "Although it may not have entered into the purposes of the framers of this bill, I know what will be said about it – that it is intended to get rid of colored suffrage. In this District where it was first established it is to be first stricken down." It was, he warned, "a precedent that will come back to plague us." It would be used by Democrats to justify the obliteration of black suffrage in the South.[62] Aaron A. Sargent of California, a loyal friend of both Grant and Shepherd, warned that this measure would transmit an unfortunate message to those struggling to maintain black suffrage in the South. Congress should not send out the word that it had been abandoned here, in the nation's capital. He, like Morton, intimated that there would be no such pressure to abandon representative government had black voting not been involved. Many other Republicans echoed their warnings, including John A. Logan of Illinois, George G. Wright of Iowa, and the carpetbag senator from Texas J. W. Flanagan. Even William Boyd Allison, who had headed the investigation of the territorial government and favored the broad outline of the Morrill bill, wished "to preserve in some form the principle of suffrage in this District."[63]

An amendment for an elective commission offered by Morton narrowly failed on a 28–28 vote. Twenty-seven Republicans voted with Morton; twelve voted with the Democrats against the amendment. Once more, those who voted to keep representation alive in the District were more likely to have supported stronger national provisions to protect the rights of African Americans, this time in the form of Charles Sumner's civil rights bill, as well as legislation to end segregation in local schools.[64] There followed a series of attempts to secure the election of one or two

---

[62] CR, 43.2:120–21, 1103–4. On Morton, see *American National Biography*, 15:956–58.

[63] CR, 43.2:165–66, 1107–8 (Sargent), 167–68 (Flanagan), 1107–8, 1160–65 (Wright); *National Republican*, February 18, 24, 1875; *Chronicle*, December 11, 15, 1874.

[64] CR, 43.2:1169–70. Few Senate roll calls on Reconstruction issues in the Forty-third Congress generated significant intraparty divisions, but if we go back to the Forty-second Congress, we find that Republican senators who voted for an elective commission were also more likely to vote for amendments that would strengthen the civil rights bill than those who voted against it. Fourteen supporters of an elective commission voted for a stronger civil rights bill more often than not; for seven, the reverse was true. Among Republican opponents of an elective commission, the equivalent numbers were 2 and 6. In voting on Sumner's local school integration bill in the same Congress, 13 supporters of an elective commission voted with Sumner more often than not; 4 more often against him. Among Republican opponents of an elective commission, the equivalent numbers were 4 and 3.

of the three commissioners, or, failing that, to retain an elected delegate to speak for the District in Congress, in which 20 or more Republicans consistently voted for an elective presence in local government, and 6 or 7, including Morrill, Stewart, the prominent Liberal Republican Carl Schurz, and, surprisingly, Sargent, voted against it.[65] In other words, at this juncture, most of the increasingly beleaguered Republican majority, including former moderates as well as former radicals, seeing their Reconstruction project come under attack in the South and increasingly, after the party's disastrous results in the November 1874 elections, in the nation as a whole, were unwilling to be seen to relax their commitment to black suffrage. This was a time, after all, when congressional Republicans were struggling to pass Sumner's civil rights bill, a stronger enforcement act, and a bill expanding the jurisdiction of the federal courts. The adoption, by 34 votes to 23, of Morton's motion to table the bill brought debate to an abrupt conclusion.[66]

Further action was delayed by a long-running controversy over the temporary government's treatment of the projects inherited from the Board of Public Works. Contrary to the assumption, no doubt unrealistic, of many members of Congress that all such projects would be terminated and no further expenditures made beyond those absolutely necessary to ensure public safety, the commissioners had entered into new contracts to complete some of the work and issued new bonds to pay for them. This occasioned a long and angry discussion of the authority of the commissioners and the nature of the government's obligation to guarantee the payment of interest on the bonds. The newly elected Democratic House majority took the occasion to rake over the history of the territory again and, by accusing the commissioners of continuing the projects, and to some extent the practices, of the Board of Public Works, to conjoin the new regime to the wickedness of the old. After giving vent to their frustration at what they saw as high-handed extravagance on the part of the commissioners, congressmen passed a law restricting any further increases in the District debt. Yet another investigation was ordered.[67]

---

[65] Other regular opponents of an elective presence included Aaron H. Cragin, John Scott, and Thomas W. Tipton. See especially the first three roll calls at *CR*, 43.2:1250. See also *CR*, 43.2:1202, 1206.

[66] Only three Republicans – Fenton, Tipton, and Sprague – voted to keep it alive. Morrill and Stewart did not vote. *CR*, 43.2:1275. See also *Evening Star*, January 8, 1875; *National Republican*, February 15, 1875.

[67] *CR*, 44.1:595–98, 679–82, 708–19, 757–69, 787–99, 818–35, 853–66, 1085–86, 1108–14, 1138–42, 1195–1201, 1232–35, 1682–87; *Evening Star*, January 16, 31, June 27, 1876; Lessoff, *Nation and Its City*, 105–12.

It was not until August 1876 that a new joint committee was appointed to frame a permanent government for the District. Although the committee's proposal was ready when Congress reassembled in December, the presidential election dispute prevented any further progress during the final session of the Forty-fourth Congress.[68]

By this time, there was a Democratic majority in the House of Representatives, although not in the Senate, and its views necessarily shaped the outcome. The Democrats faced a fundamental dilemma throughout this discussion: they believed strongly in local autonomy and wished to see popular representation in the capital, but they deplored the enfranchisement of blacks; they could not unequivocally endorse a system of government for the District that denied local democracy, nor could they welcome one in which African Americans participated equally. Their own plan for the government of the District incorporated various formulae to restrict voting, on property and educational but also, indirectly but not incidentally, on racial grounds. These most Republicans refused to accept. With the House and Senate controlled by different parties, any solution to the problem of governing the District had to be a compromise between the Democratic distaste for an unqualified suffrage and the Republican distaste for a qualified suffrage. This, in effect, ruled out the possibility of representative government at this stage.

The bill reported to the House in January 1878 represented what turned out to be a fragile bipartisan consensus in the Committee on the District of Columbia.[69] It provided for three commissioners, chosen respectively by the House of Representatives, the Senate, and the president, who were to draft local laws and ordinances and draw up estimates of District expenditures for approval by Congress, and an elective advisory council that would approve spending plans and appointments but would have no power to initiate policy. This was an attempt by the Democratic majority to retain some trace of popular sovereignty, although with a franchise restricted by means of a poll tax and strict residential

---

[68] *CR*, 44.1:3888–92, 5557, 5599. Alan Lessoff observes that the four-year delay in implementing a plan for the permanent government of the District allowed both residents and federal officials to become familiar with the operation of the temporary commission and to get used to the idea of doing without popular representation. "Federal Government and National Capital," 187.

[69] On the bill's origins, see the comments by committee members George W. Hendee, Joseph C. Blackburn, and Lorenzo Brentano *CR*, 45.2:1921–22, 1924, 2112–13, 2117. One member claimed that the bill was drawn up by the Republican Hendee and the Democrat Eppa Hunton Jr. *CR*, 45.2:2117.

qualifications. The bill also abolished the independent boards responsible for health, education, fire, and police. The United States was required to furnish 50 percent of the cost of governing the District on the grounds that it owned roughly 50 percent of the real property, although no detailed assessment had been made to confirm that ratio.[70]

In introducing the bill, one of its authors, the Vermont republican George W. Hendee, admitted his personal reservations about the elective council – "I believe it is unwise to throw back into this District at this time the right of suffrage" – and his distaste for the poll tax. It soon became clear that Republican congressmen would find it difficult to stomach the poll tax – "the most serious and the most odious innovation that has been proposed for a long time," according to John S. Jones of Ohio – and would insist that the "principle of universal political equality" be upheld in the national capital.[71] When the bill's managers called for the previous question, the motion was defeated by 94 votes to 124. A majority of the nay votes came from Republicans who found it impossible to accept the tax and residential qualifications for voting and who would rather see the franchise eliminated altogether than restricted in such a fashion, although 51 Democrats also voted against the motion, probably because they could not accept the necessity for so large a financial contribution from the federal government. "What seemed to defeat the bill," concluded the *Star*, "was the property qualification imposed on the Council."[72]

Although the elective council remained in a revised bill reported to the House in May, the committee, realizing that Republicans could not stomach suffrage restrictions and that they could not count on enough Democratic votes to get the bill through, relaxed the residential qualifications for voting. The poll tax was removed on the floor. The bill's managers fended off Democratic amendments lowering the federal contribution, arguing that some kind of permanent arrangement was necessary and that 50 percent approximated what the federal government would pay if it were assessed for taxes on its property. It was pointed out once

---

[70] CR, 45.2:1921–23; *Evening Star*, February 13, 1878; Bryan, *History of the National Capital*, 634–37.

[71] CR, 45.2:1922, 2530. See also CG, 45.2:1926 (Jones), 2527–28 (Townsend), 3215 (Hanna); *Evening Star*, February 11, March 29, 1878.

[72] CR, 45.2:2579; *Evening Star*, April 16, 19, 1878. There were also objections to the proposed ten-year residential qualification for commissioners, which would rule out the incumbent members of the temporary commission; *Evening Star*, April 20, 30, 1878. The vote in favor of the motion divided by party was Democrats 63–51, Republicans 31–73. For more detailed analysis of House voting on the bill, see Lessoff, "Federal Government and National Capital," 222–30.

again that the city's status as capital imposed extraordinary costs. An amendment reducing the federal contribution to 40 percent was rejected by 92 votes to 134, with most of the support for the lower proportion coming from Democratic members; three-quarters of the Republicans who answered the roll voted against the amendment.[73]

The Senate committee reported a quite different bill but one that retained the principle of equal allocation of costs. All three commissioners would be appointed by the president. Further, the council was eliminated: "The committee of the Senate were not able to see the necessity of the existence of such an anomalous and cumbrous and unnecessary body as this," explained John J. Ingalls of Kansas. The elective principle remained in a provision for a nonvoting Delegate to Congress, although the poll tax qualification was removed.[74] The Senate spent a great deal of time discussing residential requirements for the commissioners, tax rates, the cost of paving, the exemption of educational institutions from taxation, and the fate of the Board of Health. It devoted considerably less to the fundamental issues of representation and suffrage. All but a handful of senators agreed with Edmunds that the election of a Delegate would impose unnecessary expense on "this overtaxed, and overburdened and swamped community" in return for limited, almost wholly symbolic, benefits. Both houses had committees dedicated to the interest of the District that were always accessible to its citizens. Although Ingalls defended the retention of the office as a recognition of the principle of self-government and a gesture to local sentiment that there should be some form of representation, few of his colleagues showed much enthusiasm for the idea, and it was summarily removed by a vote of 40–9. The one remaining trace of popular representation was removed with little fuss.[75]

Most of the Senate amendments were retained in conference. The council was eliminated, and, with the removal of the Delegate, no form of popular representation remained. The roll call vote through which the House adopted the conference report demonstrated how dependent the

[73] *CR*, 45.2:3211–18, 3242–47; *Evening Star*, May 9, 1878; Lessoff, *Nation and Its City*, 121–22. The vote divided by party was Democrats 66–56, Republicans 25–75. *CR*, 45.2:3246. For a defense of the 50:50 principle, see *CR*, 45.2:2528 (Townsend), 3245 (Blackburn).

[74] *CR*, 45.2:3604–6, 3607–9; *Evening Star*, May 10, 13, 18, 1878.

[75] *CR*, 45.2:3779–80; *Evening Star*, May 22, 27, 28, 1878.

managers of the bill were on Republican votes to get it through.[76] Whereas the Democrats divided more or less equally in its favor (49–50), the Republicans supported it by an overwhelming majority (80–20); Democrats were also strikingly overrepresented in the ranks of the non-voters. Many Democrats were unhappy, in view of their party's commitment to financial retrenchment, with the size of the government's monetary contribution and unhappy, in view of their party's identification with the principle of local autonomy, with the denial of representation.[77] However, as Alan Lessoff suggests, now that the party had attained majority status in the House of Representatives and had come close to seizing the presidency, many of its national leaders had begun to adopt a more constructive attitude to policy making. Now that the responsibility of dealing with the District was theirs, they were forced to confront the problem that had earlier confronted congressional Republicans, that of determining a proper financial relationship with the District of Columbia and a form of government that would spare the federal government a repetition of the embarrassments of the recent past.[78]

Lessoff believes that the District Commission was not so much a precursor of the bureaucratic agencies established to govern cities in the Progressive Era as a typically Gilded Age expression of the drive for legislative supremacy. It served as a mechanism through which congressional control of the District could be exercised, often in great detail, down to passing laws prohibiting the flying of kites over the streets of Georgetown, questioning the need for a given number of tax officials or court messengers, or discussing the provision of water meters or library books. Hence, the commission was an agent of congressional will rather than an independent administrative body with substantial discretionary powers, such as would become a staple feature of American government in the next century. Hence, the District remained at the mercy of the vagaries of congressional decision making and the fickleness of congressional attention.

---

[76] Indeed, some of the bill's Democratic managers, such as Joseph C. S. Blackburn of Kentucky, had become distinctly unenthusiastic about it. See, for example, *CR*, 45.2:4320–21.

[77] *CR*, 45.2:4319–21, 4348; *Evening Star*, June 10, 1878. Lessoff reckons that no more than two dozen members, drawn equally from the two parties, voted against the conference report because it excluded suffrage. Only Mark Dunnell of Minnesota and Jacob D. Cox of Ohio explicitly cited that as a reason. *CR*, 45.2:4321; Lessoff, "Federal Government and National Capital," 229–30.

[78] Lessoff, *Nation and Its City*, 113.

Sadly, the imposition of direct rule would not mean that congressmen gave much more time to local affairs or that that they treated them with much more diligence and understanding than they had before.[79]

## Reasons for the End of Representative Government

In the words of Howard Gillette Jr., the establishment of direct rule "wiped out in one stroke the intensely active role of citizenship that had characterized all local jurisdictions in the aftermath of the Jacksonian revolution and left Washington residents subject to a system of administrative government not yet tested in the United States."[80] Such a government was fundamentally undemocratic. It also represented a bald contradiction of the principles on which the Republican policy of Reconstruction had been based, and it brought to an end any vestige of the Reconstruction experiment in Washington. The excesses of the territorial period did not necessarily entail the end of home rule for the District but could have been eliminated by a more careful allocation of responsibilities and a tightening of financial controls, Why, then, did Congress decide to extinguish representative local government, not only temporarily but for a hundred years?

In the first place, the signals that members were receiving from local citizens gave the overwhelming impression of a willingness to trade representation for federal cash. The Democratic House leader Samuel J. Randall noted in 1876 that "almost the entire body of propertyholders in this District desire that they shall not be handed back to the tender mercies of universal suffrage." Another leading Democratic congressman, Aylett H. Buckner of Missouri, observed that among taxpayers "there is one almost universal and according sentiment . . . that they shall have no more popular government in this District."[81] A group of prominent businessmen, apparently including both pro- and anti-Shepherd factions, petitioned Congress in November 1874 for a just apportionment of costs between the U.S. Treasury and local taxpayers and for government by

---

[79] Ibid., 114–15, 123–24. On congressional management of District affairs after 1878, see ibid., 130–63; Constance M. Green, *Washington: Capital City, 1879–1950* (Princeton, NJ: Princeton University Press, 1962), 21–28; Robert Harrison, "The Ideal of a Model City: Congress and the District of Columbia, 1905–1909," *Journal of Urban History* 15 (August 1989): 435–63; Lawrence Schmeckebeier, *The District of Columbia: Its Government and Administration* (Baltimore: Johns Hopkins University Press, 1928).

[80] Gillette, *Between Justice and Beauty*, 66.

[81] CR, 44.1:3891, 2717. See also CR, 44.1:4127 (Thurman); 45.2:1922 (Blackburn).

commission without any form of popular election. According to the *Star*, the petition had been signed by every businessman to whom it had been presented. Similar petitions in favor of the successive redactions of the commission plan were presented at regular intervals. An 1878 poll of citizens "with a stake in the community" found an overwhelming majority in favor of a commission; not one in twenty would revert to local elections, unless on a qualified franchise.[82] In repeated editorials, the *Evening Star*, which represented better than any other journal the views of the local business community, insisted that the apportionment of costs was of primary importance and reiterated its willingness to give up the right of self-government to secure an adequate financial settlement. It was not surprising, it suggested, that local taxpayers should show little nostalgia for an elective government in view of the way in which they were "so hopelessly swamped by the illiterate and untaxed." Respectable citizens viewed with extreme alarm any restoration of "the glorious right of suffrage" because they would have no voice in an elected government: "their votes are completely swamped by the floating population thrown upon us by the war." In June 1874, in requesting the repeal of the Territorial Act, a group of citizens asked Congress that there should be "no more demoralizing District elections."[83]

As Masur has demonstrated, the subtext that runs throughout this discourse is a repudiation of black voting. It was the participation of black voters that supposedly "demoralized" District elections. It was African Americans, former contrabands who had fled the perils of slavery to take refuge behind Union lines during the Civil War, who formed the bulk of the "floating population" that supposedly destabilized local politics; it was African Americans occupying the shanties and shebeens of districts like Murder Bay that supposedly provided the voting fodder for unscrupulous politicians. Although black voters constituted only about a third of the electorate and although black politicians had played a secondary role in governing the territory, they came to be blamed for most of its ills. An election held in November 1871 to authorize a $4 million improvement

---

[82] *Evening Star*, November 9, 23, December 5, 1874, January 18, February 3, 4, 6, 1875, February 16, 28, March 4, 1878; *Chronicle*, November 26, 29, 1874; *New York Times*, February 4, 1876, December 21, 1877; Lessoff, *Nation and Its City*, 118–21. The *Star* had defended the territorial regime consistently through the course of the investigations, changing course only in mid-June.

[83] *Evening Star*, November 30, December 19, 1874, January 26, 1875, April 13, 1876, January 29, February 25, 1878; Petition of Citizens of the District of Columbia, June 1, 1874, Sen43A-H8, RG 46, NARA.

loan was, in the eyes of contemporary critics and increasingly in historical memory, carried by troops of black voters who slavishly followed
their political masters to the polls. The 1872 congressional investigation
focused almost obsessively on this process, although it failed to turn up
much incriminating evidence. This mythic narrative served, in retrospect,
to invalidate the electorate's decision and with it the whole basis for the
operations of the Board of Public Works. It was through "the ignorant
negro voters, its employees," said the *Nation*, that the Board of Public
Works had maintained its control. Only black suffrage, it seemed, had
made the excesses of the Shepherd "Ring" possible.[84]

"The racist lens through which white residents interpreted their city's
recent history," says Lessoff, "goes far to explain why old-line Washingtonians had by the mid-1870s dropped their special hesitation about
appointive government."[85] The racist dimension to local support for
direct rule was very evident, and sometimes explicit. However, the experience of Washington does not stand alone. Civic elites in other cities
supported franchise restrictions, at least in municipal elections. In New
York City, for example, a taxpayers' movement, with a predominantly
elite membership, waged a campaign to restrict suffrage in city elections to save taxpayers from the heavy demands on their purses made by
Tammany politicians. It failed in that but succeeded for much of the
decade in imposing tight restrictions on municipal expenditures. Although
there was an evidently racist component to the reformers' perception of
the largely immigrant voting population of New York and other large
cities, the logic of their argument essentially centered on class: on the
manner in which, in a democratic society with extreme variations of
wealth, the many who were poor had an incentive to use the taxing
power to appropriate to their own benefit the resources of the few who
were rich. That logic applied as inexorably to William Tweed's New York

---

[84] "How Shall We Govern the National Capital?"; Horatio King to Editor, *Chronicle*,
December 17, 1874; *Evening Star*, January 2, 29, 30, February 4, March 4, May 2,
1878; Masur, "Reconstructing the Nation's Capital," 338–65. See also Walter F. Dodd,
*Government of the District of Columbia: A Study in Federal and Municipal Administra-
tion* (Washington, DC, 1909), 51; Edward Ingle, *The Negro in the District of Columbia*
(Baltimore, 1893), 67–76, 81–83. Compare this with depictions of the linkage between
allegedly corrupt carpetbag politicians and a "malleable" black electorate in the South,
as, for example, in James Shepherd Pike's *The Prostrate State: South Carolina under
Negro Government* (New York: Loring & Mussey, 1935 [1974]). See Heather Cox
Richardson, *The Death of Reconstruction: Race, Labor, and Politics in the Post-Civil
War North, 1865–1901* (Cambridge, MA: Harvard University Press, 2001), 89–121.
[85] Lessoff, *Nation and Its City*, 119.

as it did to Shepherd's Washington or, indeed, to the South under carpet-bag rule. It was a discourse in which notions of racial incapacity certainly played a part but that was perhaps more importantly about class. What David R. Quigley calls "the new politics of taxpayer conservatism" was a powerful force in urban politics during the 1870s. It was only under Washington's peculiar constitutional conditions that its objectives could be fully realized.[86]

The key problem, according to the *Nation*, was "the severance of political power from intelligence and prosperity." A city government was essentially a corporate body responsible for administering public property on behalf of its "shareholders" – that is, the property owners who contributed taxes rather than the mass of voters who did not. The problems that it posed were administrative rather than political. In the case of Washington's territorial government, the improvement loan had been submitted to the "people" as a whole rather than to the taxpayers who would be called on to pay for it. The prospective beneficiaries from the expenditure of the loan heavily outnumbered the taxpayers who would foot the bill. Hence, the votes of hundreds of "ignorant negro laborers" could saddle a debt on the property of the chief justice of the United States. The District imbroglio, like the Tweed Ring before it, demonstrated, in the eyes of the *Nation*, the failure of municipal government based on universal suffrage. As Mark W. Summers notes, the fall of Shepherd became "one more argument against leaving cities at the mercy of universal suffrage." Thus Shepherd, formerly the leader of the municipal

---

[86] David R. Quigley, "'The Proud Name of "Citizen" has Sunk': Suffrage Restriction, Class Formation, and the Tilden Commission of 1877," *American Nineteenth Century History* 3 (Summer 2002): 71 and 69–92 passim. On the Tilden Commission and the New York suffrage restriction movement, see also Sven Beckert, *The Monied Metropolis: New York City and the Consolidation of the American Bourgeoisie, 1850–1896* (Cambridge: Cambridge University Press, 2001), 211–32; Seymour Mandelbaum, *Boss Tweed's New York* (New York: John Wiley & Sons, 1965), 169–72; Scobey, *Empire City*, 257–61. On the taxpayers' movement, see especially Clifton K. Yearley, *The Money Machines: The Breakdown and Reform of Governmental and Party Finance in the North, 1860–1920* (Albany: State University of New York, 1970), chap. 1; and, for the South, Richardson, *Death of Reconstruction*, 111–21. On the antidemocratic tendency in liberal reform politics, see also Michael McGerr, *The Decline of Popular Politics: The American North, 1865–1920* (New York: Oxford University Press, 1986), 45–52; Alexander Keyssar, *The Right to Vote: The Contested History of Democracy in America* (New York: Basic Books, 2000), especially 119–27; David Quigley, *Second Founding: New York City, Reconstruction, and the Making of American Democracy* (New York: Hill & Wang, 2004), 111–74; John G. Sproat, *The "Best Men": Liberal Reformers in the Gilded Age* (New York: Oxford University Press, 1968), especially 250–57; Teaford, *Unheralded Triumph*, 17–24; Keller, *Affairs of State*, 115–21.

reform movement, was reinvented as an archetypal city boss, and the history of the territory was rewritten as a case study in machine politics, a "Republican Tammany."[87]

As Morton told the Senate in 1876, the Democrats opposed suffrage "because the negroes vote," many Republicans because they could "control the affairs themselves without suffrage." The more affluent property owners gladly acquiesced in the elimination of the representative element in the local government. After all, direct federal rule would free wealthy taxpayers from the demands of propertyless voters and the schemes of machine politicians. Of course, they themselves would not be without a voice. In the absence of formal channels of representation, well-organized groups of citizens, such as the Board of Trade, could expect to be listened to by the commissioners and the District Committees of the House and Senate. In contrast, the voice of the District's poorer inhabitants, and above all of its African American population, was rarely heard.[88]

African Americans, along with the local Republican politicians who supported them either out of ideological commitment or pragmatic interest, saw little advantage in the proposed arrangements. In 1876, the platform of the Republican Party of the District of Columbia included a statement "That taxation without representation is tyranny, and that the unjust disfranchisement of the inhabitants of this District is contrary to the spirit of Republican Institutions; a flagrant encroachment upon the inherent rights of citizenship, and an unpardonable violation of the Constitution." Yet the local Republican Party was now a rump organization with no real power; even Republicans in Congress showed little interest in its views. Grassroots black political organization tended to atrophy in the absence of a vital electoral politics, and the local Republican Party became increasingly marginalized. The voice of the advocates of home rule became fainter with time.[89] Thus, when Morton, in 1876,

---

[87] "A New Experiment of City Government," *Nation* 15 (November 21, 1872): 328–30; "How Shall We Govern the National Capital?"; "The District Investigation"; Summers, *Era of Good Stealings*, 145. For contemporary analogies with Tammany Hall, see John H. Crane, *More about the Washington Tammany* (Washington, DC: n.p., 1873); Francis C. Adams, *Our Little Monarchy* (Washington, DC, 1873).

[88] *CR*, 44.1:4122; Lessoff, *Nation and Its City*, 118–23, 208–25.

[89] Republican platform in J. H. Smallwood and A. M. Green to Sayles J. Bowen, January 19, 1876, Bowen MSS, Library of Congress. See also memorial of meeting at Lincoln Hall, January 11, 1875, SEN43A-H6; petitions for suffrage, HR44A-D1 (November 13, 1876), RG292; SEN44A-H8 (October 2, 1876), RG46, NARA; *CR*, 45.1:165; *National Republican*, December 3, 11, 18, 24, 1874; *Chronicle*, June 8, November 25, 26, December 6, 17, 1874, May 27, 1875. By this time, too, the party's leadership was almost entirely African American, which left it still further alienated from the centers of power. Johnson, "City on a Hill," 259.

complained that the people of the District were "governed as despotically as the serfs of Russia," Thurman riposted, not quite accurately, that the people of the District did not seem to petition for a return of suffrage.[90]

A number of members of Congress had also come to feel that representative government of any meaningful kind was misplaced in Washington. The influential Senator John Sherman observed in 1876 "that in the government of cities the power of popular government must be somewhat restrained in order to accomplish the purposes of municipal government." An appointive commission was "the wisest mode...to govern a municipal corporation." Stewart was another who questioned the merit of representative government in cities: "it does seem impossible, where the voters must be satisfied and where they elect the officials, to get city expenditures anywhere within reasonable bounds." Representative Jacob D. Cox, a former U.S. attorney general and governor of Ohio, agreed that "a large element of ignorant and dependent people of different races, tendencies and prejudices" constituted an unsafe foundation for local government – in Washington as in other large cities.[91] Along with the reaction to black suffrage and the waning of Reconstruction, then, the strength of the suffrage restriction movement made the late 1870s an especially propitious moment at which to terminate local democracy in the District of Columbia.

The demise of the capital's biracial democracy was facilitated by the growing disenchantment with the broader Reconstruction project to which the Republican Party had committed itself after the Civil War. As early as 1871, Stewart remarked that there was no need to demonstrate the viability of black suffrage in the District now that it was written into the Constitution in the shape of the Fifteenth Amendment.[92] There was even less point in doing so as the southern Reconstruction regimes collapsed. Republicans were increasingly governed by other considerations in their attitude toward the District, giving greater priority to physical improvement and commercial development than to equal rights and subscribing, in Carl Abbott's words, to "an economic rather than a moral vision of northernization."[93] Nonetheless, as we have seen, a large majority of Republicans voted to keep suffrage alive in the District during the

---

[90] *CR*, 44.1:4127.
[91] *CG*, 41.3:687–88; *CR*, 44.1:4125; 43.1:2088–9; 45.2:2114. See also *CG*, 41.3: 642–43 (Cook and Wood); *CR*, 43.2:166–67 (Saulsbury); 45.2:1922 (Hendee).
[92] *CG*, 41.3:687.
[93] Abbott, *Political Terrain*, 71. On the growing influence of a business-orientated Republicanism in shaping policy towards the District, see Lessoff, *Nation and Its City*, 41–71; Gillette, *Between Justice and Beauty*, 61–68.

winter of 1874–75. They also fought for the principle of equal suffrage during 1878, against Democratic attempts to introduce discriminatory voting qualifications. Where they did divide, there was no tight correlation between Republican voting on the successive governmental reorganizations and on aspects of what was usually termed "Southern policy." Morrill, for example, the principal cheerleader for commission government, was generally found voting against the more rigorous provisions in enforcement and civil rights measures, whereas Stewart more often voted with the radicals; Morton compiled a fairly comprehensive record for radical voting on Reconstruction issues, whereas Sargent tended to side with the moderates. Stewart, while proclaiming the necessity of protecting suffrage rights in the South, denied that it had any bearing on the provision of good government in the District of Columbia. There was no clear and direct causal connection between the waning of Reconstruction, a slower and more hesitant process than is often recognized, and the removal of suffrage rights from the District. Decisions about the governance of the District were influenced by the politics of Reconstruction, but they were certainly not determined by them.[94]

The various forms of government under which Washington's citizens lived during this period were manifestations of a number of underlying dilemmas that lay at the heart of congressional management of the District. On one hand, Congress was reluctant to delegate authority to

---

[94] *CR*, 43.1:4166–67; 43.2:1105–6. For varying explanations of the end of Reconstruction, see William Gillette, *Retreat from Reconstruction, 1867–1879* (Baton Rouge: Louisiana State University Press, 1979); Richardson, *Death of Reconstruction*; Michael Les Benedict, "Reform Republicans and the Retreat from Reconstruction," in Eric Anderson and Alfred A. Moss Jr., eds., *The Facts of Reconstruction: Essays in Honor of John Hope Franklin* (Baton Rouge: Louisiana State University Press, 1991, 53–77; Eric Foner, *Reconstruction: America's Unfinished Revolution, 1863–1877* (New York: Harper, 1988), esp. 524–87; Richard H. Abbott, *The Republican Party and the South: The First Southern Strategy, 1855–1877* (Chapel Hill: University of North Carolina Press, 1986), 204–32; Stanley P. Hirshson, *Farewell to the Bloody Shirt: Northern Republicans and the Southern Negro, 1877–1893* (Bloomington: University of Indiana Press, 1962); Vincent P. De Santis, *Republicans Face the Southern Question: The New Departure Years, 1877–1897* (Baltimore: Johns Hopkins University Press, 1959); W. R. Brock, *An American Crisis: Congress and Reconstruction, 1865–1867* (London: Macmillan, 1963), 274–304; C. Vann Woodward, "Seeds of Failure in Radical Race Policy," in Woodward, *American Counterpoint: Slavery and Racism in the North-South Dialogue* (Boston: Little, Brown, 1971), 163–83; Patrick W. Riddleberger, "The Radicals' Abandonment of the Negro during Reconstruction," *Journal of Negro History* 45 (April 1960): 88–102; Xi Wang, *The Trial of Democracy: Black Suffrage and Northern Republicans, 1860–1910* (Athens: University of Georgia Press, 1997). Wang is especially helpful in tracing continuing Republican support for black suffrage after 1877.

local agencies of government and became more reluctant to do so as the political condition and physical appearance of the capital acquired added symbolic significance after the Civil War. In many ways, the government of the capital embodied the honor and self-image of the nation. The expansion of the federal government, and the renewed sense of national purpose that went along with it, put new pressure on the structures of municipal government and raised the stakes of local politics. It was in this mood of heightened postwar nationalism that Congressmen began to search for new ways of ordering District affairs. They became more aware of the capital's special status and its need both for greater federal assistance and greater federal supervision. The management of what, as Shepherd later acknowledged, was "really a big government reservation," was too important to be left to local voters.[95] On the other hand, Congress was equally reluctant to devote time to District affairs. It was still more reluctant to appropriate money for District projects. During the post–Civil War era, Congress turned to a number of solutions to the problem of governing the capital. First, it encouraged a "reconstruction" of local government under Republican leadership, in the hope that it would display more vigor and efficiency than its antebellum predecessors; then it created a territorial government that, in theory, permitted greater federal control but in practice allowed an unacceptable degree of latitude to local agencies; finally, it resorted to direct rule by commission. The attraction of the commission scheme was that it appeared to solve the problem of local governance by increasing congressional control without increasing the time and attention that Congress would need to devote to the task.

As this chapter clearly shows, the governance of the capital posed a recurrent problem for the nation's lawmakers, but the decisions that they made were shaped by the particular political conditions that operated in the 1870s. Members of Congress were primarily concerned with solving a troublesome set of constitutional problems, and the practical difficulties that flowed from them, but it is unlikely that they would have arrived at the radical solution they did without the particular political circumstances that occurred during the twilight years of Reconstruction. Although their actions were not simply part of a broader sequence of decisions to wind down Reconstruction, they reflected a similar conjunction of political forces. Washington's constitutional status, as the nation's capital, made it a special case unlike any other, but, as the nation's capital, it was also a site where the various forces shaping the politics of

---

[95] Shepherd quoted in Gillette, *Between Justice and Beauty*, 68.

Reconstruction can be seen at work. Thus, the ending of Reconstruction in the District illuminates the broader process. It shows the influence of a resurgent Democracy, pledged to the ideal of local autonomy but generally hostile to the implementation of black suffrage. Any solution to the problem of governing the District after 1875 had to take account of their desires. It illustrates the importance of reform Republicanism – not just the bolters of 1872 but the broader liberal strand within the party – in eroding northern support for Reconstruction. It illustrates the manner in which a discourse about political corruption and the vagaries of a mass urban electorate interacted with policy making for the reconstructed states. And it provides further evidence of the complex relationship between the Reconstruction of the North and the Reconstruction of the South.[96] Policy making for the District, of course, was never just about the District. As George Frisbie Hoar observed, the government of the capital "peculiarly affect[ed] the national honor."[97] It was because it touched on so many different political projects and found a place in so many alternative narratives of the nation's future that the determination of the future government of the District of Columbia proved so problematic and, ultimately, so paradoxical in its outcome.

[96] On the impact of the reform Republicans, see Benedict, "Reform Republicans and Retreat from Reconstruction"; Riddleberger, "Radicals' Abandonment of the Negro"; Sproat, *"Best Men,"* 29–44. On the interrelatedness of the Reconstruction of the South and the "Reconstruction of the North," see Foner, *Reconstruction*, 461–88; Richardson, *Death of Reconstruction*; Scobey, *Empire City*, 251–61; Quigley, *Second Founding*.

[97] CR, 43.1:2331.

# 9

# Reconstruction in the Nation's Capital

### "The Capital of the Whole Nation"

In 1877, in a speech delivered in the neighboring city of Baltimore, Frederick Douglass, the District's most eminent black resident, painted Washington's recent progress in glowing terms:

> The vast and wonderful revolution which has, during the last dozen years, taken place in the condition and relations of the American people is nowhere more visible, striking, and complete, than in Washington.... Outside of the public buildings, some of which have been vastly changed and improved, all the older landmarks of the city have been obscured, or have wholly disappeared. The spade, the plough and the pick-axe of the Freedman have changed the face of the earth upon which the city stands. Hills have been leveled, valleys filled up, canals, gulleys, ditches, and other hiding places of putridity and pestilence, have been arched, drained, and purified, and their neighborhood made healthy, sweet, and habitable....
>
> Magnificent thoroughfares, for which Washington has no rival, have been lately graded, paved, and parked, and richly adorned on either side with beautiful and flourishing shade trees.

The "new dispensation of liberty," proclaimed Douglass, had lifted the capital "out of more than sixty years of mud and mire." It had "broken up the inaction and stagnation, snapped the iron chain of conservatism which anchored the city to a barbarous past . . . and opened for the city a future of glory undreamed of by its people fifteen years ago." This "marvelous transformation of Washington" had at last given Americans a capital that was commensurate with the authority and stature of the reconstructed Union. "At no time in its previous history, has it been so truly as now, the capital of the whole nation."[1]

After the Civil War the city underwent a major transformation, particularly under the guidance of the Board of Public Works between 1871 and 1874. The grading and paving of streets, the building of sewers, the filling in of the noisome Washington City Canal, and the construction of new market buildings, in combination with the improvements made by the federal government on its own property, went a long way toward converting Washington into a more tolerable place to live and a more presentable capital city. "This is just part of a process to make Washington fully worthy of the nation," observed the *Evening Star* in 1873. Alexander R. Shepherd, the mastermind behind the rebuilding program, in a speech delivered after his fall from grace, lauded the improvements which, he said, had "redeemed the national metropolis from the squalor and filth in which it had lain mouldering for nearly half a century, a bye-word and a reproach among the cities of the earth and transformed it into a thing of beauty, making it worthy of the hallowed name it bears." No intelligent resident, remarked Republican senator Aaron Sargent in 1876, would wish "that this District should be plunged back into the misery, the filth, the sickness, the squalor of ten years ago." As Alan Lessoff notes, although congressmen and civic leaders "might have found the improvers' character and methods unsettling, the goals and actual programs of the movement fit in well with their notion of what kind of city Washington should become." Hence, the program of improvements resumed, in a more restrained and controlled fashion, after the death of the territory.[2]

Many scholars have noted that Americans began to look differently on their capital city after the Civil War. Indeed, it was not until after the war that Americans began consistently to use the word "capital" to describe

---

[1] "Our National Capital: An Address Delivered in Baltimore, Maryland, on 8 May 1877," in John W. Blassingame and John R. McKivigan, eds., *The Frederick Douglass Papers. Series One: Speeches, Debates and Interviews. Volume 4: 1864–80* (New Haven, CT: Yale University Press, 1991), 446–48. An earlier version of the speech was delivered six months earlier in Washington. See *Chronicle*, November 26, 1875. For similar assessments of the new Washington, see Mary Clemmer Ames, *Ten Years in Washington: Life and Scenes in the National Capital as a Woman Sees Them* (Hartford, CT: A.D. Worthington, 1875); George A. Townsend, *New Washington, or The Renovated Capital City* (Washington, DC: Chronicle Publishing Co., 1874).

[2] *Evening Star*, March 3, 1873, November 8, 1875; CR, 44.1:822–23; Alan Lessoff, *The Nation and Its City: Politics, "Corruption," and Progress in Washington, D.C., 1861–1902* (Baltimore: Johns Hopkins University Press, 1994), 83.

what before 1860 had been most commonly referred to as the "seat of government" or the "federal city." "In the last decades of the nineteenth century," notes Carl Abbott, "Washington became what it had never been before – an object of patriotic regard and pilgrimage with a growing number of architectural monuments and national institutions." Washington, said President Ulysses S. Grant, was "rapidly assuming the appearance of a capital of which the nation may well be proud." It was becoming a capital city "in which the entire people are interested." The struggle to save the Union, along with its successful resolution, had transformed the relationship between the capital and the nation. Rather than a remote political center of little consequence to ordinary Americans, Washington had become the seat of a more potent federal government and the symbol of a renewed and more vigorous nationalism. Its transformation, says Morton Keller, was "the most visible expression of America's rejuvenated post-war nationalism."[3]

"We are here to make this capital city exemplify the civilization of our country," Senator Thomas C. Platt told Shepherd in 1876.[4] The exclusive control that Congress held over the District of Columbia gave

[3] Carl Abbott, "Washington and Berlin: National Capitals in a Networked World," in Andreas W. Daum and Christof Mauch, eds., *Berlin – Washington, 1800–2000: Capital Cities, Cultural Representation, and National Identity* (Cambridge: Cambridge University Press, 2005), 109–10; Kenneth R. Bowling, "From 'Federal Town' to 'National Capital': Ulysses S. Grant and the Reconstruction of Washington, D.C.," *Washington History* 14 (2002): 8–25; James L. Richardson, ed., *A Compilation of the Messages and Papers of the Presidents, 1789–1897* (10 vols., Washington, DC: National Bureau of Art and Literature, 1904), 7:165, 254; Morton Keller, *Affairs of State: Public Life in Late Nineteenth-Century America* (Cambridge, MA: Harvard University Press, 1977), 98–101, 106. See also Walter Erhart, "Written Capitals and Capital Topography: Berlin and Washington in Travel Literature," in Daum and Mauch, eds., *Berlin – Washington,* 68–69; Kenneth R. Bowling and Ulrike Gerhard, "Siting Federal Capitals: The American and German Debates," in ibid., 31–32; Alan Lessoff, "Gilded Age Washington: Promotional Capital of the Nation," in Lothar Hönnighausen and Andreas Falke, eds., *Washington, D.C.: Interdisciplinary Approaches* (Tübingen: Francke Verlag, 1993), 35–36. On the growth of federal power after 1865, see Richard F. Bensel, *Yankee Leviathan: The Origins of Central State Authority, 1859–1877* (Cambridge: Cambridge University Press, 1990); Keller, *Affairs of State,* Part One. On the impact of the war on American nationalism, see ibid., 38–46; Melinda Lawson, *Patriotic Fires: Forging a New Nationalism in the Civil War North* (Lawrence: University Press of Kansas, 2002); Cecilia O'Leary, *To Die For: The Paradox of American Patriotism* (Princeton, NJ: Princeton University Press, 1999); Susan-Mary Grant, "From Union to Nation? The Civil War and the Development of American Nationalism," in Susan-Mary Grant and Brian Holden Reid, eds., *The American Civil War: Explorations and Reconsiderations* (Harlow, Essex: Longman, 2000), 333–57.

[4] Thomas C. Platt to Alexander R. Shepherd, June 3, 1876, Shepherd MSS, Library of Congress.

added significance to whatever social and political institutions it might establish there. The federal government, it was argued, should be seen to apply within its own territory the same enlightened standards that it would wish to see applied elsewhere. "It should be as a city set upon a hill," said Frederick Douglass. The Board of Trustees of Public Schools, in asking for federal assistance for the District's schools, reminded members of Congress

> That the District, including as it does the Nation's capital, and being under the direct control and special care of Congress, stands in a peculiar relation to the entire country.... Its public institutions are not, like those of most other sections, matters of merely local concern, but the whole nation has an interest in, and should have a special guardian care, over them.... The Capital of a Republic, surely, should possess, and should exhibit to all sections of the country, not to say to other lands, a model of that "peculiar institution" which is conceded to be most essential to the existence and perpetuity of such a form of government, namely, the Public School.

The District should be a "model municipality," exhibiting to the world the best features of American institutions.[5]

Acceptance of that principle did not signify agreement on just what a "model municipality" would look like and which features of American institutions it should exemplify. For many decades, the existence of slavery in the nation's capital had provided a point of attack for the enemies of the institution. Its abolition marked a decisive change in the relationship between Congress and the seat of government: whereas before 1862, the nation's lawmakers had been largely content to accept the institutions that they found there, now they set out to reshape them according to what they saw as the demands of the higher conscience of the nation. In the following years, congressional Republicans used the District as "a proving ground for federal race and reconstruction policies." In the heightened atmosphere of the immediate postwar years, even a moderate like John Sherman could enthusiastically embrace the Reconstruction agenda. "I have always thought, and I have often been taunted for saying, that this District was the paradise of free negroes," said Sherman during the suffrage debate. "It is the paradise of free negroes, and it ought to be." Although other Republicans wavered in their commitment to the enforcement of equal rights, Charles Sumner and other radical Republicans retained their emphasis on issues of human rights and racial equality

---

[5] "Our National Capital," 453; Memorial from boards of trustees having authority over public schools, January 19, 1870, SEN41A-H5.2, RG46, NARA; *CR*, 44.1.

for many years after the Civil War.[6] Others laid stress on the physical improvement of the city. Increasingly, in the eyes of national policy makers, the objectives of Reconstruction took second place to architecture and city planning, to the paving of streets and the installation of sewers. The builders of the new Washington focused their attention on the physical beautification of the capital rather than the attainment of racial justice. Conflicts over priorities bedeviled efforts to reconstruct the nation's capital throughout the postbellum era.

Postwar efforts to create a "model city" on federal soil had ironic consequences. A writer in the *Atlantic Monthly* noted in 1909 that "Washington, the capital city of our nation, instead of affording, as it should, the most striking model of self-government in the whole country, is as a matter of fact a most horrible example of just the reverse." Further, "this, happening at the seat of a nation which boasts of its democratic government, constitutes a solecism of the first magnitude."[7] Yet any specific plan for a "model city" might have to be executed over the will of its inhabitants. Thus, it was when Congress abolished slavery and imposed black suffrage in the face of an almost unanimous opposition from local voters. To the *National Intelligencer*, echoing Roger Taney's dismissive comment in *Dred Scott v. Sandford*, that a black man had no rights that a white man need respect, it appeared as if Republicans in Congress believed "that the white people of the District have no rights which they are bound to respect." Instead, they were treated as "slaves of Congress and *experimented upon* in various forms of legislation, odious to its citizens." Andrew Johnson in his veto message on the suffrage bill berated Congress for its failure to respect "the will and interest of its inhabitants." However, Republicans refused to allow the wishes of the "handful of voters who temporarily encamp under the shadow of the Capitol" to stand in the way of a great national policy.[8]

So it was also when Congress deprived all District residents of the right to representation to facilitate a more efficient and economical reconstruction of the capital. Just as white Conservatives had condemned congressional indifference to local opinion immediately after the war, so now, a

---

[6] Steven J. Diner, "Statehood and the Governance of the District of Columbia: An Historical Analysis of the Policy Issues," *Journal of Policy History* 4 (1992): 395; *CG*, 39.2:308.

[7] Clinton R. Woodruff, "Charter Making in America," *Atlantic Monthly* 103 (May 1909): 631–33.

[8] *National Intelligencer*, December 13, 1867; Veto Message on "An act to regulate the franchise in the District of Columbia," January 5, 1867, in Richardson, ed., *Messages and Papers of the Presidents*, 6:474; *Evening Star*, December 13, 14, 1865; *CG*, 39.1:282.

decade later, did black Republicans. Their appeals to "the spirit of Republican Institutions" and "the inherent rights of citizenship" carried no more
weight than those of the Conservatives a decade earlier.[9] The experience
of the postwar years seemed to show that a "model city" that would
make a worthy capital for the Republic could only, in the last analysis, be
achieved under a system of direct federal rule. Congress used the District
for varying purposes but ultimately for what it believed to be the good
of the nation rather than the welfare of local residents. It should be governed, said Republican Congressman M. Russell Thayer, "in accordance
with the best interests of the people of the United States."[10] Paradoxi-
cally, then, even the use of the District to demonstrate the possibilities of
universal male suffrage was contingent on the willingness of Congress to
allow local inhabitants to vote at all. That the "trial balloon" for black
suffrage that was floated over the District of Columbia should be the
first to explode and fall to earth was altogether typical of the paradoxical
nature of its relationship with the federal government that ruled over it.

## Reconstruction in the District of Columbia

The operation of federal Reconstruction policies in the District of
Columbia reveals important lessons about the process of Reconstruction
across the nation. It shows us how Republican congressmen approached
the problem of Reconstruction under special conditions in which the writ
of the federal government ruled supreme, without the intervention of any
intermediate state authority, and where they could give legal form to
their political principles without the constitutional restraints that operated elsewhere. It shows us how Reconstruction worked under urban
conditions. Further, because of the liminal status of Washington, D.C.,
cutting across the boundary between the two sections, it provides an
interesting case study of the ways in which the Reconstruction of the
South interacted with the "Reconstruction of the North."

Untroubled by the constitutional restrictions that affected their actions
in the states of the former Confederacy, Republican congressmen were
free to give expression to their underlying ideas about freedom and racial
equality. Michael Les Benedict, Harold M. Hyman, Herman Belz, and
others have pointed to the conservative manner in which they addressed

---

[9] Republican platform enclosed in J. H. Smallwood and A. M. Green to Sayles J. Bowen,
January 19, 1876, Bowen MSS, Library of Congress.
[10] CG, 39.1:282.

issues of federalism. Their program of Reconstruction utilized reconstituted state governments to protect the civil and political rights of freedmen, rather than creating new federal administrative structures to enforce the Thirteenth, Fourteenth, and Fifteenth Amendments.[11] In the federal District there were no such constraints on the exercise of federal power. There congressmen were free to pass a series of quite radical measures to remove slavery from the District and then to expunge its traces from the statute book. They were forced to consider the full implications of emancipation and to determine which rights and liberties freedpeople should enjoy. As Eric Foner explains, "by the war's end many Republicans had come to embrace the old abolitionist view that the abolition of slavery must bring not only an end to bondage but a national citizenship whose members enjoyed the equal protection of the laws regardless of race."[12] That included removing racial distinctions from local laws and ordinances, enfranchising African American males, barring discrimination on the city's streetcars and, rather less effectively, in other public places, and laying the foundations for a black school system. It did not extend to mandating integrated schools, a step that many moderate Republicans believed crossed the line separating the public from the private sphere and many more believed to be politically foolhardy.[13] In other respects,

---

[11] Michael Les Benedict, *A Compromise of Principle: Congressional Republicans and Reconstruction, 1863–1869* (New York: Norton, 1974); Benedict, "Preserving the Constitution: The Conservative Basis of Radical Reconstruction," *Journal of American History* 61 (June 1974): 65–90; Harold M. Hyman, *A More Perfect Union: The Impact of the Civil War and Reconstruction on the Constitution* (New York: Knopf, 1973); Herman Belz, "Equality and the Fourteenth Amendment: The Original Understanding," in *Abraham Lincoln, Constitutionalism, and Equal Rights in the Civil War Era* (New York: Fordham University Press, 1998), 170–86; Earl M. Maltz, *Civil Rights, the Constitution, and Congress, 1863–1869* (Lawrence: University Press of Kansas, 1990). However, cf. Robert J. Kaczorowski, "To Begin the Nation Anew: Congress, Citizenship, and Equal Rights after the Civil War, *American Historical Review* 92 (February 1987): 45–68, which sees Republican Reconstruction legislation as substantially enlarging federal power.

[12] Eric Foner, "The Ideology of the Republican Party," in Robert F. Engs and Randall M. Miller, eds. *The Birth of the Grand Old Party: The Republicans' First Generation* (Philadelphia: University of Pennsylvania Press, 2002), 11–13. See also Jean Baker, "Defining Postwar Republicanism: Congressional Republicans and the Boundaries of Citizenship," in ibid., Eric Foner, *The Story of American Freedom* (New York: Norton, 1998), 100–13.

[13] However, as Howard N. Rabinowitz argues, integrated public facilities were not a priority for most African Americans after emancipation or for their Republican allies; at this stage, they were much more concerned with overcoming exclusion than achieving integration. "From Exclusion to Segregation: Southern Race Relations 1865–1900," *Journal of American History* 63 (September 1976): 325–50.

congressional Republicans moved early and comprehensively to inscribe the principles of racial equality in the laws of the District.

It was not just Washington's peculiar constitutional status that made the capital city a fit testing ground for the policies of emancipation and Reconstruction. Washington's well-established free black community, with its substantial cohort of able and educated leaders, played an important role in driving through the Reconstruction agenda. Local black leaders lobbied effectively for the enfranchisement of African Americans and, that being achieved, for the removal of other restrictions on their civil and political rights. They campaigned vigorously and persistently for equitable funding for colored schools against repeated attempts by Conservative and even Republican city officials to deny them the share of the school fund prescribed by Congress.[14] Furthermore, it was the local black community that presented the most articulate case for integrated schools. "In the warfare for equal rights you are the advance guard," Sumner told District blacks, through the columns of the *New National Era*. "You are animated to move forward, not only for your own immediate good, but because through you the whole colored population of the country will be benefited."[15]

A serious limitation on the vision of the architects of Reconstruction was their failure to incorporate an economic agenda. This was especially unfortunate in a city like Washington with its large population of uprooted fugitives from slavery who clung to the protection of federal territory despite the shortage of work and shelter. The federal government devised few programs to deal with their needs. The major exception was, of course, the Freedmen's Bureau, the impressive achievements of which give some indication of the kind of intervention that was needed to alleviate the problems of Washington's black poor. The bureau wound up most of its operations at the end of 1868, and, even though many of the social conditions that had brought the agency into the District in the first place remained in force, nothing took its place. The corporation provided some charitable relief and, more important, some work on the streets. As

---

[14] The role of blacks in initiating and driving forward the movement for public education in the postbellum South is emphasized in, among others, James D. Anderson, *The Education of Blacks in the South, 1860–1935* (Chapel Hill: University of North Carolina Press, 1988); Heather A. Williams, *Self-Taught: African American Education in Slavery and Freedom* (Chapel Hill: University of North Carolina Press, 2005).

[15] *New National Era*, August 7, 1873. Cf. Katherine Masur, "Reconstructing the Nation's Capital: The Politics of Race and Citizenship in the District of Columbia, 1862–1878" (Ph.D. diss., University of Michigan, 2001), 168–77.

we have seen, the need to provide work for unemployed black laborers was a driving force behind Sayles J. Bowen's improvement program and, to some degree, that of the Board of Public Works that followed. Given voice through Republican ward clubs, the compelling pressure of economic distress was a powerful and unsettling force in municipal politics until the end of direct rule in 1874.

Although its most prominent leaders were white, Washington's Republican Party was largely a black party that responded to the concerns of the black laborers who filled the meetings of Republican ward clubs and filed by their thousands into the polling booths, and those concerns, although embracing abstract issues of civil rights and a more practical concern with the provision of schools, amounted above all to the promotion of an economic agenda. "The great want is work," said the Seventh Ward activist Anthony Bowen. Whatever other issues may have moved across the political horizon, for a large number of black Republican voters, and therefore for their representatives in local government, the generation of employment remained a central preoccupation. At the same time, African Americans were beginning to demand a larger share of municipal offices, as well as occupying many of the leading positions in the party organization. As was to occur in many southern states a few years later, a Republican Party with a large black majority could not long resist the implications of that fact in terms of leadership and policy. Black Washingtonians converted the local Republican Party to their own economic agenda, used it as "a forum for collective decision-making" within the black community, and inspired it with their own intensely democratic ethos.[16]

Urban emancipation, as Michael W. Fitzgerald has shown for Mobile, took a distinctive form. Reconstruction followed a different trajectory in a city like Mobile, with its distinctive population mix and its flammable mass of economic discontent, from that which it followed in the surrounding rural counties.[17] In Washington, too, Reconstruction policies at a local level were directed by white Republicans and by descendents of the antebellum African American elite but largely driven by the economic needs of the former contrabands. That gave politics a hard intensity and a

[16] *Evening Star*, May 7, 1869; Michael W. Fitzgerald, *The Union League Movement in the Deep South: Politics and Agricultural Change during Reconstruction* (Baton Rouge: Louisiana State University Press, 1989), 57.

[17] Michael Fitzgerald, *Urban Emancipation: Popular Politics in Reconstruction Mobile, 1860–1890* (Baton Rouge: Louisiana State University Press, 2002).

pronounced aura of class warfare. Many white Washingtonians, including some Republicans, felt uncomfortable with this new kind of politics.
Their acquiescence in the end of representative democracy in the District
was facilitated by their perception of its character. The antidemocratic
démarche was, among other things, a reaction to the character of the
Republican Party that dominated local politics from 1867 until the end
of home rule.

The end of Reconstruction came early in Washington. The establishment of the territorial government was, among other things, an attempt
to defang the black vote and to dethrone the vibrant biracial politics that
had flourished in the city since 1867. According to Carl Abbott, "Territorial Washington ... was an effort to tone down a Radical Republican
city administration and find a more socially conservative but economically progressive Republican middle ground."[18] Its failure led directly to
the removal of home rule in 1874 and, more conclusively, in 1878. The
reason for the imposition of direct rule, according to Abbott, along with
Alan Lessoff and Howard Gillette Jr., was because a concern with issues
of civil rights had been pushed to one side by an alternative version of
"northernization" that stressed the economic development and physical
refurbishment of the capital rather than the pursuit of social justice and
racial equality. This transition was made easier by the general disengagement from Reconstruction that occurred during the course of the 1870s.
Although the ending of Reconstruction in the District preceded that in
much of the South, many of the same factors were at work, including a
resurgent Democracy and a reform Republicanism that reacted against
the alleged extravagance and corruption of Reconstruction regimes. Like
their equivalents in the South, Washington's Republican governments
faced a recurrent crisis of legitimacy. Many white citizens were reluctant
to acknowledge the authority of municipal governments that relied for
their electoral support on newly enfranchised black voters, many of them
former slaves and many of them newcomers to the city, and for their
leadership on northern "carpetbaggers," whose elevation to positions of
authority seemed wholly artificial. At the same time, the legitimacy of
the Republican regime was undermined by endemic financial difficulties,
caused, as we have seen, by the persistent refusal of Congress to make

---

[18] Carl Abbott, *Political Terrain: Washington, D.C. from Tidewater Town to Global
Metropolis* (Chapel Hill: University of North Carolina Press, 1999), 71.

an adequate or equitable contribution to funding the government of the capital.[19]

The early demise of Washington's biracial democracy was accelerated by the fiscal crisis precipitated by Bowen's and then Shepherd's improvement schemes. In that sense, it reflected circumstances peculiar to the District. The reform of Washington's government was driven by the need to create decision-making mechanisms that were more conducive to managing the complex and expensive improvement schemes that were set in motion during the postbellum years. However, there were other, more general, factors at work. The issues of Reconstruction in the South were inextricably linked to concerns about local government in the North. A series of municipal scandals, especially those surrounding the Tweed Ring, led a number of prominent citizens in cities like New York to argue that a representative government based on manhood suffrage was perhaps not the most appropriate way to manage the affairs of the nation's cities. Popular government as it worked in New York under Tammany Hall and in Washington under Shepherd and the Board of Public Works, as well as in the "carpetbagger" regimes of the South, they believed, meant corruption and financial extravagance precisely because the majority who benefited from lavish spending programs did not have to foot the bill, and the taxpaying minority was outnumbered at the polls. The particular ethnic or racial complexion of the majority was secondary; the primary concern was its capacity to utilize its numerical superiority to effect policies that were essentially distributive in their impact. In that sense, the antidemocratic discourse was as much about class as it was about race. Various expedients, including taxpayer suffrage and commission government, were put forward to correct the perceived difficulty, but only in Washington, with its peculiar constitutional arrangements, could they be put wholly into effect.

---

[19] Ibid.; Howard Gillette Jr., *Between Justice and Beauty: Race, Planning, and the Failure of Urban Policy in Washington, D.C.* (Baltimore: Johns Hopkins University Press, 1995), 58–72; Lessoff, *Nation and Its City.* For interpretations that emphasize issues of race and Reconstruction, see Diner, "Statehood and the Governance of the District of Columbia," 397; Katherine Masur, "Reconstructing the Nation's Capital: The Politics of Race and Citizenship in the District of Columbia, 1862–1878" (Ph.D. diss., University of Michigan, 2001), 338–89; William M. Maury, *Alexander "Boss" Shepherd and the Board of Public Works* (Washington, DC: George Washington University Press, 1975).

### "The Paradise of Free Negroes"?

As the bars came down on representative democracy in the nation's capital, Frederick Douglass continued to speak optimistically about the state of race relations. In Washington, he said, "all Americans are created equal.... the rights and immunities of the National capital are no longer limited by reason of race, color or previous condition of servitude.... no American is now too black to call Washington his home, and no American is so mean as to deny him that right." It might seem, looking at the pattern of race relations at the end of the period of Reconstruction, and, still more, at the life experiences of the great majority of the city's African American residents, that Washington was anything but "the paradise of free negroes." Yet even as the heroic days of Reconstruction receded into historical memory, there remained a kernel of truth in Sherman's claim. Washington remained a place where African Americans felt safer and where they believed their opportunities to be greater than almost anywhere else in the country, and this was largely because of the presence there of the U.S. government.[20]

Despite the end of home rule and despite the loss of voting rights, Washington remained a relatively attractive location for educated and economically successful African Americans. During the late nineteenth century, it became, in Abbott's words, "a center for black America." Until well into the next century, Republicans retained enough influence in the federal government to ensure that at least a small proportion of posts were open to African Americans, most of them, admittedly, at a clerical level or below. Although local civil rights laws were unevenly enforced and soon fell into desuetude, African Americans enjoyed a degree of legal protection that was unmatched in the South. As the *Washington Sentinel* observed in 1883, "The colored people of Washington enjoy all the social and political rights that law can give them, without protest and without annoyance. The public conveyances, are open to them, and the theatres, the jury boxes, the spoils of party power are theirs." In Howard University, Washington possessed the most distinguished black institution of higher education in the country. That and the capital's relatively well-funded system of colored schools encouraged blacks from

---

[20] *Chronicle*, November 26, 1875. See also Douglass, "Our National Capital," 451. For an example of a city that did not really undergo Reconstruction and that offered much less favorable conditions for black economic advancement and community development, see George C. Wright, *Life behind a Veil: Blacks in Louisville, Kentucky, 1865–1930* (Baton Rouge: Louisiana State University Press, 1985).

other cities to settle there. As a result, a self-conscious African American elite developed, proud and ambitious but at the same time vulnerable and insecure, uncertain of its social position in relation to, on the one hand, the white elites against which it judged itself and, on the other hand, the black majority from which its members sought to distinguish themselves.[21]

For that black majority, life was precarious. As Allan John Johnston observes, in postbellum Washington, blacks fell well behind whites according to all basic social indicators. Of employed male African Americans in 1880, 85.9 percent were engaged in some form of unskilled or semiskilled labor, 12.3 percent in some form of skilled manual labor, and only 2.6 percent in white-collar or professional work. Johnston could find little evidence of occupational mobility, either over individual careers or between generations, in his sample of black residents of Washington. Although government employment offered some security, most of the work available to African American laborers was irregular or seasonal in nature, with the result that high levels of unemployment were endemic. Thirty-nine percent of unskilled black laborers were idle for a month or more during the twelve months preceding the 1880 census. The overall rate of black unemployment in 1880 stood at 13 percent, twice the rate for white workers.[22] It is hard to find unambiguous indicators of the extent of poverty among the black population, but it is telling that the death rate among black residents was markedly higher than, even double,

[21] Abbott, *Political Terrain*, 73; *Washington Sentinel*, quoted in Constance M. Green, *The Secret City: A History of Race Relations in the Nation's Capital* (Princeton, NJ: Princeton University Press, 1967), 140. On the experience of African Americans in the District after 1865, see also Allan John Johnston, "Surviving Freedom: The Black Community in Washington, D.C., 1860–1880" (Ph.D. diss., Duke University, 1980); Thomas R. Johnson, "The City on the Hill: Race Relations in Washington, D.C., 1865–1885" (Ph.D. diss., University of Maryland, 1975). On the development of a black elite, see also Jacqueline M. Moore, *Leading the Race: The Transformation of the Black Elite in the Nation's Capital, 1880–1920* (Charlottesville: University of Virginia Press, 1999); Willard B. Gatewood Jr., *Aristocrats of Color: The Black Elite, 1880–1920* (Bloomington: University of Indiana Press, 1990), chap. 2.

[22] The occupational distribution is derived from Johnston, "Surviving Freedom," 35–37. Lois Elaine Horton, using a different sample, finds 82.0 percent unskilled and semiskilled, 14.1 percent skilled manual, and 3.9 percent white collar. Horton, "The Development of Federal Social Policy for Blacks in Washington, D.C. after Emancipation" (Ph.D. diss., Brandeis University, 1977), 188. For unemployment figures, see ibid., 187; Johnston, "Surviving Freedom," 41–43. On the absence of occupational mobility, see ibid., 314–21. See also James Borchert, *Alley Life in Washington: Family, Community, Religion and Folklore in the City, 1850–1970* (Urbana: University of Illinois Press, 1980), 167–69; Green, *Secret City*, 131–33; Johnson, "City on a Hill," 351–55.

that among whites and that the discrepancy between the rates of infant mortality was even higher. Their greater vulnerability is suggested by the fact that of the medicines dispensed to the poor, about two-thirds went to African Americans. Black adults were more likely to be illiterate, more likely to be arrested by the police, although mostly for minor offenses, and more likely to be committed to the workhouse for vagrancy or disorderly behavior, and black children were more likely to be born out of wedlock than their white contemporaries. Overall, it is hard to escape the conclusion that freedom had brought scanty rewards to the great majority of black Washingtonians.[23]

As the *Sentinel* went on to remark in 1883, "the colored race lives as separate and exclusive a life as in the days of slavery." Churches, schools, and social and cultural institutions were all completely separate.[24] There was also a significant measure of residential segregation. Although African American families were distributed widely across the city and although the sharply defined racial boundaries that demarcated neighborhoods in the twentieth-century city were not yet apparent, a number of black residential clusters can be identified: one along North Capitol Street just below Boundary Street, three in Northwest Washington centered on 19th and R Streets, Connecticut Avenue and L Street, and New York Avenue and M Street, and a larger one south of the Mall between 4$\frac{1}{2}$ Street and 1st Street, SW, an enclave covering twenty-six blocks that housed 10 percent of the city's black population in 1880 and supported a growing black retail and service sector. At the same time, many black families occupied alley dwellings located behind the main streets. Washington's extensive city blocks provided space for a maze of minor streets, on which, as population pressures increased during and after the Civil War, a motley collection of shacks and shanties was constructed, varying greatly in their mode of construction and fitness for habitation. In 1880, 10,614 persons were recorded as living in 210 alleys, 87 percent of whom were black. Even when the street population was mostly white, the residents of the alley dwellings hidden behind the street were likely to be predominately black. The alleys were private worlds that most white residents were hardly aware of and rarely visited. They were rather frightening places where intruders were made to feel unwelcome and where the

---

[23] Johnston, "Surviving Freedom," 104–10; Green, *Secret City*, 147–48; Horton, "Development of Federal Social Policy," 203–15.

[24] Quoted in Green, *Secret City*, 140 and 119–54 passim; Johnson, "City on a Hill," 291–95, 308–12.

police usually patrolled in pairs. Although the dwellings were cramped and often unsanitary and although the alley communities harbored a great deal of deprivation and hardship, they offered the black families that lived there a degree of control over their own space, a degree of freedom from white scrutiny, and a degree of social autonomy. James Borchert has investigated the tight-knit and in many respects vigorous communities that developed there, drawing on elements of slave culture as well as adapting to the harsh conditions that confronted African Americans in the late nineteenth-century city.[25]

Segregated, discriminated against, and disfranchised, most of Washington's African American population seems to have been unable to realize the fruits of emancipation. Yet it is difficult to believe that they fared worse than the equivalent populations in other southern cities. In 1880, 59,596 of the inhabitants of the District of Columbia were black, an increase of 41,503 since 1860. Of the newcomers, an estimated 15,000 had arrived since 1870, demonstrating that the qualities that had made the federal territory attractive to African Americans during the Civil War era continued to make it attractive in the following decades.[26] These included a reputation as a "judicial haven" for blacks. The presence of African Americans on juries – roughly one-third of jurors on average were black – ensured a fairer hearing in court than was likely elsewhere in the South. The system of black schools that had been nurtured during the Civil War and Reconstruction continued to grow after 1878. Although black schools were systematically underfunded relative to white schools, although the physical plant and equipment was generally inferior and the classes invariably larger, and although black teachers were paid less than white teachers, the differentials were less than in most other southern school systems. After the Board of Trustees of Colored Schools was disbanded in the course of the governmental reorganization of 1874, the District Commissioners ensured that three members of the board of education were African American, and the black community as a whole

---

[25] Borchert, *Alley Life in Washington*; Johnston, "Surviving Freedom," 20–34; Johnson, "City on a Hill," 299–308; Paul A. Groves, "The Development of a Black Residential Community in Southwest Washington, 1860–1897," *Records of the Columbia Historical Society, 1973–74* (Washington, DC, 1976), 260–75; Groves, "The 'Hidden Population': Washington Alley Dwellers in the Late Nineteenth Century," *Professional Geographer* 26 (August 1974): 270–76; Groves and Edward K. Muller, "The Evolution of Black Residential Areas in Late Nineteenth-Century Cities," *Journal of Historical Geography* 1 (April 1975): 169–91.

[26] For population figures, see Green, *Secret City*, 33, 200.

retained some influence over the management and personnel of the black schools.[27] Above all, perhaps, the spatial geography of Washington, as well as its political status, made it possible for African Americans to enjoy a measure of autonomy, a control over their own lives, which was not so easily attained elsewhere. This made possible the reconstitution of extended families and the construction and maintenance of communities under relatively favorable conditions. The considerations that made freedpeople reluctant to leave sometimes appalling living conditions in Washington immediately after the Civil War, to the puzzlement of Freedmen's Bureau agents and social reformers, still applied ten or twenty years later. As a number of recent historians have argued, the creation of an autonomous black social life was one of the lasting legacies of Reconstruction, and Washington's peculiar political status made that easier to achieve than elsewhere in the South.

### Congress and the District

Because Washington was the nation's capital, the newly installed Republican majority in Congress was free to pursue a program of emancipation and Reconstruction that converted the city, at least comparatively speaking, into a "paradise of free negroes." The enfranchisement of African American males and the encouragement and support of its supporters on Capitol Hill enabled the local Republican Party to rise to a position of dominance. That party, in its internal workings, fostered a vigorous grassroots democracy that empowered the freed community to a degree that would otherwise have been inconceivable and that pushed the city government toward broadly distributive policies that would otherwise have been improbable. Although for the most part the strings of power remained in the hands of white Republican leaders and members of the antebellum free black community, the ward clubs provided a forum within which freed blacks could give voice to their opinions and a vehicle through which they could put pressure on municipal officials to accede to their demands. For a few years, the nation's capital harbored a vibrant biracial politics that went a long way toward putting the professed ideals of Reconstruction into effect.

Because Washington was the nation's capital, however, these changes were all too easily reversed. Holding exclusive authority over the District, Congress was under no obligation to respect the wishes of the local

---

[27] Johnson, "City on a Hill," 314–27.

majority or to give it a voice in the management of its own affairs. Once it began to find fault with the workings of local government, and once it began to find the rambunctious processes of local democracy an embarrassment, Congress elected to cut away the ground from under the local democracy and rule the District through its own appointed agents. The result was in most respects an honest and efficient government but one that by its very nature did not listen equally to the voice of all its citizens. Nevertheless, federal control of municipal affairs ensured that most of the legislation protecting the rights of African Americans remained on the statute books and that at least some of it continued to work to their advantage. It ensured that the District was spared for a time the worst excesses of Jim Crow.

Because Washington was the nation's capital, its governance posed a series of structural problems that were never effectively resolved. Local government, lacking much of the authority that it needed to govern effectively and without representation in Congress, was incompetent to deal decisively with the challenges facing the city after the Civil War. It was unable to pursue coherent and purposeful lines of policy in relation, for example, to the acquisition of adequate railroad facilities, the clearing out of the Washington City Canal, or the construction of a new central market-house, and it dealt with street railroads and other utilities from a position of considerable weakness. The agency that did hold the authority, the national Congress, was intermittent in its attention and indifferent in its attitude to the government of the capital, except when affairs reached a crisis point and demanded immediate attention, as in the death throes of the territory. With roughly half the real property in the city exempt from municipal taxation and with Congress congenitally miserly with appropriations for District projects, the local authorities lacked the resources to carry out their functions satisfactorily. The outcome of this was most evident in the condition of the broad streets and avenues that stretched to the far horizons, occupying roughly half the area of the city and presenting a huge challenge to those that were required to grade and pave them, to construct sewers beneath them, and in general to render them passable and presentable to citizens and strangers alike. This was a double challenge: on one hand, the state of Washington's streets rendered life uncomfortable for its inhabitants; on the other hand, their physical appearance rendered nugatory any plan to realize the ambitions of the city's founders and create a city that was truly "worthy of the nation." The city government not only needed the resources to make the city habitable but also to contribute to the building of a new Washington, and it fell far short of achieving this. Therefore, the government of Washington, and then of the District of Columbia, bumped along from one crisis to another until Congress resolved the impasse by removing local government from the District altogether.

For all the manifest failings of local officials like Bowen and Shepherd, this was largely a problem of Congress's own making. As Republican Senator Lot M. Morrill acknowledged in 1876, the United States had consistently shirked its duties toward the District and failed to make adequate appropriations for improvements.[28] Had federal legislators been willing to make a fair contribution to the running of local government and the construction of a modern capital, then it is likely that many of the structural difficulties that beset those entrusted with governing the District might have been avoided, and the whole story might have ended differently.

As Washington emerged from the Civil War, it faced a number of challenges. In the first place, its Republican masters on the Hill had resolved to eradicate all traces of slavery and to engraft on the local statute books the principle of equal rights. Second, a reinvigorated nation required a capital that expressed its newfound authority. Third, approximately 30,000 former contrabands had to be assimilated into the life of the city, economically and socially, as well as politically. It might be argued that the failure of either federal or local policy makers to do anything constructive about this third challenge detracted from their ability to deal effectively with the first two. If Reconstruction, considered as a program of legislation designed to protect the rights of African Americans, and reconstruction, considered as a program of physical improvements, were incompatible, as many distinguished historians of the District have suggested, then that was largely because of the conditions under which they were carried out. In the first place, the limited financial resources available to local government made it impossible for it to carry out its various functions successfully. Second, the economic interests of the black majority proved an unsettling element in local politics, and the identification of the Republican Party with the mass of "contrabands" provided its enemies with a powerful set of ideological cudgels with which to belabor it. The government of the capital was perceived as one in which "contraband suffrage" exerted control and in which the interests of property holders were at the mercy of the propertyless majority. This contributed to the climate in which local representation could be curtailed and then

[28] CR, 44.1:767.

removed. The association of equal rights with a particular kind of class politics made the local Reconstruction project all the more vulnerable to attack.[29] In Washington, as in the states farther south, the financial problems confronted by a Republican regime detracted from its capacity to govern effectively and undermined its credibility, and the economic vulnerability of the majority of freedpeople fueled an angry form of class politics that proved highly damaging to the Reconstruction project. The failure of Reconstruction can never be fully understood without giving some thought to its economic dimension.[30]

As Frederick Douglass remarked in 1877, Washington had undergone a "vast and wonderful revolution" since the Civil War. It was no longer the "straggling awkward village" that had confronted visitors before the war but had been transformed to become, in Douglass's words, "the most luminous territory." It was no longer an outpost of the slave South but had become a testing ground for Republican policies of emancipation and Reconstruction, and even if congressional enthusiasm for liberal racial policies soon waned, the resultant reaction was less damaging than in most of the former slave states.[31] The new status of the capital was, of course, inextricably linked to the Republicans' nationalizing project.

[29] See, in particular, Masur, "Reconstructing the Nation's Capital."

[30] Mark W. Summers, *Railroads, Reconstruction, and the Gospel of Prosperity: Aid under the Radical Republicans, 1865–1877* (Princeton, NJ: Princeton University Press, 1984); Lawrence N. Powell, "The Politics of Livelihood: Carpetbaggers in the Deep South," in J. Morgan Kousser and James M. McPherson, eds., *Region, Race, and Reconstruction: Essays in Honor of C. Vann Woodward* (New York: Oxford University Press, 1982), 315–48; J. Mills Thornton III, "Fiscal Policy and the Failure of Radical Reconstruction in the Lower South," in ibid., 349–94; Bensel, *Yankee Leviathan*, 380–95; Perman, *Emancipation and Reconstruction*, 73–102; Carl H. Moneyhon, "The Failure of Southern Republicanism, 1867–1876," in Eric Anderson and Alfred A. Moss Jr., eds., *The Facts of Reconstruction: Essays in Honor of John Hope Franklin* (Baton Rouge: Louisiana State University Press, 1991), 99–119; Otto H. Olsen, ed., *Reconstruction and Redemption in the South* (Baton Rouge: Louisiana State University Press, 1980); Fitzgerald, *Urban Emancipation*. See also Michael W. Fitzgerald, "Reconstruction Politics and the Politics of Reconstruction," in Thomas J. Brown, ed., *Reconstructions: New Perspectives on the Postbellum United States* (New York: Oxford University Press, 2006), 106–8. On the treatment of southern Republican regimes by Congress, see Terry L. Seip, *The South Returns to Congress: Men, Economic Measures, and Interpersonal Relationships, 1868–1879* (Baton Rouge: Louisiana State University Press, 1983). On class divisions between Republicans during Reconstruction, see Thomas Holt, *Black over White: Black Political Leadership in South Carolina during Reconstruction* (Urbana: University of Illinois Press, 1977); Fitzgerald, *Urban Emancipation*.

[31] Douglass, "Our National Capital," 446; Douglass, "The Freedman's Monument to Abraham Lincoln: An Address Delivered in Washington, D.C., on 14 April 1876," in Blassingame and McKivigan, eds., *Frederick Douglass Papers*, 4:429.

According to Eric Foner, the "activist national state" that emerged from the Civil War and Reconstruction expressed "a new set of purposes, including an unprecedented commitment to the idea of a national citizenship whose equal rights belonged to all Americans regardless of race."[32] As at other times in the nation's history, the governance of the capital reflected the priorities of the American state and the preoccupations of the American people. If a capital is meant to articulate the national identity and provide an expression of the nation's image of itself, one must question how significant to America's self-image in the long term were the attainment of equal rights and the welfare of freedpeople.[33]

[32] Foner, *Reconstruction*, xxvi; Heather Cox Richardson, *The Greatest Nation of the Earth: Republican Economic Policies during the Civil War* (Cambridge, MA: Harvard University Press, 1997); Richardson, "North and West of Reconstruction," in Brown, ed., *Reconstructions*, 66–90.

[33] Relevant here is the recent literature on Civil War memory, especially David A. Blight, *Race and Reunion: The Civil War in American Memory* (Cambridge, MA: Belknap Press of Harvard University Press, 2001). See also the review of this literature in Matthew J. Grow, "The Shadow of the Civil War: A Historiography of Civil War Memory," *American Nineteenth Century History* 4 (Summer 2003): 77–103.

# Index